# GROW YOUR WINGS!

## Life Empowerment for the Ultimate Life

by

*Sandie Duncan*

Copyright © 2015 Sandie Duncan
All rights reserved.

This book or any portion thereof
may not be reproduced or used in any manner whatsoever
without the express written permission of the publisher
except for the use of brief quotations in a book review.

**ISBN: 9781517316822**

## ABOUT THE AUTHOR

A life of continuous twists and turns, roller-coaster rides, amazing and terrible experiences can certainly make for some interesting challenges! But, at the grand age of 56, those challenges have been a full-on set of steep learning curves and an education for life....

I can now breathe easy knowing that I have come out on the winning side far more knowledgeable and stronger than ever before..
And, using that valuable strength and education has brought me to write this series of books on Life Empowerment.

You obviously can't get through life without encountering several kinds of emotions, especially when family is involved....
Pride is one of those emotions that I am lucky enough to have on my side.
And my most proud achievement is my beautiful daughter, who has been by my side constantly and is my best friend. She's the reason for keeping me ever optimistic and forward-looking.

***And I dedicate this series of books to her.***

Married life was both tough and happy. Following an emotional divorce after the '*seven year itch*', I raised my daughter single-handed to become the unique and totally amazingly creative individual that she has turned out to be. *Another reason to be proud.*
But from tough comes more strength and lessons to be learnt and passed onto the next journey...

Working life has certainly spanned across a variety of avenues with periods of high level incomes versus having to rely on benefits to get by.
And that's *very* humbling.
But you do what you gotta do to keep the wolf from the door and I have gone from making a good living at some extremely stressful managerial positions to actually ripping up paper to get a few coppers together to keep a roof over our heads, when my circumstances have taken a dramatic change.

And all the while, I've spent my time trying to make a better life for both myself and my daughter.

My entrepreneurial spirit has pushed me forward to follow various 'dreams' that I thought at the time I had a passion for, but soon realised that they were more by circumstance rather than anything else and I have just gone along merrily finding my way because I was quite good at those roles using the skills I had picked up along the way.
But I now know that I was never *really* following what was in my heart or being my *true* self. I didn't realise this at the time, because I hadn't really matured or 'found' myself properly yet.

*This has taken many years to discover (and I am still learning).*

But even so, I like to think that I have always tried to do the best job I possibly could in every scenario I have found myself in.
And with every new experience, brings new skills and new knowledge to take with me....

There's certainly been some stubborn characters to deal with along the way. A battle of wills and ego's and attempts at making me feel inadequate and belittled has taught me to find a way of dealing with things, whilst all the while still keeping an eye on my eventual goal(s).

All of my achievements, no matter how small have been invaluable to me and I keep them tucked under my arm and carry them with pride (...there's that word again...).

Each string to my bow has added to my capabilities and served me well in some particular way or another.

Each experience, challenge, emotion, success or 'failure' has added to my sense of empowerment.

There's been many crossroads that have caused me to re-evaluate my life's direction and those changes have been both scary and exciting, but necessary.

One of those direction-changing times sent me off on a mid-life degree where I was 'proud' to gain a high 2:1 with honours, and off I went on a brand new high-flying marketing career, which has held me in very good stead ever since.

Growing up with a father in the army, we moved around constantly as a family, which unfortunately, or fortunately, gave me itchy feet and made me carry on moving. I've never had a proper network of childhood friends to grow up with and my family eventually split into different directions, and so now we only see each other through infrequent visits.

This is a character toughening-up situation and you soon learn to make friends easily and adapt to changes quickly. Lots of new learning curves with new schools, new homes, new jobs, new friends, new lives...

However, living at home and abroad has allowed me to experience quite a few different cultures and I've also had to learn to work within new constraints and ways of doing things, particularly when I set up in business abroad.

Sometimes some of those new challenges have caused something of a nightmare for me, but even so, they have all been part of a valuable education that have helped me to fulfil so many things *because* of them and not in spite of them.
That even includes having to deal with little mini-mafia's, cowboys, very dodgy characters and also having all my money robbed from me and being forced to come back home with my tail between my legs and start all over again from scratch!

Health issues have been a little bit scary too, with some very near misses to contend with!

Fitness has always been part of my normal life and so I wasn't expecting an aerobics class to be interrupted by a brain haemorrhage at the very early age of 43....

That was one of my nine lives, but I live to tell the tale and thankfully came out the other side practically unscathed, all bar losing a few brain cells that have affected my memory a little!

I've also fallen down the side of a mountain when living abroad and cracked my head open on a large rock, knocking me out with no-one around to help!

Add to this a couple of skin cancers to deal with too, but that's all solved and all's well that ends well...

An early menopause starting at only 37 put my body in turmoil and has caused me to have to live with certain ailments that I could do without, as well as some debilitating food intolerances that have needed some dealing with, but because of my general interest in health and well-being, I have found help with this.

My continuous study of nutrition and fitness has also lead me to some exciting jobs in this industry, including owning a health store and being a keep-fit and wellness instructor.

This education has given me a totally healthy perspective on life and a yearning to keep myself as fit and youthful for as long as absolutely possible.
Having this outlook means I get to do more active and adventurous things that allow me to enjoy my life to the maximum I am able to.

Some of my higher-level career choices have been extremely pressurised and with one deadline after another have caused some severe stress.
After several years of this continuous condition, I suffered a breakdown which ended up as depression and made me have to give up work for a while.

This put me in position where I had to rethink my life strategy (again) and ever since then, I have been searching for complete balance in my life and making strides to live more calmly and within my own true values and beliefs.

It has taken time to get to this point, and I still seek absolute harmony.

*This may eventually come - I have faith and hope.*

My weight has fluctuated a little over time and although I now have a little 'middle-age' spread, I still work hard at keeping it even and my body in good condition for my age. This is a constant prerequisite for me. When I am in peak condition, I feel absolutely wonderful and can only highly recommend it to everyone.

Like most people, I have also had my fair share of losses – both my parents, my mother very young at only 64 died of a massive heart attack after years of hypertension following a stroke at only 42, and my father of dementia, like his mother before him.
Losing a baby through miscarriage was also traumatic, even though I put a brave face on it at the time.

Animals have been a constant in my life and a real comfort. I love the therapy and wonderful companionship animals give.

Art and creativity have also been a strong force in my life and have given me great pleasure and where I've had the honour of meeting some truly inspirational people.

I have also found spirituality in the great outdoors. It's where I fare best and feel at total peace, especially in the countryside or by the sea where I'm lucky enough to live. I've had the chance to take part in some exhilarating outdoor pursuit challenges that have built up great self-confidence and esteem.

Positivity and optimism are definitely my outlook on life - always looking towards the future and never back to the past.

I truly believe that everything happens for a reason, even if you don't see it right at the time, you will realise exactly why later....

Success to me comes in all ways and varieties – *whatever is your version for you is correct.*

I had the good fortune to work on building a business with a very knowledgeable and experienced multi-millionaire who introduced me to the concept of spirituality and looking to the universe for help and guidance, believing in who you are and connecting with the depths of your consciousness.

It was a very thought-provoking and enlightening period and has made me look at life in a totally different way and start my journey towards following a new path to my ultimate destiny.

It was whilst working with him that it occurred to me that a book had not really been written to totally cover the many *different* aspects of how to empower yourself, rather than it being just a way of building strength and confidence.

So, having spent my life tapping into and actually living out, all the many areas that encompass 'ultimate empowerment for life', I decided to follow through on my idea and put together 3 simple volumes that consolidate several different books on various subject matters....

There are three in the range covering separate areas – The Ultimate Life; Health, Diet and Fitness and Business and Achievement. They all contain very similar information with the content crossing over each volume, but each book has guidance and a leaning towards the people who are engaged in, or want to know more about those specific fields of interest.

Everything that has been written in the series, I have either lived through and been influenced by or learnt from at some point in my life – whether that's self-taught or properly educated and trained. I'm now passing this knowledge and experience on to you.

I believe wholeheartedly that people should totally be who they are born to be and exploit their own innate skills to their full advantage, so they are completely happy in their life and achievements.

People should do everything they can to follow their dreams and be their true selves.....

I hope you find at least something of value that can help enhance and empower you in your life, however minor. It will make me very happy indeed that I have contributed in some small way to your happiness and ultimate fulfilment...

*Enjoy*!

# *GROW YOUR WINGS!*

## Life Empowerment
## for the
## Ultimate Life

*…..is your life stuck where it shouldn't be, like a wheel wedged in the sand where it can't move or function as it should, making no progress, momentum or direction and cemented in a place it has no business being….?*

*…..let's get that wheel rolling again….*

**……empowered living…….**
*Who doesn't want to live their ultimate life?*
Everything as you want it to be, relationships solid, career exactly as it should be – satisfying, fulfilling and enjoyable, emotions balanced, body fit and healthy, finances in order, your day to day life lots of fun, you're calm, there are no stresses, everyone respecting you for who you are and you're feeling like the success you deserve to be……wonderful…..

*This is true empowerment.*

Empowered living means so much more than just feeling strong in attitude, confidence and motivation.
It's all about feeling balanced in all aspects of life, feeling energised through being healthy and strong enough in body, mind and spirit so it gets you through life with ultimate success.

It's when you are able to thrive in *all* conditions and have the ability to cope in circumstances that cross your path.

*It's for you to shine and feel fit, alive and full of energy.*

It's to enable you to live a positive life and remove the negativity from your world, so you have the space to move forward towards your *clear* destiny along your *own* path as a *free* spirit.

It's to not be burdened by emotional baggage, stress and unwanted distractions and frustrations. It's so you are able to eat, drink and be merry without it affecting your overall well-being.

It's empowerment to be able to hold good, strong and healthy relationships with people that you *choose* to be around you and embrace challenges and opportunities with a powerful mental attitude, where your decision-making is firm and is what *you* choose for *yourself*.

*It's where the choices you make are yours and you can face any issues with your head held high.*

It is where you live an enriching life, that has all the rewards you want and you are achieving your goals, fulfilling your dreams and accomplishing your desires.
It is where you are developing yourself and have the right mindset to live your ultimate life and where *you* choose the steps you want to put in place to get you there.
And where you realise your full potential and succeed to the level you want to.
It's a state where you can let go of negativity and all that you don't need, so you can follow a path of excellence towards your amazing life.
The full meaning behind health and fitness is not just to ensure against heart attacks, high blood pressure and weight-loss, etc., but it is a *state of mind* where you think of it as the best possible way of living, so that you get the most out of life and can live it to the full!

All of these things combined are ways that add up to *total* empowerment of mind, body, spirit – physically, mentally, emotionally and intellectually.

*It's an attitude, a way of living, a mindset.....*

It's about you enjoying your life to the full and making the most of it. In the sections that follow, you will find a whole variety of ways and means for you to embrace that state of empowerment, to help you find a path to satisfaction, happiness and fulfilment.

They take spiritual routes, practical help, physical possibilities, mental and emotional solutions, suggestions for overall health and well-being, looking at different therapies, how to follow your dreams, change your mindset, live your life for *you* and ways to become the true and genuine person you *should* be, so you can live your ultimate life-style and make the most of who you are as a *unique* individual.

Some areas will cross over, some areas may contradict others, some thoughts, ideas and strategies may be reiterated – but will apply to different aspects of life and looked at from another perspective, some you may be interested in, some may not be for you – but they are all about *your* choice.

A lot of things will work together, some are opposite, but bear with the crux of the messages.

*They are all there to help empower you, whether you take on only one strategy, or try them all as a comprehensive 'life package'......*

Choose to take what you want from the advice and leave behind what you feel is not your belief. There are things that you might read and like to try out, but give it *all* a chance before you make a judgement.

There are areas you might want to explore further.
There are many books, classes and pieces of information available that can expand on any of the theories and go into more detail, should you wish to follow them through in more depth.

There will also be updates on certain facts and theories, as information and knowledge inevitably evolves, and sometimes very quickly....

However you look at this book, it's hoped you find at least some of it helpful and you take away some useful knowledge and practical advice that helps empower you towards the best life you can have, along an enjoyable and exciting path to the ultimate *you*.

*And that's exactly what it's all about!*

**Enjoy.......**


### ....your life....your direction....
*The very first thing you need to think about on your journey to empowerment is never to feel weak, never to feel powerless and never to feel out of control.*
Always remember, this is *your* life to lead, this is *your* life to live. You have the power in your hands to lay out the foundations of your path and to walk it in the way you feel fit – as an individual in this realm, as you in this universe.

Without you and all your being, your instincts, your feelings, your thoughts, your ideas and creativity, you have no way, no direction. Your direction is yours alone. Yours to be proud of and yours to decide upon.
Yours to live....

*Your life is the one for you.*

If you allow others to lead you, to tell you, to take you over and think for you, then you are not you and you have lost control of who you are and why you're here.
Each person, as an individual, makes this place what it is, makes life unique and turns the world in an interesting revolution.

*Set out your own strategy in life.*

Empower yourself with your own strength of conviction and creative thinking. Allow your own thoughts to control you as you yourself have set them out to do.

As long as you feel your own control, you will feel empowered to make you own decisions and live your life how you must, how you decide, how you, as a unique being, wants.
Be calm, be focussed, be inwardly happy and content that you are leading your path along your own way and you will really feel like you own yourself.

This is the only way for the world to go round. The only way for the universe to accept your positive energy and allow you to move forward towards your own goals and destiny.

*And let each person do the same......*

**....so here we go then...another year, another me......**
*As every new year dawns, so we all feel very empowered at the time to make this year, **the** year of great resolution!*
We've all made those unattainable new years resolutions that we never stick to beyond the first week of January – you know it's true! What is yours?
To get that business going? To become fit and healthy? To get that degree? To make more money? To achieve something you've always wanted to do? To become successful at something you know you could do if you really put your mind to it?
So many goals, so little time, so much procrastination.....!

So here's the rub......maybe it would be wiser to do just the one thing instead that will make all your future resolutions far more achievable.........and that is, to **change your mindset**.

The most important thing about making any kind of change or decision in your life, is to have the right mindset – the perspective on your life that makes you determined to see something through, but also to lock into your mind, new ways of thinking.

This, in turn, will instil in you, new behaviours and actions that will set you up **for life**.

This is never more prevalent than when it comes to your own empowerment.

So, as one door does open – whether this is at the new year, or at any other point in your life, you are in a wonderful position to grasp those opportunities with open arms and a totally willing mind.
Instead of staring continuously at closed doors, make sure you are mindful enough to recognise those open doors and opportunities when they do arrive.

*Don't just sit in regret, anger or resentment at what has happened in the past – that time has gone.*

You need to learn from those experiences and put whatever you have gleaned from them into making fabulous new positive actions for your future.
Reflect back on your past year and understand what actions and inactions you took and how you can move forward on your journey with renewed vigour and determination.

Don't mess about with this – look at yourself *honestly* – it's your life, your goals, so you aren't going to fool anyone except yourself, so be brave!
Take a really balanced look at all your successes and 'failures', or lack of actions you meant to take, but didn't.
*Are they even relevant to you any more?*

Think of things you are proud of, things that gave you a sense of pleasure or satisfaction and why that was?
Why didn't you do what you wish you had done, what were your relationships like – good, bad, indifferent, and why?
Do you need to cut out any dead wood and get rid of the negative people in your life, and how do you hang on to the good relationships?
What can you do to enhance and improve them, what important things did you learn and how are you going to use them from this point on...?

*How can all this valuable information influence your future plans?*

Have a session with yourself and write it all down.
Think hard and deeply.
Give yourself the time....
Then spend time developing and editing it all.

Every aspect of this exercise will help in your quest for empowerment over your life.
Because, if you want things to happen in your life, you need to change your attitude towards things. If you look back and on reflection, you find that you didn't achieve anything that you wanted to, then you were the only one stopping yourself.

*Think seriously about that......*

Changing your mindset to positive motivation and seeing yourself with the successful outcomes, will get you there, in time.

No-one's mind changes over night, so don't expect it.
It takes time to develop a positive, life-altering mindset, but it *is* achievable, so you need to allow yourself the time it needs to get there.
(There is more about helping you to do all this further into this book).
If you just sit back in your comfort zone, you will stay the same.
It's your choice.
It really is.....

But!

Enjoy the ride whilst it's happening, after all, you can only live today, not yesterday or tomorrow, just **_now_**.

Keep your well-being in good shape so you can take pleasure from living every moment.
Earn enough to keep comfortable, but not so that it becomes the *only* thing you focus on and worry about so it eventually ends up compromising your health.
Try to keep yourself calm and relaxed, so you can live how you want to live, without worry and stress blighting your every move.

*You surely want to know, as you near your end, that you have lived a full and happy life, one without regret and where you can leave a positive legacy behind you.*

Feel the strength in this.

**.....so now....take care of your body, it's the only place you have to live in.....**

*And when you put it like that, it sounds serious enough to make sure you do something about living in a wonderfully healthy body, doesn't it....?*

Why abuse or neglect the very thing that keeps you alive?
Don't be afraid!
Looking after it really doesn't have to be a chore. In fact, once you get going, it soon becomes fun and a natural part of your life.

*Believe it, it's true!*

Feeling good by putting good energy into your body with good food and exercise is not a luxury for the few, it's available to everyone, everyday.
All you have to do to have a fulfilling, great life and enjoy a feeling of total well-being, confidence and happiness, is *join in*.

The full meaning behind health and fitness is not just to insure against disease and illness or to live a long life, but for it also to be the very best possible way of living that you can have, so that you are happy, get the most out of every moment and opportunity and you can really live life to the full!

Having a *clean* body contributes to a clean mind.

By using this outlook as your strategy, you can put in place several exercises and ways of living that empower you in all aspects of your life, giving you the right tools and mindset to feel totally healthy in body, mind and spirit.

*Your success is your own vision and purpose – whatever that means to you.*

Be good to yourself and in doing so, you can feel truly strong enough to surge ahead and achieve your ultimate desires and wishes, or simply live a calm, healthy, fulfilled and vibrant life. Totally imagine how that feels...

*And that's the ultimate empowerment......*

**....I feel a touch of personal mastery coming on....**

*If you truly want to spend your life feeling really fulfilled and happy, attaining your goals and ultimately reaching your desired destiny, then you should realise that personal mastery is what is going to get you there.*

There will be pertinent times in your life when you emerge from the chaos or mundane and think, "*What's going on with my life? Is this really the journey I wanted to take, or have I just drifted along on automatic, conforming and fulfilling the desires of others, rather than myself....*"?

Well, **Boo!**
*What now.......?*

If you want to reach that ultimate life, embark on a career or business that enhances your spirit, taps into and exploits your innate skills, feel fantastically fit, have beautiful relationships and a stress-free existence where you feel calm, proud, confident and totally motivated, then you need to set yourself on that path of self-discovery towards self-mastery.

*You need to set yourself on your very own journey of development and improvement.*

This doesn't mean you have to find success in money, in getting to the top or being the biggest and the best at something – it's all about what you, *personally* feel is your own destiny.
Your success is what your inner guide is telling you is the *true* you – the person you really *want* to be, following your *own* set of skills, along your *own* ultimate path.
No matter where you are in life, or what stage you are at, it's still achievable.
It's all from your own perspective.
It's all about what your own personal vision is, what you feel your purpose is, what your principles are and how your beliefs determine your route.

So it's a real journey of discovery, as you ask yourself what you *truly* know is in your heart, mind and soul, and how you propose to put the steps in place to get there.

*You will really need to take time understanding <u>exactly</u> how you think and feel, and how and why you do things.*

Really consider whether any of it is actually in your purpose for life and sending you in the right direction, or are you totally veering off course, resulting in unhappiness, feeling unfulfilled and dissatisfied with life......

To do this, you need to give yourself the space and time to sit down and think very clearly about exactly what your destiny is. You can't make changes unless you know *precisely* what to change. So, you have to really get to know yourself *intimately* first, because you cannot start any new chapters in your life until you stop rereading the last ones!
Plotting your next moves and becoming the new you will not happen overnight – *so don't expect it.*
It's too easy to think you can do quick fixes, but you need to get into the *right mindset* to *believe* in yourself and go forward with spirit and self-belief – which may mean big changes!

So this is not a immediate 'plaster over the cracks' job.
It's your transformation, your self-mastery, your life story.

Remember also, *you want to enjoy the journey along the way.*

Self-discovery is a wonderful thing. You will have some eureka moments and you will have some knock-backs and mistakes. This is part of it all.
Challenging though it will be – it's a wonderful way to see what suits you best and what to throw out of your life – discovering the negatives and positives that will enhance your life and bring out the true you.

As you do so, so you will feel the self-satisfaction, recognise your successes (no matter how small), the fulfilments you have and the happiness you've enjoyed, as you acknowledge who you really are.

This exercise will bring out your strengths and weaknesses and make you look at the decisions you take and really make you think deeply about yourself. Plus this will help to shape who you are and move forwards towards the mastery of yourself and your life.

After all, most people want to live their lives with some kind of purpose, some kind of meaning. What's the point of spending your life sitting on the couch, going to a job that you hate, not having the best of relationships with people, allowing your health to deteriorate, all sending you on a downward spiral of disease and illness.

*What really is the point of that?*

You were only given one life (in this realm anyway), so you might as well live it to the best of your ability and get the most out of it!
As you go through this, your sense of empowerment will begin to kick in as you begin to feel stronger and more alive.
The more you feel good inside, so this will enable you to feel strong enough to take your journey of positive wealth, wellness and fitness.

*If you feel balanced and well rounded, with the right kind of mindset and are getting all aspects of your life in order, you will be in a perfect position to become and feel wonderfully empowered to get on and live in fantastic health, well-being, success and achievement.*

**…..well, I'll just learn to love myself…then everything will be all right……**
*Do you actually love who you are?*
Is it time to put a structure into place so you can feel good about yourself and start loving yourself?
*If you love yourself, you are in a much better position to love others.*
You have healthier relationships with people because you feel inner contentment and that puts you in the right frame of mind to be open, kind and expressive.

If you love yourself and who you are, you can be confident in your beliefs and feelings, and this in turn, means you can express yourself unashamedly – because you feel good enough to. You have nothing to hide behind or be embarrassed about.

*This doesn't mean giving yourself a free reign of arrogance and egotism though.*

That's a totally different story……

Once you know what path you are going on, you've decided who you are, what you believe, what needs to be done and the steps you need to take, then it's paramount that you *focus* on that goal. Not necessarily in a dogmatic, inflexible way to the detriment of your sanity, because life is an ever moving feast that has it's twists and turns, and you need to *accept* that and *go with the flow,* readjusting the goal-posts from time to time as circumstances and you, change along the way.

But you still have to keep your eye on your ball, be disciplined and committed to your personal goal, while you enjoy the journey.
You may well have spent the best part of your life just reacting to things as and when they have come up, and that is how you have ended up where you are today.
Time to start being '*proactive*' instead!

*That means that you are making the decisions for yourself, you are taking your own steps, you are making your own action plan.*

Look for opportunities, don't wait for them to come to you – you may be missing out!
As you put your actions into place and you know exactly where you are going, you will see opportunities more clearly, you will know how to go out there and find them, where to look, what to discard, what to follow up on.

*It makes life far more fun – because you are the one in control, not someone else controlling you.* That's because you now understand yourself and where you really want to go.

You are being the *true* you.
You have become alert and aware and *you* are the one setting the pace.

When you know who you are, you have learnt how to love yourself and you are fulfilling your own personal ambitions, you will be in a better position to contribute to other things and other people. This will make you feel good and part of society, rather than just being your own 'island'.

*You will need to keep a positive mental attitude as much as possible.*

Of course there will be times when you feel down in the dumps, when things get on top of you, when other people get in the way of your happiness or have an opinion on how and what you should be doing, but you need to hold your head up high and get past these days.

*Ridding yourself of negativity and people who bring you down is all part of self-mastery.*

You need to be shaping positive thoughts and giving yourself positive energy at all times.
It's all about your attitude to life.
Feel positive.
Feel empowered.
Be the best you can be – for you!
Confront you fears, get past them and move on. You cannot improve your life if you have these millstones hanging round your neck bringing you down all the time.

*Look at them as positive challenges, as part of your journey to your ultimate life.*

Stop them limiting you from progressing. Stop them hindering your confidence.
Be strong!
Get help if you need it....
If you want this transformation, you will want the life-balance that it gives you.
Being in control and mastering all the aspects of your life will give you the time and energy you need to spend on the *important* things in life. You get the satisfaction out of your work and you get the improvement in your relationships and also give yourself the time you need for *yourself*.

Whatever path you choose on your course for a successful life, as you master all those necessary steps you need to get there, you will feel yourself achieving, brimming with positivity, developing your talents and skills and feeling more and more strong with every day.

You will feel yourself accelerating, energy rising and your whole life having meaning and purpose once again!

Add all these ingredients together and you have happiness.
Your goal in sight.
Your true self coming through.
Your destiny laid out in front of you.
Your own personal transformation.
*Your ultimate life.*
So then, who's in control now?
Who's creating your life now?
Who's making all the choices and decisions now?
Whose journey are you on now?
Who's happiness, fulfilment and success is this now?
Yours, of course!
It's all your own development, your own achievements, your own dreams.
It's your goal, your destiny.
Your self-mastery.
Be proud.
Sit down with yourself and work on who you are.....

*Enjoy your transformation.*
*Enjoy your empowerment.*
*Enjoy your ultimate life.....*

> **"You need to wake up to your own magnificence.**
> **Until you understand the hidden depths of yourself,**
> **you are only half awake.**
> **Make the time to awaken from the dream**
> **and create a life of passion and purpose**
> **and unlock the gateway to your glorious self".**

**...it's time to unlock your own inner capabilities, change your mindset and change your life..**
*If being a winner is your ultimate aspiration, visualising what you want to achieve can turn your ideas into wealth and success.*

Dig deep and unlock your true potential!

You can convert your aspirations into real money and success so you are rewarded for your great ideas and hard work once and for all.

You just need to make smart decisions using a new invigorated mindset – *a mindset that is focussed and determined.*

*Why not let the world know you are an expert in your field?*

If you have done the homework to get there and have become knowledgeable and experienced in your area of work, you should be broadcasting it and getting yourself into a fabulous position where you can treat yourself to a new life!

*Everyone has unique capabilities hidden away inside them, so it's time to release the power of your potential and be at the forefront.*

Find the leader in you!

Anyone can be rich in lifestyle with the right formula.
You're holding your life in your hands, so make it the best it can be.
Step out of the turmoil and into success! Be a winner in life.
*Fluff up you feathers and be proud of what you are capable of and who you truly are.*
Feel the empowerment in this.
So, if you've got a brilliant idea, what are you going to do about it?
You've just got to take that leap of faith....
So don't stay asleep and dream – wake up and start living!
*Make that transformation, for the sake of yourself.....*

**…. it doesn't matter how hard you try, if you haven't got the right mindset.....**
*Do you really have the right mindset to succeed in life?*
It's all very well having knowledge, education, skills, opportunities, stamina and a hard working ethic, but, if you haven't got the right *mindset,* all that will just be wasted, if success, in any capacity, is your life path.

*Personal excellence should be part of your overall mission in life if you want to succeed, make money and have the lifestyle you've always dreamed of.*

However, in that pursuit of excellence, you need to have the right mindset to follow it through – that's if you genuinely have a thirst to reach that ultimate dream....
Successful people are those that do what unsuccessful people aren't willing to do.

To get there, you should be making the most of your time by updating and increasing your skills. *Go the extra mile.*
Broaden your mind.
Set aside time to study.
Develop and exploit the natural talents and abilities you were born with.
Put together a plan to get where you want to be.
Do not use a lack of ability as an excuse not to get there, or to go backwards. Just learn how, or get someone's help. Tap into someone else's expertise if needs be.
If at first you don't succeed, try again.

New skills and experiences don't always go right the first time, so therefore don't simply feel inadequate and inferior.
Stick with it until you do succeed.

Remember, you're developing a skill that gives you the ability to provide for yourself and your family and to reach that ultimate life.
If you are going to excel, you may have to do things you don't always enjoy, but must develop in order to get to your goal. Don't view doing these things as negative, instead, view it as a small price to pay for your chosen success.
Everybody has talent, but ability takes hard work, and hard work opens the door to success and the freedom to do what you want, when you want.
There are always going to be people who are better at certain things than you are.
However, there's also a *high* chance that you are better at other things than *they* are.

*We all have our own unique capabilities and talents.*

But, all skills can be learned if you really apply yourself.
Even if you're not the best, if it helps you understand your field better and move up the ladder and earn more.

Then, even if it is a good understanding, it will certainly help in the process.

*If you want that goal badly enough, you will be willing to achieve what it takes to make it happen.*

Empowering mindset!

Out of mistakes can come golden opportunities. *Look for them.*
See how you can spin a mistake into a positive outcome. Learn from your mistakes and try and glean something out of them to take you forward.
Always focus on you and what you are doing, what your plan and ultimate goal is.

There are bound to be others that are doing better than you, even if you are really successful. But focussing on those above you just creates feelings of inadequacy and jealousy, which is negative. Instead, use it as inspiration that you too can succeed.

Set it into your mind.

*You are the most important person in your life.*

Without it sounding selfish, if you don't take care of yourself first, *how are you going to be able to care for anyone else?*

Be practical about your time and efforts and don't offer it to others until you are right yourself.
The more peace of mind and better equipped you are, the happier you will be, and in turn, you will extend that happiness onto others and be able to give them your time far more effectively.
If needs be, use someone you may view as an 'enemy' to motivate you and spur you on to greater achievements.
If there is someone out there that has belittled you or not believed in you and your skills for whatever reason, use that as motivation to show them what you're made of.

Think about how good your success will make you feel when they see how well you've done!

Focus on your own success before trying to change the world and the things that you have no control over.
It is a waste of energy worrying and fretting about things, as you will only frustrate yourself and hinder your own progress. Accept there are things that you cannot change and focus on your own goal first.

*Your energy will be much better spent.*

You can always be concerned about external issues more once you have reached a comfortable position and have more time, and possibly money, to do so.
Sometimes it's necessary to prioritise your time better and downsize your jobs or thins that you believe need to be done, so you can focus on the most important goal or goals. You cannot do everything at once, so try and establish what your highest priority is and use your energy on that first.

If you cannot change someone's mind, then move on.
Spending lots of time and effort on opening up a closed mind is fruitless. Accept that's the situation and use your energy on trying to get to where you are going instead.

Focus your mind on it.....

Everyone has a bad day. Don't take it to heart and think the whole world is going to end.
Accept it, take a deep breath and start again tomorrow.

If a job's worth doing, do it with a centred, controlled and dedicated mind that is fresh and able to concentrate.

Your success and goal depends on your motivation and best efforts, so just put your bad day down to experience, wake up fresh the next day and ready to go get 'em!

It's always a good idea to evaluate.
Look back on your achievements, your mistakes, what you have learnt and look at ways of doing things better. Life is all about learning and using your experiences to take you forward with renewed vigour and intelligence.

*Be patient.*

All goals take time and all schedules and agendas move. Things don't always have to be done yesterday. Plans need to be achieved one step at a time. Skills need to be learnt. Improvements need to be made steadily.
Don't be discouraged if thins aren't moving at a great pace. Be more productive every day and develop a better attitude to yourself and well-being.
Set your mind to be fully concentrated and drive towards your goals and destiny.
Each step and experience, no matter how small, will enhance your life and make you a better and more valuable person, with peace of mind, less stress and more wealth and good health.
Make a lifelong commitment to personal excellence.
What is meant to be will happen, if you have faith and let it do it's thing....

*Commit to developing this mindset and your empowerment will be sure to follow...*


**"Your intelligence is always with you overseeing your body, even though you may not be aware of its work".**


**.....so they say that chance favours the prepared mind....**
*It's obvious that if you want to get on in life, rather than just sit and stagnate, be bored out of your wits, or regret that you never did anything with your time, then you need to develop the right mentality to get rid of this inertia.*
And you need to be open to all opportunities and possibilities that come your way – without which, life drifts along, going nowhere, and doing not very much at all!
Even if you come up with your own opportunities, you still need to be prepared to carry them through.....

You will need to have the correct mindset to enable you to follow through any new intentions and add extra processes and acquisitions onto whatever work you may already have created.

Being prepared and in the right frame of mind enables you to embrace new networks of thought, with the ability to sense, understand, decide and act upon any observations and opportunities that suddenly appear to you.

They say that '*luck is when preparation and opportunity meet*', so being prepared allows you to be ready to change chance into good fortune.
They also say that things follow a law, have their own regular 'periods' and also repeat themselves.
Every that has happened will happen over again, sometimes more than once.
You therefore need to be open and ready for things when they come your way, in order to take complete advantage of those opportunities and make the most out of them, so you can successfully enhance your life.

*One thing is for sure, luck always changes and so you surely must stay observant and have your eyes open to creative opportunities and solutions in your world.*

It's always better to remain optimistic so you can look forward, rather than be pessimistic about your life and maintain a negative view on what will happen to you.
Because you can't possibly stay open to whatever arises, if you are too busy feeling sorry for yourself, or being jealous of other peoples' good fortune.
This is no a good perspective to have if you want to feel empowered about your future.

*You need to stay alert and really expect great opportunities to come your way!*

> **"You have to acknowledge the power within you
> to overcome your circumstances.
> Believe in yourself enough to follow your intuition
> and allow yourself to make the changes
> that will 'free' you".**

**....your world is amazing and a mirror of your thoughts.....
bringing you success and enlightenment...**

*If you make a considered effort to understand and believe in the positive energy that is passed between you and the earth, you can develop a wonderful state of being at one with the world, nature and the universe as a whole.*

Through this '*intelligence*', you can have an actual *organic* effect on the health of this ever-evolving planet.

Embracing this philosophy should allow you to accept that the universe provides for you and as you take *from* it, so you can also give back. This brings a cycle of sharing. As you explore and expand this understanding and acceptance, you will open up a realisation and naturally build a passion and zest for what life truly has to offer you......

Subsequently, by passing on this message of positive energy, love and acceptance to others, you set in motion the continuing cycle of an enhanced world where everyone can collectively live more harmoniously together.

*Because, when you learn to appreciate what this planet has to offer, you can jump to a higher level of understanding of how it functions.*

And, whether you realise it or not, you are using your own energy quite naturally to develop your understanding and place in the universe. And as you gradually move up in that intelligence, you can begin to realise that everyone and everything is actually *connected*. And by showing your love and gratitude to the world and what it has to offer you and each other, all that energy starts to resonate at a higher level.

As this understanding and acceptance continues to be passed on and appreciated, so it becomes a self-fulfilling prophecy.
*Everyone has a responsibility to both themselves and the planet.*
Through this new understanding of the world, you can learn how to create a valuable existence in it. You can find your own path and go on a personal journey to betterment, wealth, health, success, peace and happiness.

And thereby, ultimate empowerment.

Through your new insight and intelligence, you can use the power of your own positive energy, together with the energies of the universe and mould the life you really want.
You do this through your *thought creation*.

*Because, your thoughts are a mirror of your life.*
Whatever you think, so you create your life with those thoughts.

*You can get anything you want, fulfil your dreams and become a master of your own mind and personal universe.*

You will begin to see the true meaning of life through your thoughts. By having total and focussed consideration for your own world and nature itself and what that can ultimately do for you, you can reap the rewards of this and pass on the benefits to others along the way.
You can '*anchor*' your new positive way of thinking and feeling and personally aim at getting more out of your life.
You can develop a brand new mindset that remains within you for ever....
Your new intellect and awareness of how life can work will automatically alert you to all the opportunities that come your way, because you will be totally *mindful* of them.
Your new positive thoughts will give you the attributes needed to enhance your life in a meaningful way. You will begin to evolve through the repetition of your positive thoughts and start to manifest outcomes that you yourself *personally* create.

You will be part of your <u>own</u> story, helping to cultivate happiness in your life, having built up the knowledge and intelligence to help you live more happily and contently.
Adopting this philosophy and 'openness' will develop your skills in *mindfulness* and the tools for achieving the perfect life, fantastic relationships and a fulfilling, satisfying career.
You will be going through a total process of personal empowerment. The single most important investment you can make in your life, is to create a new positive mindset, to be open to learning, to release the clutter from your life and to reconnect with nature, thereby becoming energised and motivated. That's if you want to become successful in all aspects of your world.

*Reprogramming your mind will change your life forever.*

It will even change the life of those around you.
*You will create your own* destiny, instead of allowing others or circumstances to dictate them for you.

*Remember, it's all about choice.*

Allow a new way of thinking into your consciousness and give yourself the energy and power you need to get ahead and become fully in charge of yourself.
You no longer need to talk yourself down or out of things, you just need to learn how to plug into your new power of positive thoughts and create your own destiny.
You don't have to fear anything any more, because you know you are creating your life *yourself*.

*And by having certain faith in yourself and remembering that the universe is always providing for you, you can allow your world to take shape, without having to enforce anything at all......*

**……so then…..tell me a bit about my unconscious mind…..I can control it myself, can't I…**
*What you think you do and what you actually do, can be very different.*
From what you eat and drink to how you work and who you love – you can be almost certain that you are working on *automatic*.
But the unconscious mind is very powerful…..!
And you can cleverly use this information to enhance your achievements and fulfil your goals.

So, are you really in control of your life or are you living in a hectic blur?
Only a very minute part of your mind is played by the conscious mind…….it's your unconscious mind that is actually in control…..

Apparently, we're all *optimists*.

Because, despite all the risks we face or know about, we *still* carry on regardless anyway. From health to finance and how we drive, negative information doesn't seem to sink in....

For example - getting stressed at work, eating fatty, salty foods, smoking, drinking and lying on the couch all day - we all know is bad for us, yet we still do it anyway!

So, how do you remain optimistic in the face of actual reality?
As you go through life taking on all kinds of hardships and negative events.....you tend to ignore negative information, *even when you are given the statistics.*
The part of your brain that deals with negative events is less active than the positive part.
Your brain sees the world through rose-tinted glasses, in other words, inaccurately!

It *is* very good for your health to *expect* positive things to happen in the future. Plus, if you want to get ahead, it motivates you to put in the effort – that's why your brain has evolved to become optimistic, and this has been essential to our success as a species.

As an example, look at our ancestors who left Africa to find something new....
In order to explore, they had to know there was *something* to discover that was better than what they already had.
It's the same with us now..... Knowing there is something better out there, keeps us striving for a better future.

So seeing the world through rose-tinted glasses can actually equal optimism.
Having a sense that you're in control of everything you do is just an illusion.
Your very survival has long depended on everything your unconscious does for you behind the scenes.
All the skills you have learnt and perfected over the years become automatic in time and unconsciously controlled.

By becoming automatic in some areas, it frees up your conscious mind to do other things.
Your unconscious decides what information, in a very busy world, is worthy of your conscious attention – what's interesting, what's worth exploring, etc.
*Harnessing* these signals may help you to cope with the data overload you face in today's world.

The unconscious is the sophisticated centre of everything you do – when it comes down to it, your brain runs mostly unconsciously – on auto pilot.

*By tapping into and using it's immense power, send your unconscious mind lots of motivating, inspiring and positive thoughts to 'log' into, so they also become automatic, giving you the absolute potential to change your life and fortunes for the better, forever!*

**……getting your life in order…..means getting your own life strategy together…..**
*Enhance that sense of empowerment by making up your own strategy for life – one that is totally personal to you.*
By writing down what you want out of your life – whether that's being successful or just simply feeling free, you can aim towards achieving and becoming it.
Do this by thinking about what it is you want **exactly**, and then planning the steps you need to get there.
So, how can you be in control enough to follow this *unique* path….?
There may be a fundamental foundation that you need to lay first before you can actually move forward.

*And to start building up the strength to do that, you will need to eliminate any barriers that may be getting in the way.*

Your particular goal may mean you need money to get there.
So start gradually increasing your bank balance, either by saving a little every time you get paid, by saving on bills and squirrelling bits of cash away, or by getting a better or additional job that allows you to build up your nest egg for achievement.

*Spring clean your circumstances by removing meaningless chores and tasks to make some extra time for your changes.*

Remove any negative people and influences, so you can feel more empowered to move upwards with your goal and be in a position to make your *own* decisions about your life and the strategy you want to put in place.
Perhaps a de-clutter of your mind also needs to happen - ridding yourself of all those things in your head that keep rearing up and standing in your way.

If this is deeply emotional, you may need some outside help with this or use some of the strategies further in this book.

Deal with any debts you may have by setting up payment plans to gradually settle accounts, so you can feel like you are once again in control of your finances and life!
Whatever it is that is personal to you to make your changes – set it out in a workable strategy.

Use the *big picture* to start with and then add in the tactics and actions to get there, so you can really start living your life as it was meant to be!
As you gradually clean up your situation and clear your mind, you will be open to exciting new things and become aware of opportunities as they arise.

The whole exercise will also give you a renewed sense of vigour and focus.
*How empowering will that feel.....!?*

**......you know that nothing will ever change unless you do......**
*If you want to be successful, you need to have something to offer.*
Something of worth....
You have to make yourself valuable and stand out from the rest.
If you don't feel this is already a strong part of who you are, then things will obviously need to change.
And change will only come from your willingness to make the effort and develop your inner strength – which can take a lot of courage.
But, through this strategy, you can really transform every aspect of your life!

If you truly want that change or success, you need to be prepared to work a little bit harder and go the extra mile.
You need to study more to get the skills and knowledge you require under your belt.
You need to become more intelligent.

If you want to become an expert in your field and command more money and a higher profile, you need to put aside the time to become better than you are now.

But don't worry, because by being just 1% better than you are now, or than your colleagues or the competition are, makes you more valuable than them and increases your chances of higher success. All because you have that extra 1% edge!

However, that doesn't need to be as scary as it may seem!
It doesn't necessarily mean spending 3-5 years at university....
You can learn whatever you need to become that bit better, or even an expert, in your own time for just an hour or 2 a day using the extensive resources available to you publicly, like online or the library.
Or you could take a course that only requires a few months to get the knowledge, rather than the years it takes with further education.

*This new process of development and thinking will force your attitude to change and so your relationship with your own 'inner reality' changes as well.*

And this will form a self-fulfilling prophecy.
If you want something to change, you need to switch your outlook on life to the *centre* of your inner self, rather than expect things to change from the *outside*.
Once you transform to this way of seeing things, everything becomes possible.

So, if you want to empower yourself to take the next step and make yourself really valuable, start making your plans and looking around for the means to get you there....

*....because nothing will change, unless you do......*

**......because it's YOUR choices and YOUR life that make you who you are......**
*It's so easy to lose focus if you allow your control to be looosened by outside things and people.*
But, never forget that you have *choices* in life.
Every choice you make is yours alone.
Even if someone makes a choice for you, you are making the choice to allow them to do so – thereby giving permission for the control to be taken out of your hands.

Everything you have done, or has happened in your life is through the choices *you* have made – whether good, bad, indifferent or major.

*And each and every one of those choices has made your life what it is today.*

If you don't like where you have landed, you have to come to terms with the fact that *you* put yourself there, and look yourself straight in the face with honesty and frankness about that situation.
Don't delude yourself (and it's very easy to do that if you're not *completely* honest).
See yourself and your life EXACTLY for what it is.

If don't like what you can see or where you are, then make a choice to change things.
If you don't make changes in life, then everything will stay exactly as it is......and that's a **fact**!
If there is a negative influence in your life obstructing the progress of your health and fitness, weight, work, people, your environment, or your money, achievement and success ladder, whatever it is, *it is destructive*.
It is a force and an energy that will have a bad effect on how you think and feel.
It dominates your every move – if you *allow* it to.
It's YOUR choice if you let it!
If you don't like how it is, then it's YOUR own responsibility to change things, no-one else's.

*After all, you are here to fulfil YOUR own life.*

And it's your responsibility to get the most out of your innate talent and make it as good as it can be, for the time you are given on this beautiful planet.
This *may* mean you being selfish, but it's really just about you looking after yourself, which in turn will benefit those around you in so many ways too anyway.....
All relationships around you, all connections to you, will feed from the positive energy that you generate through you looking after yourself first.
It has a knock-on effect.

*When you are happy, well and relaxed, so you pass those influences onto those you come into contact with.*

It's self-fulfilling empowerment...!

If everyone looked after themselves by feeding their soul, by creating positive vibes, by looking after themselves, by making the right choices for themselves, then the energy flow between us all will always be positive, and when energy is positive, so happiness can be spread.

Think about it......

If you are around happy, lively people who smile and laugh their way through life, who conduct themselves well because they have made all the right choices in life for THEM as an *individual*, then you will naturally feel their high, their good energy flow, their internal peace and calm.

*It passes on naturally. It's good vibrations.*

Even if you only smiled at someone as you walk along, they usually smile back.
This puts you in good spirits, makes you feel nice and so they will too. You're all set up for the day and will continue to smile at others who smile at others and so on...

*The positive energy is being passed on and on and on between us all.*

When anyone feels good and calm inside, it projects outwardly too. You will skip through the day doing tasks in a relaxed manner, feeling confident and getting jobs done more efficiently. Thereby passing on good work, which in turn has good energy. Your boss or partner, or whoever else is concerned, will be happy with you, and so the positive vibe has been passed around through so many ways.

As each day passes and you make the right choices for you, so you become happier, things work out better for you, ambitions are fulfilled and success is imminent – whether that is success in business, achievement or just inner peace.

*It's all part of your life empowerment....and others' too.*

Everyday you wake up feeling good and fresh and motivated from all the achievements you've made and the happy energy you've passed between others, who will in turn pass their positive energy onto others in their own surroundings and so the world will turn in a much better way.

Thoughtfulness, charity and consideration will be amplified as patience and goodness radiates out from your inner happiness and positive energy which you are transferring on, and more and more circles of positivity are rotated round and round the world.

*All because of the good choices you made!*

When you feel happier and lighter and your positive energy is flowing so freely, you will open up to how your heart is feeling, how love flows through it and you can begin to build up more friendships and relationships.
Bringing you back to the *basics* in life.

By sharing what you have, you'll become more receptive to the Universe's bounty.
In this positive state, you can clear the clutter from your head and heart of past negative relationships, events and experiences and make way for renewed thoughts, opening yourself up to a realm of possibilities and opportunities.
Because you will feel wide awake and totally receptive.

*Your world will begin to see prospects and the truth that is designed just for you....*

Those opportunities that you have now consciously noticed and possibly acted upon, will then open out into more available choices. Choices that you will have the right frame of mind to consider and initiate, making you more contented or successful in your life.
Free up space in your head.
Clear out the old unused or no longer wanted.

*Make room for your life!*

Unblocking your mind will allow you to think more clearly, see more clearly and decide more clearly.

*When you are in this position, you cannot help but feel an empowering force surging through you!*

> **"Be the person you want to be.**
> **Believe it through and through and you will surely have**
> **the best possible life you can have**
> **in this beautiful world".**


**……..grow and let go…………**
*If you truly want to grow as a person because you feel you are stuck in a rut, still doing the same old things day after day and getting nowhere, then create some of those positive changes in your life.*
Doing this will get you out of that repetitive groove and onto the road to better and improved circumstances.
Where has your vision and ambitious plan gone...?
Buried under a pile of stale dreams?

As you know, nothing changes unless you do, so you cannot expect to go on in the same old way and wait for a miracle to happen. Everyone makes their own luck and you have to be prepared and ready to take on new opportunities and challenges that present themselves, or that you particularly want to look for.
Make this happen with your new, changed mindset.

*Change is essential for your growth and development as a person, particularly if your current path lacks meaning and satisfaction, or you feel totally lacking in power over your life.*

You may well be sitting on a mountain of obstacles that you have *unconsciously* created and that you believe you really *need* in your life. It's quite possibly because they create 'comfort' for you, they have purpose, or they help you feel in control and accepted within your circle, or your own mind.

But those very obstacles are really no longer beneficial to you and are now just in the way of your progress.

*They have developed into burdensome barriers that are preventing you from growing.*

You probably think you're not able to change any more, because you have allowed yourself to become complacent. You have coveted all that baggage you have dragged along with you since childhood and through adulthood and held onto it for dear life. This may well have created low self-esteem, fear, perfectionism, anger and the need to please or be in control.

All this added together has caused you to behave, think and feel a certain way, and you now can't shake this off - even though deep inside, you know full well that this isn't the *real* you.

*This whole situation is totally unproductive and sabotaging your growth, progress and success.*

How can you make positive changes with all this hanging round your neck, constantly bringing you down...?
These negative things that have now turned into daily habits, have penetrated your thoughts and emotions and are driving your behaviour, because your brain is now totally wired that way!

But, if you sincerely want that positive change in your life, you will need to clear out those negative emotions, that anger and frustration, that feeling of hopelessness and that fear of failure.
It is worth the risk because what's on the other side is precious freedom and satisfaction!

It's time to move past those barriers and make the most out of your life.

It's time to step out of your comfort zone, stop listening to those in your surrounding environment that are keeping you safe and warm, and begin to build the strength to grow past those obstacles and reinforcements and start being who you *truly* want to be, *once and for all*.

*Start living a happy life and achieving your goals, instead of listening to negative discouragement – even if it's your own inner self telling you this.*

It's time to take back control!
It may seem daunting at first – of course it will, you've got used to living your certain way in your comfort zone, and it will certainly be challenging – but then, that's what life is all about, isn't it?

*It's about challenging yourself and growing with the experiences, whilst on your journey to the best you can be...!*

You will need to instil determination and energy....
You will need to stretch yourself and change your mindset in order to get there.
You need to find a purpose, a goal to aim for, that's if you *really* want to move forward.
Hopefully you will find all the tools you need in here to help change your mindset and become fully empowered to fulfil your dreams and start living the life you deserve.
Tell yourself that you goals *are achievable*.

*If you think you can do it, then you will.*

You really wouldn't seriously think about becoming something that is *totally* not **you** anyway. Because if you are going to change your life for the better, it is naturally going to be something that you *want* and therefore feel you *can do or be*.

If you really want to be a successful electrician, you wouldn't be thinking about being an artist.
That would make it something you really have no innate skill for. Even though you could probably *learn* how to be an artist – it certainly *won't* be coming from a place in your heart and soul.
You will be thinking of something more *inwardly* rewarding that you know full well will be the making of you, because you secretly know you would be good at it, and what's more, happy doing it too...!

*You just need an intelligent approach to your goal.*

Don't try any *quick-fix* approaches. They really don't work.

You wouldn't be giving yourself the time or the proper application to get your new, empowered mindset in order.
You need to change emotionally, mentally and sometimes physically, in order to take yourself on the journey to your destiny <u>and stay there</u>.

You don't want to take the short-cut and find you didn't have the right tools *inwardly* to <u>sustain and maintain</u> that life. You will fall out of love with yourself and be back to square one again, sitting with all your previous anxieties and insecurities, frustrations and despondency.
It would be soul destroying.

Whatever changes you decide to make, even if it's big (and why not....everyone needs to dream big!), take small, manageable steps to get there. Don't fall at the first hurdle because you swamped yourself with too many high expectations or a massive workload, and then feel like a failure because it was all too much!

Each small step is a *change*.
Any percentage of change is a positive shift.
Each positive shift, ends up with a big positive change and you in the driving seat again, feeling good and satisfied, fulfilling dreams, living your life.

When it comes to any change, only worry about things that *concern you*, not things that are out of your control.
That's just a futile exercise and an added stress.
If you cannot change those things, then why spend time concerning yourself with them? Just think about how much head-space you will be freeing up for yourself?!

Take advice from others by all means, but don't spend too much time juggling all their suggestions and trying to please them! You will know instinctively what feels right for you, if any of it at all.

*Go by your own intuition – then you will feel good and comfortable about any decisions you make.*

During your conversations, research and experiences, be ready and prepared.

Because, along the way you will undoubtedly come up with some fantastic ideas and brilliant, motivating insights that will spur you on towards new resolutions and what you *really* want to be doing, including some exciting challenges for your future.
When you are awake and alert, fabulous opportunities arise and doors open waiting for you to cross their threshold into a new and wonderful world.

*Everyone's journey is totally unique to each person.*

Find your own glove that fits you!

Go with your own flow, don't swim against it or fight to be something you are not, or that you don't believe or that just doesn't match anywhere near what's going on in your own mind, body and soul! But remember to push through your comfort zone if you want that personal change for the better.

*You may only have to turn the screw* **1 degree** *to the right for your whole life to take on a completely different perspective!*

A perspective that *transforms* you.

No matter how insignificant you think it might be, it could be the very thing that has a *massive* impact on you and moves you into action, removing all those negative obstacles and instilling pure quality into your life - sending you soaring through the sky!
*How wonderful!*

Allow your new-found philosophies and strategies for the future to become your *'truth'* that you live by, that your every day consists of being, that shapes how you feel about life and how you act towards it.
Empower yourself with those principles and grow with them.

*It's positive change for personal growth.....*

**........I one hundred percent believe that I am valuable.......**
*You should be valuing yourself above all else.*
How and the way you live and who you surround yourself by, should be to enhance and complement you, not hinder and stress you.

Your life should not be about constant conflict and turmoil, worry and discontent.
Consider this very seriously....

This kind of life is not an acceptable way to spend your journey while you are here....
There are strategies that you can put in place to ensure your life is *right for you.*

*A life that is balanced and happy with an open mind and heart ready to learn, engage and see every opportunity that comes your way.*

A life without negativity and unwanted threats to your inner peace.
If you feel that you have become a product of your own making, *then you are **right**!*
But, just as this may be negative, so it can be positive too.
It's all about '*cause and effect*'.
For every decision, choice, action you make, so there will be a result, a consequence for that thought - no matter whether it is good, bad or indifferent.
No-one is to blame for anything that happens in your life except you.
*You have to **accept** this.*

You are wholly responsible for every choice you make. It is not possible for anyone else to make a choice for you, even if you are being encouraged and coerced by someone to make a particular decision, it is ultimately up to you to follow that advice.

*You have the right and choice to say yes or no......*

If you agree with their decision, it is *you* who has agreed to it. You have made that choice and you cannot blame anyone else for it.

This is *your* life.

Everything that has happened in your life, all events, people and circumstances in it, are there because you decided and allowed them to be there.
So, therefore, in this respect, you can choose to add and subtract certain things into or out of your life.
You decide.....

That means then, if things are not going your way, you have the utmost power to turn things around and make positive choices and decisions.

*You must always believe you are worthy of good things.*

Why shouldn't you be.....?
Believe good things will happen and your heart and brain cannot go against this. You are telling them this and they will react to that demand and request accordingly.

*You must truly commit to this **100 percent** without **any** doubt.*

Any doubt inside your mind will not be wholeheartedly accepted, and therefore is not a complete conviction that your brain can understand.
If you feel you are having to 'expect' too much from people, then this is in conflict with you as a person, as the *true you*.
You are compromising yourself, as those expectations are not being met by the people around you and therefore cannot be a correct '*fit*' for you.
You shouldn't *have* to try too hard with people for them to be an acceptable part of your life and destiny.
*Why compromise yourself to be acceptable to others?*
<u>You are you and can only be you</u>.

It is absolutely *impossible* to be anyone else!
If things don't suit you, then they are not an 'innate' part of who you are.
You shouldn't have to try too hard to be the person you are, because ultimately, you are not being that person by having to try so hard.
You should be able to be the *true* you, just by being *you* - calmly and <u>naturally</u>.

Obviously, if you have to remove negative people and situations from your life, then you can make the space for bigger, better and much more amazing people and things instead.
Your head, heart and world will be open to accepting every opportunity that shows itself to you.

You cannot be in this position of calm and openness if you are being closed down by the negativity of stress and tension caused by outside forces....
How can you allow your true colours to shine through, if you are too busy trying to be something else for someone else or because of someone else?

*You owe it to yourself to allow good things into your life.*

You need to be ready and prepared to let these things in.
You need to know that your time, effort and love are being spent in the right places and on the right people.
Right people for *you*.
People that allow you to breathe and *be*.
People who appreciate you for you, just the way you are, without having to try to bend or shape you, and without you having to be a *different* person.

If you spend your life in negativity, the only possible option is to attract more negativity.

*Think hard about this.*

Equate it to your life. Watch how things have happened, or will happen.
Do the reverse if necessary!
Positive energy will attract more positive energy, so why waste your time holding onto negativity if the world is full of good things you can attract instead?
*Always* know that you deserve good things. No-one deserves bad.

Remember, as Winston Churchill once said:

'A *pessimist sees the difficulty in every opportunity; an optimist sees the opportunity in every difficulty'*.

Start living your own life of value and positivity.

*Open up your world to a realm beyond your expectations.*
*That is true empowerment....*

**…...first though......you have to be responsible for your own life and destiny...**

*As part of being responsible for yourself and your life, if you want to succeed, you will need to **think** more.*

Instead of being reactive to events happening, look ahead....

Have the foresight to stop, look and listen to what is going on around you in your life and the world.
How are things changing and progressing and how can you adapt and move to respond to those changes?
Or better, improve on those changes?

*You need to be alert and ahead of the game if you want to get past any problems and move forwards and upwards.*

Be proactive, **not** reactive.

Being reactive means that you will never be prepared.
You will always be waiting for things to happen and reacting to them at the time they occur.
If you are not ready and able, both physically and financially, even emotionally and mentally, then you will quite probably fail.

*So be ready by being proactive.*

Be in control of what is happening *yourself* and not by other forces being in control of you and your life and well-being.

In this modern age where things change so quickly in front of your eyes, you cannot sit back on your laurels and wait for things to turn out okay, because that may not be an accurate assumption.
Especially if you are already struggling anyway.

Get some empowerment back in your life if you want to survive and grow.
Wake up and take a good look around you.
Find ways of making positive things happen **for** you instead of waiting for them to happen **to** you.....
Set up your *own* brand new way of living.

*Don't wait for **it** to set you up......*

**…...so, are you just living without actually *living*.....**
*To most people, achieving their dream is very important....*
However, so many people still insist on living within boring, mundane routines and the built up boundaries and limitations they have set for themselves – whether they realise they have or not......

Too many people walk the Earth without actually living their life. They go from day to day without even noticing the beautiful things in life, or even really noticing what they are actually doing *themselves*. Everything's on 'automatic'.......

Are you one of those people that puts their dreams on hold because you believe that achieving them means a lot of work?
Perhaps you believe your dream is just not realistic? But, if you haven't really tried working on it, how can you possibly know it is actually unrealistic?

*You won't know until you've actually tried....*

Do you think that by not following your dreams, you will be consumed by regret when your final day comes?

*People usually regret the things they didn't do, rather than the things they failed in doing....*

Don't you think that you owe it to yourself, your family and everyone around you to try?
Life doesn't have to be about how big your house is, how much money you have coming in, how luxurious your car is, whether you can afford a yacht and expensive holidays or not.
Life is really about *living* it and doing what you *want* to do – otherwise, what really is the point?

As you go through the physical process of fulfilling your dream, so you will build on your wisdom and character.
If you think you are already happy, how deep do you think that happiness really is? Happiness is great, but are you truly contented, or is it just shallow pleasure?

By not doing what you are innately *supposed* to do – which is usually what your dream is, *you are only getting second best out of life.*

Don't spend your life in a bubble of *'what ifs'* and *'what could've beens'* – this is such a waste......

It may be scary – it probably *will* be.
It may well be risky.
But regardless of your age, financial status and responsibilities in life, it's never too late to achieve your dream!
Those that have tried have never regretted it – why should they?
They're living their dream!

Isn't it time you took that step and started living the life you deserve.....?


**"You can discover a world and life you never thought possible.
You can make your dreams come true,
fulfil all your ambitions, find inner peace and
a confidence that will all become part of
your everyday life".**


**....... so then....begin doing what you want now.....**
In the words of Marie Ray (Professional Counsellor)...."*We only have this moment, sparkling like a star in our hand and melting like a snow flake*".
You need to remind yourself of this very regularly.....
**Every day!**
So often you put your life on hold waiting for some *'given'* time when you will be thinner, richer or the stars are aligned in your favour......
*When you do this, you're not being powerful in the **present** and are essentially wishing your life away....*

**....and in the process.....learn to love yourself for the greater good.....**
*How much do you love yourself?*
This doesn't mean in a massively egotistic way, rather that you love who and what you are inwardly and outwardly?
And that means so you can conduct your life in a meaningful and

valuable way, where others recognise your confidence as well as you do....

Knowing who you are allows you to carry on life in a structured and focussed way, because you will accept yourself and all your flaws, know you can change things as and when you want or need to, and *really* be the person you want to be.
That's all without allowing others to control you and change for *their* benefit, instead of your own.

Feeling and being yourself will help you love yourself, and as you love yourself, so you allow others into your heart to love you too.
It's all about being the *true* you.

*As the true you, you can live an empowered life that fulfils all your desires and dreams.*

Knowing this gives you ultimate peace and satisfaction, acceptance and freedom.
You are happy to be you, improve you and change you according to your own self.

If you are happy in yourself, then you are happy for others to be themselves too. And feeling like this, stops you spending your time being judgemental and critical, selfish and controlling – both towards yourself and others. It eliminates so much negativity – which we can all live without.
It gives you confidence and pride to live as *yourself* and feel totally contented with who you are – as a total and unique individual – no matter how sane or eccentric that may be!
Your self-esteem will be high and you will attract others to you (as in the '*Law of Attraction*' – *more about this later*).

You open up your world to love, luck, hope and optimism and in doing so, you also open up a world of opportunities that have the potential to make your life the best it can be.

*You will naturally be a kind and positive person because you don't feel like you are competing with anyone, because you are totally happy within yourself.*

Build up the love for yourself by being kind and positive to yourself – praise your good work, praise your good health and praise your wonderful life.

Empower your thoughts with good things that support your development and life in general. Acknowledge that all your efforts are for the good, that they are enhancing your life and building your skills, which ultimately brings good results.

Release any worry you are holding onto that is getting in the way of your space to love yourself – it's just a hindrance.

Get help with anything you need, so you can remove those stresses from your life and you can make yourself feel SO much better for freeing yourself from the responsibility of them all.

Keep supporting your path, building up images and visualising yourself making the best out of your life, living it to the full, achieving your desires.

*Feel confident at all times that everything you want out of life will happen.*

Don't be down on yourself and your dreams by thinking they won't ever happen. That's negative talking getting into your head and is not conducive with feeling love for yourself.

Take heart that you can make *anything* you want happen, as long as you believe you have the power to make it so.

Let go of past mistakes and hurts that have been playing on your mind.

They are gone – it's the present and future that is important now on your path to good and better things.

Always remember that you **are** worthy of happiness and achievement, so forgive yourself and move on to more wonderful and exciting events.

If you are feeling happy, be happy, if you are feeling sad, be sad – but acknowledge why you are having those feelings and learn from them. Don't wallow in negativity for so long that is not helpful to anyone and certainly not for the love of yourself.

Be truthful about your emotions and learn how to deal with them in a positive way.

Make them useful and allow them to guide you. Knowing your thoughts and feelings is a good way of healing yourself and allowing you to grow as a person.
Get in touch with your spirituality, as it's a wonderful place to grow from.

*If you can get in touch with your senses, allow yourself to find the inner you, feel connected to the world and universe, you will feel like you really belong to, and are part of, this beautiful and extraordinary place we all live in.*

In doing so, you will become more nurtured and in love with yourself and in turn, become more loving and compassionate outwardly.
Tell yourself that you love and accept yourself <u>constantly</u> – get it into your heart and mind!
Feel good about it and tell yourself you are proud and happy *every day*.

*All these positive affirmations will resonate in your brain and the more you do it, the more it will accept it as fact!*

Always remember how grateful you are for the person you are and the things you have in your life, including all those skills and attributes that make you such a unique person.
Feel strong and empowered by the gifts you were given - that you are healthy and alive and in total control of your life every day!
Find something that you know you are, or could be really good at, and hone those skills.

*Knowing you have something special in those skills to offer the world, is a fabulous and powerful motivator and confidence booster!*

Allow yourself to dream.
Allow yourself to **believe** in those dreams.

The only person stopping you is you – so nurture your dreams and make them happen!
As part of knowing who you are and loving yourself, make sure you

know when to stop, have a break and some 'me-time'.
Love your health and your body too.
Take time to relax and do things that you like to do.
Spend time looking after yourself.
Do things that nourish your soul.
And don't forget that life needs a little bit of fun too!

Man does not live by work and seriousness alone, so do something that makes you let go, laugh out loud and feel free!

Part of loving yourself is loving your body – which means your well-being!
Ditch the cigarettes, the alcohol, the drugs, the junk food and couch and eat well.
Nourish your body, get some exercise and fresh air and feel the real benefits of feeling strong and healthy, so you can make the most out of your life with a clear head, flexibility and a great stand-point for a long life.

If you love yourself, you love your body naturally, hand-in-hand as part of your everyday 'self-love' empowerment.

Start looking at the beauty around you.
Love it and it will help you to learn to love yourself. Really begin to notice the world in all it's resplendent glory. Fully appreciate it and you will then truly treasure your place in it.....

At the end of the day, you can only be you and you have to value that, because there is no-one else like you – you are *authentically unique*.
And within that person that is *only you*, you have your own choices, you have ownership of you, yourself, your body, your feelings, actions and thoughts, as they are yours to cherish.
They are yours to make decisions, fantasise, dream, hope, be a success and be the owner of your own fears, mistakes and failures, but *you* choose how you handle them – no-one else.
You can genuinely love yourself wholly, in all aspects and all parts and no-one can take that away from you.

*You are a friend of yourself, so take care of you!*

Be a true survivor in an unknown, but ever-changing world of fantastic opportunities, people and events and situations.
Use your unique and personal gifts and tools to have the life you want.

*Believe in yourself and you and all your efforts will truly be okay in the world....*

**…..money, money, money..... how much does it really matter....?**
*What kind of position would you really, ultimately like to be in....?*
Think about if money were no object, if it really didn't matter, that it wasn't the be all and end all?
What would you be doing right now?
As an absolute certainty, it would be something you *totally* enjoy doing!
You surely wouldn't be slaving over a hot desk, head down a toilet, or getting down and dirty under a car bonnet (unless any of these were your perfect dream of course)!

If money really was no object, most people would be thinking about their dream career or their innate vocation – something that really stimulates them and gets their juices flowing. This may be anything from writing, poetry, riding horses, being out on the sea, or maybe being some kind of artist....

*Whatever you ultimately choose!*

But, if it were any of these things, you have probably been told that these kind of vocations are no way to earn a crust, you can't make a living out of doing any of them.....
So you just have to soldier on in your unfulfilling job role, slaving for someone else or working to keep grumpy customers happy and just getting on with it. Boo!

Yet, why not do what inspires you, what makes you happy, what lifts your spirits and forget about building up funds.... ?
If your main ruling is that it's all about the money because that is the most important thing in life, then you may be in danger of completely wasting your life! Because you will end up spending all your time concentrating on bringing the money in, just so you can go on living.

That will be your mindset. *Enough is never enough.*

You go on in a cycle, always wanting better and more, never satisfied. And the people around you will expect that from you and *keep* expecting it from you. So you continue on doing the same things you don't like and your life is one big, fat vicious money-chasing mercenary circle.
Stress, pressure, high expectations, short tempers, very little free time.....
How does that sound to you?

*Don't you think it's better to have a more fulfilling life where you truly enjoy doing the things you love doing, rather than having a miserable life busting a gut?*

How about doing that something you really like and become proficient at it - a *master of skills*? People will always be looking for skilled experts in all sorts of fields and will pay good money for it. There will always be people out there looking for the same thing that you are interested in!

Why spend your life in turmoil and passing that strategy down to your children and then them in turn, onto their children, educating them all to follow in your footsteps and do exactly the same thing as you are doing?

The cycle never ends and generations later, you've got people still running around doing things they really don't like and not making the most out of their lives.

*Sounds like a strange sort of plan - even a nightmare, doesn't it.....?*

You spend your time educating your children to do the same things, to justify what you are doing and so you can have some satisfaction that you have been doing the right thing all this time.......
So, it's really important to ask yourself, and to get your children to ask themselves, what is it you *really* want from life?
What is your **ultimate** aim.....?

*Then follow it through and begin to live life how it should be lived – in harmony with your inner self and your ultimate desires....*

**...by following your star..you will end up where you need to be..**
*Determine for yourself what your **star** is.......an achievement, a perfect state, a wonderful relationship, a secret yearning, a business aim....whatever it is – make it your own personal *star.**
Focussing on your *star* will motivate you to get on with your life and fulfil your goals and ambitions.

Bit by bit, piece by piece and day by day you will get closer to your *star*, as you take the steps required to reach it.
Invent something that you can use to continuously remind you of your *star*.

Always keep your *star* in mind as you go through your day, as you take on hard knocks and when life seems like such a chore. Always try to perceive it as you are *using* this time to achieve something, no matter how small and no matter how insignificant it seems.

*If you have your *star* in mind, you will always know that what you are doing is part of your journey and therefore,* **very** *worthwhile.*
It's part of your '*flow*'....

Constantly focussing on your *star* will mean that you will be making choices to realise your destination. You will be making the *right* choices, because that is your ultimate goal.
You will be instilling empowerment into every aspect of your life to realise your aim.

So, by following your *star*, you can only end up where you need to be!

Don't just wish on your *star* – **<u>manifest</u>** it!

**…...focussing on yourself internally will create a better you …...**
*Creating the best in you, will in turn, help to create a better world....*
*A world that radiates more positive energy that will connect you and ultimately, everyone around you and beyond.*
To make this happen, you will essentially need to change and improve yourself at a fundamental level, in areas that you feel could do with an '*overhaul*'.

When you master yourself from *within*, you'll be far more prepared to face your journey ahead.

Do this with good nutrition, developing a strong connection with nature, instilling more balance and spirituality and having more *faith*.

*In essence, you need to love yourself and others.*

Become *true* and proud of yourself.
Open your eyes to the beauty of the world around you.
Learn to appreciate what you have been given here on earth.
Appreciate the wonders of creation.
Spend as much time as you can with nature.
Observe, learn and question through all the masterpieces all around you.
Use nature to clean your energy and *raise your vibrations*.
Find help to understand and achieve this, if necessary.

Through your own intelligent mind, use *reasoning* and *logic* to discover your goals and destiny, rather than flailing about aimlessly not knowing who or what you really are, or living a shallow existence without much regard to anything at all.
Focus on the *basics* and get back to what's important in life.

You have been created for a reason.
Achieve your purpose.
Enrich your mind, your body and your soul.
If you can achieve this, then you will be passing on your true spirit to the world and those you are surrounded by, thus creating good positivity to bring to the circle of life.

*Find your truth....*

**......just be an 'inverse paranoid'......your challenges are sent to try you......**
*Sincerely believe that the universe is always conspiring to do you* **good**, *rather than thinking of yourself as a 'victim' that everyone is out to get!*
Use the power of your *'inverse paranoia'* to change your mindset to the opposite of this, so that you recognise and are thankful for your life being <u>good</u> and that *no-one* is actually plotting against you!

As an inverse paranoid, you will be able to see each situation and challenge as being *given* for your own benefit and that will provide you with a *valuable* experience in life that you can learn from.

*Know that you are being taught via the problems and difficulties that you may face in order for you to develop and grow.*

Really think about how empowering that is....!

If you are continually faced with the same problems over and over again, then maybe the universe is telling you that you have something to learn from it that you just haven't picked up on yet....
If you don't notice any of it, then your subconscious mind is likely to keep on repeating it until you do!

It really is all an important part of your growth, not just someone having a go at you, or making your life miserable on purpose.
If you wake up in the morning and adopt the attitude that whatever life throws your way is just another challenge for you to develop from, then you will have a *healthy perspective* and will understand more about the *importance* of those things being sent to you.

You can then begin to look forward to your days full of expectancy, because you know that special things will happen to you to guide you and make your life a more fulfilling and valuable experience, rather than just one chore after another.

Who are you going to meet today that may become important in your life?
What will you be taught by the events of the day that will enhance your life?
What experiences will you learn valuable lessons from today?
What skills will you need to develop today that will make your life progress in a more positive and fulfilling way?

Adopting this more positive attitude, will allow you to be open to the amazing things that will start to occur and give you the confidence of facing each day with renewed enthusiasm and enjoyment.

*Your attitude will be one of optimism and power.*

You will feel that your life is guiding you with more strength to become the person you need to be, in order to follow your path and destiny with hope and happiness, and not just think of it as conspiring to make you fail.
*So therefore, being an inverse paranoid is truly empowering and can have an amazing impact on your whole life!*

**....so what's all this about positive energy....?**
*Positive energy can transform your life.....!*
You constantly emit positive and negative energy.
As you emit this energy, so people pick up on it and gravitate towards you, or move away from you accordingly.

This is part of the *'Law of Attraction'*.
Like attracts like.

You will surround yourself with those who are attracted by your energy. So if people are draining your energy and are negative, chances are that is what you yourself are transmitting.
If you are emitting good positive energy, you will probably have people who are uplifting and encouraging.
Stands to reason really, even if you didn't know anything about the law of attraction!

*Emitting positive energy will enable you to grow and heal and become stronger.*

You will undoubtedly see good qualities in others and feel compassion towards the world.
You will also probably be a good listener, seeing others' perspectives, as well as be open-minded, understanding, non-judgemental and giving people the benefit of the doubt.
You will be honest in your thoughts and actions and allow others to do the same, admitting your negative emotions and persevering in fear and defeat.
You will be able to celebrate and appreciate others' success and happiness and follow your own desires and dreams.

*So, send out positive energy and get it back.*

Feed from it and live in peace and happiness.

Your negative energy will come out in acting out your weaknesses and darker side, focussing on others' mistakes, making you obsessed about being perfect and trying to change others' perspectives and opinions to meet your own.
You will be unbalanced, allow other's moods to dictate yours, resent others' success and happiness, have a hard heart, be cynical, fearful, bitter and suffocate your own dreams and ambitions as a result.
These are not actions or emotions of an empowered mind.

*Be empowered with positive energy that makes you determined to do your best and see the world as* **good**.

Don't idealise about 'impossible-to-live-up-to' expectations.
Maintain a sense of humour and have an open heart, mind and soul.
You don't have to keep up with the Jones'!
Be creative and manifest what you want in your personal life, for *yourself and your own purpose*.

*Own up to your mistakes, have open communication with people, feel connected to the world as a whole, and don't be fazed by disagreements and failures - it's just all part of living!*

.....**I think therefore I am**........
*It is your thoughts that create and shape your life....*
If you can get a proper understanding of how your brain works, then you will be in a *very* good position to be in *charge* of who you are and how you work.

Your thoughts make you who you are.
Every thought you have, as you know, has a *physical outcome*.
Everything that's happened in your life so far, has been manifested through the power of your own thoughts – formed in *your* own mind.
Everything you do is part and parcel of your thoughts.
You command your *super-conscious* via these thoughts and it **obeys**, making the events and things in your life become actuality.
It has no choice.

All the decisions you've made have been as a result of the thoughts in your head, some or most of them, conditioned through your previous events and influences. And that includes everything you have done concerning your achievements and ambitions!

*If you want to change anything in your life, all you need to do then, is change your thought patterns and act upon them.*

So, if you are still doing things in the *same* old way, blame your thoughts!
If you continue to think how you have always thought, then nothing will ever change and you will never be able to create anything new or make anything better.
If you are in a poor position, then that is as a result of everything that has happened to you over time.
Because all negative things occur due to your thoughts, so positive ones obviously do as well.

*Therefore, you can change your life for the better by reversing those unhappy thoughts into good, beneficial ones.*

You are in control and you cause what happens to you.....
If your thoughts are working on happy goals, then you will undoubtedly be striving towards those. Get creating the very opposite of unhappy, sad or negative.
Be happy, positive and achieving instead!

*Also, stop giving your thoughts a battle between positive and negative patterns, or you will spend your life constantly at war with yourself!*

With your renewed thoughts and adopting that positive, enlightened feeling, you will change as an individual and get the life you really want.
More optimistic things will begin to happen, setting you on your path to *riches* – in whatever form you want it.
If you want to bring those thought patterns into proper alignment so they bring about your ultimate wishes and desires, then you can use a '*mantra*' to unify them.

By writing down your list of ultimate desires, you can see what track you need to be on in order to get to those goals.

For instance, if it's a better *job* you want, the probability is that it's the *rewards* and *benefits* that go along with it that will be motivating you towards that particular target.
So list this under a **'Career'** section.
If it's better family and friendships you want, then this will go under a **'Relationships'** section. Material wants like cars, houses and holidays will be listed under **'Abundance and Prosperity'**, and so on.

Once you have got your list of desires and rewards written down, you will probably see a pattern taking shape.
This can then give you the form for creating a *positive mantra* towards achieving those things, such as:

"*I* **AM** *happy and rich in abundance and prosperity*" or
"*I* **HAVE** *a beautiful and fulfilling life*".

Say them out loud and genuinely *believe* it!
Use your mantra often with *power and conviction* to stimulate your super-conscious mind into believing it and taking action!

**Command it to be <u>real</u> for you!**

Repeat it regularly to yourself, before bed, upon waking, in the mirror, whenever you can to instil it *fully* into your mind.

Become the *master of your own destiny.*

This dominating force will help to bring about health, strength and vitality in your physical body and will therefore empower you.
Telling your super-conscious mind that you **ARE** already the things you want to be, will instil into it that's *who you are* and you are not in a 'state of lack' in any aspects of your life.

*This is a positive path to go forward with, in order to manifest all your desires.*

If you find negative thoughts creeping into your head, cancel them out with your positive mantra.

Your super-conscious knows exactly what to do because it is a strong force that does not judge, but is there for you, to empower you towards accomplishing anything you want.
It is an excellent resource to tap into and can literally *transform your life*.

As you grow and evolve, let your mantra's grow and evolve with you, so you move to achieving one desire after another.
You control your thoughts and back them up with your positive mantra's.

*Your life literally is what you think about.....*

### ........I'm all out of balance.......
*When it comes to getting your life in balance, you have to realise that it is YOUR life that you must be concentrating on.*
And that means not trying to be someone else or live the life of someone else....
Everyone is an individual and as such, what's good for one, may not be good for another.

*So you should steer away from constantly wanting what other people have got.*

If it's the millionaire lifestyle that you desire, how do you *really* know that it's actually suited to you?
You may find that you are quite happy living a simple life where all your bills are covered, you're debt-free, you live in the right area, in the right environment, with the right friends and family around you, and enough time and funds to just relax and be content.

So, why would you want the probable stress of what comes with striving for that millionaire lifestyle? It could be a nightmare for you!

*So, you need to define your OWN success – what do you want for* **you**?

Think about the steps you need to have your ultimate life.
Small steps – not huge, unimaginable ones that look so unachievable that you end up doing nothing, because you think there's no way you can get there. It's just all too much!

*Small steps make big ones in the end!*

There's no way you can transform your life overnight, so do things one at a time, so you avoid being so overwhelmed that it all terrifies you.
Pick what you are most passionate about first, whether it's starting your own business, losing weight, getting your well-being sorted out, clearing debts, owning something fabulous, etc.
Make it something you know fills you with excitement.

**Then go for it!**

Little by little, day by day, however small the task, you will be making your dream closer to reality, giving you an ultimate aim.

*Stick with it and you will make your life both balanced in your favour as well as successful......*

**…..and now you need to move forward with clear intention……**
*It may seem obvious that in order to move forward in life, you should have a clear intention...*
But are you one of those people who just drifts along, following the herd, doing what is *expected* of you, without any *clear intention* about what you're doing and where you're going at all....?
If you asked most people what they wanted, they would probably say more money.
It's a natural response.
More money gives you the freedom to do what you want, when you want.
*It makes life easier, that's for sure.*

You may dream of beautiful holidays, a fantastic house in an idyllic location with a big car in the driveway and wonderful food on the table.

*But actually, money is just the goal, the outcome, the result - it's not the <u>intention</u>.*

It's not creating a clear path to that wealth, or how you get there in the first place.

There's *no* process.
And without a process, how do you know what to do to actually get to this wonderful life?
What kind of journey do you need to go on in order for all your wishes to manifest themselves?

*Are these desires actually what you truly want?*

Do they make you feel passionate, give you a feeling in your gut that makes your heart pound, or are they just something you think or believe would be good, but not really what you are *actually* about?
What direction do you want to go in that *truly* makes your creative juices flow and gives you something to get up in the morning and jump out of bed for....?

You have to get **to** the money and in doing so, you need to go on your creative journey to get there.
You have to make sure that you actually *live* your life in the process, rather than blindly ploughing on to reach that monetary goal, without even looking up and realising that you forgot to enjoy your life along the way!

*That's time you cannot get back....!*

You need to live in *total awareness* of your thoughts and feelings, actions and intentions and actually feel *alive*, whilst you travel along your path. Not only go through the motions just to reach that wealth. You want to experience things *using all your senses* and you need to ask yourself **why** you are doing what you are doing?
What point or relevance does this have to you and your journey?
Is this part of your intention at all?

*Ask yourself why, why, and why again.......*

Why do I want this, why is that the reason, why do I think that?
Until you drill right down to what it is that you do *really* want.
How do you actually feel about that, does it make you feel good or uncomfortable?
Do you feel confident about your decision?

Is it really material things you want, or is it more about how you *feel inside*, whether you feel good about what you are doing or will experience, or is it really about your own development?
This is all about forming your *clear intention* that you can properly move forward with towards your vision, your dream, your destiny.

*Feel it, smell it, sense it.*

Keep it close and refer to it every day to remind you of the journey you are going on.

Remember, this is an ongoing, *flexible* intention – as you grow and change, so it will grow and change with you.

Once you realise and declare your intention to the world, you will open up and be mindful and aware of it and the things that you need to put it into place will magnetise towards you, and opportunities, events and experiences will show themselves to you!

Without doubt, you will also be faced with obstacles, because as you change, so your mind and body will naturally resist and put up a protection barrier.

*But you mustn't be put off by any distractions or blockages that get in the way.*

Just knock them back and return to your course, knowing that the path you are taking is real to you and nothing is going to stop you from your intention.

This is all part of your creative process and will help you grow and move forward with added strength and empowerment.
Don't allow yourself to fall back into that old comfortable place where nothing moves and nothing changes, wasting your life and ignoring your destiny.

There will be frustrations and delays, old fears and insecurities, but if you expect them, then you will know how to handle them and get on with your progress regardless.
Feel the energy surging through you as you move forward with clear intention towards your goal, enjoying your journey along the way,

sucking up the experiences and feeling your senses strong and electrifying.

*Remember,* **you** *are the one in control.*

When setting your intentions, make sure you are *absolutely specific* about how you will implement them. It's no good being vague or indecisive – this will not get you there. You need to have concrete plans of action and steps to follow.

Write up your plan in bite-size, short-term, manageable chunks. Don't make them so massive that they just feel totally unachievable, otherwise you may just swamp yourself and make yourself feel like you just can't manage it.
Do easy things that you are perfectly comfortable doing, otherwise, if they are too difficult you may end up just demotivating yourself and throwing the towel in.

You can then just tick things off as you watch your progress. As you do this, you will feel great and more motivated to carry on.

*It's a great way to feel empowered and in control of your life.*

It will give you a plan to stick to and where you can measure your advancement as you go along, keeping you in check and showing yourself what you have achieved and what needs to be done next.

The more you do, the stronger and more confident you will become and so the more risks and higher actions you can take.

Remember to enjoy the ride along the way – that's the whole point!

*And, bit by bit, you will get to your destination – where, you will undoubtedly find a new path to go along and new goals to reach that you set brand new clear intentions for!*

**…...all you need is to get the power back into your life……**
*Everyone wants to know that they have total power over their life.* God forbid if someone points out to you that they don't think this is the case, because the likelihood is that you will automatically go on the defensive!

It's a natural reaction.

You will, of course, view your life, your reactions, your feelings, your circumstances, etc., as your *own way of life* that suits *you*.......
After all, you are the one that has created your life up to this point.
You are the one that acts within it, you are the one that responds to everything that comes up according to your own beliefs.

Of course you do – that's *you*, isn't it?

You've made yourself the way you are now.
You are consistent with the way you see life.
You move along effortlessly, going into situations as you see fit, as you are used to, as **you**.
You suffer one set of circumstances after another, because your emotions are embedded in your psyche.
That's how you cope.

*However, if you are going from one disaster to another and you keep reacting to them in the same old way, you are just recreating those catastrophes and they keep coming back time and time again.*

They are a reflection of how you relate to life.
Things will never change, because *you* aren't changing.
You aren't allowing yourself to move on from those disastrous circumstances. Life isn't working out in certain areas to your advantage or benefit, because your set of circumstances are merely a symptom of an underlying problem or condition that you are *hanging on to*.
Something that has instilled fear, or upset, or an inability to see clearly – are all forcing you to act in a certain way that you have got *used* to, rather than resolving the problem. So, every time this area of your life is not working, so your underlying condition will be ever present, rearing it's ugly head, producing exactly the same result as before *again*.

And so, your life stays exactly the same!

Therefore, if you truly want to solve this problem area, you need to focus on removing that very thing that creates the problem in the

first place.
As soon as you do this – everything changes, you find a solution and your life gets it's balance back and happiness ensues.....
It's a process that can be achieved.
You can turn your life around and relate to the world in a much more positive way.
For everything that you do, no matter how small, has an effect......
*It's the law.*

There is a natural relationship between everything that happens.
A simple analogy would be, if we put the kettle on, the water will boil.
You have provided a cause – the kettle, it's had an effect – the water boils.
Your whole life and the whole world revolves around this law.
It's obvious.
It stands to reason.

So, therefore, whatever happens to you in life, you will react according to that event.
Everything you do, everything everyone does, everything in the universe, has a cause and an effect.
You react to something, it reacts to you.
How you personally react to things as they happen around you, will produce your own experience of them and will determine your quality of life and everything that happens in it.
But, if you think that you are only *the effect* of something, rather than the cause, so you will think you are the victim of your circumstances.

You will believe you have no power over what is happening to you and naturally this will produce a negative reaction to your own life.
You will begin to lack confidence and eventually lose your ability to react effectively to circumstances.
You will become upset, think your life isn't working and the whole world is against you.
You totally believe that you have no control over *anything*.

*However, you can turn your situation around by simply taking some action and making your own effect instead.*

Think about how good it felt the last time this may have happened to you...
Did you feel confident and abundant in energy and creativity?
Did you feel empowered?

Yet all you did was to change the way you thought about the circumstances - you were on top of them and didn't allow them to have any power over you, and in doing so, you *changed your course*!

By doing this and taking the control and power back, you can expect to fulfil your dreams just through the power of your own thoughts!

If you can be specific about those areas in your life that continuously don't work over and over again, you can address them and take some action to gain control back.
You will be able to see just exactly where you need to work on things, which things affect your confidence and happiness and what is having an effect on your life.

Sit down and take a serious look at where you are allowing the power to be taken away from you, and where you can regain it and shift the power back in your favour instead.

This is a very useful exercise and could reveal some surprising revelations.

Once you've done his, think about how much more empowered you will be, how the quality of your life will improve and become different.....

.....*and how this can really feed your ability to fulfil your dreams*.....!

**Your job is to continually hold up a mirror to yourself
and refuse to work at anything
that is not an expression of everything
that is good and capable within you!**

**………come to terms with your 'free will'………**
*Discover your place and what you are.*
From this you can go ahead and do whatever you want and not spend your whole life suppressed and frustrated.

*Everyone has a purpose in life, including you….*

Everyone is put on earth to achieve certain goals, including you……
The purpose of being on earth is to discover what that destiny is and to follow it – no matter what. This is the idea of *'true will'*.
Use your skills to improve your lot.

When you discover your true will, you should put all your energies into it and you will succeed, *because that is your **true will***.
It may take a little while to work out what it is, but when you discover it, you'll find it's all there living within you……

*Dig deep.*

**…..use the potential you were born with………**
*Not allowing your natural gifts to flourish is a dire shame and will dampen your spirit.*
Whoever you are, wherever you're from, whatever your background, you will have innate skills and talents that you were born with and that you are good at.
You should home in on these, develop them and make the most out of them.
Doing this will allow your potential to increase and give you something you can be spirited about and believe in.

*Make this your career and it will be something you will naturally excel at!*

If you just allow yourself to drift along in a dead-end job or doing something that bores and depresses you, what impact do you think this will have on your life?

Tap into your natural gift and *really* make it something you are passionate and enthusiastic about. You will feel so much more alive and motivated towards achieving your goals, making your life and career successful and the best it can possibly be.

*And for this you will be grateful.*

When you get to the end of your days, you can rest assured that you have made the most of what you were given and you enjoyed your own adventure on this earth. You will be proud and go with a smile on your face, knowing you did good and your life was meaningful and valuable!
Your spirit will shine and take you to the next place with honour.

*So find that special gift as quickly as you can and allow it to take you through life with zest, joyfulness and worth.*

**…...first find your motivation and focus on that …..**
*Dig deep into your soul and search out what motivates you.*
Is it money, freedom, a big house, a life full of adventure, a stress-free life, a big wedding, to be a successful entrepreneur, to have peace in your life, to be part of a Thai commune being at one with yourself, to build security for your family, to get that special ticket to some adventure you've wanted to go on for years, or just to feel like a success in life?

Whatever it is, if you remain focussed and keep this at the forefront of your mind, you will undoubtedly achieve it.....
So, think long and hard about what your motivation is.

What is it that keeps you going?
What are you passionate about?
What floats your boat?
What makes you get through your days?

Do you even know?
If not, you need to tune in and find that motivation, because it is an important way to achieving your destiny.
You need to find that *something* that makes you determined to get there. Something that makes you committed to your own success.
What is your goal and why do you want to get there?
Set that as your motivation.
Use it as your inspiration for moving forward and getting to that special thing or place.

Focus on that goal so you feel committed to reaching it and keeping going.

*Create the right mindset to achieving it and you will surely get there in time and will feel true bliss has arrived at last!*

**......your true calling has power and meaning.......**
*Before you spend far too much time, stress and emphasis on wanting more and more, being mercenary and always chasing bigger and better things in your pursuit of happiness, you should really think about who you truly are and what needs to be done to reach your 'inner' self.*
Only then will you be *genuinely* happy and life can expand beyond your dreams.

Just harness the desire to be who you rightfully are or where you sincerely want to be.
Instil the belief in yourself and what you want to achieve.

*Be absolutely certain in your soul that you will get there and accept that you actually will.*

With all these definite intentions, you will be sure to manifest all your desires.

If, when you try certain things out and it just feels wrong, the chances are that they were not really your *true inner* goals at all. You will therefore need to have a rethink from a *deeper level* into exactly what it is that is totally appropriate for *you*.

*If you really want to be good at your job, you must do what you love.*

But, knowing what you love to do may not be as easy as it first seems and may well require a *period of discovery* as you try to realise just exactly what it is.

One of the reasons you may not realise straight away, is probably because you've gone along all your life on *automatic*, doing what is expected of you, without really looking inside and discovering, or allowing yourself to do exactly what is right for you, *personally*.

You've probably been too busy pleasing other people or striving to make money, without blinking or stopping to think about what your actual *true* calling is.

Maybe you want to know why it is you are just not successful in life....?

*It may be time to stop and look honestly at yourself.*

Why you are not happy in your work?
Are your inner talents and abilities being used just for other people to achieve their goals instead of your own?

Success comes from being excellent at what you do and how you feel. And what you do needs to be something that you *know* makes you feel happy, satisfied and fulfilled *inside and out*.
Only then, can you know, in your heart, that you are following your true calling.

Your true calling will make your feel **good** inside.
You'll know what it is, because you will *feel it in your soul, it will excite you, make your heart pound and will be what makes you* **excellent**.

If you are not following it, you will feel cheated (or you will be cheating yourself), and you may even feel helpless and out of control.
Because of the lack of control, you may feel unable to change things in your life.

By being in control and following your true calling and being able to become *brilliant* at whatever that is, you will be able to improve your life and increase your earnings, because you will be following your innate talents and making the best and most out of them.

*You can become an expert and command a value for what it is you do.*

Even if it isn't about money, by fulfilling your true calling, you will feel at peace inside, knowing that you are doing what you are meant to do and not going through life just 'existing'.

But first you have to *find* it, which means you will probably have to change. Without change, everything stays the same. It's up to *you* to be true to yourself and enable that change to happen.

*Your aim in life should be to become everything that you are capable of becoming.*

You should be able to use your talents to maximum use, express who you are, use your innate skills and abilities to the full, so you can develop as a strong, empowered person who feels on top of the world and who enjoys every day, because you know you are doing a *great* job.
*You need to wake up in the morning and feel joyful and look forward to the events ahead of you.*

And at the end of the day, you should feel satisfied that you have fulfilled something wonderful.
You will look forward to all your forthcoming adventures.
You need to constantly look at your life to be sure that what you are doing is right for you, that makes you feel good about yourself and those around you.

*You need to be an absolute expression of who you are and what you should be. You should feel like you are working for the good of your soul and that your capabilities are being used as a true extension of what's inside your heart.*

If you follow your true calling, you will be a fantastic example of who you're meant to be and your innate skills will develop and shine to become extraordinary too. This excellent performance should, and will be, excellently rewarded.
You will be of value – whether that's in the workplace or if you are self-employed. People will want you and you can use that to your advantage. You can demand a price for that particular quality that you are *uniquely* offering.

Equally, if you are drifting along being something for someone else, a puppet slogging your heart out for another's gain, or are just being *average*, or becoming bored and may be producing lack-lustre results, then you can only expect to be rewarded with low or average pay.

*Horses for courses....*

If you don't want that in your life, if you don't want to be that person who feels threatened and under the thumb of another person, out of control, unable to make your own decisions, or are not being real and true to yourself, then you need to think long and hard about what changes you can make.

*Engage your empowerment to get out of that rut and get onto your true course in life.*

Even if that means that you do have to take or continue in meagre jobs while you make your plans for that improvement.
So, whilst you're going through your period of discovery, it's important that you are dedicated and devoted to your current job. Be good at it and accept that you were placed there for a *reason*.

*It may not be clear or evident at first, but in retrospect and in time, you will come to realise just exactly why you were there.*

The experience you gain and lessons you learn from your current job, and indeed, any previous jobs before that, will have been accumulated on purpose, *for the greater role you have in your destiny.*
And in any case, you might as well try to enjoy and get the most out of your current work, because doing a good job will still be satisfying and make you feel good and better about yourself. Even if you think it's unimportant – at least you will feel like you're *accomplishing* something - and that's always got to be a good feeling.....

Behind the scenes, you can be laying down the foundations of your new, rewarding, superior and more fulfilling life.
One that suits you far more than you are just putting up with right now.
One that you *should* be doing.
One that makes you happy, contented, alive and excited!

*This is your journey, and your destination is to be your true self, whilst savouring every taste of life along the way.*

A destination should never be reached however – as even if you

think you have got there, you will be planning and developing even further for your upcoming future.
If you think you have got there, then you would have given up and settled.....

Your life is a total journey, as it has it's twists and turns, challenges and adventures.
Thank goodness!

We all have different lives as different people. We owe it to ourselves to embrace that individualism and uniqueness. And be proud of it.
When you do find your true calling, and you *should*, everyday you will feel motivated, ready to take on challenges, pay any price to be that person and overcome all obstacles and negativities that you encounter along the way.

*You will naturally develop to be the very best version of yourself.*

This is a brand new mindset.
You will want to learn more, you will be driven and you will want to embrace your field in order to be great at it and allow yourself to grow. You will feel your value expanding and extending within you, as you increase and improve your skills and knowledge with every waking moment.
Even if it means trying to get into the head and psyche of your top role models, seeing how they operate and how they make decisions, how they got to where they are and how you can too. If necessary, allow them to be your guide as you learn on the job and gain insight into how your role will fit alongside theirs, if not overtake them!
But nobody is going to wave a magic wand. ....

You have to make it happen *yourself*.

Your life is *your* responsibility and it is because of your decisions and mindset that you are where you are today. Therefore, it is also this that will drive you to where you want to be tomorrow – upwards and onwards to your true calling.

*You want it, you do it!*

Make no mistake, you may have to have a few goes at it.....
You may think you want to be something, but find that it just doesn't feel right.
So, move on to the next thing.
*It doesn't matter.*
Life is a series of journeys and crossroads until you get to your true calling. Expect it and you won't feel disappointed, because you know you are having a go and trying to get there, with a few blips along the way.

*If you want to become good, then you have to do the work.*

If the inner desire isn't there for you, then maybe you are doing the wrong job or going down the wrong route.
Ask those close to you what they think you should be doing. They may have noticed something in you that you didn't really consider and that may just turn on a bright light for you, and you can say "that's it!" and off you go....

If you need help, don't be afraid to ask someone. Maybe a life coach could help you get deeper into your inner workings and help you discover who you should really be.

When you start to seriously consider what it is you are meant to be doing as part of your destiny, things will begin to become clear and unfold in front of you, as you properly tune into the reasons why you've done things and been in certain situations.

Keep an open mind and be aware of the messages that come to you from each incident as they happen, as these will help to uncover the mystery of your fate and life path.

*If you want to discover just exactly what it is you need to be doing both spirituality and materially, then a bit of deep soul searching and evaluation may be required.*

There's a high chance that it may not be feasible to just give up your current job whilst you sit and contemplate your destiny, so whilst you're going about your daily duties, you can be thinking and searching for questions and coming up with answers, where hopefully, things will begin to reveal themselves to you.

Anything can happen whilst you're getting on with your job. As you work diligently and get better at it, you may find yourself in line for a promotion, or you may be meeting objectives that can work towards something better, or even doing something that points in the direction of what you want to be doing more of.
You may even realise that you have out-lived your current job and it's time to move on.

*Any of these outcomes will give you a boost in self-esteem and confidence, which will help you move onto the next level of your life.*

Whatever you discover your true calling is, you should feel like you are making a contribution and doing something amazing with your life.

Use your natural skills and talents to enable you to overcome any obstacles and achieve any goal you set for yourself – with aplomb and success.
Your true calling, your empowered self, will allow you to throw yourself wholeheartedly into your life, removing all limits and allowing you to be who you want, have what you want and do what you want.

*What can be more enriching and fulfilling than that......?*
**Go for it!**

**....everything you do in life counts towards your enrichment and destiny.....**
*No matter how small or insignificant the things that you do are, nothing is ever wasted....*
Everything is part of a learning curve and has a reason.

And whether or not you realise it at the time, you will undoubtedly find out later why you had to do it all.

When you do begin to realise what your *true calling* is, you will understand that you have all the equipment and tools you need to fulfil it.

Even the family you were born into, your education, your unique life experiences – they're all part of it. They're all there to facilitate your growth and allow you to fulfil your potential – even if any of it was negative, it's all part of your learning and development towards better things.....

You have to give life time, so be patient and you will get to where you want to be in the end.

Even if you think that you are doing everything yourself and are not being controlled by anything – and that it's all about your own effort and you know your own destiny, it cannot unfold of it's own accord.

*It's all only as good as the effort you make to bring it to reality.*

Of course, you will need self-effort to get through all the difficulties of life. You need to find a good harmonious balance, so you can move on to the next thing without giving up.

*Knowing what your true calling and destiny is, gives you the strength to keep on going, no matter how disappointing things may become.*

There will be times when you have to face some battles in order to get there, but you must then try to be the warrior and fight through them to become the winner. With each challenge, you become stronger, your patience and stamina are discovered, along with the determination to get through and out the other side more able to move onto your next challenge.

*No one can keep you from bringing about your true destiny.*

While you are discovering your genuine desire in life, you have to accept that there are always consequences to everything you do and that every action counts as you take that journey.
So, you need to adopt some courage to make the changes that may be necessary along the way.
You're bound to come across contention and obstacles, so if you can get someone on your side who can help you, so much the better, otherwise you need the strength to face and win through the battles for yourself.

Be ready for inevitable difficulties and the possibility that things will be tough, but each challenge you overcome will be a new lesson and another building block to living an empowered life and fulfilling all your desires.

**……I do have aspirations for success…….**
*Most people aspire to be 'successful', but that term doesn't necessarily mean having pots of money.*
Success comes in any form that is personal to *you*, whether that's in your career, your business, achieving a personal goal, becoming fit and healthy, or even just living a simple, but peaceful life. Whatever it is that you are setting out to attain will be your *own* defined success.

There's quite a difference between *aspiration and ambition.*

Perhaps you perceive ambition in a more negative light to aspiration? Maybe that's because you see it in the context of being power-hungry and just wanting control and possessions.
Aspiration is definitely more about personal growth and a thirst for nurturing experience of *all* kinds in life.

*Aspiration is about going on a journey of your dreams.*

It's about growing and propelling yourself forward on your own personal adventure.
It's not about helping someone else to achieve their goals.
It's about working on your *own* goals - those things that *you* aspire to have, when and how.

However, without any kind of deadline, any aspiration you have is just *something that you* **wish for**, *but will never really* **<u>achieve</u>**.
If you genuinely *want* something to happen, then it's time to make a <u>plan</u>.
Are you like a lot of people who have a special dream that's been running around in your head for years, particularly during those mundane periods? That ambition always seems to come to the *fore* then.
You think - "*What am I doing, where am I going, is this all there is…?*"

You know that it isn't, but you are still sitting back on those aspirations and not really doing anything about them.

If you really want that desire to come true and not just remain a pipe dream, then you need to set a *time and plan to achieve it*.

As an illustration - if you have to go somewhere, you always make a Travel Plan, with timings, dates, what to do, how to get there, routes, what to pack, how much it's going to cost, etc.
Then you set out to achieve that journey.

This is exactly how you need to look at your dream and build that plan in order to make it happen.
Within that process, you will need to make some commitments and take some necessary actions to get your aspiration to fruition.

*You can then start enjoying your life and really begin being where you should be in life - living your ultimate dream.*

So start making some decisions, begin to put your plans into place. Open up your mind to your own world of possibilities, let the light in and start setting out the steps for your amazing journey and adventure.

You may find that this process evokes a lot of questions, so you will need to come up with some solutions.
You may also have some hurdles to get over, but, if you are *real, positive and determined*, you will instinctively know what you need to do to achieve your dream.
And you will also know what to clear out of your way and what to keep, including what's negative and what's going to help you get there. You will know what barriers are in the way and why you need to smash through them to get where you want to be.
If not, get help!

Because ultimately, it's *your* life that you need to lead and so therefore you are the one that needs to make the decisions and stick to them.
If you think you can do better than you are doing right now, and you spend your time just looking up to people all the time, then why not aim to be even better than them....?

Your aspirations come first!

*You really can fly......if you let yourself!*

**…..visualise what you want and magic happens before your eyes....**
*So, what can help you produce positive changes in your life......?*
Using the art of *mental imagery and affirmations* will definitely help you and your achievements.
With all the things that happen to you in your life, the ups and downs, the challenges, the people you come across, the adventures you take, the emotions you go through and your connection with the world and all it's beauty and offerings, your life is definitely a unique **work of art**.

*If you are mindful,* every day, when things happen to you, with your thoughts and feelings, *you can actually feel the art working*, you can truly see yourself as a real *artist*.
And in this vein, you can make your life exactly as you want your piece of art to look.

*Each possibility and opportunity is an actual moment of creation.*

Something that you create for yourself.
*Really* believe that and you can choose to create something very wonderful with your life.
It's a free choice that you have at your fingertips.
You can try new things, make different decisions, find alternative ways of operating, or you can do things exactly as you have always done them.
Whatever you find rewarding, makes *your* piece of art.
*Each moment offers something unique.*

Every moment is the part of the puzzle in the wonderful game of life.
Using your own imagination you can create whatever you want in your life.
You are already doing this quite naturally on a daily basis, but probably don't even realise it! However, you can *actively* become extremely aware of it by being totally *mindful*, and use this fantastic skill to your advantage on your road towards complete happiness and fulfilment.

Everything and everyone, including you, is composed of tiny particles of pure energy, nothing is actually solid or separate from each other, even the space between us.

*We are all part of one great big energy field, all vibrating at different speeds and density.*

In that field of vibrations, 'thought' is light, quick, easy to change, affected easily by things and can manifest instantaneously. Matter however, is more dense, compact, slower to change and more difficult to affect.

Everything and everyone is *interrelated and affected* by each other. Things of similar quality and vibrations tend to attract to one another – just like when you have a thought or feeling about something and then you bump into something related to it.

It's just about using this basic energy of the universe to work automatically for you in a positive way......

If you are *unconsciously* and without thinking, using this energy to create limitations, difficulties, problems and lack in your life, so alternately, you can reverse that direction instead into one of love, health, beauty, peace, enjoyment, fulfilment, good relationships, rewarding work, prosperity, abundance, success, and so on......

....just by *using your imagination to creatively visualise what you truly want for yourself.*

Athletes can condition their bodies to move with efficiency and strength, by directing their thoughts towards a positive outlook and rehearsing a **_win_**, by the practise of *visualization*.

By generating that sense and feeling, that image, that mental picture clearly in your imagination of what you wish to manifest and then focussing positive energy towards it, you use that power to achieve whatever it is you are requesting of the universe.

It can be anything – emotional, mental, physical or spiritual – *you control your own choices.*

*You* believe that those things you want are possible, *you* desire it, *you* open your mind to the concept and you will *naturally lean towards enrichment in your life.*

Your spirit will be positive and you will *embrace wanting to find new knowledge and experiences* in order to follow that path you have created in your imagination.

*Consciously* align yourself with these principles, *open up your closed, rational mind*, feel the possibilities and understand and accept that the universe is composed of energy *that is there for your advantage......*

You first create a thought before you manifest it through physical energy, just like when you go to do something – you obviously have to think about doing it first. If you just hold the thought in your mind, it will probably eventually manifest itself via attraction and the flow of energy, like feeling beautiful – *if you properly think it,* **you will be**!

Whatever you put into the universe will be reflected back to you. Whatever you think about most strongly and deeply, so you will always attract it into your life – including all negative feelings, such as fearfulness and anxiety.

*You will attract situations that you actually want to avoid, by holding those negativities in your mind.*

Reverse this into a positive mental attitude instead, like pleasure, happiness, joyfulness and success, and then you will attract those types of experiences and people into your life instead.

When you begin to develop this strategy by being <u>mindful</u> of your thoughts and feelings, by watching your perspectives on certain situations and people, by making observations about your life as you go on your daily business, etc., you will *really* start to <u>take note</u> of your reactions to things.

And, as you begin to explore and discover your basic attitudes towards life, you may notice how you have been holding back and blocking satisfaction and fulfilment in your life - quite unconsciously, *without even realising it....*

When you are *open* and able to *see more clearly what is happening right in front of your nose (*as this strategy will lead you to that*)*, you can remove those limiting attitudes by using creative visualisation, and giving yourself the space in your head and heart to find greater happiness and love.

*You **truly** are the creator of your own life.*

The way to start a visualisation is with deep-breathing, becoming relaxed and producing an image of your chosen desire in your mind to focus on – and using positive affirmations in the **present** tense, to make it as strong as possible.

*You need to make sure you are owning your desire **now** - as if you already have it!*

Tell yourself you've already acquired it - the big house is *yours*, the wonderful holiday is *yours*, the perfect relationship is *yours*, the fantastic career is *already yours, the peaceful calm life - yours*!

*Don't have any doubts or contradictions telling you that you don't deserve it, otherwise it won't happen!*

You will just be causing conflict by conceiving two opposite ends of the scale...
And if these thoughts do come into your head, allow them to flow in and out, *without giving them any power*, and then just return to your positive statements.
Relax and enjoy the favourable experience and repeat the process whenever you can, because the more you get it into your brain, *the more it will believe it.*

The more relaxed you are, the more effective your visualisation will be, so you can replace all your worrying and negative thinking with these positive thoughts instead.

Get any help you may need learning to relax through yoga and/or meditation or deep breathing, and you will also see the added benefits in your physical, mental and emotional health too.

Choose the best times when you are most relaxed, like when going to sleep or waking up, because your mind and body are far more receptive then.

If you are having problems not seeing any mental images at first, then try not to worry too much. This will come in time, as long as you remain relaxed about it and you don't start getting aggravated and stressed. It may be that you are trying too hard and just blocking the process.

It may be you are scared of what you might see, or there are emotions you don't really want to acknowledge or confront.

*But, if you are willing to take the time to look them fully in the eye, allow them to flow in and out, then they will gradually lose their power over you and begin to diminish.*

If you need any help with stronger issues that you are being blocked by, then perhaps you could get some help from an appropriate therapist.

There may be times during the process when you are receptive to whatever comes into your mind without choosing anything in particular, and you can just allow it to flow quite naturally in and out.

At other times, you may want to be totally active with your visualisations and focus on certain issues and bring in your own images. Working them out of your system....

Remember not to try and force anything when it comes to your affirmations – allow a free flow and don't be addicted to getting results from them, always knowing that whatever improvement you get out of them, will be an added bonus for you.

Everyone, including you, has a part to play on this planet and the more you practise creative visualisation and affirmations, so you will begin to tune into who you truly are and what you should really be doing with your life.

*You have natural gifts and should be doing what you genuinely love.*

Look out for messages sent through dreams and fantasies, as well as being aware of the every day things you find yourself doing and the actions you ultimately take, because they all have meaning and

purpose in your life and they could well be telling you which path you should be taking.
Keep tuning into your inner guidance and you will begin to notice things unfolding perfectly for you.

You can use visualisation and affirmations as a tool to keep yourself fit and healthy. Keeping a healthy body, helps to maintain a healthy mind, and if you feel ill, you will be able to talk yourself up, rather than into a more diseased state of mind.

*The messages that go to and from your brain can have a powerful impact on your belief system.*

You don't *have* to inherit a family illness or think it's inevitable that you will get ill for some reason or other. You can keep yourself positive and well nourished so that you maintain good well-being and then you can communicate to yourself that you are a healthy person.

And, if it does come about that you do become ill, then you need to use the time to be peaceful and quiet and allow your body to heal and relax, bringing in wholesome energy to help you get well again. Use the time to talk to yourself about any inner problems you may have and try to come up with ways to resolve them.

*Become wise and listen to the messages you are being given, using them to learn and grow.*

Utilise your visualisations and affirmations to create good images of yourself in absolute health and wellness.
If you are stuck with a chronic illness, then use the affirmations to help you to accept your ailment and the limitations it has for you, in order that you can live the best and most rewarding life possible with those conditions.

*Remember, that your life is a work of art – everything in it is part of your creativity and you are your own artist.*

Every moment you are here is time to be creative, do the things you should be doing and look for all the opportunities that come your way.

Look for new ways of doing things and new challenges that give you more rewards.

*We are all playing the game, so you might as well make the most of it and give it your all....*

**…..you need to have a purpose to feel valued and enthused about life...**
*Do you actually feel like you know what your purpose is in life?*
If you do, whatever it is, it should be *specific to you* and no-one else.
You will instinctively be aware of that *buzz* that flows with sheer enthusiasm through your veins.
It's what keeps you alive and motivated.
But, to follow that passion through, you may well need to step out of your comfort zone.....

*Unclog your mind and heart and listen to what they say.*

Get past all the noise that's going on inside you, especially all the negativities and problems that may be stopping you from *really* listening. Even though you have probably got other people's input and opinions, you *must* listen to your *own* voice, as it's the only one that matters to you!
No-one else can properly concentrate on yourself but you.

*You owe it to yourself for your own personal and spiritual growth.*

This will also have a strong impact on your business development and achievement.

Focus on your skills.
Find your own purpose by listening and taking notes about your own particular thoughts.

Getting it all down on paper will actually get everything out of your head and help to quieten your mind.
Build up a proper and true picture of what you really want to accomplish in your life and what you want to be remembered for.
Listening to your mind and inner voice will make things clearer for you.

As you feel things coming to you, allow yourself to get a deeper understanding of what it is you desire, researching and getting inspiration to drive your motivation.
Everything that interests you, write down and you will gradually get a clearer picture of what you want to become and who you want to be.

*Feel the empowerment driving you on as you come to realise just exactly what your real purpose is and how you can transform your life dramatically.*

The vast majority of people have goals that aren't really a *genuine* part of who they truly are.

Maybe you are becoming attached to things and feelings that you *believe* will make you happy, but it's causing you stress and tension in your pursuit of them. You may well find that when you get there, they don't actually bring you the happiness you expected at all!

You can find you are living in your 'outside' world, setting goals from that particular perspective and *not* from your true inner self.
It's usually at this point that you realise there *must* be more to life than the constant struggling, working hard and stressing. It can cause you to become a lot more spiritual as you go on a search to find what that purpose *really* is.

When you've found it, you will begin to feel like you are *living* life and plugging all the emptiness you've created over the years.

*Learn to let go, relax and go with the flow more.*

Live in the present and let yourself just '*be*', because then you will discover that you are actually perfectly okay, <u>without</u> all the striving. If you just stop attaching yourself to things you don't really need any more, you will feel far freer and more open to new opportunities and creativity.
You can use your energy to channel into your *higher self*, seeing new experiences and fulfilling fresh goals, or just feeling basically good about yourself and life in general.

Use creative visualisation to help you think more clearly, move out of feeling frustrated or worried and into a new way of living instead. Get away from those negative patterns of thinking with lots of positive visualisation practise, and gradually move away from some of those bad lifelong habits that may have formed over the years and slowed down your efforts to get somewhere in life.

Be patient with it and gradually you will be able to transform your life.

*Through perseverance you can overcome those old negative patterns, begin to grow and become inspired and encouraged to live a much better life – even through the most difficult of times.*

> **"'Chance favours the prepared mind' –
> in other words,
> be ready for any luck and
> opportunities that come your way".**

**....so be the leader in your life, get that vision out of your head and into action....**
*You know by now that you should be making every effort to run your own life and not letting your life run you!*
There's got to be a real difference between successful people and unsuccessful people.....and it appears that there are certain principles that every successful person has....

And that is *having a compelling vision of a future that is in line with their values, interests and desires*.

This gives them the *edge* for bringing it all into reality.
Therefore, you need to get down to establishing where you *really* see yourself further down the line.

So, do you want to be wealthy or healthy, build a prosperous business or teach yoga?
Whatever it is, make it more powerful by writing down a clear and specific, well-defined picture that you see of your life and *refer to it often*.

It is one of the most powerful ways to maintaining a focus on what it is you desire your life to be and also keeps you motivated to achieving that ultimate position.

Being able to visualize the end result can yield a certain clarity, inspiration and direction. It creates a purpose and becomes a measurement for your success.
If you have no real vision, you run the risk of experiencing a certain amount of anxiety and frustration as a result. If you do not have a vision of who you want to be, how you want to succeed, or what you want out of life, you begin to lack drive and your life becomes just a simple *order of events.*

*Outside influences can also disconnect you from your deeper values, purpose, potential and wisdom.*

But don't let that deter you from the principle of creating a vision. Your vision needs to be powerful, current, up-to-date and something that really connects you with your deepest passions, triggers your highest potential and helps you to know why and what you're doing. It's how you get your own life in order.

It can be the difference between you making it or not succeeding.

To succeed, you need the ability to envision your desirable future with such clarity that you can plainly see the steps you have to take to get there. You keep a clear picture of an ambitious and prosperous future. You grasp the importance of your vision and embrace it with both arms, in order for it to come to realisation. Your vision is your reference point for success, your target, your focus and your horizon for your ultimate purpose.

You need your vision to be specific and ambitious and the key to your success and magnificence.
It must be an idea of what you have in your mind for yourself or anything you desire, if this is going to happen.

*It will help you pursue your dreams and achieve your goals.*

It's strength will help you to overcome any obstacles and hold on tight when times get tough.

It will become your measurement of success.
It's actual importance is to inspire you to reach something that you want in life and to keep your focus and motivation for achieving it. A vision will open up your mind to many possibilities and a brighter and bigger future.

When you can envision a future that is better, happier and more productive, you are more likely to make the changes that are necessary for you to reach that type of wonderful life.
A successful leader can see the future.
They have the ability to see it *today*, calculate an improving and growing *future*, yet still stay focused in the *present*.

*Their vision is a **reality** waiting to happen, not just a dream.*

With strong dedication and confidence, leaders are driven, spending hours, like a force within, to manifest their visions.

*A vision is essential for successful people.*

It's used as a target to focus resources and energy upon and is motivating against forces of resistance such as failure, business and emotional hardships and negative feedback.
If you want to become 'someone' or 'something', you first have to be clear and know yourself - emotionally, physically, spiritually and intellectually, otherwise, how will you know who you want to be and if you can actually succeed?

*Know exactly what you want.*

Ask yourself, specifically, where and how you want to see yourself in a specific amount of years. Anything is possible within a vision, so get passionate and think **BIG**!

Set a plan of action to reach your vision.
Gradually, over time, you will begin to see parts of your vision coming true, until one day you are actually *living* it!

Remember, if you don't change, then nothing changes – everything stays the same, so think beyond your current reality and be creative by inventing, mind-mapping, imagining and dreaming about what doesn't exist now, but will in the future, including all aspects of life.

*Focus on things that give your life purpose and meaning and don't put limits on your dreams.*

A vision that is clear, will open your mind to the endless possibilities of the future.
Having a vision is utterly important in your path to success. You feel much more valuable as a person when you set and achieve visions and goals.
*So, become empowered and be the leader in your own story of success....*

**.......following your vision whilst swimming against the tide...**
*So you now know you're passionate about this new inspiration that has come to you...*
You've done your dreaming and searching and you really feel you're ready to go – but what's holding you back.....?
Is it those nagging doubts that others close to you are planting in your mind?

They are probably not ready for your transformation and are actively discouraging you from moving forward with your new journey. You can then begin to lose faith, because you are so used to listening to the advice of others, and now you're not trusting your own instincts about what you should really be doing with your life – that is, *fulfilling your dream.*

Others will undoubtedly be hesitant about it, because it means you will change and they will not be ready for that change like you are, however well meaning they may seem.

*But, you must use your own drive and ambition to project yourself forwards.*

You should be following what you are meant to be doing in life as part of your own path and destiny.
You should be feeling like you are achieving something fantastic and allowing yourself to be happy with that satisfying feeling of success and fulfilment. You should be able to enjoy the excitement and exhilaration of starting something new, that you have longed to

do and that you believe will be the making of you.

*So you must push through the negativity from others who may not share your vision or who could doubt your capability.*

If you know full well that you will need some training, do some research and really develop yourself to get to that dream.
You are certain deep in your heart that you can and *will* do it!

It may be that those close to you are just trying to protect you, or are threatened by this *new* you, and that's fine. But, you need to know how to sensitively remove yourself from their well-intentioned advice and accept that you *can* move forward with strength on your own, without them holding you back.

Obviously, what you want is to have a powerful support network behind you, motivating you all the way and picking you up when you are struggling mentally or emotionally.
So, if you can find people like this, then surround yourself by them and use them as an asset to your development and growth.

*Your journey and accomplishments will be so much stronger with this network behind you.*

Perhaps if you cannot find these kind of people within your own group of close friends, family or colleagues, then you could start getting involved in a networking group that will have like-minded people who are also striving to succeed in their chosen field, who can spur you on and encourage you to keep going.

These are people who can offer constructive advice and who have an excellent understanding of how your chosen goal works and can offer some of their expertise and knowledge, that you can actively use every day.

Having the right mindset yourself, as well as having those around you giving support, will move you forwards in leaps and bounds towards achieving great outcomes, and could be key to you finding success with your personal venture.

So instil your drive towards your goals firmly in your mind.

Let your loved ones watch you grow and thrive, which will be all the motivation and understanding they will need to know that you can make it, even though they are in a totally different place to you.

It will soon become clear to them and they'll learn that you are achieving what you set out to do, and so this will gradually make them more positive towards you and your goals.

This, in turn, will make you feel less guilty about doing it, without, or despite their initial 'advice' or negativity.

You never know, you may be just the inspiration that provokes them out of their inertia or familiarity and into *adopting your courage and following their own dreams!*

What a fantastic way to go!

*And what a fantastic way to empower not only yourself, but your loved ones too!*

**…..allow the universe to help you get to your ultimate life……..**
*Come to realise and understand that the power of your subconscious mind is an extremely strong tool that can help you achieve any of your personal or business goals.*
Be aware of the connection between your *subconscious mind and the law of attraction* in helping you achieve success and prosperity.

People are extremely capable of developing themselves through *free will and choice*, and this, with the power of your subconscious, is one of your greatest gifts.

You can be totally capable of manipulating them to work in your favour and can give yourself a much healthier and successful life.

*You realise by now that you, and everything around you, is energy and it's vibrations.*

Your subconscious mind is no different and it's power works by sending and acknowledging the different vibrations within your body. As such, whatever your wants and desires are, so your body responds by being attracted to those things.

As you open up and begin to notice them more, this will stimulate you into making certain strategies about how to achieve your goals.

Using this principle, whatever you are now and what you are experiencing, is the product of your subconscious conditioning, because the vibrations within your body are pulling you towards the things you want.....

*Stop and give this some deep and serious thought to properly understand and take in it's full meaning......*

**…...so therefore, use the law of the universe to your supreme benefit.....**
*You can see that by tapping into your super-conscious, being intelligent, as well as spiritual, and using the law of the universe, you can mould the life you want and fulfil your dreams.*

If you want to have the greatest life you could possibly have, you need to be super positive and have that unwavering **total** belief that you never have to worry any more.

With this overall principle in mind, *you really can revolutionize your life.*

You can also use it to put your business goals and ambitions into place, by understanding how to ask your super-conscious to fulfil those desires.
Start to be more aware of yourself, how you think, what you watch and what you pick up on.
It's all too easy to walk around in a daze on *automatic*.

So begin to have more *conscious* thoughts about what you are doing day to day, rather than just allowing those subconscious thoughts, some of which have been built up through past conditioning and influences, to just allow things to happen to you *without you even thinking about it....*

You naturally pick up energy through how the world generally works and you also create energy yourself. You can harness that energy in a positive way, so you can experience new outcomes and have a completely different life.

*Because, everyone is connected to each other and this universe, whether you like it or not....*

And because, everything in the world is created as a result of just being *conscious*.....
By using your '*super-conscious'*, you can create anything that lies within the realms of your own mind, by tuning in and harmonising with it, thus *bringing everything you desire into actuality.*

Why not....it's your natural given right...

Allow your spiritual side to flow into your physical thoughts, beliefs, feelings and emotions.
If you can begin to understand your super-conscious mind, it will enhance your ability to actually manifest your inner desires.
It is *limitless*.

It's not rocket science, it's just a natural process –think about it....

*You have the potential for any conceivable outcome* - everything from good, bad and all that exists in-between.

Whether your desired outcome is physical or non-physical, there are no limitations or boundaries within this *infinite field* of potential and possibilities. It exists everywhere and is within everything, encompassing ALL things created – those already in existence, that have already happened and that is about to happen, and in all probabilities both seen and unseen, from rags to riches, tangible and spiritual.

*Accept this.*
You don't have to argue with it.

Give it some deep thought so you **fully understand** the meaning surrounding this actual philosophy....

Because, whatever has the capability to be conceived or focused on in your mind, or a thought followed by an action, can be manifested in a physical form, regardless of whatever it is.

And with every feeling and emotion, whether it's happy, sad, bitter or bad, if you focus your super-conscious mind on it, you are *choosing to experience it* and it will therefore be manifested in a physical form.

Think about it hard enough and you will conclude to yourself that this is actually <u>*obvious*</u>.

ALL things, whether they are seen or unseen, basically comprise of pure energy or light. Everything in life consists of a vibrating mass of energy which serves as the fundamental building blocks for every conceivable outcome - right out into infinity.
Your ability to think and reason exists within your super-consciousness.

The way you personally decide to think, feel and act, determines what you are choosing to draw from your super-conscious mind, and these choices determine the series of events, conditions and circumstances that together make up your life experiences.
You have your own freedom to use and make your own choices.
You tap into your own *unlimited* potential.

You use what you have been given – either negatively or positively – to your detriment or to your advantage.

*You choose......*

Your perception of your own reality will ultimately determine the choices you make, and the more you tune into yourself and become consciously aware of the choices you are making, so you will begin to understand yourself as an individual, and how you draw from your super-conscious mind to gain your experiences in life.

You need to fully recognise and acknowledge the limitless power provided to you to be, do and have whatever you choose.

Whatever you choose to believe in, how everything came to be, how we all got here, and your current reality exists as a result of your super-conscious mind. Where you came from was as a result of thought and this extends to the whole universe around you.

You have been provided the ability to consciously direct your energy to create your reality through your own thought projection.
You just have to consciously and intentionally conceive it all.

If you are not experiencing all you want, it is because your conscious thought patterns are in conflict and not harmonising with your programmed core beliefs stored in your subconscious, and this is what is being communicated to your super-conscious, thus determining your physical results – good or bad!

Therefore, if you have a desire to be rich, but subconsciously you don't think you will ever be, due to previously created beliefs and programming, you are effectively broadcasting an unharmonious energy frequency that is blocking that reality of ever being rich!

*Although you may have a strong desire to be rich as a conscious desire, it's the underlying unconscious beliefs that you hold, that determine and create events, conditions and circumstances in your life.*

You are planting the seed and projecting your subconscious beliefs about money and as such, turning this into your reality. This all affects what you are asking your super-conscious mind to deliver to you.
The trick is to make a conscious and consistent effort to focus on what you *do* want and not on what you *don't* want, because if you place your conscious focus on not having any money, you are still, in effect, placing your focus on the *opposite* of what you desire.

*Your super-conscious will draw from that dominant focus, i.e. being broke!*

Therefore, you need to change those vibrations to being *rich*, telling yourself that it's an *already existing reality,* thereby intensifying the energy to make your desire come true.
You can never create a desired outcome by placing your predominant focus on the absence of it's polar opposite.

*Focus on attainment, **not** lack or absence.*

Your super-conscious does not judge, but always provides an outcome.
It does not say yes to some things and no to others.
You have **free will** and your limitations are based merely on what you believe is possible for yourself.

Remember '*cause and effect*'.
Your beliefs are the cause, the outcomes that you experience are the effect.
Whatever you choose in every area of your life is yours when you are consciously aware that *all things are possible.*
Whatever you believe and perceive your truth to be, so it will become the truth of your life experiences and will unfold *just as you instruct it.*

There is no right or wrong in your own truth and reality, because whatever your choices are, they are *correct,* they are your right.
You can choose to have a higher quality of life if you are aware of your own individual power to create it. You can become empowered to believe it and manifest it, just as you wish.

Your super-conscious mind will deliver whatever you ask for without judgement and your desired outcomes will in turn allow you to achieve the ultimate self-mastery for a life that you want, fulfilling your dreams *without limit*.

*You will be rewarded with fulfilment, peace, happiness, a sense of purpose and limitless abundance in all aspects of your life.*

**…..using the 7 spiritual laws to help you succeed in life…..**
*According to ancient wisdom, there are seven spiritual laws that you need to follow if you want a successful life.*
They are:

- **The Law Of Pure Potential**
- **The Law Of Giving And Receiving**
- **The Law Of Karma (Cause And Effect)**
- **The Law Of Least Effort**
- **The Law Of Intention And Desire**
- **The Law Of Detachment**
- **The Law Of Dharma**

A successful life can obviously mean more than just wealth and monetary value.
It can be successfully peaceful, successfully spiritual, successful of mind and successful of body. As you go through all the many stages of your life, you will know at which point you are looking for a *specific* type of success.
You may want to add these strategies towards fulfilling your desire to achieve ultimate empowerment.

Here is an brief understanding of those laws.
You can, of course, get a more in-depth insight into these laws by looking for more information on this subject.

**The Law Of Pure Potential** *is when you come to realise that your* **true** *self is one of pure potentiality.*
You align with the power that manifests everything in the universe, which is that of *creation*.
To properly commit to the law of pure potentiality, you need to take time twice every day to sit alone in silent meditation for thirty minutes.
You need to commune with nature and hold witness to the intelligence that exists within every living thing and releasing the field of pure potentiality and unbounded creativity.
*Do not judge anything.*

**The Law of Giving and Receiving** *are different aspects of the flow of energy in the universe.*
As it operates through a dynamic exchange of giving and receiving, so you need to give out what you wish to seek, to keep the abundance circulating in your life.
To apply this law, you need to commit to bringing a gift – this may be given as a compliment, a flower or perhaps a prayer to others you intend to encounter and thereby begin the process of circulating joy, wealth and affluence in your life and the lives of others.
You also need to be grateful for all the gifts that life has to offer – in nature, sunlight, sound of birds singing, spring flowers or first snow of winter.
Also be open to receiving from others, either in the form of material gifts, money, a compliment or a prayer and in doing so, *keeping wealth circulating in your life.*

***The Law of Karma*** *is the action of 'Cause And Effect'.*
Every action you take generates a force of energy that is returned to you in like kind, like the saying, *'we reap what we sow'*.
When you choose actions that bring happiness and success to others, the fruit of your karma is happiness and success.
You can apply this law by being consciously aware of the choices you make in each moment and therefore their consequences. For example, who will be affected by those choices, in preparation of what will happen in your future, such as bringing fulfilment and happiness to yourself and others. Be guided by what you feel in your heart and how comfortable you feel about it.
Ask yourself, *'does this feel right'*?

***The Law of Least Effort*** *harnesses the forces of harmony, joy and love.*
This is natures intelligence that functions with sheer ease and carefreeness, enabling us to create success and good fortune without effort.
To apply this law you need to practise accepting people, situations, circumstances and events as they occur, accepting that things are as they should be moving within the universe. You cannot struggle against the whole universe by struggling against this moment to make them as *you* wish they were.
Once you have accepted things as they are, take responsibility for your situation and for all the events you see as problems, such as not blaming anyone or anything for your situation.
Instead, be alert to every problem as being an opportunity in disguise, that will allow you to transform it into greater benefit.
You should feel no need to convince or persuade others to accept your point of view and you should remain open to all points of view, but not be rigidly attached to any one of them.

**The Law of Intention and Desire** *is the power of organising the mechanics for the fulfilment of what it is you wish for.*
Make a list of all your desires, carry it with you and look at it before you go into your silence, meditation, before you go to sleep at night and when you wake up in the morning.
You need to surrender this list to the womb of creation and trust that there is a reason for when things don't seem to go your way and that the cosmic plan has designs for you, much grander than even

those that you have conceived.
You need to constantly remind yourself that obstacles should not get the better of your intentions and desires and that *things are as they are for a reason.*
Accept this.

**The Law of Detachment** *makes you step into the unknown, frees you from your past and your prison of past conditioning into a field of all possibilities, surrendering you to the creative mind within the universe.*
Allow yourself and those around you the freedom to be as they are and not rigidly impose your idea of how things should be. Do not force solutions on problems, thereby creating new problems.
Participate in everything with detached involvement.
Factor in uncertainty as an essential ingredient of your experience, allowing solutions to spontaneously emerge out of the problem, out of the confusion, disorder and chaos. The more uncertain things seem to be, the more secure you will feel, because uncertainty is your path to freedom and you will find your security.
Step into the field of all possibilities and anticipate the excitement that can occur when you remain open to an infinity of choices.
When you step into this field, *you will experience all the fun, adventure, magic and mystery of life.*

**The Law of Dharma** *concerns everyone's purpose in life, your unique or special talent to give to others, so that you can experience the ecstasy and exultation of your own spirit, which is the ultimate goal of all goals.*
Apply this law by committing to lovingly nurturing the god or goddess deep within your soul and paying attention to the spirit within you that animates both your body and mind.
Make a list of your unique talents and then list all the things that you love to do while expressing your unique talents. Use them in the service of humanity and lose track of time and create abundance in your life as well as others.
Ask yourself daily, how can I serve and how can I help?
The answers to these questions will allow you to help and serve your fellow human beings with love.
*See how positively different you feel when you embrace these laws fully......*

### …..and then there's the law of attraction….

*As already mentioned, this law says that whatever you give your attention to, or whatever it is you desire, will cause you to emit a vibrational frequency, and so that desire will become real.*
However, in the same way, if you don't want something, so it will match that vibration.
As such, even if you focus your attention for a short while on there being a **lack** of something, it will become so and you would therefore feel discouragement, pessimism, depression, insecurity, worry, anger, and the host of negative emotions that are induced by you *wanting* something and *not having* it.

*It makes perfect sense then to always plan for what you **DO** really want!*

Your thoughts are working for you as you invite them into the process of the *'Law of Attraction'*.
Believe that as you go with this flow, there is absolutely nothing that you cannot achieve. The whole of your well-being will reap the benefits of allowing this flow to physically manifest your desires. Don't work against it and try not to resist it, or you will counteract it's very purpose.

What creates your world is governed by who you are and what you think, and that is caused by a powerful focus of energy and vibration on your thoughts, which then becomes a belief.

*You really have to harness it to make it work for you.*

It's a natural force that's all around you, operating all the time. Your unconscious mind does the attracting and it is far more important in your thinking than your conscious mind.

Gradually, as you understand and trust the power of the law of attraction and things actually begin to appear around you, so you will develop stronger vibrational habits.

You will then start to feel stronger and gain more control over your life, and through this power, *you can guide your own experiences in any way you choose your life to be.*

When you sit down and seriously think deeply about it, everyone is free to create their own joy and happiness purely through how they project their thoughts.
This can act as part of your own empowerment.

As you may have gathered by now, there is a very important rule that you have to remember when asking for your desires, and that is not to unwittingly work against your vibrations by reinforcing things that you *don't* want, rather than what you *do* want.
Because, if you do, your desires just cannot come through.

In other words, you shouldn't be saying you **don't** want to be poor, but rather, you should be saying you **want** to be rich!
You are bound to have these '*counter intentions*' - those hidden beliefs that block you, perhaps carried through from childhood or previous situations and events that have happened to you and are holding you back. What you have to do is bring your counter intentions to the surface and remove them to make way for *abundance*.

You have to look into the mirror of your mind - search for and find your own limiting beliefs and eliminate them.

If you think positively consistently, it can't turn out badly, and in reverse, if you think negatively, it usually won't turn out well. That has surely shown itself to you time and time again....
Guide your thoughts through your feelings and by activating a more dominant and positive vibration, direct your energy with focus and control to achieve what you want.

*What you see around you is a projection of yourself.*

Once you change your inner, so your outer will change with it.
Look at your own reflection.
Get rid of old beliefs that are holding you back.
*Speak to and deliver good messages to yourself.*
Unlock your unconscious and bring your conscious mind into alignment with each other. Take inspired action to free yourself from limiting beliefs.
Become clear in your mind by unblocking filters.

Open yourself up to receiving and then acting upon it. The universe will listen to intentions and your visualisations will no longer be blocked. Take small actions and become open to more and more opportunities.

*Become aware of your doubts.*

Then get some conviction and clarity of who and what you are and where you want to go.
Shift your thinking for the better and allow this positive flow of energy to bring you goodness and enrichment.

*Everyone is meant to live a good life, thrive, feel well and enjoy love and happiness.*

So, by accepting yourself as a vibrational being who attracts things, and by understanding the way thoughts reflect your life, you hold the keys to get from wherever you are to wherever you want to be.

*Allow the law of attraction to align with your ultimate desires through really feeling the passion and pleasure towards your wishes.*

Do not allow negative feelings to bring you out of harmony and connection with the universal energy, thereby affecting your direction.
Deliberately choose good thoughts and in doing so, hold absolute power over your experiences – always remembering that you get what you think about – whether you want it or not.

As you get good at it, you will begin a fantastic journey to whatever you can imagine.
Trust that the universe will deliver and has the ability to do so – desire, request, granted, fulfilled!
Attract enrichment from the inside out.
You need a supercharged sub-conscious mind to attract abundance.

*Open up a life of magic and miracles.*

Be true to yourself, connect to the energy, be positive and you *can* have happiness and bring it to others too.
*This is true empowerment!*

**.....so the Universe is conspiring to deliver your desires...**
*As you can see, as a living being, you are vibrating and creating emotions through every experience you go through.*
And to *truly* know and understand who you really are and why your world is the way it is, you need to start paying attention to these emotional signals and connections.
This way you will get everything you desire out of your life and become who you really want to be. *You are the creator of your own life.*
You are a totally free person and you now know that with help from your own thoughts, you make your own choices.

Therefore, have faith in the system, and like the air that you breathe, relax and allow the energy to flow through you.
Have faith that as this 'vibrational being', by transmitting your desires to the universe, it will understand and answer whatever you want, whether spoken out loud or not.

*But you need to be **open** to receiving.*

Firstly, you need to understand that you must *enjoy your journey in life*, because life is <u>now</u>, *in this moment*, not in the future, not in the past.

You also need to know that there is *nothing* that you cannot do or be, because you have the freedom to create your own reality and experiences, using the innate knowledge you already possess.

You may be pulled in all different directions trying to please someone else, only to discover that you can't move in a proper direction that is consistent with pleasing both of you, and in doing so, *neither* of you are being pleased!

*Therefore you are not going along your own path of desires or achieving what is meant for you.*

Your life is totally up to you, because you make your own choices and should not be satisfied with anyone else attempting to create your life *for* you....

Actually, when you seriously think about it, it is actually impossible for anyone else to do that for you, because ultimately, it is *you* who is making all your own decisions – whether they are good or bad or influenced by someone else – you are *still* the one making the choices.

*Because you can say **yes** or **no**.....*

On your quest and journey, always be happy with who you are and what you have, whilst still being eager for more.
Your vibrations, through the power of your focussed thought and attention, are constantly transmitted to the universe and they are answered to fulfil your desires, so you need to remain open to allow yourself to receive it.

*You just need to ask for it.....*

Feel optimistic as you anticipate what is coming to you.
Don't doubt, fear, feel unworthy or impatient, otherwise you will block the flow - the current that runs through everything.

Any resistant thoughts you have like anger, frustration, tension, etc., will be holding the opposite vibrational pattern to that which you desire, and this mismatch will be responsible for you not getting what you want from life.
You are working *against* it.
It does takes a lot of courage to admit, but you have to realise that whatever you have done in life, it is only you, and you alone, that has created it.

*No-one else is responsible for your reality.*

Once you accept this situation, it will really empower you.
Just be aware of, and understand that, your world is all about this energy and you can create your own experiences and reap the benefits of the results that happen.
If you always remember that whatever your desires and beliefs are, they are just thoughts. *Through these thoughts, you are 'asking'.*
And with every new idea you would like to experience or have, believe that the universe will always answer those desires and that they will be realised.

*Be ready, open and prepared to receive them.*
*Once you are moving in the direction of your desires, you can begin to relax and enjoy your fantastic journey.*

### ...making a statement to manifest your desires.....
*You may find it helpful to write down a current life statement to yourself as a confirmation of your desires, as something you can refer to, every day.*
*Take a very* **bold** *look at what you want, where you are in your life and how you see your desires unfolding.*
*What is your goal, how can you get there, what skills do you need and what will this ultimately bring you?*

Here is an example of a statement:

*"I wish to become at one with the world and strong through my daily positive actions.*
*I am currently in transition to become what I desire.*
*I am moving up my scale of possibilities by being open and learning about the universe and what it is offering me.*
*Although this is the middle of my 'growth line', and I am sometimes a little stressed and overwhelmed by it all, that is what needs to be done to achieve manifestation of my goals, I know that my character, stamina and expectations will pay off for me.*
*I need to instil patience and endurance, remain open-minded and committed to my development and responsibilities to achieve my personal goals and thereby manifest my desires, and be in control and enjoy the journey!*
*This will bring me excellent peace, calm, tranquillity, good health, strength, satisfaction and happiness.*
*This is all I ask....."*

You can adapt this statement to whatever your ultimate desire is and your steps to get there.
Pin your positive statement up somewhere to refer to when you need.
Adapt and amend it as you see fit, so it is always relevant over the course of your journey and keeps you motivated and empowered along the way....

**..reach out to the cosmos for help in achieving what you want...**
*If you've ever been curious about how it works, 'Cosmic Ordering' is another way of asking the universe for your wishes, wants and needs, and then trusting in it to fulfil those desires.*
So, you could potentially use this school of thought to benefit your goals and success path.

There are 7 Principles of Cosmic Ordering to follow:

**First** - *you have to decide what it is that you want.*
This can actually be quite challenging, so it will need to be thought through carefully, as this is what you are *wishing* for and what you *really* want to happen.

**Second** - *it is very important that you make sure your orders are positive, in the present tense and ultimately personal to you.*
You have to avoid negative words such as 'not' and 'no', and only order things that are beneficial to you, from a loving place in your heart.
Any orders that are hateful, negative or vengeful are likely to backfire.

**Third** - *you must order in a way that suits and works <u>uniquely</u> for you and how you feel about your connection to the Universe, empowering yourself through your own ritual and mood.*

**Fourth** - *you must <u>trust</u> the Cosmic Ordering process.*
Start by making simple orders, until you build sufficient trust and understanding of *letting go*, not feeling automatically in control.
Leave the Cosmos to deliver your order in perfect timing and in the best possible way for you.
Be relaxed and not be too prescriptive about how and when your order is going to be delivered. You don't need to interfere or restrict the creative possibilities open to the Universe to deliver your order.

**Fifth** - *you must trust your inner wisdom to guide you in your choices, when stating exactly what you want and when you want it delivered by, and that strikes the right balance between action and allowing.*
In allowing the Universe to bring you your order, you have to let go of all anxiety and have *complete* belief that the Cosmos *will* deliver your order to you.
At the same time as this, you still need to be open, aware and ready to take the opportunities that the universe may bring you as part of it's delivery.

**Sixth** - *you need to believe and accept that you deserve to have a wonderful life.*
You need to *live it* because the Universe is *infinitely* abundant.
If you cannot bring yourself to believe that you deserve good things, it becomes difficult to ask for them with an open and honest heart.
So, therefore, your Cosmic Order might be "*I have a beautiful car*!", but if your actual thoughts are "*I don't deserve it.*" ... that is the *true* belief of your message and so that is what the Cosmos will deliver!
**Seventh** - *you must acknowledge your successes.*
Recognise the fantastic power of Cosmic Ordering by feeling gratitude when the universe delivers, even if you think it may just be a coincidence.
You have to recognise it *really* was delivered!

*Therefore, be triumphant in your ordering success and allow it to reinforce your belief for any of your future orders!*

So, put your trust in Cosmic Ordering and get asking for that fabulous wish.....!

**…….on your path to total life empowerment, you need to look at your relationship with yourself.....**
*You should have a sense of self – and this doesn't mean having a big ego.*
We all have an ego in some way or another, if we really think about it.
It may rear it's head when we think or do something in particular, but no-one needs to go along life barging their way through situations and relationships being all big and pompous.

*No one will thank you for it!*

However, you do need to be aware of yourself as you are moving through your day.
Because, it's all too easy to walk through life not really looking left or right, up or down, in or out, but just being in your own little bubble within your own little world – probably in a very shallow and purposeless kind of way.
You may just be drifting from one situation to another and from one relationship to another, without really having any realisation of what bearing any of this has on your *true position in the world*.

But, being aware of who and how you are, will help you to see your position as it is now, how you want to be known and where you stand in life.
You will be able to tune into your role and purpose and keep connected and grounded to your environment. It will also help you to build crucial relationships and move forward consciously on a day to day basis.

*It'll make you consider where you are on your path line and where you want to actually be.*

By being aware of yourself, you can home in on what you are doing with yourself in *actuality* and whether you are fulfilling your proper potential or not.
It will also make you aware of your surroundings and where you sit within them and how you fit into the world as a whole........

Do not be shy of who you are. Be proud.

*Use this 'positioning' of yourself to look at how you feel regarding your goals and where you want to be in the future with them – including the next few months up to a year.*

> ***"This is an amazing world, with amazing opportunities, fantastic beauty and spectacular nature to die for, with extraordinary people living extraordinary lives....***
> ***You need to be part of this and you can be.***
> ***It's all about creating the life you***
> ***want to live in this wonderful place.***
> ***It's not about spending your life being bored, unhappy and just existing.***
> ***That's not why you are here".***

**……..if you are able to come to terms with acceptance, it can be very liberating……**
*Learning to accept certain situations that are beyond your control can truly set you free, in so many ways…..*
If you find yourself in circumstances that you can't *really* do anything

about, then instead of butting up against them so they cause you undue stress, anger and frustration, just *accept* things are the way they are....

You don't *have* to submit to those confrontational situations that you come up against – those negative challenges that crop up in everyone's day to day life. Rather come to realise that certain events and people just *won't* be flexible and therefore, have the strength to **accept** those circumstances as they are and leave well alone.

So many things can arise in your personal surroundings that may affect you in this way, particularly with peoples' characters or methods of doing things possibly annoying you.
However, sometimes you just need to *trust* people to get on with the task they have been assigned to deliver, *before* you start trying to control the way they are and the way they execute the job......

*This can be extremely empowering.....*

In doing so, it can reduce the irritation and frustration in your life, releasing you from any stubbornness you bear just for the sake of it.

*You get to live a life that's more free because you have less to argue and worry about.*

Your concern for those things that are actually out of your control, will no longer take a hold of you. You can begin to calm down and just see things for what they are, without judging them and then allow yourself and those people or situations to go on their merry way, without a conflict of interests.

Just take a breath and trust those people....

You can allow yourself to be yourself and allow others that courtesy too.
You will gain more respect for being this way and you will have more self-respect for yourself too. People will begin to perceive you in a different way and *that perception can be powerful.*
You don't <u>*have*</u> to be influenced by conditions that really have no business being in your life.

*You can choose what you want to accept and what you don't want in your life.*

If there are things in your life that are just an absolute pain, but you know you cannot do anything about them and you're just spending your time knocking your head against a brick wall trying to resolve things to *your* way of thinking, then it's time to take your foot **off** that control pedal and just accept and allow others to be who they are and certain situations to be what they are.

If all your efforts are ineffective because you cannot be fully in control, or you find yourself constantly adopting submissive behaviour, then changing your attitude more towards being trusting of the other party and not disapproving or judgemental, can help you be free of all the emotions that come along with it.

Don't expect this change in attitude to happen overnight, because you will have to adjust your mindset to embrace these circumstances. But if you adopt this philosophy, gradually with practise, you will find yourself trusting and becoming more emotionally mature, less judging, critical and casting blame.

*Let go of what you can't control, accept people and situations for what they are and begin to enjoy a far freer life emotionally with a greater sense of empowerment.*

### …..be comfortable with yourself……
*It's very hard to be happy if you are constantly comparing yourself to others – whether that's in looks, assets, opinions, achievements, or anything else.*
No-body is perfect, nor should we be.
You should be happy that your imperfections make you unique, individual and who you are.

So, you cannot spend your life comparing your inside to other people's outside, or what you see and *perceive* to be real.
Dwelling on what you aren't and haven't got, rather than what you are and have got, will eventually eat you away.

If you truly want to enjoy your life, learning to love who you are, accepting who you are and being thankful for who you are, will totally increase your resilience and well-being.

*Self acceptance is a major part of life empowerment.*

Being better and improving yourself all comes as part of life, but firstly you have to accept who you are in order to progress in the world.
But you really need to be kinder to yourself.
Being kind to yourself in turn, will project out to being kind to others and the chain goes on from there....
If you want to be accepted, then you have to accept yourself first.

Going through life with constant criticism in your head or telling yourself you are not good enough, will only descend into unhappiness.
Accepting that you are just you and that life is a kaleidoscope of ups and downs, trials and tribulations, weaknesses and strength, is a very normal part of life.
Overcoming, living through and moving on from things, is how life is meant to be and it's not just you being paranoid, insecure, low in self-esteem or inferior in any way.
*Having this ability takes away the focus of feeling this paranoia when times get rough, and helps to enable and empower you to progress forward along your life path.*

Being able to function at a good level is a natural part of your overall welfare, and being able to accept yourself for who you are is key to how good, strong and happy you feel.

You obviously need to feel positive about yourself, and knowing all your strengths and weaknesses contribute to enabling that. Along with coming to terms with those things that you may be clinging on to that have happened in the past.

Properly letting go of those feelings and removing them from your mind can be a lengthy process, depending on how long you have been affected by them and the limitations they have put on you.
But to be able to move on, you need to look them in the eye and realise what it is about those things, mistakes, bad relationships, etc., that you can work *with*, rather than *against*, if you want to

function with efficient capability.

*Glean the positives about them - what lessons have you learnt that you can take forward?*

Then gradually remove the negative thinking and feelings to make a clear path ahead, empowering you to achieve what you want to make your life as wonderful as it should be.
If you have big goals to achieve, it is totally necessary to accept yourself and your limitations, especially if you have set your sights on major success. Because if things don't work out quite as they should, you really need to know that you are not a loser or a failure, just because they didn't happen or turn out *exactly* as you wanted them to.

Know then, that life has a path for you and if you accept your mistakes or inabilities in certain areas, you can go for it <u>again</u>, or along a *new* path or strategy, using all that you learnt along the way to make a better job of it next time.
Perhaps it's the universe telling you that it wasn't the right path for you anyway, or you need to gain better skills to achieve better results, or even take on new expertise to help get you where you want to be.

Each time you try, you challenge yourself and this is a very important part of life's journey, without which, it would be extremely dull indeed.
Just accept that all things happen as part of life from which you must learn and empower yourself, ready for the next move.

Being low on self-acceptance can mean that you spend too much time and inner effort on being troubled by what you think you *should* be, making you believe that there is something wrong with you and causing lots of negative self-talk.
This does nothing to your happiness and really gets in the way of making the most of yourself.

It stands to reason that if you have a reasonably balanced sense of self-worth and judge yourself to be valuable and good, you will naturally experience more happiness, have more optimism about life and feel less negative, depressed or anxious.

This obviously doesn't apply to those with over-inflated ego's, self-delusion and exaggerated positivity, because if you are like this, then when that state is threatened, you can be quite sensitive about any negative feedback, which in turn can cause anger and aggression and make any chance of improvement quite difficult.

Your self-esteem is likely to be affected by the last set of judgements others made about you and your performance.
So you will naturally feel good if you have been praised and complimented about a recent success, or feel terrible if it was 'deemed' a failure.
However, taking your idea of your own self-esteem to extremes where you judge yourself as superior to others will fall down when it has the judgement of others, causing a separation in the ranks and disconnecting you with people in the long run, so you need to be careful with this.

As in *Buddhism*, you need to explore showing yourself some compassion, as they say it is linked to greater happiness, resilience, less depression and anxiety, optimism and higher self-esteem, promoting connections with others.

*Be kind and understanding to yourself, especially if you are feeling inadequate and insecure.*

Recognise that, as a human being, pain and failure are unavoidable in life and you therefore need a sense of balance without drama, and awareness without exaggeration or self-pity, when it comes to your emotions, thoughts and feelings.

By being compassionate towards yourself, you can promote your own improvement and lessen your comparison of yourself to others, reducing any self-pity and therefore allowing you to work positively through your challenges and learn from your mistakes, which helps to develop new skills and knowledge along the way.

You shouldn't be spending your life sending yourself self-hate messages, as it can only lead to misery, low self-confidence and self-esteem, which is not the motivation you need to get on with your life!

*Instead start treating yourself with the respect and gratitude you deserve.*

Along the way, this state of mind is likely to increase your effectiveness at work, as well as your personal life, health and well-being.
You may recognise your self-criticism telling you that you don't have any willpower, that your body is terrible, that life is about depriving yourself, that you cannot succeed....
Yet in the next move you're stuffing chocolate cake into your mouth, you're lounging on the sofa and you're basically living an unhealthy and unbalanced lifestyle!
In other words the total opposite to what you are wanting to achieve in your life!
But hating yourself for being like it does no-one any good at all.

*Decide to love and be kind to yourself instead.*
Why not?

Don't believe that self-criticism means you are keeping yourself in line, or that if you stray from this thought pattern, you will become self-indulgent.
It doesn't have to be that way.

Instead of telling yourself you're bound to fail - **prepare**.
Instead of thinking you will miss a deadline, **focus** and give it your best.
Instead of thinking you don't know about something, **learn** it.
Instead of thinking you don't have the energy to exercise and become fit, start slowly and **build** it up.
Instead of thinking you are doing everything wrong, ask yourself what is the **best** you can do.

*Turn all negative talk into positive talk.*

Stop blaming yourself for things and start respecting yourself instead.
It's far more constructive, gives you a lot more confidence and also makes a real difference to both *your* life and those in it.
It's no good being angry with yourself for not being someone else.

Your journey will only turn out miserable.

*Always look at the positive actions you can take and you will feel far more motivated and your spirits will be lifted.*

And you can get on and achieve things!

If there are common self-criticisms that keep recurring in your head, then write them down and promise yourself that you will turn them into a positive, so that you can begin accomplishing your goals once and for all.
Get them out of your head and give yourself that space back!
There's bound to be things that you like about yourself, so always have them at the forefront of your mind, reminding you that *you are good and valuable.*

If you want to feel empowered, build your confidence and give yourself the capacity to really create the life you want, then it's all about respecting yourself.

*Start liking yourself, loving yourself, being yourself and accepting yourself.*

And stop being so hard on yourself!
At the end of the day, you are the *only* one who will definitely look after yourself.
*It's your responsibility.*
You have a life to lead.
Make it wonderful.
Make some memories and make your journey a work of art.
You owe it to yourself.
*You **deserve** it!*

> ***"By helping yourself, you in turn can give all the help you want to give to those you love and you can all live in a better place.
> You will begin to see the world in all it's glory and have a first hand in bringing out it's beauty".***

**……begin being at peace with yourself……..**
*Are you truly at peace with yourself?*
To find real peace, you need to feel content inside with who you are, warts and all.
However, you should still accept there is *still* so much in the world yet to learn and see, and embrace the potential you have to be *great*.

Life is a total stream of challenges and that's good, because without them, it would be extremely monotonous indeed.
You can still be grateful for all the things you have already - like your home, your relationships, your means and income, your support network and all the <u>free</u> things this world offers you *everyday*.

Accepting who you are enables you to celebrate your life, your qualities, your skills and just being you – *a highly unique individual*. And accepting yourself as who you are allows you to laugh, sing, have fun and cry, learn and develop and just simply look at life in the face and enjoy it! Because you are not dragging unnecessary issues around with you all day long.....

At the end of the day, you can only be you, but you *can* be the *best* of you, and being at peace with yourself means making the most of who you are.
You are able to feel confident about this and therefore grow with it every day.

So instead of striving to be something you are not, or someone who you can never truly be (because it's someone else!), start to love who you are as that exceptional and beautiful person in the world, and begin to be at peace with yourself, once and for all.

If you want to find that inner peace, it means you have to give yourself the time to disconnect with all the hustle and bustle of the daily grind that you live in day in, day out, so you can give yourself the space to reconnect with exactly who you truly are.

Remove stress and only concentrate on your own life, without being affected by things that you have no control over or that don't really concern you.

If you cannot change something, then why worry yourself about it?

You can spend too much time and energy worrying about what others think of you – even though you may not even know what they're thinking!
That's just u*nnecessary* stress that is totally *avoidable*.
Give yourself back that space in your mind. It's one more step towards inner peace.

Find something peaceful and quiet to sooth your mind, soul and spirit and that will help you to re-energise, like meditation, for instance. Just a few minutes a day will make all the difference.
Get out in the fresh air, away from the congestion, the pollution and all the noise.
Tap into what nature has given you – breathe and feel good, tranquil and relaxed. Find inspiration and calm in the trees, flowers, sky and wildlife, and all the other wonderful gifts given to you.

*Just listen......*

Release the happy hormones generated from laughter and smiling! Let them free and remove a large amount of your stress and negativity. Something so small, yet so powerful, can make such a *huge* impact.
Look *beyond* yourself for a while. Take yourself away from your own problems and realise how small and insignificant they are when you think about what else is going on in the world.

Be grateful.....

Engaging in acts of kindness towards others helps to solidify your own inner peace, because being good to others makes *you* feel good inside.
It removes you from being consumed by your own wants all the time and allows you to get closer to people and feel less selfish or self-absorbed.
When you are at your wits end, always remember how many times you have possibly been in that situation before and have always come out of the other end, *absolutely fine* - usually having learnt something from it and grown as a result.

Hope is always a good feeling to rely on when you're feeling overwhelmed by anything.
It can help you to realise that this is just a blip, it's not the end of the world and everything will be all right. Just hold on to that positivity and it will help you to remain calm.

Help instil your inner peace with whatever it is you have faith in – whatever that may be that's personal to you. Having that faith will guide you towards peace and wisdom and help keep you sane and calm.

Remembering that life is one long journey of constant learning and challenges, development and growth should help you to realise that solutions come along to help you strive and survive.

And if you don't know something right *now*, it doesn't matter, because you can learn as you go along your path.

Realising and accepting that you don't have to have all the answers, is surely a positive way towards tranquillity and inner peace.

Being at peace with yourself also means not holding onto the past - that's already gone and cannot now be changed.
Equally, don't spend too much time worrying about the future - that hasn't even happened yet.

So, by living in the *present*, you can enjoy each moment, be aware and *mindful* of what's happening *right* **here** and **now**.
As you live in this moment, you can only deal with *now* and in doing so, feel far more peaceful and serene than you can imagine.

*Feel your own truth inside.....*

Know that you will overcome all eventualities and come out stronger and more empowered, satisfied and content with yourself.

*No matter how much money or possessions you have, you cannot put a price on your own peace*, so be sure it's your priority.

Everything you have done in your life up to now, including all your mistakes, trials and tribulations have made you who you are – there

is no escaping that fact.
You have made yourself you, through your own thoughts and actions.
This applies to all your personal achievements too....

*Choose to accept yourself and be at peace.*

**You make your own luck by putting yourself in a place where you can benefit from fortune.**

**......vanity can possess you.....**
*It's great to feel beautiful.*
Of course it is...!
No doubt you like to feel good about yourself, because when you do, it makes you feel strong, able to rise up and feel empowered to take on the world.
And you probably realise that how you feel on the outside affects how you feel on the inside and can therefore affect your psychological well-being – both positively and negatively.

But beauty isn't only skin deep, you also need to feel beautiful deep *inside,* so that you can be a beautiful person *outside.*
Someone who is confident and has good self-esteem, will spend their life projecting that confidence and sense of well-being throughout their daily lives.

However, there are so many people who don't feel so good about themselves, who ignore their fantastic qualities, like inner beauty, skills, knowledge, caring personalities, etc., in place of feeling the need to look better to the external world, as well as themselves.

This thinking has possibly originated from someone being negative towards them, or perhaps media hype has created an unhealthy view of how they feel about how they look.
This then has caused them to yearn to be some far reaching air-brushed and unrealistic model type, and this, as a consequence, has negatively affected their emotional well-being.

Maybe you are also like this......?

You are subjected to too many pressures to conform to stereotypes and the 'perfect' body shape, size and look. You may find that because you are not happy with the way you look, it can often lead to becoming very self-conscious, lacking in confidence, feeling anything *but* beautiful and even obsessive about your image.

You probably tend to forget that everyone is an individual with a different look, shape and size and it is *this* that is your true natural beauty.
You should be able to be happy with the way you look, however you look.

But, when the way you *look* takes over your life and the obsession becomes out of control, then you are spending far too much time and energy on the shallow pursuit of 'beauty', to the detriment of *real* life.
In doing this, you are not allowing yourself to actually live a balanced and considerate life because sense has been taken over by the obsession. Your mind is in another place with new priorities and you are unable to see the world in it's proper state.

You will be missing out on all the fun.....!

Not only that, but anything you do, will always be dominated by how you look as being the most important aspect of your world, and everything else needs to fit around it.

It other words, *vanity will possess you.*

That is not empowering you to get ahead in life.
You cannot be at peace and living in a calm state, if all you think about constantly is what you look like.

*You need time to step back from that mindset and outlook and start living in the real world.*

By all means spend time looking after yourself, and feeling fit and healthy is the best way to do this. It will also release those 'feel-good' endorphins and build up strength and well-being, which in turn will make you look and feel good about yourself, increase your confidence and self-esteem and replace those negative views of yourself.

*You can then tackle the world and take control of your path, instead of physical appearance taking you over.*

If you come out of your vanity 'bubble', you may see a lot more opportunities in front of you that will help you get ahead and ultimately allow you to become far more successful.

*The most important thing in life is that you have to be yourself instead of trying to be someone else.*

Enjoy your natural beauty, feel more contented, maintain your emotional well-being and you will enjoy life a whole lot more.

*Break out and feel the freedom in this...!*

**.......wake up to your own magnificence......**
*Until you understand the hidden depths of yourself, you are only half awake.*
Make the time to awaken from your *dream-like state* so you can begin to create a life of passion and purpose and unlock the gateway to your wonderful self.

You have to *acknowledge the power within you* to overcome any circumstances you need to conquer.

Be a success in life.
Your *own* version of success.

Begin to believe in yourself enough to follow your gut intuition and allow yourself to make the changes that will free you from any restrictions in your life.

Achieve what you *want* to achieve.

Never think you are lacking or unworthy, otherwise the chances are, you will conduct your life as that kind of person.
Go for your goals with strength and confidence.

Follow the rhythm of your natural *ebb and flow* and be yourself without stress and worry, so you can enjoy life in a world that has been given to you experience and make the most of.

*You are magnificent.*
*Believe it!*

**.…."I am me and that's all I can be, but I can be the best I can be, to be the best of me"….**
*You are you and that's all you can be…..*
Be happy with this.
After all, at the end of the day, who else can you be?

Even with pressure and heavy influence trying to bend and shape you, you can still only be yourself and after a lot of trying, pushing and pulling in directions that don't suit you or are not really meant for you, your own personality and feelings will come to the fore in the end.

*You were born a unique individual, so it's your right to be one.*

Embrace it and look at the many ways of using your individualism to make the right personal choices, decisions and path in life, so you may enjoy it's full potential and get the most out of what you are here to do and be.

*To live as who you truly are is a wonderful state to the ultimate life.*

To know who you truly are is sometimes something that needs a lot of thorough thinking about, because so many of us trundle along on *automatic*, blindly following a path that we didn't necessarily choose for ourselves, *but it keeps up the equilibrium.*

To better realise just exactly who you are, what you should be doing and where you really want to be, means you need to get in touch with your inner self and come to terms with the possibility of change. Because you will need to go into a period of '*self-actualization*'.

What you think you are or want to be, may not necessarily be the *exact* calling for you.

And you have already seen that it may have been borne out of life's circumstances and events, including your relationships, all having a strong influence on your life.

You need to get to the *depths* of who you genuinely are and then begin to grow and blossom into the true version of yourself, start achieving what you want and living a *complete* life.
You may need help getting to those depths, if you think you may find it difficult on your own.

Living a life of true empowerment is all about being all you can be and reaching your full potential, whilst exploiting your innate talents and gifts and using your skills to enjoy your place in this world to the highest level you can, with total passion and purpose.

Learning to love yourself is part of this process, as having a good relationship with yourself will bring up all you need to know about yourself. You've already seen how that may be achieved.....

In nurturing this love and relationship with yourself, you will be able to highlight exactly what you *uniquely* have to offer, and as such you can be more specific about how to use your gifts for the good of yourself and the world around you.

In doing so, you will build complete courage to follow exactly what it is that your inner voice is calling you to do.

*Listen to what it's saying.....*

Having the strength and vision to ask yourself *exactly* what you would want to do if you knew *absolutely no part of it would fail* – is a true and real picture of what it is you are *genuinely* being asked to do.
Without the usual barriers and restrictions you can put up around you, you can be free to allow yourself to dig deep and allow your real thoughts, ideas and opinions to emerge, because nothing is blocking your way.

In going through this evaluation, your real personality and characteristics will come to the fore and you will be guided to your true calling. You will then be able to put together your plan of action to follow it through, building in all the challenges, tasks, requirements and steps you need to go through to set your vocation in place.

Being realistic about what you need to do and all the inevitable hurdles you will cross along your path, is all part of the self-actualization process.

Believing in yourself, feeling worthy, confident in your choices and knowing now that everything starts by a thought and then manifests into an action, is a vital part of understanding how living out your innate talents and going along your own journey, *leads to ultimate living*.
Obviously this is an ongoing process that will chop and change throughout your life as certain journeys will enlighten you along the way, reconnecting you with who you truly are.

As you develop and grow, become more wise and capable, you can exceed your potential and open up a wealth of new extended opportunities.
You will begin to value yourself more and discard the expectations of others that you may have been living under. In other words, *false layers* of conditioning that has shaped you up to this point.

*You will soon begin to see your place in the world from your own point of view and inner knowledge.*

It is down to you how brave and willing you are to step out of your comfort zone and the restraints of your own restrictive fears, in order to achieve the *real* you - away from old people and habits and into new exploration, new insights, perspectives and learning.
With this courage comes growth, expansion and joy!
And of course, empowerment.

In order to get to ultimate self-actualization, you must first go through some basic, but challenging steps to make sure that you are ready, and these include having all your physical needs and safety  covered, so you feel free and content to start your new journey.

You also need to feel a sense of belonging and love in order that you have that inner peace.

Once these things are achieved, you need to work on your confidence and self esteem.

With this you will feel proud, strong and empowered enough to get to your goal.

Circumstances of life may get in the way of your progress, however, you will gradually begin to fulfil each requirement and get through each level and eventually be in a place where you know you are ready to take on the world.

When you are at the point where you really feel satisfied having conquered your desires, you will be in a very good place to do good for others, which in return will give you even more satisfaction in life and give you that ultimate feeling of self-actualization and at the same time, *self-acceptance*.

*When you have self-acceptance, then you can accept and respect others for who they are too.*

You can be realistic, rational and logical about the world in a positive way.
You can be in a position of strength and be able to take responsibility for yourself and your decisions, because you know who you are and what path you are on.

Being on this road to discovery helps you spend healthy time alone, as well as in company and you have a balanced sense of humour, knowing that you are not bound by stringent rules in life and that *you are on a journey of enjoyment, enrichment and achievement.*

**….people may forget what you said and what you did, but they will never forget how you made them feel….**
*This is so true.*
If you are the type that can be quite thoughtless with your words at times, then you should start to take the consequences of your actions into serious consideration.

Think about how harsh or cruel language has felt yourself when the boot's been on the other foot.....
When you do or say something negative towards someone else, it will always have an impact on how they feel.

*And that feeling can stay with people for years....*

As such, it can have a knock-on effect and influence all manner of things related to it for a very long time afterwards (whether you realise it or not....).
If that particular person is very sensitive, or is not the type who has a thick-skin that enables them to just dismiss unpleasant words quite easily, or, if they don't have the right mindset not allow it to affect their life in such a way that they can just move on regardless, then there is a *strong* possibility that it will stay *within* them until it naturally dies away with time – that's if it ever does at all....

*Therefore, think **hard** about this.*

If you want to feel empowered in life, it does not mean riding roughshod over people, having a huge ego, talking *at* them in a belittling way, blinding them with science to look big, lying to worm your way out of something you don't want to take responsibility for, bullying someone into submission, or shirking your duties and passing it onto someone else because you don't want to do it yourself, or any other manner of negative behaviour or language that will have a bad impact on the other person or group.

*None of this is big or clever.*

Nor does it consider the other party in any way.
You are ultimately responsible for your life, your actions and your words and you should bear all this in mind as you go about your everyday activities.

If you want to live in a peaceful world, then you need to be happy in your own skin and as an individual in your own right, with thoughts and feelings that you own, without fear of someone making you feel bad or like the underdog.

*Essentially, by allowing them to take away your power.*

And this goes for everyone you deal with too.....
So therefore, think about what you say and do, and how you say and do it, and if it is likely to affect someone else around you.

*Bear in mind that they may carry whatever you do or say around with them for years.*

And anyway, wouldn't it be nice to be known as someone who has a *positive memorable* impact on people, who instils sheer admiration and respect in others, rather than as an ill-natured, bad-mannered, arrogant person that people don't really like and would rather avoid? Your life has surely got to feel a whole lot better for being kind and caring, happy and cheerful, considerate and thoughtful hasn't it? Your family and friends will certainly thank you for it!

*Keep your power within you, don't surrender it to negativity.*

**......be joyful and live life in freedom......**
Enjoy your own peace, harmony and satisfaction, otherwise, what really is the point?

If you cannot live fully with an absolute knowledge that you are achieving your own potential and thereby feeling satisfied in yourself, your work, your relationships and standing in this world, then you cannot feel fully happy and at peace with yourself, and you cannot be *totally free*......

*Live a rich and rewarding life, it's your destiny.*

**......take your time.......stop, look, listen.....**
Take time to breathe in the world around you.
Be *part of it* - appreciate nature and what you have....
As people continuously run around in the fast lane trying to live longer, they seem to be more sad and ill because of it - with stress, depression, dementia, anxiety and obesity all abundant problems.

If you are worried that this may be you, then you need to start bringing the joy, colour and imagination back into your life and improving it's *quality*, not it's quantity.

Take your foot off the accelerator and your finger off the 'want' button and start to appreciate what the world has to offer, rather than just taking it for granted or even ignoring it.
Just by slowing down and taking your time, speaking, eating and exercising are improved dramatically.

Calm yourself by simply breathing slowly, because a relaxed body will be more flexible and fast.
A calm, less tense mind can learn new things and solve problems much better and quicker than when you are uptight.

*It's obvious that one of the fundamental strategies for well-being is to create an improved life balance, where it's not all go, go, go!*

So what if you ignore your phone or your email for a while? Just because it's there, it doesn't necessarily mean it has to be on....
By learning to ignore some of these things in life, you can make time for more important activities and people, rather than feeling like you're being bullied into other people's urgency!
Take some time to have adventures and build closer relationships.

*Enjoy who you are and who your friends and family are.*

Think about what and where your life is going and how properly in tune you are with it, rather than just running along at a fast pace without even thinking about it.
Look at yourself and your relationship with life in an *honest* way - thinking carefully about what you *really* care about and desire, and who you actually want in your life. Give special attention to those close relationships that you hold very dearly.

*Live your life with passion and adventure and most importantly, enjoy it!*

Take your time in your world.
Be happy, relaxed, thoughtful and warm-hearted.

*This is an empowering state to be in.*

***"You have so little time on this earth that
the biggest risk is to spend it dissatisfied".***

**.....look at life as a work of art....**
*The world is a work of art constantly changing shapes and textures.*
Every time you look at something, it changes form and structure.
From different angles, it shows a different face.
In different lights, it shows a different shade.
You move and things move with you.
Colours change as the day goes on and, as light falls on things, so they produce different hues.
The world is full of angles, curves, dips, soft, hard, transparent, dense, smooth, jagged textures and configurations.
If you view things from above, below, at eye-level, underneath and on top, everything looks different, like a brand new object.

Each time it resonates in your brain as something brand new.
Each thing comes with a sound of it's own.
Another property that makes it unique and enhances your experience of it.
Everything comes with its own smell, further heightening your experience of it.

Some things seem ugly, some beautiful and some indifferent.
But each thing is a fantastic work of art to behold.
Whether man-made or natural, whether worn out or new, whether alive and breathing or 'dead' and inert, each thing has been placed on this earth over time and through progress.

*Each item has been borne out of someone or something's creativity.*

It has been landscaped and worn into its place, it's position in life, it's use and it's purpose.
It all 'fits' like a magic and magnificent giant puzzle.

*It's all there for a reason.*

It all exists as a huge and fantastic 4D painting.

A creation of shapes without spaces. All connected to each other whether close and touching or far away and distant.
There are no gaps. It is all filled with energy – whether dense or thin, dark or light. It is all interlinked and being used by each other to exist, to function, to activate and produce or just pass by.

Every movement or action changes it's structure.
Every ebb and flow allows regeneration.
Every life and death has an effect on everything around it.
Every new or old thing, thought, feeling and action has a cause and consequence.

*Whether seen or unseen, each thing produces it's own* **'work of art'**.

The universe is truly a very special place and you should value and enjoy every part of it.
Each stroke you make in each day, you are making a unique contribution.
You are making a choice, a difference, an effect.
Choose wisely, think carefully and walk tall with happiness, sincerity, humanity, care and love.
Pass on your joyous effect.
*Be a good messenger.*

Be your own proud work of art and watch your life unfold in a fulfilling and truly positive way.
Your ultimate life.

Live it.
Love it.
*Be empowered by your own special existence.*

**…..it's time to start living in the moment……**
*How much time do you spend actually 'living in the moment' - taking time just to be at one with yourself and nature?*
You can spend so much time being *busy* - on your phone, watching TV, running around chasing your tail, staring at a computer, etc., but you need to *stop and take stock*, give yourself a break and just allow yourself to wind down.

*Don't lose contact with who you are and your place on this earth.*

Turn off your mobile and whatever else is polluting your environment and turn on your senses. Tune in your body and focus on what is actually *around* you.
There is nothing wrong with having a plan in life, but it has to be flexible, one that moves and sways with your life, as opportunities come your way.

However, you need to be awake and aware enough to see them. You have to learn to be able to go with the flow if the promise of a better life appears via those opportunities, right in front of your face. Instead of racing along a narrow path, you should remember to enjoy your journey and not just sail *alongside* it.
The journey is just as important as arriving (if you ever do arrive, as life is a constant journey!).

Look around you, remove any internal judgements about anything and just reflect on all the positive things in your life, like your family, the ones you love, your home comforts, the beauty of nature and the sky above you.

Take time to just appreciate exactly what you have right **_now_**.

Get yourself a sense of humour!
Who wants to be around a constant grump or whinger? Be the joker, the warm person that makes people smile – it's much more fun and enjoyable! Wouldn't you rather be known for having a lovely positive attitude who looks for fun in every moment instead of always looking on the negative side of everything....?
Try being spontaneous for a change, and in doing so, give yourself and everyone else in your close community the break they deserve!

*Live in the moment, experience **now** and begin to feel real - like you are indeed part of this vast and very special universe......*

## ......changing into a more positive mindset......
*To feel ultimate fulfilment in your daily life, you need to make positive choices.*
To do this, take proper control to turn your life around.
If you were to feel happy and grateful for everything you have or do every day, it will be more obvious to you to feel positive about your

achievements, surroundings, relationships and possessions.

By keeping a diary of those things, you can look back on them and feel good about your life.

Smiling at strangers makes both you and them feel good (makes them wonder what you are secretly happy about too!), and tells your brain that you are in a positive frame of mind.

Saying *'thank you'* more gives you a fuller sense of gratitude towards the things in your life.

*You need this. It gives you a sense of purpose.*

There's not really much point in spending your life without that sense.....
As you go through your day, *feel present in the moment with what you are doing.*
Feel that sense of purpose - enjoy it, benefit from it, feel good about it.
You will then feel in control of that task, that feeling and that overall sense of *being*.

Spending time with people you like, who like you and make you feel good about yourself, will liven up your day and carry on that feeling for several hours, even days afterwards.
*You need to feel loved and appreciated, so get together with those that connect with that feeling.*

Use your wisdom and intelligence in a beneficial way.
The information you pass on could have a major influence on the people you network with every day. Sharing is the best way forward. It makes everyone feel good.

Try not to think that people are judging you harshly, if at all.

Chances are, it's all in your head anyway, so don't spend too much time on negative thoughts. If you don't judge yourself, you will feel calmer and more in control of your feelings and will pass that on to others along the way.

By listing all your strengths, you are showing yourself how good you are.

*There is nothing more empowering than the feeling of knowing you are good at things and have skills, experience and expertise, in whatever that may be.*

It's so enjoyable to be spending time doing activities you love, or that you get some kind of thrill or happiness from - no matter how small that may be.
And staying on the subject of enjoyment – savouring your food can bring you that enormous feel-good factor, as you open up the senses that are involved in taste, sight and smell.
Appreciate your food.

Always remember that every decision you make is a choice and that also *includes the decision to **avoid** making a choice!*

You have the power of those choices, so be wise with your thoughts, take your time over your decisions. Never feel pressured into making a decision quickly, until you have given it your *full* consideration. And, if you choose not to do something because it is not to your benefit or health, then *own* that choice! Don't be coerced into making the wrong decisions for you and your life path.

*Own your emotions.*

Know what they are and how they act. Learn to deal with them in your own way. But be empowered by how you control them. If you need time, take the time you need to use your emotions wisely, *in accordance with your natural self.*

However, don't be a slave or martyr to them. Learn to be in control and when it's time to move on, you can make positive choices for yourself and your future.

Try not to harbour negative emotions and use them as a reason or excuse for everything you do and how you act, in such a way that it controls *you* instead and stops you from getting ahead and progressing with your life.

Laughter is a wonderful emotion which instantly lifts your spirits and has a knock-on effect on others around you at the time. It fills your heart and soul with positivity.

So make yourself laugh and pass it on!

Surround yourself with people you love and who love you.
If you can't see them every day or week, then make up a collage to remind you of them that makes you smile every time you look at it.

Equally, keeping mementoes that remind you of how great *you* are, will make you feel good about yourself, and why not?

*You are fabulous and never forget that!*

All these little, but important steps, are little but important steps in building great empowerment within yourself.

*And you can carry this positive and empowering mindset with you for life!*

**Pass this on to your children!**

**Let them grow up with a positive mind,
opening up the world of opportunities.
Awaken their creative minds allowing them to
expand their thoughts and ideas
and become unique and independent in the world.
Expose their individuality and let them express their
innate talents and skills to let them develop
and give them the
ability to listen to their inner selves.**

**Help them to be incredible...**

**.....don't keep looking back.....**
*Whatever's behind you, is behind you.*
What's done, is done.
You cannot change it. But, you *can* change the path to your future. The past doesn't *have* to have any bearing on 'now', other than you

need to learn from it, take whatever was positive, glean any new usable skills and move on with renewed vigour and energy.

*After all, what does bitterness and dwelling on previous negative experiences actually achieve?*

Only more negativity.
It stifles you.
It takes over your inner self, affects your decisions and stops you from living a full life. It stops you pursuing your dreams and enjoying your life in the '*now*', and it puts up barriers to good thoughts and energy.

Every time you find yourself looking back in a negative way, blaming and coming up with '*if onlys*' and '*what ifs*', replace them with something more positive and useful like,

'*I'm going to be.....*', '*I'm happy as I am*', '*I'm strong, confident and forward thinking*', '*I am the person who is making the most out of life and moving forwards with passion and positivity*', or '*my life is full of enrichment, abundance and prosperity*'.

These are much better thoughts that tell your brain to be positive and forward-looking.

Be the person you want to be.

*Believe it through and through and you will surely have the best possible and empowered life you can have in this beautiful world.*

**.......energise your whole body and power up.....**
*Imagine having that wonderful compelling feeling of wanting to take on the world with gusto!*
Get your whole body, internally and externally, energised through strong positivity and excellent well-being – physically, mentally, emotionally and spiritually.
Being in such a powerful state can, in effect, make you feel at peace with yourself and in control of your life, because you will feel *total and complete*.

Through this, you will begin to see the world as a beautiful place.

You will discover things you didn't notice before. Nature will spring up in front of you and you will see colour and life in the world around you. Things will seem brighter and more engaging, you will hear things better - the birds, music, the waves.
This will energise you even further...

*Because being at one with nature is part of the big 'energy system'.*

The whole world, the universe, is one giant network of energy passing between objects, buzzing around us and through us. So it's best to make use of that energy as positively as possible.

*Anything other than that is destructive. A negative force.*

And if you allow that negative force to take you over, you will begin a spiral of downward events that will only cause calamities, depression and bad thoughts.

*Why use up your energy in a bad way?*

Quickly replace it with a good thoughts to stop the rot setting in.
Think of something wonderful instead.
Whether it's something fantastic that you have personally experienced or something you wish to experience, or be near, such as a beautiful waterfall or landscape, or a wonderful time you spent with your partner or pet, or even something like skydiving, for example.

Anchor those happy and blissful thoughts and feelings about that experience into your mind and use it every time you feel like you're falling back.

Try to keep your energy upbeat.

*Remember - your choice, your life.*

If you want a bad life, then think negative thoughts....

But obviously you want a good, healthy successful life, so clear out those bad thoughts and replace it with something substantially better.

Always think, 'I **AM**', never 'I *want*' or 'I *wish*' or '*If only*', because these words are saying you '*lack*' something.

They tell your brain and body that something is missing, is wanted – thereby saying you haven't got it.
This is a negative thought.

Telling yourself 'I **AM**' is communicating to your brain that this is who you *already* are and it accepts it as gospel.

"*I am successful*", "*I am healthy and slim*", "*I am a good, beautiful person*' are all good examples of telling your brain that you are something *already*.

You can apply this to any aspect of your life, whether you want to build a business, lose weight or be a certain type of person.

Telling yourself that you **are** something is passing on a positive statement to your brain, which in turn produces positive energy.

If you want your dreams to come true, you can't spend all day telling yourself, "*I can't do this*", "*I'm no good at that*", "*I'm useless*", "*I've got no chance of achieving that*" - these are all negative statements communicating that *lack* of something.

Replace these words with "*I am a slim, fit, healthy, beautiful person*" for example, and you will be giving your very clever brain and body the positive instructions to produce the lively energy that it needs to achieve the outcome you want.

So, think very carefully about the messages you send to your brain if you want something or are feeling down, because it is *always* listening and will *always* respond accordingly....

Always produce positive energy within all aspects of your life – mentally, physically, emotionally and spiritually.
Choose to live an upbeat life.

*Empower your brain to empower you...!*

## ....clear away the clutter from your life to empower your future......

*Apart from clearing any emotional and mental clutter from your heart and head that has been holding you prisoner for years, if you want to move forward in a far more constructive and motivated way, you also need to clear the clutter from your surroundings and environment.*

Getting rid of rubbish and excessive things around you, will help enormously in getting your life into some semblance of order.
It will also give you the space that you need to get on with the things that you have been holding back on, due to total lack of organisation.
If you cannot face this clear-up yourself, then get someone to help you.

There are plenty of professional people out there who would relish getting you organised!
If you're doing it yourself, step by step, go through your home and work area and start getting rid of things that have been hanging around for years and have never been used. Or find a place for things to 'live', so you know exactly where they are when you need them, and can put them back there when you've finished.

Take back space on the floor and surfaces that were once yours and you will be amazed how much better your life will feel. You will be able to breathe again and this will put your mindset into a positive frame, ready to take on the world.

And, with your emotional 'clutter', don't just paper over the cracks, otherwise you will never be able to move ahead with confidence and strength, because you will always have those old issues rearing their ugly head again and getting in the way of your good progress.

It will obviously take time to clear your clutter and leave it all behind you, because these are emotional connections you are dealing with.

*But just doing shallow things to help remove old issues will **not** work for long.*

Take your time, eliminate and replace negativity with positivity, clear your head, heart and environment, balance yourself, be healthy, become renewed, invigorated and energised.

Then you will move forward towards your ultimate goals and lifestyle into a position where you can *fully embrace your future with new-found confidence and empowerment.*

**......you will never be poor when you have sincere gratitude.....**
*Imagine if you spent life being grateful for what you have and the opportunities that you have been given, instead of always wanting more and never being satisfied.....?*
How much more settled and balanced would you feel?
People do tend to spend too much of their energy on living in the future or the past and not actually paying attention to themselves *right now* and just being *thankful.*

A life with an **'*attitude of gratitude'*** is surely a great way of living...

There's a strong possibility that you have far more now than you have had in the past, so it's only proper that you should be grateful for the progression that you have made over time. And there's nothing to say that you could be less well off in the future.
But you can be assured that *right at this moment*, you have probably got a lot to be grateful for and you should really acknowledge that.

Jealousy, envy and pride will get in the way of allowing you to actually feel in *this* moment, so don't judge yourself by everyone else.

*If you can be happy with what you have, who you are and what you want to become, then that is your right and honour.*

Do you *really* think you will win the lottery or inherit a fortune from some long lost uncle you don't even know about?
Have you *really* put in the effort to deserve and expect that fantastic promotion at work?
If not, then you are living in a land of *false expectations,* and while you are *living in the future*, you are not concentrating properly on the present.

And if you are not concentrating properly on the present, you are not *living in full awareness of your own life.*

As you live in the present, so you will naturally be making progressions towards your future anyway, because you will be focussing properly on what you are doing and really *making the most out of every moment.*

In doing so, you will be automatically taking steps forward.

And, by living in the moment, as you read, as you work, as you walk, you will be aware of every action you make and enjoy the steps you are taking along your journey. You will be engrossed in your actions and making sure you are doing exactly what you *want* to be doing with your life, making the right choices and having the right thoughts.

And you can therefore be grateful for all the little things in life that give you pleasure, being aware of the beauty around you and all the connections you have and make along the way.
*And you will also be conscious of those around you who impact your life, who make sense to you and who fit into your puzzle.*

You will notice the 'haves' and 'have-nots' and you will be in touch with your humanitarian and philanthropic side, because you will want to give more. And the more you give, the more you receive, and this reciprocation really is the *essence of gratitude*, and will instil a type of love that will endure.

By being grateful for all the little and big things you have around you, you will begin to enjoy increased happiness and loving relationships, which in turn, will automatically have a very beneficial impact on your health and general well-being.
Don't wait around for all the big things to happen, relish the smaller things that make your day more joyful and comfortable.

Take stock and write down all the little things as they happen, so you can reflect on them and you will begin a journey of sincere happiness. It will be an empowering process and will generate a wonderful state of mind knowing that what you *do* have, you can be sincerely grateful for, because it doesn't leave you wanting.....

Start to *want what you have* and don't dwell so much on the 'better' things, that may or may not lie around the corner.

*If you appreciate what you have, you will never be poor!*

**....so then, you need to appreciate what you have and not what you haven't got....**
*Because it seems that in this day and age, everyone is reaching for what they haven't got, feeling that unless they have 'everything', then they have <u>nothing</u>.*
It's that feeling that any success will only be measured by how much they have in the bank, what they look like and who they are. And if they haven't got all of these attributes, then they are nothing and nobody.

It seems that wanting fame and fortune comes before actually appreciating exactly what's right in front of you.
It isn't until you move away from yourself, either by staying somewhere different, spending time in strangers' company or having something removed from you, that you realise just what you *have* got and then count yourself lucky for it.

Instead of acknowledging what you *do* have, you harbour the feeling that you just aren't good enough, you've been *so* unlucky and cheated in life. This state of mind ends up spiralling into feelings of low self-worth, low self-respect, low self-esteem and a lack of confidence.
Far from being part of a society built up by the media, you are in fact part of the *real* world, a *real* person, with *real* issues and outcomes.

*But you are still special!*

It doesn't mean that you have to have several figures in your bank account to feel contented, or the latest gadget to make you feel good, or have the best figure in the world otherwise you're a failure.
It takes some time to realise that you can genuinely be *you* without all the shallow 'add-ons' and *you can actually function*, you <u>are</u> okay and you're a vital part of this world.

When you know this, you can just appreciate the things that you do actually have.

At the end of the day, as long as you have shelter, food and a comfortable way of living, everything else *can* be irrelevant. Holding onto the love in your heart, being kind, being loved, connecting with others and the world, can truly *make you content just as you are.*

Appreciating that you have far more than others who have nothing at all, but still survive, who are quite happy with far less, who just appreciate what nature has given them and enjoy their lives anyway, can be quite humbling.
A far cry from what may be your normal existence of running around at 100mph just to feather someone else's nest.

And this may be the total *opposite* of what you genuinely are as a person.

But you have just got *used* to that way of living, having drifted into, or been conditioned by others to get to the position you are in today......
You may well be more suited to quite happily living a much simpler life, or even using your 100mph days to help others and grow yourself a beautiful heart instead. Your significance in the world may be gained through living in a far more philanthropic way, rather than battling for the buck day in day out!

Having a sense of where your life is, in comparison to those who don't have a bed to sleep in or food on the table, or maybe have a terminal illness, can put your world into serious perspective.

*So it may be time to cultivate yourself towards being more grateful, as it is probable that you are materially much better off than most.*

In cultivating that gratitude, you can begin to fully acknowledge that, whether you're paying a high price at an expensive restaurant or sitting down to eat something cheaply cooked at home, you will stop eating when you're full, appreciating that you have enough to be grateful for.
A full belly is full whether it's costing you £500 or £2 to eat.....

What virtues do you value about yourself?

Learn to love who you are and what you are capable of, and understand and appreciate that when you are young you have youth on your side, because when you get older, all those things you worried about then, like fame and fortune and unrealistic expectations, will seem so shallow and pointless.

Remember instead, the things that **do** last, like honour, truth, honesty, good character, your family and the beauty of the natural world around you. These are all the things that make you feel strong and let you know that you have a wonderful place on this earth and within your surroundings and networks.

*If you want to feel truly empowered, just be nice!*

Feeling 'ordinary' may make you 'moody' and that can have an impact on those around you. But if you smile and make eye contact with people instead, let people talk about themselves (everyone likes doing that from time to time!), and generally make others feel good about themselves, this will, in turn, make you feel good about yourself too.

*You could well be the **one** person with a kind word who actually lifts somebody's spirit that day!*

It's important to be nice and project loving kindness.
It'll take a bit of time to get used to doing this, especially if you don't feel particularly good, but with practise, it will have a very empowering effect on you. And at the same time, make others feel worthwhile and happy too!

Keep family and friends an important aspect of your life. Relationships are important, connections are valuable and help to keep you grounded. Love them and they will love you back.

Everyone needs love in their life.

Don't hog the limelight or boast about yourself. People won't thank you for it, or be particularly impressed and will eventually try to knock you off your high pedestal and bring you back down to size. So be humble and don't be self-important.

If you exercise humility for things that you have done, you will naturally get the appreciation and appropriate praise without all the bragging anyway! And that is a far better way to feel satisfied about your accomplishments.

Be of service to others.
There's nothing quite like the feeling of humble satisfaction than helping others less fortunate than yourself. Volunteering, giving and gifting - whatever you can do, all builds a healthy and loving heart.

*Someone being grateful to you for the help you have given them is a satisfaction that stays in your heart forever.*

Due to their gratitude, it will help you understand and realise that you and the way you live, are not only good enough, but absolutely brilliant!
If you want to impress people and feel worthy and valued, then you must feel impressed by yourself too.
Doing something wonderful for someone else gives you that wonderful sense!

Feeling part of the bigger universe gives you something to believe in.
Use whatever faith you have to help you work through your life so you feel like an important and vital part of this world. Pray, meditate or confide in someone - it all helps and adds to you feeling whole and worthy, helping you to appreciate what you *do* have to be grateful for.
*Try not to use someone else's life or accomplishments as a benchmark to measure your own life by.*

All people are flawed and all people are perfect in their *own* way.
There will be those at the top, in the middle and at the bottom.
There are people who have and have not, who are experts at one thing and not another.
Everyone is different and individual.

*So it's no good comparing your own worth and value against someone else's.*

There will always be people faster and slower than you.

There will always be people slimmer and bigger than you.
You are you and you fit into the world just as they do and just as importantly.
The person who is last will think you are faster.
The person who is less clever and achieving will think you are more clever and achieving!

You have to rise up and live your life as a valuable member of the world – even if you are not rich and famous. Value the fact that you are not wanting and in need of the essential tools to live with, and that you are healthy and have family and friends around you.

If you want more, then the world is your oyster if you empower yourself inside to go for it - *always remembering that you have what you need right at your fingertips....*

Take the time to be at one with yourself, listening to your own thoughts, exploring your inner self. With the right mindset, you can make the positive changes in your life necessary to be happy.
If you feel that your life isn't exciting, then you have every opportunity in the world to make it more so.
Everything is right there for you, just use your time to engage yourself in new challenges, be productive and get that sense of satisfaction that new skills give you and that help to make your life better.

If you want it enough, you will.....

*Otherwise, be happy, content and at peace with yourself.....*

**We all have a desire to be important,
to be recognised and to be of service to people.
Why not choose to appreciate others?
Offer real praise, not shallow flattery that always feels false.
Congratulate someone on their work, their efforts or
what makes them unique.
People take a real interest in those
who show them interest first.
Pass it on......**

**......create yourself happy.......**
*Everyone can be happy.*
You would think that people with power, money and everything they want would be happy, but this is not always the case.
It isn't necessarily about material things, it's more about the contentment and peace inside. People with nothing can be happy. It's to do with perspective and subjectivity.

*There are many things that you can do to induce happiness.*

Happiness doesn't necessarily mean you have to spend everyday smiling and laughing your head off. You can feel a deep inner sensation of happiness.
This can be achieved by doing some very simple things every day to bring about a feeling of being happy. And if it brings about a change in you that means you can progress with your life, by empowering you to drive and achieve your goals, then it's really worth taking a look at.

In fact, once you start routinely doing certain exercises to induce happier feelings, they will become habit-forming and eventually just a natural part of your daily life, massively impacting your whole world!
You may think having money will make you happy, but actually spending money will only give you a short-term fix and will not lead to great, *inner* happiness.

*You can program your mind to be happier.*

You may have already programmed your mind to be sad and depressed and therefore, if you can programme your brain to be like that, then you can certainly *reprogramme it to be the opposite!*
*It's just a case of reinforcement and changing the messages you send to your brain.*

Your body produces chemicals that make you happy, like Serotonin, and if they fall to a low level, it can make your mood low.
However, you *do* have the capacity to make more happy chemicals and lift your mood - because your mind and body are obviously linked!

Physical action automatically causes an affect in your brain, like when you relax, your thoughts relax too. Yoga and meditation are a perfect illustration of this.

Even having good strong posture will make you feel much more confident and therefore happier. Slouching can also make your mood low, whilst standing tall and smiling to yourself can make you feel much better. Apart from anything else, you feel far more comfortable and can breathe better – which in turn gets more oxygen circulating around your body, which is wonderfully healthy!

If you do suffer with sadness, depression and unhappiness, there's a probability that it comes from past experiences that have stayed with you for years. If this is true, then it's time to replace those bad feelings with happy ones instead, so your brain and body become more used to associations of happiness in their place.

*The more you remember to do this, the more you will get into the habit of it and thereby feel better and more uplifted.*

If you constantly move around staring at the ground, try lifting your head up and looking out and forward. This difference will have a strong influence on your thinking and instil a sense of freedom and space, instead of feeling *closed down*. This is a simple way to induce a change in brain activity that causes feelings of peace and well-being.

*So look at the sky and tops of buildings, so it triggers the brain to reinforce good feelings!*

Mimicking someone else's happiness can also induce good feelings. Or thinking about and imagining happy times can help to create thoughts of happiness and well-being.
When you feel happy, it can open up a world of opportunities, because your frame of mind becomes receptive and welcoming.

If you've ever been in a situation in the past that has caused negative thoughts that you are now dragging around with you, try thinking it through again to see if there was anything about that situation that you learnt from and can take positivity out of?

*There's always something to glean from experiences that you can take with you on your next adventure, or skills that you gained to add new strings to your bow.*

Perhaps then, you can be more grateful for that experience (*everything happens for a reason*), and therefore not look so badly on it from now on!
Learning becomes a habit in your unconscious mind – the more you do something, the more it will sit inside your brain and will eventually become habit.

*When you think about it, habits form your life, they make you who you are.*

The more you repeat something, so it paves a pathway in your brain, which becomes stronger each time. Unhappy people have habits that cause that state of mind, in the same way as happy people sustain that with their habits.

*So, you can get a different outcome through gaining new habits.*

As they become stronger and more powerful, they can completely alter your level of happiness, replacing your old habits with new ones to make you feel good.
Even pretending to smile or laugh can alter your mood to a positive one, because it produces that serotonin and endorphins that make you feel good.

Laughing also boosts the immune system, clears out toxins, gives you better digestion and fewer bouts of colds and flu.

*What's not to like about laughing....?!*

And when you smile, others smile too - passing on the happy signal. Try smiling 40 times a day and laughing 20 times a day and see the difference!
If you add 20 minutes of exercise into your day as well, you can change from being depressed to extremely optimistic.

*Physical exercise makes you happier than if you didn't do it....*

It stimulates adrenaline and more endorphins, increasing alertness and energy, giving a sense of satisfaction and relaxation, clearing out stress chemicals and rebalancing your neurology and body chemistry.

All this, in turn, physically changes your state of mind and is an effective treatment for depression and better quality of sleep.

Try some exercise, even just walking, to help get those happy feelings into your soul! Just try moving a bit more – every little helps! A 15 minute walk or 2000 steps can be the difference between a slim and an overweight person! Exercise outdoors in the fresh air and this will lift your mood even more – giving you a boost and increasing your self-esteem.

*Putting little happiness reminders around the house can help instil positive feelings and make your mood lighter.*
Think about some good times in your life or things you want in the future, put them on little notes and place them in spaces where you know you can see them as you move about your business.
Doing this can change the neurology of your brain as well.

Are you the type of depressed person who continually says negative things to themselves such as, "*I can't cope on my own*", "*When will it all go wrong?*", "*I never have any luck*"....?

This does *nothing* to help you feel any better!
However, you *can* get past this quite simply by adding a positive saying onto the end of the negative one, such as, "*I've just got another day to get through and then I'm going to sit in the sun and chill out. Aaaah, bliss!*". Or something similar......

The more you practise this, the negative thought will be replaced by that positive one.
Negative thinking shuts the door on positive possibilities, ruling them out of your imagination.

*If you continually think of having bad luck, you won't have your mind open to the thousands of possibilities that could be happening in your life....!*

If you are having a bad day, try not to exaggerate things that happen to you into huge situations, like, *"No-one understands me..."*, but rather say something like *"so-and-so didn't understand what I said"* – then think about how you can get that person to understand what you *did* say, thereby removing the negative and turning it into a positive *solution*.

*Don't burn yourself out by driving and striving.*

This can affect your happiness levels and bring you down quite hard in your quest to achieve great things. If you are running around at 100mph, then try making a simple to-do list, prioritising what is '*essential* to get done today', what is '*important* but can wait', and then '*everything else*'.
Get your essentials done and out of the way and that overwhelming feeling of drowning will dissipate.

If you take a good look around, you may have noticed that happy people usually have common characteristics. They don't carry the burden of the past around with them, because they have let go of any former mistakes and bad experiences, knowing that there really isn't anything that can be done about the past.

They therefore focus their energy on the present instead with an eye on their future.
It's also about how they respond to certain situations and circumstances.

If you want to be happy, be like them and take responsibility for yourself, don't keep blaming others for your misgivings, because you have to realise that you have the freedom to choose your own decisions and events in your life.

Know that you can choose to get upset if someone annoys you. Or not.....

Anyone can, because we are all blessed with the *freedom of choice*. It does take courage though, because people and circumstances have an impact on your life everyday, so you have to be strong enough to make your freedom *your own responsibility*.

You have to empower yourself to make your own choices and being content with those choices will ultimately make you happy, with all the knock-on positive effects that come with it.

Don't submit and allow those little things to get on top of you and constantly bug you, chipping away at your happiness in the process. Take control of them and don't allow them to take over your world and ruin your life.

To be truly happy, you also need to be strong in your relationships. Being surrounded by the people you love and who love you back, gives you the ultimate feeling of happiness.
Make this one of your priorities in your quest for joy in life.

You've probably heard the saying '*You reap what you sow*'.. in this case it means that when you make others happy, you in turn, make *yourself* happy.
It's one of life's vicious circles – but a nice one!
Practising compassion and helping other people through being selfless, is a certain road to happiness.

Add new strings to your bow by enjoying new passions, exploring the worlds' gifts and finding out about new and interesting things. There is so much that surrounds you, so get involved and start getting excited.

*Create **new** ways of being happy.*

Learning and developing is all part of your constant growth, which in turn, only adds to that feeling of happiness. Adding new skills to your abilities will naturally help you achieve new levels too.

*Start building up your character. Make yourself known as a true and trustworthy person.*

Be loved for who you are.
Deliver what you say you will and keep your promises. You will gain more respect, which in turn will make you feel really happy about yourself.
What are you at your *core*?
Do some work on this and start becoming that person. You can only

be you, no-one else, but you have to *be* yourself. It's the *only* way you can be happy.

*You certainly can't by trying and striving to be someone you're not!*

Everyone needs a purpose in life.
Without it you feel lost and unfulfilled, whiling away the days drifting from one thing to another, or nothing at all, without even realising what life is all about. Take stock of what that purpose is for you and take it by the horns.

*Use your courage to follow your purpose and be proud of it.*

Create yourself a positive mantra unique to you that you can take full advantage of and keep repeating it to yourself in as many ways as possible, as a constant reminder of what your mission is!

Doing your best to improve yourself by having an ambition is absolutely fine, but try not to allow yourself to get *so* obsessed with it that it turns from making you feel excited and motivated, into just hitting your happiness where it hurts!

Finding what your innate talents are and then using them to the fullest is the best way of being satisfied and enjoying your work. No-one is happier than when they are spending time doing something they love and are good at - achieving great things because they know they will be doing their best in the process.

You must have things to be grateful for, no matter how small, but maybe you take them for granted and are always wanting more, never being satisfied.

How lost would you be if those things were taken away from you?

Take note and be thankful for them. One day, you may be without them! It's time to appreciate your comforts and loves in life. Being grateful and not constantly looking for the greener grass will instil a feeling of being happy with what you have.

At the end of the day, life isn't about how much money you have in the bank, it's about what you are getting out of life.

You don't need to have a high powered job stressing you to the maximum to be happy. You can be content with less.

*Stop, think and give it a try.*

As long as you are comfortable and the bailiffs aren't beating down the door, why do you need to strive, using all your time and energy to get a bigger house, a bigger bank balance, a bigger car, when that time and energy could be spent on much nice things closer to your heart that make you feel good and happy?

Get yourself into a positive frame of mind, so that when you are tasked with things you'd rather not confront, you can take something from the experience.

So don't allow negative thoughts to creep in and take over your head. No matter how bad they seem at the time, things generally can be dealt with. Be in control of your thoughts, don't allow them to control you. This is what happy people do.

*Instead of working hard, work creatively!*

As you go with the flow, you won't even notice the time so much and your production rate will excel.
As you achieve, so you will feel happy inside and proud of what you have accomplished.
Feel that sense of empowerment surging through your veins.
And always remember that it's YOU who decides whether or not you are happy in life.

CHOOSE to be happy......

***Change your morning alarm to something soothing....***
***Who likes getting up in the morning to a horrible noise demanding you to get up <u>now</u>?!***
***Change the tone to something you really like instead, so you wake up feeling like the day is greeting you in a much more pleasurable way, with a smile instead of grunt!***
***What a better way to look forward to your day.....***

**.....move forward to a new year and new you......**
*Do you feel like you need something to keep you motivated at the beginning of the year, or at ANY time in your life for that matter (you are not restricted to the new year to make changes for the better!)?*
Then make a little, but important pact with yourself to write down whatever your ambition or resolution is - and then keep looking at it, reflecting on it and updating it every month to keep that, and any new goals in the forefront of your mind at all times.
So think really hard about what you would like to achieve this year (or from now on....), and what this year is going to **really *mean*** to you, and then focus on it every day to help keep you motivated.

Do you want a year of working towards your wealth and ultimate freedom?
Do you want to achieve something specific this year that you have been meaning to do and had in mind for a long time but keep putting it off?

*Then make this a year of being selfish with your goals and ambitions* – remembering the more you achieve for yourself, the happier you will be, and in turn, the happier you will be around your friends and family - which can only benefit you all.

If there are some sacrifices you need to make in order to get these things done, then think carefully about what they may have to be, and how you can make them without upsetting too many people around you.

Bear in mind that these sacrifices will be made to the advantage of those around you too....

Your ambitions and resolutions don't necessarily need to be about work.
They could just as easily be about adventure and fun stuff, family, or health and fitness.

Whatever they are – make up your pact to yourself and put it in the front of your diary for easy reference on a regular basis and to keep you upbeat and enthusiastic.

Make sure you put it down in a *positive way and mean what you say*.
Upbeat, positive affirmations are the way forward – no *'ifs', 'ands'* or *'buts'* in the way.

Remember – this is your own selfish goal for you to achieve, so make your *own* mind up.

*Take strength and heart from the commitment you make for yourself, that you are fulfilling one of your dreams and that the decisions you make are going to transform not only your life, but those close to you, forever.....*

**…..too much work....not enough life.....**
Getting the right balance where everyone is happy can be a bit of a struggle, but with the right strategy, (and the right attitude), you can work things out so you can still get the most out of your life and achieve the things you want.
Being realistic and honest when you go about setting your goals is *imperative* – without being too optimistic or pessimistic about your options.

Remember you are the one in control of your life, so *set goals that are yours and no-one else's*.

If you are hoping to rely on others to help you achieve your goals, remember that people can change their minds and behaviour, so don't *totally depend* on them to realise your plans.

If you are a risk taker, then fine, but if not, *really consider and research* if your plans are definitely within reach or can actually be achieved within your immediate constraints.

This exercise could also reveal that the outcomes may not turn out quite as badly as you first thought.....
Then you can let go of any fear you may have had and really feel free to take that risk and go for it!

If you can, get a good, like-minded support group around you. Make sure these are positive people that can help or motivate you when you need it.

This could include any part of your family or friends, as well as experts in the field you will be working in that could help get things off the ground and keep them running.
Even if you just use them for advice or a sounding board to talk at when you need to air some views, or if you have a new idea you want to get feedback on.

*Whatever you end up doing, planning is all important.*

Without a laid-out plan, you have no focus or goals to aim for and could end up flailing about in the dark, procrastinating for all you're worth and just shuffling papers around instead of getting on with what needs to be done – that's if you actually *know* what needs to be done – without the plan!

You need a plan to put your deadlines into.
Working backwards from your target date, place in the required actions you need to take to get to your goal. Within that plan, you can also assign all the tasks and money you will require on a working basis to achieve it.
It's best to have an overall outline plan for 5 years, then one for a year with more detail and then a 6-month plan containing all your actions.
Keeping a daily plan of tasks and actions will help keep you focused too.
Remember to build in any contingency required in case of hold-ups or if things go wrong, and also make it flexible to allow for life changes and things that may get in the way that will need your time as well.
Take into account that you are a human being with relationships, so build in personal time and people as well, *without* taking away the focus of your goal.

Once you get into action and start executing your plan, it may be tweaked, added to, or deleted as appropriate. Whatever isn't working for you will become apparent and therefore, will need to be either eliminated completely or reworked in a way that produces better results for you.

Some things will be successful and some things will 'fail' (or rather, will challenge you or teach you something precious....).

It's all part of life and trying to achieve something, so don't lose heart and never feel guilty about doing what you want in life.

*You could be using that precious energy on positive progress instead!*

Keep all your guilts and frustrations within the boundaries of where they belong, so don't bring your family matters to work and vice versa. Otherwise you'll never get on with anything of any merit, if you're wasting your time worrying about what's going on at home, whilst trying to concentrate on your next business meeting.
Neither do your family want you bringing the stresses of your work day to the dinner table and taking it out on their digestion!

However, always remember to give yourself a well deserved pat on the back when you do something good or achieve something you've been working hard at!
You need your successes to keep you warm – no matter how small……
Many small things build up to a big pile of achievements!

And never take your eye off the fact that your life is about *you,* so your work-life balance is essential and individual to you and *your* personal needs.

*Don't be all work and no play!*

Even if people depend on you, a happy, healthy and well-balanced *you* will be a far more lovable, effective and giving you, who can be depended upon.

*It's **not** a selfish act to look after yourself, so don't feel guilty about it.*
*If your family and friends see a confident, glowing person in front of them, this will keep them inspired to be like you too, so everyone's a winner!*

**…..whatever you cause to do will have an effect……**
*Everything you do will have an effect – no matter how small or how insignificant.*
You cause something to happen by the sheer action of *doing*.

Makes sense doesn't it.....

So, bearing this in mind, should you wish to '*receive*' something, then you will need to do something to make that thing happen. That's obvious......

In an ancient wisdom that reveals how the universe and life work, '*Kabballa*', which means '*to receive*', says that all joy, love and happiness comes from the light of the creator.
To get more joy, love and happiness, you need to become like that light and then you will receive more fulfilment.
The **ego** - '*having a sense of self in which you are only interested in your own gain*', separates us from this light.
Kabballa says our sole desire to share, enables the transformation, so you need to become more akin to it.

*Change yourself from an ego, into having a nature of desire to share.*

For the process of transformation you need to constantly work and delve into Kabballa-thinking for never-ending fulfilment.

*This is not a quick fix.*

It is something that needs to be worked on constantly.
You need to understand the world and yourself and then you can become the person you truly want to become. You need to have the understanding and wisdom to grow and change to achieve the life for which you were created.
Words are easy, relatively speaking.
But words that produce no result are lost.
Words need to have an effect on behaviour.

Ultimately, it's actions that count.
Actions are a way of proving words.
Actions are a way of testing the reality that words uphold.
Practise is an adventure.
A refuge.
A pleasure.
A statement of intention.

It is a means of making clear to yourself, not just by words, but by deeds, all your aspirations.

*It is also a way of taking practical steps towards change.
If you feel like the Kabballa way of thinking will assist you on your road to life empowerment, then it may be helpful for you to look further into this, to get more clarity and a deeper understanding.*

**…...talk yourself *into* things……not out of them……**
How many times do you hear yourself saying, *"I just can't be bothered"*, or *"What's the point?"* or *"It'll never work out anyway"*, or *" I never have any luck, so I might as well not even try"!…..??*
Reading this back, how do you think it sounds?
How does it make you feel?
Does it seem like a majorly negative way of looking at life?
Well, it is, and what exactly is the point of being like this, when it comes down to it?

It's just far too easy to just give in to the day, to your apathy, to your laziness, to your lack of enthusiasm, to your procrastination, because you don't have to do anything about anything, just let it all slide, sit back and let life pass you by without any effort.
Is this the kind of life that you had pictured for yourself?
Because if it isn't, then you've got to start talking yourself INTO things and not out of them!

No-one's going to wave a magic wand over you.
Everyone has to make their own luck.

Think about all the exciting, life-changing things you could be part of and all the challenges and events that could be making your life exciting and happy.
All those things that could be making you laugh, feel vibrant and causing you to interact with people and the world around you…..

Life isn't really for watching yourself slowly die, waiting till it's all over, so you can close your eyes and say goodbye to the world, not having done anything to show for all the years you have been blessed to be on this beautiful earth.

Life is supposed to be full of adventures, learning new stuff, getting involved, making friends, having wonderful relationships, exploring all the exciting and interesting things the earth has to offer, making the most out of why you are here, using your time to fulfil your capacity as a person and maximising all the skills that you have been blessed with.

So, if you are spending your precious time in a heap on the sofa waiting for things to happen, without making any effort at all and just telling yourself that you really can't be bothered, then you need to rethink your life strategy and get into a whole new mindset.

A mindset that will enable you to take on life in a more positive and proactive way, get your dreams and ambitions up and running, so that you can be happy at the end of it all, because you have had a satisfying and fulfilling time that you can be proud of and that others can be proud of too.

A full life so others can celebrate you as the vibrant, pleasant and adventurous person that you really are, who made the most out of every second you were given and having left a lasting effect on those around you, with a smile and a great feeling in their hearts whenever they think of you.

*Don't waste it, it's yours to live.*

*Be grateful. Be thankful. Be happy!*

> **"The key to realising a dream is
> to focus not on success, but 'significance' –
> and then even the small steps and little victories
> along your path will take on greater meaning."**
>
> Oprah Winfrey

**.....search for the opportunity in every crisis.....**
*Generally there will always be an opportunity to be found in every crisis.*
That is, if you possess the open mind to *see* it and have the strength to endure whatever the crisis throws at you, and you don't

lose heart or become emotional, start panicking and slide downwards instead.

*As one door closes, another one always opens....*

You just have to wait for it to reveal itself.
However, you will be tested during the chaos. But whatever happens during any crisis, it will inevitably make you change and progress in life.
The trick is not to admit defeat and be a victim within those circumstances.
It is a time to be courageous and face the fear, 'go with the flow', stop panicking and allow solutions to come to you.

*Each time something happens, so it will open up all kinds of possibilities to you.*

If you allow yourself to go with the flow, you will know when the time is right to take action, but also when the time is right to just sit and do nothing.
Life has a habit of chopping and changing and whatever is right for you, will happen.

*You never know, you may find that crisis, or forced change was all a blessing in disguise anyway....*

If you've tried everything you can think of to remedy the crisis and it's still not worked out for you, then just stop what you are doing and sit back....

*It's at this time that you will probably find that having a clear head will show you the way to go.*

Try not to get too anxious or stressed, just gather up your inner strength and you can focus on what needs to be done with new found energy and empowerment, and you will then be able to get your desired result or embrace a new life strategy more easily.

*Don't let a crisis get in the way of your progress.*

See it as a challenge that you can overcome instead.

Seize every opportunity from it to help you move forwards and not backwards, and you will surely come out with a successful outcome.

*Everything is sent to try us.....for a reason......*

### ......optimism breeds success.......
*When it comes to successful people, most of them have a vein of optimism running through them.* They can see all the *positivity* in problems, challenges, failures and knock-backs.
They can face them head on and if they don't work out, they can learn from the situation and use that lesson to progress forward.

Optimism can be learnt – it's a mindset, a choice you can make to be that way, instead of being negative about things and dragging yourself down in the process.

*It's all about your approach to life.*

Do you want yours to be an adventure or a story of blame, depression, doom and gloom....?
Because it doesn't have to be that way.
If you're spending your life moaning about nothing ever going your way, you need to take a leaf out of a successful person's book and start looking at what *you need to know*, what could be different, what you can do or should have done when dealing with knock-backs, and how you can get a successful outcome in the future instead.

*Don't be a victim of circumstance - be a creator of your life.*

Be responsible for what happens in it!
If you are in a situation that doesn't feel right to you, or it's something that makes you unhappy, stressed or bored, etc., then this is telling you that things aren't right and need to change.
What is the lesson that you can learn from this situation?
Keep asking yourself until you exhaust the reasons and have got deep into the core of the matter.

If you cannot do this yourself, then perhaps the help of a life coach could be helpful to you, but either way, this exercise can help you make a difference to your life.

However, you have to take whatever it is that you learn and *apply* it, because if you don't, you will continue to make the same mistakes over and over again.

*Nothing changes until you do.*

Be an optimist and look forwards, not backwards.
Be positive, not negative.
Don't spend precious time thinking about what you don't want, but rather focus on what you *do* want and how you can achieve it.

Ask yourself - "*how can I acquire something I yearn for?*", "*how can I get a promotion?*", "*how can I move to an area I really want to live in?*", "*what skills do I need to get that job or build that business?*", "*how can I maximise my chances of working in that environment?*", "*how can I get the money to buy that car?*"........etc.

*Get your mindset into the action mode and be willing to follow it through.*

If you want something – you have to *believe you can get it* and you have to *accept you need to take action*, and be *willing* to do so, in order to achieve it.

Find the good in things, not the bad all the time....

If things don't work out according to plan, instead of blaming the world and getting angry, understand that you will learn from it and that lesson will be useful to you further down the line.

*Everything happens for a reason and even if you don't see it at the time, it will become clear later on.*

Don't' dwell on the negativity of it, but continue to get on with your life and look for new opportunities.
Keep your eyes, your mind and your heart alert and then you will be open to them when they come.

If you are stuck with your head down in depression and misery mode with the notion - '*why does this always happen to me?*', then you will miss those chances and life will slip you by.

Read positive, motivational writing, surround yourself with upbeat people, feed your mind, experience new challenges, try new food, communicate with different people, travel, think big, build your knowledge, push your boundaries, spread your outlook on life, don't quit, don't give in!

*You are what you do!*
*You are what you think!*

If you want it, you can make it happen....
If you do more, expand more, develop more, you can manifest your dreams.
You can become the *true* you.
Be an optimist and have a positive outlook on life – increase your chances and probability of getting there.

*Change your behaviour. Be a success.*

**…..it's all a matter of your mind…..**
'Mind over matter' is so much more than that old-fashioned saying - one that tends to wash over you whenever you hear it mentioned.
It is actually a *way* of living – of moving forwards with life, thinking through situations and circumstances - no matter how small or large.

Think about it…..

Look at all the extreme sports people, the doctors who put themselves through endlessly long hard shifts, those big successful business people and ultimate salesmen with unbelievable targets to reach and others who put themselves in impossible scenario's....?

They all come through to achieve amazing goals and results, maintain ultimate stamina and conquer death-defying feats of strength and endurance in hazardous situations.

They all have a strong mindset outdoing and superseding the task put in front of them and pushing through barriers that, to the everyday eye, would seem totally out of reach for the normal person.

But, these people *know* they will do what is necessary to win, to succeed, to get to their ultimate goal.

They will certainly be embracing *mind over matter.*

*You tell your mind what you want and as sure as night and day, your brain will answer and respond.*

The old adage '*you can do whatever you want to do, achieve whatever you want to achieve*' is not just some half-hearted saying thrown randomly at people without any back-up or forethought.
If you can tell your mind that you *cannot* do something – you know full well, you won't do it. So why then, can't you tell your mind that you *CAN* do something - and **_do it_**?

*Practise makes perfect....*

If you set your mind to something and practise it, if you want it badly enough and you keep telling yourself it *is* achievable and you *ARE* it, then your mind and body will accept what you are telling it and follow through.

Of course you will have to keep on at yourself, telling yourself you *can* do it, you *are* it and keep practising – after all, Rome wasn't built in a day.
You cannot expect to suddenly become an expert at something you've only tried twice or half-heartedly put a feeble amount of effort into.

*So, no matter how passionate you are, you will still need to practise until you are able to master your goal.*

But with your mind dealing positively with the matter, in time, your goal and ambition will be realised and you will get what you want out of life.
*It is ultimately your choice to talk yourself up and into, not _out_ of something*, if it is what you truly want out of life.

*Use your mind to full advantage and in a matter of time, your desires will come to you....*

**…..is it your time to take a leap of faith…….**
*When times are unsettled it may not seem appropriate for a 'leap of faith', but if you don't take chances, then your life won't change.*
If you compulsively throw yourself into something new, it could just be a way of escaping from difficulties in your life, rather than dealing with them.

*But sometimes by taking a real chance and trying something different, it can be just what you really needed and exactly what turns your life around for the better…!*

Don't expect it to be easy though, it's not called a '*comfort zone*' for nothing and getting out of it can feel quite painful.
If you lift yourself up, use your strength and courage and believe in yourself, you can get to where you want……

*…..if you take that* **leap of faith**……

**"You can have a new invigorated and satisfying life,
where every choice you make is strong
and puts your future exactly where it should be –
fulfilled, enhanced, enriched and happy,
and where you are inspired and motivated".**


**…living your life as you should….**
*They say that you are more likely to 'live as you should if you live your life as though it were someone else's'…….*
Chances are that you are probably able give *others* very good advice, but find it a bit lacking when it comes to the same intention for yourself.

However, by pretending that your life *is* someone else's, it gives you a *new-found freedom* to make decisions and take actions that you may not necessarily have the courage to take by being *yourself*….

This is because, when you are in this position, you don't have the *fear or criticism* of yourself and you are therefore more likely to take chances you might not *personally* take.

Then suddenly, by being more *impartial*, more opportunities are revealed.
You will feel stronger about making transformations in your life.
In fact, *they* say that your life isn't really yours anyway, because the majority of people live in their *heads*, which is not necessarily their *true* self.
All those hopes, fears and fantasies stuck in your head, aren't really real, so living as though you are someone else can *free you from your own limitations* – usually those set by yourself - where you are *trapped by who and what you **think** you are*, but aren't really....

It's all in your mind.....

Start freeing yourself from your own issues and limitations and live as though you are someone else....! It will certainly be interesting and empowering!
*You never know, this may well lead onto the path to your dreams.....*

**.....the sacrifices you make will be worth everything.....**
*As you go on your journey towards fulfilling your ultimate empowered life, you will have to be prepared to make some initial sacrifices.*
This will be inevitable.
Those sacrifices may be in terms of time, effort, finance, relationships or changes to your life, including relocating. But come to terms with the fact that if you want to get to the stage in your life that is authentically '*you*' and where you dream to be, changes *have* to happen.
Sometimes that means making certain choices that may not be popular, but in the long-term will reap rewards.

*Be honest and frank with yourself.*

Whatever is negative and stopping you going along your path and reaching your ultimate self, will be hampering your progress and you need to make the choice as to whether or not it, or they, really have a place in your life?

*Approach this with caution but commitment.*

Explain fully to both yourself and those that may be effected, exactly why you are doing whatever it is and that it will be for the *most benefit and advantage in the long run.*

Get their understanding by using your strength of purpose and resolve. Be empowered to show them you are making the most out of your life, and if they love and respect you, they will realise that it is all for the good and will have empathy towards it and support you.

*Then you can go for your dream, or ultimate state, with calm and determined intention.*
**Good luck!**

**.......your very own wealth creation......**
*Every new day should be embraced as another step along your path of total 'wealth creation'.*
The wealth of the riches of life, not just money, but health, happiness, contentment, peace, love and any other aspect of you that you feel deserves enriching.
Each positive thought towards that enrichment will bring you closer to who you are meant to be and why you're here.

Each minute of the day offers you new chances and opportunities to take advantage of – if you remain *conscious and awake* to their existence.

There is no gain in negativity – it is a destructive force that only impinges on your feelings, attitude and subsequent actions and progress.
There is absolutely no merit in clinging onto anything that will stop you moving forwards and attaining a life of purpose, serenity and joy - your creation of wealth.

Focussing on making positive steps, slowly and surely will move you to your personal peace – even if that peace is financially motivated, it is *your* dream aim to attain that kind of wealth.

Losing sight of who you are and what you want will mean you are only living a *part* of life, or even *no part at all*, if you are *only subsumed by all the negative things that you either once had, or think are coming.....*

This does nothing except stunt your growth.
It does nothing to help you feel empowered in your life.
It does nothing to create the enrichment and wealth you deserve.

Think hard about how you will feel when your time has come and you look back and say that you did nothing but waste your life....
You were given so many golden opportunities to make something of yourself and *now they're gone*.
You had your time and you spent it eaten up by bad feelings that stopped you achieving your peace in life.
Create your very own wealth, whatever you choose that to be...
It is time to let go and be free.

*Free to let the sun shine on your days and be who you are really meant to be.*

> **"To move forward, you really have to tell yourself that negativity is not an option!**
> **Love who you are and what you are doing....**
> **Everything has a place in life,**
> **so surge ahead with passion and conviction.**
> **Don't be brought down by people trying to control you**
> **or your thoughts and feelings,**
> **because the only ones that are important to you**
> **are the ones you make for yourself!"**

**…..halting negativity in order to live your life to the full…..**
*If you are scared of something, like a dog, for instance, ask yourself how long you have had that fear for and how long you have allowed it to live within you?*
How long has it stopped you from getting on with your life?

Who put that fear there in the first place?

Have you inherited it from one of your parents or siblings because they are scared of whatever it is, like the dog, too?
Imagine if you didn't have that ball and chain around your neck getting in the way of your progress, living in your head, heart and mind, taking over control of your day to day movements.

*Apply that perspective to your life.*

It's just a little dog, probably not really interested in you anyway, walking past you on their daily routine, getting on with enjoying their walk or playing in their garden, totally unaware of your irrational fear. They're not bothered about how you feel, they're perfectly happy.

Take that thinking and apply it to your particular fearful position in life and consider how allowing it to get in the way has stopped you from achieving what you want.

Holding onto fears, bitterness, hurt, pain, negative emotions are just ruling your life *for* you, instead of you governing your *own* thoughts for yourself.
If someone or something has placed that fear in your head, why are you living with someone else's bad concept of things...?

If you stop and think about it, you may even realise that their fear would not actually affect you that badly at all if you made the conscious decision about it yourself – however, you have just clung onto their projected anxieties out of sheer conditioning over time....

You therefore need to put in a strategy that will remove all that negativity from your body and mind and give yourself a chance to get on, leave the past behind and empower yourself to start achieving your goals and ambitions.
Whether that's something big like career accomplishments or personal freedom and peace of mind, get help for your fears, put them in a box, lock them away and let yourself move on into a fuller, freer and calmer future.

You owe it to yourself.......

**....about your thinking.....**
*All the thoughts that come and go throughout your mind every day, shape who you are.*
Your feelings, your creativity and your experiences are a direct result of what happens to you in life.
Half the time, you aren't even consciously aware of the stream of things going on in your mind all the time, but they influence

everything you do. These thoughts have stemmed from years of conditioning and events that have happened over time, programming you and replaying over and over again in your head.

Some of the negative thoughts that have come from past influences really have no meaning or bearing on your life *today*. A lot of the time, they are self-defeating thoughts that constantly tell you that you can't do things, or that things just aren't going to turn out positively, or that you're just not good enough.

Are they stopping you carrying out your plans for achievement? Are they affecting your empowerment?

*Do you want those thoughts to dictate your life.....?*

**...who's controlling who......**
*If your health, wealth, success, peace and contentment are afflicted by your own and other people's negative thinking, then you have to begin to remove and replace it with new, better, more inspirational and motivating thoughts.*
Getting rid of negativity that is caused by people, the stresses of certain situations or your health, etc., is a major helpful step in moving forward towards your goals.

It is absolutely amazing how different you will feel as you begin to remove your negativities one by one - with each elimination calming down your addled mind, soothing your heart and building your confidence.

*Don't allow others to bring you down.*

Don't let them get in the way of your goals – whether business or personal.
Move away from them if they are in the way of your happiness.
Don't let yourself to be controlled by someone else. This is not *your* own destiny and this kind of negativity and control is not your *own* life being played out, as a *unique individual*.

So, if someone is zapping your energy, think about whether you should actually be in their company.

If all you feel from them is bad energy, then you need to remove that unfavourable element from your life.

Take some time to consider if anyone is controlling you, pulling your strings or trying to lead you along a path that is not your own. If you have these kind of people around you, you need to seriously think about how you can distance them from your life, so you can move forward in a far more positive way.

*The control is totally in your hands and you will feel so much more empowered by doing this.*

### ....but we need negative experiences don't we......
*You do need negative experiences to get to where you need to go, to help you endure and build up your strength and feel more powerful, so you can be in a good place to reap the rewards of success.*
You have to get through the night to get to the sunshine of the day.
**But**, you don't need to dwell on the negative and the dark side of things, as that will run the risk of sending you on a downward spiral, making you feel worse than ever.....

Negative thinking just isn't productive, it just batters your confidence and stops you from making any progress.
Along the road you are bound to come up against negativities, that's inevitable - whether it is coming from other people or from your own personal insecurities and feelings about your life, successes and ambitions.
These negative feelings could pop up time and time again, but the trick is not to yield to them, just ignore them.

*Don't give them any creedence.*

### .....why aren't successful people negative then......
*Even the most positive of people can come up against negative feelings from time to time.*
Not all successful people are happy and cheerful 24/7 – even if it looks like
it from the outside - inside they could be struggling.
But their trick is to keep on going, by focussing on their goals and ignoring those negativities.

They know these tendencies would just get in the way and pull them down, if they allowed themselves to listen to that inner voice telling them they can't do things.

*They focus on being successful instead.*

They probably still curse and swear their way to the top, but each day they work through it and achieve what needs to be done instead. They don't get caught in the trap that brings them down. Nor do they spend years trying to be in a positive state of mind and changing their behaviour *first,* before they can even step on their road to success.

They also divert any negative energy of jealousy and envy, etc., to help push them upwards and forwards, surpassing those that make them feel that way and inducing it in those individuals instead!

Get your own back on those who have angered or hurt you, by being successful and prosperous instead.

*Use your worry to motivate and empower you into showing them exactly what you are capable of and realising your dreams in front of their eyes!*

**…..there's always someone who tries to bring me down….**
Try and keep a distance from ruthless and cunning people who will try and knock you back and interfere with your peace and serenity, or threaten your career and personal objectives.
The likelihood is that they just have an inferiority complex or problems in their own life and are therefore spending their time resenting their particular lot in life.
Keep them at arms length if you want to get on.

You don't necessarily need them onside to enable your progression – there will always be other ways and other people who can help you instead, if you are serious about your goals or changing things.

*Remember, you cannot please all of the people all of the time (but you can please yourself)!*

Don't allow them to control and manipulate you to the point that it

affects your way forward. Don't let them turn you into a negative person.
If you can get at least *some* people on your side, then your path to victory and success, whatever that may be specific to you, becomes so much more achievable.

*Choose for yourself who's help you need to further yourself.*

So, if you come across cunning and ruthless people, just refuse to participate in their games, don't get involved and just detach yourself from them.

*Be your own person – strong and empowered.*

**…..yes, but, I just can't get things out of my head…..**
It's very easy to let yourself go into a rant in your head, re-living and re-argueing situations over and over again.
Be aware of what you are doing and shake yourself out of it.
Smile, say, "*bygones*", and replace it with a new distraction – something more positive.
Do not let it spiral you down into deeper negativity and stress.

What you need is either a solution to your problem that you can activate, or delete the situation from your mind and move on.
Perhaps learn something from the situation – either from your own perspective or the other person's or situations perspective.

*Ask yourself what you can learn about yourself in this predicament?*

Is there something in the argument or situation that allows you to realign your thoughts and actions so that you are much better prepared if it happens again?

*Or perhaps there's an element that you can take forward that helps you build your life in a much stronger and empowered way....*

**…..I get so depressed sometimes….**
When you feel yourself going on a downward spiral, try to bring yourself back up quickly, before the negativity takes over.
You will need to identify just what it is that is causing this and removing your power, and begin to take that power back, before it

grips a hold and becomes out of your control.
Make a decision.

Either you allow this 'fog' to break you down, or you look it in the eye and say you're going to break through it instead.
Get rid of the mindset that is making you a victim of it all and tell yourself this is *your* life, *your* choice and therefore you are not going to let it beat you, before any damage happens.

*Make a conscious decision to change your outlook.*

You may well need some support in doing this and that's absolutely fine – whatever gets you there. It won't happen overnight, but each step in the right direction is progress and a rung up the ladder to your own valuable empowerment.

If you're feeling down or negative, try to talk yourself up, not down.
Keep doing nice things that feed your soul.
Think of how well you've done and the things you are gradually building up every day towards your goals.

*So look forward, not back or down.*

Accomplish something small every day and give yourself a pat on the back for every little thing you achieve, no matter what it is - work, health or personal related.

And keep smiling - send those endorphins whizzing round your body!

Dance as though no-one is watching!
Love as though you have never loved before!
Sing as though no-one can hear you!
*Live as though heaven is on earth!*

**…..they said I was bad…..**
*Are those negative beliefs continually popping up, making you put yourself down as a result…?*

Then consider asking yourself if you have any *real* proof that these bad things you keep feeling or telling yourself are *genuinely* true?

How is having this negative state of mind actually benefiting you? Search for evidence that in reality, the total opposite is true and then replace the 'bad' stuff with far more positive self-talk and beliefs.

If you wouldn't tell a friend they have the kind of unfavourable qualities that you keep reiterating to yourself, then why be so self-inflicting towards yourself?
This attitude and set of bad thoughts certainly won't help you progress forward in life.

*Why get yourself into such a bad space and then complain that life is so terrible?*

You need to let go of these negative self-beliefs – some of which you may have picked up from your past experiences. However, just because you were told whatever it was *then*, it does not necessarily mean that the same situation still applies right *now* - that's if it ever *really* did......

This preoccupation could have been something as simple as a passing remark from your parent or teacher that has sat in your subconscious mind and meant *far* too much to you ever since.

Weed it out, throw it away and try to stop putting yourself down forever more as a result of it.

To help you do this, this little exercise may help (or if it's *really* bad, get some professional help):

So then, write down:
**My negative belief is....**"*My life isn't going anywhere fast*".
**This affects my life by....** '*making me feel like a loser and I end up not believing in myself*'.
**I got this belief from....** '*my high school teacher*'.
**It stops me....**'*making the effort to try and better myself*'.
**I could replace this with a more positive belief like....**'*I am intelligent and perfectly capable, with excellent skills*'.
**I really believe this because the difference it would make to my life is.....** '*I would be far more satisfied with my life and I could get a gratifying position and be a lot happier and more fulfilled*'.

*The more you replace negative thoughts with positive ones, the more you increase your chances of inviting in positive outcomes,* because the more you focus on them, the more you attract similar situations, people and relationships.

It stands to reason that if you are focussed positively, then you will not want negative things and people around you. If you don't wallow in negativity when bad things happen to you, then things will *almost definitely soon pass.*
So you need to keep telling yourself that.

*Time is a very good healer.*

You will already know this from past events and circumstances that you have been in.
Seriously try to bear that in mind.
Problems and dramas invariably don't get solved from a negative standpoint....

*Empower yourself to overcome....!*

**…..so just change things then.....**
By actively changing scenario's from bad to good, you change negative situations into positive ones.
You talk to your brain and tell it what you want.
*It listens.....*

Just make a *serious* effort to cut out the negative and bring in the positive.
Find things and people that <u>uplift</u> you and avoid those that bring you down or drain all your energy.

Take a *good* look at what those relationships and circumstances are actually doing to you and whether they are genuinely helping you or just hindering you.

*You are the only one who lives in your mind and therefore, you are the only one who has the power to change your outlook on things.*

It can't be said often enough...

### ....but I need my emotions, don't I......
*Allow yourself to feel your negative emotions, but don't let them overtake you.*
Take ownership and then let them go.
Then you will begin to take control of your thoughts and feelings.

*Feel confident and walk tall.*

### .....what will they think of me though.....
*Adopt the thinking that, whatever other people think of you, is none of your business.*
If you *don't know* about it, it won't affect you and you won't worry about it.
You will then spend more time focussing on yourself and how you feel about *you*, instead of paying any attention to what is going on in other people's minds.
So live your life as you want to live it and really enjoy yourself.

*If you don't live your life, who will?*

Because it is within your own dreams and aspirations that you find your golden opportunities.
You open up the door to possibilities, challenges and fulfilment.
You can make your dreams and aspirations a reality.

*You know deep down inside that you can do it, so let it out and make it happen.*

It's only you who can take care of your own life.
Let the others take care of theirs, whilst you put yours into a shape that fits you perfectly. Only then will you feel the happiness and glory for yourself and your own achievements.

*Each small inspirational thought will lead to another, and in time, to materialisation.*

### ....I just can't help feeling low....
*Are you someone who can't help but wallow?*
Start a new strategy for when you get into situations that are likely to get you down, by giving yourself a time limit on how long you'll allow yourself to be like that.

That way, you don't end up spending days in a slump and running the risk of everything overwhelming you - otherwise you will never get out of those bad thoughts and feelings.

Do all the things you need to do when you wallow, but spend only a short amount of time on it – minutes, rather than hours or days, obviously depending on the severity of the situation.

*Get it all out of your system and then move on.*

Lift up your head, smile and do something that makes you feel nice instead - perhaps a nice walk in the fresh air, some time at a spa, listen to you favourite music or doing something creative.
It's your choice.

Make some room in your head to allow some happy and positive thoughts, rather than spending it all on how you could possibly have done things differently, or said something in a different way, etc.

Life is meant to be enjoyed after all, not spent in deep reflection on how awful it is!

Be grateful for all the good things you have that give you pleasure and make you happy. Things that make you feel great and vibrant. And do more of them!
Or if you haven't got anything like these things in your life – start making room for them!

*Everyone deserves to have wonderful things to uplift them......*

**….that's just the way I am, I can't change.....**
You **can** change your mindset from a negative outlook – that's if you really want to.....
Use your *present tense* positive affirmations, visualisations and anchoring.
These methods are extremely helpful, because you can replace those worn out 'stories' that may be going round and round in your head and heart, with far better concepts and ideas that will help you progress with your life right *now*, in the <u>present</u>.

This powerful technique can transform your life through changing your attitude towards certain situations. It also permits you to have some higher expectations for yourself.

*You can create whatever you want in your own mind.*

Whether you follow this process by speaking out loud, writing things down, saying them in your mind, or through chanting - it all works in the same beneficial way.

Every time you find yourself looking back in a negative way, or blaming yourself and coming up with '*if onlys*' and '*what ifs*', replace them with something more positive and useful like, "*I am an achiever*", or "*I am strong, confident, forward thinking and successful*", or "*I am the person who is making the most out of my life and moving forward with passion and positivity*", or, "*my life is full of enrichment, abundance and prosperity*".

Whatever suits your own personal circumstances and works best for you.

Visualise what you want to be and desire and anchor those thoughts and feelings into your psyche. Doing this as often as you can will help give you the effective tools to get beyond negative experiences and tap into your subconscious, *instilling positive outcomes into your brain.*

*This is an empowering system that can sincerely facilitate the changes you want to make.*

So you see, you **can** change....
*Try it and see for yourself!*

**....new messages for your brain to act upon.....**
*Retraining your brain with new positive messages will make you enjoy your life more.*
Keep chipping away with those good words, that uplifting self-talk, your encouraging motivational language....
This will ultimately contribute to making you far more successful and fulfilled and also help you get over things a lot more quickly than you would otherwise have done, if you'd just carried on allowing yourself to feel bad or dispirited.

Use this strategy to gain inroads into feeling much better about life in general and to keep you driven towards your goals.

*In doing so, your renewed strength will help you to progress far more productively, as well as fortify your overall sense of empowerment.*

**….I AM good enough.....*I AM*.....**
*So, whenever you feel that negative chatter telling you that you are incapable of something, or you're not good enough, you should 'recreate' that thought into something more positive.*
Something that tells you that you are perfectly able and that you deserve the happiness and fulfilment it will bring you.

You become the *master* of your own thoughts and you continuously tell yourself how much you are attracting good things into your life and how satisfied you are with all the positive things that are happening to you **right now.**

Remember to use those affirmations in the present tense – like it already exists *right now.*
Don't forget to affirm what you *DO* want and not what you *don't* want – so you are creating an image that you have complete ownership of.

It's only about *you* - so it should feel *exactly* right for you.

Change and adapt it according to your own resonance and make it clear, strong and concise. This will create a far more effective affirmation. It needs to cause the biggest and most powerful impact on your consciousness.
It should be something fresh and new that you are creating for *yourself.*

Develop a brand new outlook and use it as an opportunity to request something that you *really* desire in life. Something that will enable more exciting and satisfying experiences into your life that will ultimately make *you, and you alone,* **happy**!
Instil the belief that your desire is yours already, really feeling the power surging through you as you create your own, true reality.

*You **ARE** good enough!*

You can achieve whatever you want!

**...I'm going to start living my life without negativity....**
*Start planting the seeds for your ultimate growth right **now**.*
Start to unlock the key to your infinite intelligence and your own deserving success.
Look forward, not back.
Look for the optimism, not the pessimism.
Be great, not resigned.
Conquer your goal-seeking dreams.

*This is the way life should be.....*

**...I'm telling myself that negativity is not an option....**
*Surge ahead with your life with passion, energy and vitality.*
Love who you are and what you are doing.
It all has a place in life.
The role you have given yourself has a purpose and a meaning that you will learn from.
*Believe in it.*
And don't be brought down by people trying to control you and your thoughts.
Don't get dragged into their negativity net!

*Be the owner of yourself!*

***Always tell yourself***
***"Nothing can hurt me!***
***I am protected by the good spirit,***
***power and energy of the Universe"!***

**...because you are the power of your own thoughts...**
*If you think that you are weak, then you will be.....*
And, if you think you are *strong* then that is exactly what you will be too!

Because, whatever you think affects the whole of your body, including each and every individual cell.

*So, learn to think more positively and you will be able to achieve so much more.*
(well, thinking negatively doesn't really get you that far, does it....?)

When all else fails, look to your *inner* strength - your passion to be *you*.
You can be whoever you choose to be, even if this is to relax and do nothing with your life!
If you truly believe that your chosen path is this, then be happy as you are, with that in mind.

*Stop fighting it and accept it as your path in life.*

Always feel satisfied and content that the choices you make are the right ones for *you*, that they sit well within your heart, head, body and soul, then you will glide through life knowing you are doing exactly the right thing – *just for you*.

*Choose your open doors wisely.*

Step across the threshold with your personal path in mind.
Opportunities are there for you.
See them, look at them and make the right choices.

*You think, therefore you are.*

*Your life awaits....*

**....get someone positive to try to keep you motivated.....**
*Find that special person who will help to keep you motivated in times of weakness.*
Make it someone you know believes in you and your ambitions.
Make sure they are a positive person.
You do not need a negative influence that will just use a weaker moment as an excuse to put you down, ruin your agenda or make you stray from your achievements.

*Choose wisely....*

**....to spend time judging others....is a waste of <u>your</u> time.....**
*Do not judge others.....*
What use does this have to you? Where does it get you exactly?
Being judgemental is a negative activity. ….
It removes you from yourself and allows your emotions to become involved in someone else's business that usually has no bearing on your own.

*And even if it does, it is not about you.*

Whatever anyone else gets up to, does, looks like, owns or thinks is *their* business. Allow them to do that, be that, think that or have that, as you would expect them to do the same for you.
Focussing on someone else's business and being judgemental, means you are invoking negative feelings in yourself that you really have no need for. This action can cause embitterment.
Why waste precious energy on it?

What does it *actually* achieve?

Whatever another person is, does not have to affect you.

*Your life is yours to control, their life is theirs.*

If you stop judging, there will be a fresh stress-free space in your life to replace with more positive things instead, that have a better effect on your life, far more than such wasted energy.

*You will be amazed how much better you will feel if you remove judgement from your life!*

Why be affected by someone else's business when you can go on your own way enjoying your own life, doing your own thing?
You can be motivating yourself to accomplish all the things *you* want instead.

*Let others be and you just be yourself.*

By spending time on judging, you are taking positivity away from yourself and affecting your own peace and harmony.

*Use that energy for the good instead – for improving your life and empowering it to be the best it can be......*

**...whatever happens, you *can* adapt and overcome...**
*There are going to be times in your life when you may have no control over some circumstances.*
This is likely to be an illness or disability that you have no choice but to live with.
At first, it is bound to cause upset, shock and a period of grief.
This is absolutely natural.

Get all the help you can from doctors, family and friends to assist you in coming to terms with this new change, so you can make sure you are able to move forward with your life in the best way possible.

Once you have become used to your new circumstances, you need to adopt a positive attitude to how you can carry on and still continue to really enjoy your life, using all the resources you have at your disposal.

*Try not to sink into despair and depression.*

It's time to adapt to your new way of living and overcome all the possible knock-on effects of what has happened to you. Don't give into the down-side of your condition – it's all too easy to just give in and give up!

Feeding on the negative aspects of your condition will do nothing for you but make your life more intolerable, or make you more ill, more depressed, more insular and insecure.

Have the nerve and strength to lift up your spirit and still continue to do things in your life that challenge you, are full of adventure and make you happy.

Your circumstances may even jolt you into doing things you have always wanted to do, but never bothered. Or if not, why not indulge in inspiring new opportunities that weren't in your imagination or perception before?

Can you modify or alter your aspirations to something else, that are just as exciting instead?

*Learn to adapt to your new life and overcome your ailments, so you can empower yourself to take life head on with vitality, positivity and sheer optimism.*

*"Just because something good ends, doesn't mean something better won't begin...."*

**.....always remember.....if you got over it before, you can get over it again.....**
*You know how life has challenged you over the years.*
You know how many things have been '*sent to try you*'.....
And you also know that you have always got over them and come out the other side, probably having learnt something along the way. You probably also realised it happened because it was making way for something else, something new, or to clear some issues or dead wood out of the way once and for all.

*Always bear this in mind when you are faced with challenging or problematic situations in the future.*
When you do come across tricky times, beware the downward spiral that could send you plummeting into the negative.
Always think about how you managed to get past things before, how much stronger you can be this time and how you know all will be well, if not better, after it's sorted out this time.
And anyway, it may not be anywhere near as scary as you think!

*It could actually be the making of you....*

Even losing your job or a relationship, for instance, should be viewed not as a loss, but the perfect chance to bring about new opportunities.

That stab at promotion that 'failed' – didn't actually *fail* – it taught you something vital....
It taught you how to do things *better* in future....
It taught you what your next job could be....

It taught you what your next goal may be....
*It taught you how to win next time!*

So start being optimistic instead of thinking your whole world has collapsed and will never be the same ever again.
*Well, it's true, it probably won't be!*

But change could certainly be for the *better*, rather than for the worse.
View it as *everything does happen for a reason*, even if you can't see it at the time. It will probably show itself later.

So, if you've recently had a rough time, you are finding it very difficult to get over and it's making you lose your mojo and is just depressing you, then think back to a time when something similar or of equal measure may have happened to you. Although you may have found it difficult then too, what lessons did you learn from it.....?

*One's thing's for sure – you got over it, otherwise you wouldn't be still standing today!*

And if there's anything you can take from that last incident – it's that it all worked out in the end and you can therefore get over it again this time. This time though, you use the lessons you learnt from last time and employ them in a much better and more efficient way.

Things always seem bigger and more dreadful than they actually are when it first happens. When you're totally embroiled in it, you think there's no way out. But, you can always look back on it and know that it was never quite as bad as you thought it was at the time.

Whatever consequences came from it, you survived, you came out the other end and you got on with your life.

So, instead of wallowing in self-pity, anger, frustration, and depression, lift up your head and your heart, look yourself straight in the eye, build a strategy to get you through it and move on with your life.

Feel strong and empowered to tackle anything, rise above it and turn your path into a far clearer way forward, for not only you, but for those close to you as well.....

Don't drag all your woes around with you like a huge concrete burden for years on end.
Use every circumstance as a learning curve and useful experience.

There's a lot to live out there, so go get 'em!

*You did it before.....so you can do it again....but this time - much better!*

**....but before you can change anything...you must be honest and frank with yourself...**
*So you've decided you want some definite changes in your life....*
Then to implement those transformations, you mustn't be 'delusional' about who and what you are.....
It's unbelievably easy to do.

But, if you are going to get anywhere or establish changes, make something of yourself, be a successful achiever, or just feel better and more confident, then you need to have a serious word with yourself about who you are, what you are doing, where you are and what you want to be.

*And, in order to do that, you HAVE to be honest with yourself.*

It's no good deluding yourself that you and everything in your life is fantastic, that nothing is your fault and everyone else is to blame - if it really isn't *genuinely* like that.
If you don't make any changes in life, then everything will stay exactly as it is, so look at yourself with a very *truthful* and *open* mind.

*See yourself, your life, EXACTLY for what it is.*

If you don't like what you see or where you are, then make a concerted choice to alter things.

If there are negative influences in your life, whether it's work, people, your environment, fitness, weight, or lack of money, whatever it is, those influences are destructive.
They cause a force, an energy that has a bad effect on how you think and feel.
It can dominate your every move – if you allow it to.
It's YOUR choice!

*If you don't like this position, then it's YOUR responsibility to modify it, no-one else's.*

So if you're not happy, then you are the *only* one that can do something about it.
Take that deep and frank look at yourself and your *self-limitations* – those things that you can and can't do. That doesn't mean what you *think* you can do, but what you actually **can** do, nor who you *think* you are, but who you really **are**.

You can't make changes unless you know where and what to change......

Being truthful with yourself means not deluding yourself.
Not deluding yourself may mean asking other people's perception of you, versus your own perception of yourself.

This may upset you at first, especially if you don't like what you hear, but if you calmly take on-board what they say, you can take a deep breath and start putting firm plans and actions into place to build up the requirements you need mentally, physically and emotionally to achieve those changes.
Also, doing this will help get you into the right mindset for your own success – whatever that means to you

*Without the truth, you can't really move forward in a constructive way.*

Otherwise, you will still continue to move through life in the same old way, believing you are doing right, or being a negative person who is pessimistic about your life and options.
But how can you feel completely satisfied with your existence if you don't move forwards and upwards...?

Empowerment is positive when it means you are fulfilling what you are meant to with your life.
If you aren't feeling good, aren't doing good and aren't getting anywhere, you need this positive enforcement to help you advance forward.

*So, you need to look yourself in the eye and recognise those faults and failings that are getting in the way of what you want - no holds barred.*

It's no good telling yourself that you are definitely going to make changes and then following that with '*yeh, but*' and '*I can't because*', or '*I'm not really like that, so therefore....*'

If there are things that are stopping you, like apathy, procrastination, lack of self-confidence, or previous failures dogging you at every angle, or you're allowing yourself to be dominated by someone or something, or you lack motivation or appropriate skills, then you need to tell yourself that these are *real* issues that need to be tackled and resolved.

*So, address them and go out there and find those solutions.*

It may take time, particularly if you have conditioned yourself over the years to feel and be a certain way, because nothing changes overnight.

So don't be too hard on yourself if things don't have an effect straight away, it will come with time, as long as you stick at it, have a goal and don't be put off by outside, or inner forces getting in your way.

Feel the progress everyday, pat yourself on the back for all the achievements you have made, however small, and keep on going.....

You will get there in the end and on your journey, you will find your life opening up and opportunities coming your way, because you will be more <u>alert</u> to them, as you change and improve.

*So, sit down with yourself and start looking deep within, get to work on **you**, feel more empowered and start living your ultimate life - the life you deserve.*

Help is out there if you need it!

> *"This is not a sprint or a quick fix.*
> *It will take you time to clear all the clutter and*
> *change your mindset for the better,*
> *so that it all comes quite naturally.*
> *Give it the time it deserves".*

**….life is a series of challenges....so why not make them fabulous ones.....**
*Begin to make plans to do something challenging that you have always wanted to do.*
Whether it's something big like sky-diving or just something simple that you've always wanted to do, but just never got round to doing it.

*Start thinking about how you can achieve it....*

Perhaps it's something as small as taking a stroll along an area you've seen that looks really nice, but just never stopped to take the time, or reading a book you've always been curious about.
It can be something quick or something that takes time.

<u>Make the time!</u>

Begin to build up a list of things you really want to get out of life, even if you tick off one of those things, you have achieved something for yourself that you've always yearned to do.
Accomplishing that one thing will undoubtedly make you motivated to continue on and do more things that invigorate you or make you feel vibrant and happy.

*Doing something out of your ordinary routine makes you feel **alive**!*

**....and even those everyday challenges can be empowering.....**
*Challenging yourself as often as you can is all part of improving and building your life, because it helps give you strength and aids your development.*
By pushing yourself into doing things that you are a little afraid of, you are growing as a person and this will help you to become more and more empowered as you build up your confidence and inner toughness.
This applies to both personal and work life.

If you find it difficult to make tough decisions, by starting small and building up, you can put yourself in great stead for a much stronger future.
Naturally, the more you do something, the easier it becomes and the more proficient you will become at it. This can only be for your own benefit, because it gives you the potential to get what you want out of life, including success in whatever you desire.
It will help you to make much bigger decisions in life and even increase your level of happiness.

*With this new empowerment, you will be in a wonderful position of enablement which will allow you to look at situations and events from a better and higher viewpoint.*

This will give you the tools to be courageous in your needs and wants, as you will see things far more clearly and your path can lead to exactly where you want it to be, without prejudice.
It will stretch you to levels that you may have previously thought were beyond your reach or potential. You will feel more professional, more able, more improved, more focussed, more productive and obviously more happy!

Even the simple word *'no'* can have a profound effect on you if you are used to saying '"yes" to everyone all the time in order to please them, no matter how small the request. It's always difficult to do at first because you will probably be riddled with guilt.

But not always feeling obliged to do the right thing for someone else every time they ask, is a big step in reducing the internal turmoil you may be having because of never being able to say no!

The reduction in stress and tension will be apparent to you as you begin to learn that your own time and efforts should be acknowledged in their own right.

So, think about something you are normally quite afraid to do and have a go at facing it, no matter how silly or small this may be. It's your own unique challenge to yourself and only you will know what it is.

*Never mind what anyone else thinks!*

Do something as often as you can that challenges you that you can overcome – whether in the workplace or at home.

*Each little thing you do will help you to make tough decisions in the future and will certainly help you to redesign your life, and even make you come up with some **amazing** opportunities.*

**Hooray!**

**....and the moral of the little donkey story is......**
*You may have heard the one about the donkey that got stuck down a well and despite his greatest efforts, it's owner couldn't rescue it and he felt, due to it's age, it wasn't worth the hassle of continuing his feat of saving it.....?*
So he decides to fill the well in on top of the donkey, with the help of his friends and neighbours, and closes up the top.

However, after a while, the donkey emerges out of the well and runs off unscathed.

This was because, with each shovel full of dirt and rubble they had thrown into the well and on top of the donkeys back, he had shaken it off and used the built-up dirt underneath him to keep taking a step up, until the well was full and he was right back up to the entrance. He then just stepped out - free and alive and raring to go again!
A fantastic feat!

And the moral of this story is that life will shovel dirt onto you of varying kinds. The trick is to shake it off each time and take a step up.....!

Our troubles are the mere stepping-stones of life and even when in the deepest of 'wells', don't ever stop and give up, just shake it off and step up!
What other choice do you have?

If your life is getting you down, get some advice so you can carry on and make it more exciting again.
Happiness should be a given and in order to reap the benefits of it, you need to forgive and free your heart from any hatred you may have built up that is getting in your way.
You need to stop worrying about things that may never even happen – most things don't – so you can free your mind and give yourself some well deserved peace.

*Always appreciate what you have got, because some have nothing.*

Try living simply instead of yearning for more and more all the time and never being satisfied.
If you have, then give. It will really make you feel good.
And if you live by expecting less from others but more from yourself, then you will live more in total harmony.

*And above all, **smile** and pass it on.......*

**......stop driving and striving and just be you.....**
Are you spending your life chasing your tail, being stressed out, or racing up the ladder in an out-and-out bid to get to the top?
Is that feeling empowering...?

**Stop for a minute.**

Is this really what you want?
Is this really you?
Why are you doing it?
What are you trying to accomplish?
Are you trying to achieve the impossible?
Is this what your life is really all about?

Fine, if it is, but if it is seriously getting you down, causing you to run at 100 mph all the time, having a negative effect on your health, damaging your relationships and scaring you half to death because you're just 'winging' it, then you need to sit down and have a serious rethink!

Get some paper and start writing down the *fors* and *againsts* - the pros and cons of what you are doing with your life – personally and career-wise.

*Ask yourself what you would really rather be doing and if what you are doing right now, is even going to get you to your goal of personal contentment?*

Think about your innate skills and talents.
Are you tapping into them and making the absolute most of what they are, honing them and becoming an expert in that field?
Are you clambering up a corporate ladder you really have no interest in?
Should you really be teaching yoga instead, for instance?
Are you running a business you have no real connection with, when you should be learning how to become a chef maybe?
Are you on a 4-year course to nowhere when you would rather be out in the fresh air teaching wind-surfing perhaps?

Remember you only have **one life** on this earth – you should be making the most of it.

And by following a career path that doesn't suit you, or enduring an occupation that someone else has paved out for you, you are not taking the way best way forward if you *seriously want a happy and balanced life.*
Your reason for being here is to make the most of who you are and in doing so, you 'gift' not only yourself, but others too.

*The knock-on effect of you being the true you is immense.*

You get the best out of your life, you become an expert in your own subject and you pass on your knowledge and wisdom to others. In turn, you are a happier person and by passing on your skills, you make others happy too.

*It's a win-win situation and one that makes the world go round in a harmonious way.*

And having that kind of overall positioning is truly empowering!

<u>So, just stop for a minute.</u>

Step off that roller-coaster and ask yourself why you are 'driving and striving'?

*Are you really fulfilling your potential in the right way, and if not, don't you think it's time that you did, for you own sake, as well as other people around you?*

### ....this job is boring me to death....
*If you are engaged in work that doesn't inspire you, the chances are you will get bored and disinterested.*
It can tire you out and you can become a negative person, even if you aren't necessarily that kind of person in the first place!
It's so much easier to enjoy working when you don't have to put too much effort into it because you are really *interested* in the job.

*So, you really should look for work that will fulfil you!*

Even if that's classed by some as a *'negative activity'* – like spending all day sitting down reading.
If that's what you like doing, you could find a way of getting a job that embraces that kind of occupation, like editing, being a book critic or working in a library.
Maybe you like eating? So find a job that involves that, like being a restaurant critic or a chef.
Or if you like to watch films all day, maybe you could be a film critic....?
You could turn out to be a huge success in any of these industries, or whatever your choice is!

If there isn't a job that has been established yet that suits your nature, then why not set one up yourself?
Find the hidden assets in it and make it work for you!
Set up your own business in whatever your interests are or what you feel you're really good at. Develop yourself as an entrepreneur and you could build a very lucrative enterprise doing what impassions you.

*The more you do what you are inspired by and suits your nature, the more effortless and rewarding the job will be.*

Don't allow yourself to be judged by others' standards either.
What may be good for one person, doesn't necessarily mean it will be good for another.
You can end up making judgements about people and causing negative emotions where they are not necessarily true. For instance, just because someone gets up late, that doesn't mean they are a bad person, it just means that they are a late riser or it could just be that they work nights.
If you like to get up late, then try and find a job that suits this scenario.
Don't allow people to shame you or make you feel like a failure, just because you don't fit into *their* lifestyle or their ideals....

*Just focus on your own personal aspirations and protect yourself from their criticism.*

Spend that energy on being determined to fulfil your own dreams, building up your empowerment and becoming a success in your own right.

*Be the person you're meant to be and happiness will absolutely follow.*

### …..know yourself, brand yourself....
Whether you realise it or not, like everyone else, you have a 'brand'; an image; a value.
But have you ever *really* taken the time to sit down to establish just what that is exactly?
You have strengths and attributes that you should be proud of.

Of course there are things that challenge you, that's all part of life, but you *can* face them and become stronger for it.

Establishing what your purpose is and giving yourself a 'brand' will help you to identify just who you are and the roles you fit into, and how important you actually are to both yourself and the others you come into contact with every day.

By fully knowing who you are, you should be able to get what you want out of life because you can seriously focus on this and position yourself to get it....

You can deal with challenges on the way to success, build and grow personally and embrace who you are. You can be ambitious, set goals and be ready to deal with life's obstacles – just by implementing your *brand*.
If someone was to write a basic paragraph that generally described you, what would they say?

*Try putting yourself in their shoes and doing this for yourself as an observer of you.*

Include things like, who you are, what you do, where you work, your role, your character, what you like doing, your social life, what your activities are, what you do when you go out, fitness activities, your interests, children, marital status, how you spend your weekends, your basic beliefs and values, things you like, how you relax, where you live, the type of home you have, who your friends are, etc.

Build that whole picture up.

Then move on to consider and reflect on how you got to your life as it is now.....what experiences you've had, all your failures and successes – in fact, all the things that have made you who you are today.
Include your past activities, key things you were interested in and were good at, which people were key in your life during each decade, what you were disappointed with, etc.

By breaking it down into 10 year increments, you can watch your background unfold, see how you grew, what influences you had and which common themes ran through your stages of life.

You can establish the different and changing roles you have played on your journey, which relationships have played an important part and what expectations those people have from you, in particular your mother, manager, spouse, colleagues, etc.

Those 'job titles' that you have fulfilled throughout those periods will have a list of skills attributed to them – competent talents you had to carry out your 'brand role' – essentially, your job description.

But what makes you the unique individual that you are, over and above these brand roles?
What are your core values that guide your behaviour and make you react in your own way in certain situations, how you handle things, your thoughts and feelings regarding issues, your level of performance when things happen?
They all make you who you are right now.
They make you connect with others of similar values, or make you feel awkward or uncomfortable when those values are compromised by those who aren't on your level, or way of thinking and acting.

*It's this set of traits that make your character and soul, your authenticity.*
Essentially, *who you are.*

Your values are part of your personality, such as being caring, responsible, or compassionate. They are different to your attributes, which are your skills and capabilities, such as being accurate in your work, your professionalism and ability to remain focussed.

Although the following list is by no means exhaustive, it should give you some idea of the types of values there are.
Find **your** *top ones and live by their meaning and sense of purpose:*

Achievement, Adventure, Autonomy, Ambition, Authenticity, Calmness, Confidence, Commitment, Compassion, Contentment, Cooperation, Creativity, Dependability, Empathy, Ethics, Fairness, Flexibility, Friendliness, Graciousness, Generosity, Happiness, Honesty, Humour, Independence, Integrity, Kindness, Loyalty, Maturity, Modesty, Openness, Personal Growth, Partnership, Privacy, Responsibility, Security, Sensuality, add you own in here.....!

*When you truly know who you are, what values you hold close and become **focussed** around them, you will feel the empowerment within you leading the way to a more satisfying and fulfilling life ahead.*

### ……..sell yourself into better prospects…..

*Isn't it always the way that when it comes to your professional environment, you can sell, sell, sell, but when it comes to you, you lack that courage of conviction and confidence….*
This is especially so if you decide to break out on your own – for whatever reason.
*Even if you think you can do it in your mind*, you seem to come across certain stumbling blocks when executing it all.

You probably find that you are great at promoting all your friends and family's assets and abilities, but your own are an entirely different matter! Quite often, you can sit behind other peoples dreams, like your partners, in order for them to do well and fulfil *their* ambitions, but yours take a back seat.

*Before long, all your hopes start fading and resentment can set in.*

Everyone needs a purpose in life, something that really makes them want to get up in the morning - the buzz, the excitement, the fulfilment, their own income and means of independence.
And why not?

To follow your passion though, you will definitely need to 'sell' yourself if you want to get off the starting block and make your dreams a reality.
You will have to not only promote your project, but also yourself as a person, raising your profile and get involved in marketing yourself, your product, services and skills.
*That's if you want to make it.*

Doing your own thing will mean selling, in all aspects of the word, on a day to day basis. You need to represent yourself. This takes a bit of confidence.

There are a couple of tricks to assist you in getting into the right selling mindset, that should help you get over your initial lack of confidence and enable you to present yourself in a much stronger light.
Instead of seeing yourself as having to be in a 'full-on' sales pitch scenario that may scare you a bit, think of yourself merely as having

a *conversation* with your prospective customer or employer, for instance.

Look at it as if you are establishing how you can help them out with a problem they have that you can potentially solve, like providing them with a service or product that meets their needs, or giving them some expertise that you may have to offer.
Sell your assets!

It may help you relax into the situation more.
If you get to know your product and/or service/field inside out and back to front, you will be in a far more confident position, because you will fully see the value in what you are providing and therefore, what you are offering the other person.

*This will definitely give you far more of an 'edge' than just going in with little or no knowledge of what you are doing.*

It will also relax the other person, because you will give them confidence that you know what you are talking about too.
If you sell with personality and free yourself from the 'competition' mind-set, then people will buy from you, or accept you, because they like *you as a person....*

*With belief, perseverance and determination in what you are doing, you will stay ahead.*

## .....make your outcomes effective......
*If you want to be on top of everything in your life, you need to have the right balance of down time to work time.*
Having the space to rejuvenate is important if you want to get the most out of your working day.
It is not selfish to give yourself periods in which you can relax and indulge in your favourite pass-times.
It's essential.

There's *me-time* and there's *work-time* – and you need both if you want to keep sane and be effective, productive and empowered, and not stressed, burnt out and irritable.

Step off the gas for a change and give your life a chance.

Diarise over the next week, month or year, all the things you are going to do to be creative, relax, recharge and aid your own healthy well-being, so you know these activities are built into your day and *must* be done, just as much as your work duties.

*Think of one thing that you can get started **now**.*

Make it something you believe in - something that is a deep-seated part of who you are that respects your own values and principles. Put the bones of it in place.
Make that fulfilment your priority and if others ask you to do their stuff instead, remain focussed and ask yourself if it fits in with your own vision of what you want.

If it doesn't, it's not your priority....

*Learn to say "**no**".*

Pass the buck and responsibility onto someone who can manage things for you for a while.
If you want to change your life, it starts with *you*.

Use your visualisation techniques to see yourself experiencing and achieving what it is that you have set out for yourself.

Develop the right mindset and approach towards your relationships with people, so that you both mutually benefit from any outcome between you.

*Think **win-win** and have a balanced outlook and healthy respect in all your dealings.*

And that means actually listening to the other side and not just waiting for your chance to cut in with your own views. If you want to be listened to just as much and have your opinions taken into consideration and respected, then you need to learn to listen to the other side too. It will establish a better rapport between you, and ultimately better relationship in the long-run.

And through respecting the other person's side, however different it may be to yours, you could well come up with a much better way of doing something, or even discover an idea that neither of you had initially thought of, just through an amalgamation of two creative minds instead of two separate ones.

*So, by getting a balance of work, me-time, healthy relationships and overall belief in yourself and what you want out of your life, you will become a lot more effective in your chosen aspirations and get the outcomes you desire.*

*"Have the courage of your own convictions.*
*Be strong and assertive.*
*Stand up for yourself.*
*You are valuable and respected.*
*Make a decision and be positive about it".*


…..**turning your resolutions into proper results**…..
*So, you have made a definite decision that the time is right for a change in your life - great!*
However, you know that change doesn't come without making some sacrifices....
And apart from dealing with the practical issues, the most immediate thing that probably needs to happen is to change things on your **inside**.

You have to possess the correct mindset to change and follow through on your dreams for them to come to fruition...

It's all very well deciding that you are going to be a millionaire in a year or sometime in the future, but one of the main reasons that you may never get there is probably because the majority of the time it's all just fantasy and not actually a *feasible* proposition.
Perhaps your goals are just too high in expectations......?

*Obviously you have to start with the fantasy in the first place, otherwise where would you begin?*

But then, you have to move from fantasy mode, to a clear and proper picture of *exactly* where you want to be and by **when**.

You have to physically **see** the achievement, the lifestyle, the feeling, etc., in order to really embrace the actions you need to take to get there.
And that is all about making new habits......

*Everything you say and do is as a result of your habits.*

If you are in the habit of sitting on the sofa watching TV with a burger in your hand, then you will probably only ever be a couch potato..... Sad, but true....
Those people who have toned muscles and are in peak fitness and health, have only got there as a result of the habits they've built up over time - by going to the gym, exercising, eating healthily and having a strong and determined frame of mind......

It's a *life-style*.

Those people who have become an entrepreneurial success and are living the dream, have got there through total habitual focus and dedication.
They practise what they preach.

Whether good or bad, all your habits have become a subconscious blueprint in your brain for it to abide by. However, you **do** have the tools to change things you don't like.
You only need 21 days of repetitive behaviour to form a new habit – negative or positive.
That means you can process just about *anything* into a normal everyday function.
And by making something 'beneficial' into a habit, you can effectively work at shaping and forming yourself into **exactly** what you desire to be.

*Imagine how this could dramatically transform you in just a matter of months – depending on what it is you want.*

By progressing slowly, one thing at a time, you could eventually replace all your negative habits with positive ones....

This means working on replacing one behaviour with another, rather than just wishing something away. Because the more you think about trying to avoid doing something, the more you end up doing it, or wanting it.
That's because you end up focussing on it more and then feel more compelled towards it! You're keeping it at the forefront of your mind, nagging at your brain continuously!
So by putting something else in it's place, your mind will focus on achieving that instead.

*Your brain is an extremely clever piece of equipment!*

Think about all the positive knock-on effects that will undoubtedly accompany that new behaviour as well...
Whatever is good, will encourage more good...

For instance, instead of lying on the couch staring at the box, start researching what you need to do to get started on your dream or improve the circumstances you are currently in.  Whilst you're doing this, tell yourself how fantastic you are feeling, how you are energizing yourself, making yourself into a success, are more mentally alert and alive and feeling great about your future!

Transfer any thoughts you may be having from negative to positive and keep telling your brain you are doing something good, and gradually change that bad habit.
Keep instilling your new behaviour and thoughts into your daily life-style - make it part of your routine, so after a while, it just becomes a natural thing you do or thought you have!

*Imagine how many times you can do this and start transforming your life. You have the absolute potential to turn into something you have longed to be for years.*

How empowering is that?!

But, obviously nothing happens overnight, so never give up.......
Don't delude yourself into thinking that things will happen straight away - it's a journey to successful change you're going on, which takes time.

It entails shifting those old 'fixed' habits and finding new neurological pathways in your brain, so you develop a brand new mindset and outlook.

Start yourself off with a plan of how you want your life to look and feel in 6 months time, making a list of what you need to do in order to get there.
Make sure you put in place a structure that you can follow, with good preparations to help motivate you, especially when you are having 'off' days - as this will help to keep you going.

Visualise exactly how you want your day and life to be and imagine yourself living it out, feeling stimulated, excited and impelled to take on the world!

Do some meditation or deep breathing and really fill yourself with the *absolute certainty* that you are going to get there and your life will be saturated with everything you deserve – and really *feel positive about your choices*.

If other people can do it, so can you!

Remember not to overdo the amount of things you want to change in one go! It takes 3 weeks to form a new habit, so don't overload yourself with too many changes at once.

Little by little you will gradually achieve what you want to create in your life and turn them into the results you desire.
Pat yourself on the back for each little thing you accomplish.

*Use every step as part of your journey and make sure you enjoy it!*

### …..just keeping a routine helps keep you strong….
*Having a to-do list and ticking things off as you go gives you a wonderful sense of achievement, no matter how small the task.*
Believe it or not, this small action could be crucial to your emotional well-being, because it gives you a sense of worth and productivity.

Flailing around aimlessly without any structure or meaning in your life can cause depression and apathy.

Look at your days and see if you can instil some kind of routine and get your life back on track towards purpose and fulfilment.

Your empowerment relies on it.....

*You will feel the benefit instantly.*

**…...keeping focussed on your own wonderful goals....**
*If you want to flow through your life more effortlessly and easily, making it less of a struggle, then the action of setting goals can help facilitate this.*
It will get you on the road to realising your true purpose and in the process, give you a wonderful feeling of satisfaction.
It may seem obvious, but you must make sure that when setting your goals, they do actually have some *real* importance and value to you.

Are they appropriate to your success and your personal life....?

There might be a certain amount of procrastination that goes along with this exercise, because whilst you're thinking through things, you could have a sense of hopelessness, depression or even a feeling of being overwhelmed, and this in turn, could distract you *away* from the process.
This is quite normal and could even provide some valuable clues as to why you avoid getting what you want in life.

Here are some steps to follow to help you set your goals - *make it as fun as you can!*

Write down your goals under subject headings, such as, *'personal growth'*, *'work and career'*, *'relationships'*, *'finances'*, *'leisure'*, *'lifestyle'*, *'creativity'*, etc.
Follow it with what you have in your life at present, what you would like to change and what you want to improve for the future.
Remember, this is totally adaptable and subject to change at any time in your life, as you and your business grow and develop.

Be as adventurous, imaginative and outrageous as you like - *as though you could have anything in the world*, <u>without exception</u>.

*Don't let anybody put you off.....*

Once you have whittled your goals down, you can put them into time-scales of 6 months, 1 year and 5 years time.
Make your aims *realistic and achievable* in the time frame you have given yourself, otherwise you run the risk of them not being accomplished, and you will just feel like you have failed.

If you don't achieve them however, don't give yourself a hard time and give up.
Just decide if this really is a <u>good</u> goal for you and reframe it, or give it up and let it go.
Sometimes this happens in life.....

It may be hard to realise that you are not actually going to be *'something'* – but it is life's way of making some space to be just exactly what you *should* be and you probably need the time to pursue that particular path instead.....

Sometimes you need several goes at things before you realise just *exactly* what you *do* want out of your life, or how you *truthfully* feel about certain aspects and facets of your existence.

Acknowledge all goals that you *do* achieve, rewarding yourself each time you do and making sure you realise that *you have done something wonderful*.

Whatever you do, don't give yourself *far* too much to do.

Otherwise, you can get too stressed about achieving it all and then never actually accomplish anything, other than a big headache and a horrible feeling of non-attainment!

So, make sure you set goals that are good for you and that feel *right and possible*.

Sometimes, you just need to work on one thing at a time. With specific focus, you can get more done than trying to do too many things at once and achieving very little.

Remember, life is meant to be enjoyed and this goal-setting is supposed to be helping you to get what you want out of life, *not* hindering your progress.

Don't be unrealistic and set your goals far too high, or for something that *someone else wants* from you and not what *you* really want..

You need to truly desire it **yourself**.

All this should be pleasurable and make you feel uplifted, motivated, challenged and fulfilled.
If you feel pressure, then it just isn't right!

Now you can make up some strong and clear affirmations accordingly – remember - as if your goals have *already* been achieved.
This helps you keep assertive and forward moving.

"*I* **AM** *achieving my ultimate goal......*" (make yours relevant to *you*).

Another idea that may help you is to make up a '*treasure map*' of exactly what you want in life.

It's like a mood-board filled with colour and pictures, photos, images, writings, artwork of your desires, etc., so you have something physical that you can look at that reminds you of where you want to be in life, *with all your goals - both career-wise and personally,* **totally fulfilled**.

You can make one for each area of your life, like your career, health, relationships, etc., or one big map of everything – with you in the middle looking the epitome of success, health, wealth and happiness.
Make sure you put it in a prominent place where you can look at it regularly.

All these little tricks will keep you totally empowered to reach your goals, feel great and have a wonderful sense of purpose and value.

*No time.*
*Tired. Sore. Dirty workout clothes. Blisters.*
*It's too hot. Don't like sweating.*
*Too many bags to carry.*
*Hard day at work. Great day at work.*
*I'll eat less today.*
*Need a break. Need a reward.*
*Just one day off.*

*Excuses will always be there for you. Opportunity won't.....*


**.....so, let's use some self improvement tools.....**
*If you are looking to improve your personal development so you can attain higher success and fulfilment, there are some more approaches you can use to guarantee results.*

Writing down your thoughts and daily activities can have a hand in helping you make sense of yourself and facilitating your own enhancement and improving self-confidence.

Meditation can help significantly, because it reduces stress and helps you process any thoughts more easily that are causing you unease. Additionally, it can bring about good physical health by encouraging a lower heart rate, aiding sound sleep and speeding up recovery from any illness you may have had.

*Having a balanced mind is obviously an excellent starter in self-improvement and your empowerment.*

Being balanced is essential for your growth.
Everything you do and think will have an impact on everything else in life. So you need to be emotionally, mentally and physically 'fit' in order to drive your personal growth and thereby achieve your goals.

*Being well-rounded will help you feel more secure in your journey.*

You may not believe it, but most successful people are only as intelligent as the average person.

The simple difference is that they *expect* higher attainment, and as such, have a mindset akin to that. Their self-belief and perseverance is all the knowledge they need to push themselves forward in life.

*They expect it to happen and it usually does*, because all that expectation and belief converts itself into the action required to achieve it.

Obviously, knowing what you *do* want and what your goals are, are vital ingredients in getting to where you want to be, so writing down the objectives and strategies to get you there is essential to that success. It will give you a clearer picture of what needs to be done and how to go about building and achieving those expectations.

With every action and individual goal achieved, no matter how small, you will be one step closer to achieving your success and ultimate happiness.

Influence your subconscious mind through your positive affirmations in order to advantageously affect your personality, disposition, attributes and life as a whole, so you have the right mindset for that success.

Write out and recite on a regular basis all those affirmations that are relevant to each area of your life.

*The more you ingrain your positive affirmations into your brain, the stronger you will be in reaching your ultimate aims and life-style.*

***Write down anything you have achieved every day -
no matter how small the achievement!
You can then look back on it and
see how much progress you have made.
Do a little bit every day and you'll get there in time.
Don't rush - everything comes to those who wait.
But you do need to move in a
positive forward direction to get there.....***

**......how your values improve and empower your life.....**
*Your values will have an enormous impact on how you conduct your life.*
They will also have an impact on what kind of path you should genuinely be following.....
Are you actually living according to your own true feelings, or just those you have adopted from conditioning throughout your life?

It's almost a certainty that your life will be dictated by those influences from childhood to adulthood via your relationships with your family, particularly your parents, your colleagues, friends and those who have had a dominance in your relationships.

The choices you have made over those years have probably been determined by the values you have picked up from that conditioning and set of circumstances, but *are they the real, true you...?*
You may have built a foundation on them, *but you may also be rejecting your own internal values as a result.*

During this process, you will have determined the direction your life has gone in – including your career, your activities and your relationships. Some of which may have been chosen for you.....without you even realising it – *due to the values you have taken on as a result of this conditioning.*

Have you actually become that entrepreneur you have had buried deep down inside?
Have you gone on that course you've always yearned to do?
Have you achieved that position you deeply feel you'd be excellent at?
The biggest question of all that comes out of this is - *'are you truly happy in your current situation'*?
Have the values you have used up till now, brought you to where you want to be, or at least on the road to it...?

If you are at the point where you are really considering what meaning you have in life, what your connection is with the world and questioning your success and life fulfilment, *you may want to challenge yourself and the values you currently own or have 'adopted'.*

You may decide it's time to be honest with yourself and identify just exactly where your true values lie, particularly if you want to make the very best out of yourself as a person, so that you can continue to progress in a manner that has *true* meaning to you.

If it has been instilled in you that you *must* make as much money as possible and this has lead you on a path of pursuing material riches – possibly to the detriment of your health and sanity, when in fact, deep down inside, all you want to be is a yoga teacher, then you know your values have been *totally misplaced and your true path has been distorted.*
This applies to *any* characteristic you live by.

For example, living the epitome of 'made-up' beauty with all it's accompanying aspects because you have been *told* this is the best way to 'appear', when actually all you *really* want to do is slob out on a farm raising animals; or if you have been striving hard and slogging your heart out to get to the top of the tree in your profession just to gain status – exactly as Dad did, when your own dream is to run a little cottage industry of your own..... are all a conditioning and restrictive pathway that has been forced on you by someone else, and is therefore ***not*** your true calling.

These roads all probably came with fierce competitive stipulations and disciplines, alongside rewards and punishments for a job well done or poorly performed.
Eventually, over time, as it has all been drip fed into your soul, you have become something you're not – **by default**!

So, ask yourself, what values in particular do you think were instilled in you as a result of your upbringing?
Is what you do now who you really are?

As you are fiercely climbing that corporate ladder, are you secretly thinking that you just want to teach others?
These 2 career choices hold completely different values, for obvious reasons.

Are you engaging in activities that truly reflect your inner wishes?

Are you spending time on the golf course socialising with the hoi-poloi, when you would rather be using that spare time and energy helping out some charity? If so, then what are you doing with your life?

Another big question is, how do you spend your money - on material objects or frivolous jollys? Would you much rather be donating it to philanthropic and worthy causes that make you feel wonderful inside?

Clearly then, you are not living to your *true* values....

Have you even given yourself the time to reconsider your values, or just like these examples, have you spent all your life drifting along living the values of those you grew up with?
If you do actually feel totally dissatisfied with your life, then the chances are, you are not living to your values, you are just going along with your adopted ones.

*This is not living an empowered life.*
This is living a *false* life.
A life that is not the *real* you....

Is it time to re-evaluate and modify your values and start living a more fulfilled life?
Why not make the most out of your life?
Why not? It's yours after all..!
Your choice.....
Live dissatisfied or live happy?
Superficial or real?

Just because you may have grown up in a culture of 'success' that is known by power, money, being attractive and popular, or on the complete flip-side, 'contempt' that is identified as being poor, ugly and unpopular, it doesn't mean that you have to live by these definitions *forever and a day.....*
By applying a completely different mindset, you have many opportunities to change this state of play and live by your *own* values, create your *own* chances, empower yourself and define *your individual* path towards your *own* personalised meaning and destiny.

Remember, 'success' means both inside AND outside.

Determine your *own criteria for your success,* so you can actually cope with the movements of life and be strong, steadfast and more driven in your decision-making.

If you know who you are through your own values, then you will be more focussed in your priorities and in being so, more secure in everything you do and closely treasure.

You can list down all the values that are important to you in order of priority, such as achievement, adventurousness, assertiveness, balance, being the best, belonging, calmness, cheerfulness, excellence, expertise, fairness, faith, family, fidelity, fitness, focus, freedom, fun, stability, strength, success, support, etc.

This course of action will show you just what you really do value *most* in life, as well as giving you the precious information you need to set your intentions for life.
It will also give you some insight into whether you are actually *living* within your own values now or not.

If you need to gain skills and qualifications to attain your goals, by writing things down you will see more fully, exactly what decisions need to be made to develop and achieve them.
With this knowledge, you will be in a much better place to judge what is right for you.

You may have some difficulty in setting your values, perhaps because of challenging confrontations or unrealistic expectations, so you may be forced into making preferences between certain areas, but as you list you can decipher from your deeply-held priorities, just what you would be willingly to give up, and what your top values are that you would *never relinquish* under any circumstances – those that you *genuinely* want to follow through and actually live life by.
It will then become glaringly obvious that there are things you want *more* than others.

But this is a start and it doesn't necessarily mean that you will never get everything you want.

This list of wants and wishes will always be a movable feast and there will come a time in life when those things you can't actually have *right now,* will become more reachable and attainable later.

Your list of values may be easy to just write down, but the hard work comes when you have to put things *into action to get them in place.*

Some decisions may upset the apple-cart – either with yourself and/or those close to you - but for the sake of your own beliefs, they will need to be confronted in order to get to your ultimate destination.
You will need to be strong to look these situations straight in the eye.

*But whatever values come out on top - these are what you should spend* **most** *of your time pursuing.....*

These are the real you......

If you can see that you are spending too much time on the least values highlighted in your list, you know you are not living as you *truly* should and you need to take action!

Once you have gone through the process and found your values, stay anchored to who you *really* are and what you really believe - matching your values with your behaviours as much as you possibly can.

Choose your own career, your own ideas, your own path to peace and happiness....

Put aside the voices of other people's values and tune totally into your own, listening to your own inner voice and put a real meaning to who you authentically are.
Remember, this is about your *own* personal morality, integrity and self-respect.

Be brave!
*Feel empowered!*

Enjoy a more fulfilling journey. Be ready to evolve and mature as your life goes on.

*If you are living by your own true values, you will feel so satisfied and fulfilled, live with a clear head and conscience and remain connected to the real meaning and purpose of your life – forever.....*

**…...what a life coach can do for you.....**
*Life coaching is all about engaging with you to achieve results through action.*
You can write and think to your hearts content about the changes you are going to make in your life, but without doing any of it – it sits on the page or in your head, dormant, useless and without any power.

*Of course, without action, nothing will change – everything stays the same.*
All the dreams and self-belief in the world will not come to fruition if you just sit on those thoughts and do nothing....
Your dreams of achieving that ultimate goal will stay buried in your soul - wasted and inactive.

If you cannot motivate yourself to get into action, or you know you need to change but are unsure of how or what you really want or need, then perhaps with the help of a Life Coach, you will be able to change your mindset and become empowered to live your optimal life, *once and for all.*

Skilled in talking through your situation and circumstances so they can understand why you are in the position you are in, they will identify and design strategies that focus and motivate you into moving towards a better life and where you want to be. They will be committed to keeping you on track along the way, as you achieve your goals step by step.

Although a Life Coach is not your therapist or counsellor, it may well feel like you are being 'healed' when, through their help, you start *'living'* again. However, they are not necessarily concerned about your past, or short-term solutions, but more about taking measures to *work towards your future.*

*In doing so, you will be challenged and have to be honest with yourself.*

**But**, it will stimulate your senses and actions as your life coach guides you through a very personal process that they set up for you. You will begin to become stronger and feel your life evolving into something more creative, happy, organised and empowered.

Your coach will help you to accept who you truly are and as such, move forward into making goals for yourself to progress towards. They'll be able to get you balanced so you are not constantly striving for perfection, but are enthusiastically embracing the supportive and constructive actions you need to take.

They can make you believe that *anything is possible* (it is!), and help you to lay out in front of you what your life ambitions and desires are, lifting your self-esteem and confidence, in order to recognise what you have already achieved and reward yourself as such.
If you need to become more healthy, then they will help you to embrace the fact that doing exercise is a huge step on your road to success, keeping not only your body, but your mind, at optimum levels.

They can help you see the wood for the trees and get you working gradually on one thing at a time, instead of you having a head full of so many things you want to do, that thinking about them all is just too exhausting and you end up procrastinating and doing nothing instead!
You will be able to stretch your mind and capabilities to embrace challenges and complete the tasks set for you successfully.

*You will become really motivated so you look at life far more optimistically, knowing that you have a real and happy future ahead of you.*

Sometimes your coach will use 'visualisation' techniques (seeing yourself doing something and succeeding) to achieve all of this. It will give the strength to have the courage of your convictions and follow your ambitions through, whilst on the journey to your ultimate desires.

You will begin to feel your place in the world and how you contribute to your community, how your relationships work and how to be comfortable with yourself as a unique individual.

*You will like yourself, feel contented and proud of your successes.*

And then, because you like yourself, you will like others around you, you will feel self-respect and realise respect for others too.
Life will feel enjoyable.
Your everyday tasks and actions will make you feel good as you make plans and take steps towards a successful, fulfilling and rewarding life.
Whether for personal or business achievements, your Life Coach will take you through a life transition and balance out your life so that you can enjoy achievement, as well as peace and contentment. With a structure, support, sounding board and proper focus in place, you will end up accomplishing a lot more and making better decisions than you may be able to do alone.

*All being well, you will then sit in a wonderful position of empowerment that you can use to push yourself forward and stand tall.*

You will feel positively able to face more challenges, deal with stressful situations and instil a new life-balance that is personal to you and your own success.
All the Coach will ask for is that you be <u>committed</u> to changing aspects of your life, so you can make it better and more enriched.

*Unlocking the door to your ultimate life will be the key to enablement and empowerment, as you open your mind and make the journey to your true desires.*

**....are you someone that actually needs the benefits of a life coach.....**
*So, if you don't think you can start making those changes you want on your own, then maybe you could greatly benefit from a Life Coach.*
Perhaps you don't have a close support network, you find it difficult to get into the right mindset, you allow procrastination and frustration to get in the way of trying to move on, you are fearful of

change or you just cannot let go of attachments that keep blocking your progress.
Then consulting a Life Coach may be just what you need to give you that leg up to get you going on your path to achieving what you want in life, including a healthy dose of empowerment.

*If you need help – get it!*

No-one needs to be ashamed that they can't do '*it*' on their own......

You may need that extra injection of willpower to jump-start you into the right mindset for self-control and moving on to a better life, so a Life Coach is one way to go for it.

If you are truly committed to your own success and want to make sure you get the most out of life, fulfil your potential and start living as the true you, then the personal support you can get from a life coach, will help you develop your strategy and encourage you on your road to personal growth, and make a positive difference to your outlook and future.

If you feel like the direction of your life is being dictated by your job or well meaning friends and family, or you don't always feel supported, then perhaps it's time to find more effective help elsewhere.
You may well be interested in your job but just cannot get passionate about it, or you even feel stuck in an unfulfilling position because your innate skills are just going to waste or are being overlooked.
You should feel proud of your experiences and abilities, so it could be time to open up your possibilities and see opportunities for what they are.
You should be making the most out of your study and training.

*Take yourself on a personal development journey and surpass all of your own expectations, reprogramme yourself and regain your energy and enthusiasm for life.*

You need to be heard and feel valued and seen for who you really are.
Your skills need to be honoured and you need to unlock all of your

potential and allow your inner light to shine through.
Get your goals and life on track.
Study and train more if you need to reach certain goals to make you feel happy and satisfied.
Think about how you can do things differently to regain your confidence.

**See it as a lifetime <u>investment</u>.**

Continuous development is important and can only benefit you and those you come into contact with either professionally or personally.

You need to believe in yourself and start to expand your horizons.

*Don't expect it to be an easy quick fix – nobody is lucky enough to have that magic wand.*

But every successful person knows that it takes time, energy and involves a lot of research.

Use modern technology to your advantage. So much is mobile nowadays that you can easily work on the go, learn, research and spend time outside away from the desk and still get on with developing your life.

If you want to move your life forward and reach your highest potential, you must realise that work will need to be done, with new challenges, different perspectives, motivation and commitment.

*Get things clear in your mind, devise a plan that will help you move forward to obtain your goals.*

If you are stuck, then find a life coach or someone who can help you to focus on your objectives and make you see the wood for the trees.

You may need to challenge those belief systems and behaviour patterns that could be keeping you from moving forward, so you become aware of what you are doing and it helps you change things, if necessary. Your life coach can assist you with this.

Go on a journey of change and enjoy every second of it, as you begin to find the answers to achieving your new life.

*Become strong and powerful in your own skin, moving into a wider and better way of living and reaching your highest potential.*

Extract your life out of inertia.....

### …..using your creativity to build intelligence....
*If you're thinking about progression and growth, then being creative can be extremely important.*
So don't underestimate it or view it as something that is just a waste of your precious time.
Being creative is a great aide and key function in problem-solving and making decisions, something that on average, you can spend 50-60% of your work-life doing.
So the better you get at thinking up creative ways to solve problems, the more effective you will be.
Your problem-solving ability will determine how much you can gain in status, esteem and recognition.
By being more productive, better, faster and performing more proficiently, becoming more intelligent through creativity is one way to get to the top of your game.

There's a chance that your creative intelligence is buried and needs to be tapped into and opened up more fully. Most people really function on very little creativity, because they fail to use their hidden reserves.

The brain is a powerful organ and people can always learn new ideas and new skills – by forming new or stronger connections between nerve cells.
Therefore fully use your mental potential instead of spending too much time on the same old day to day tasks that you do all the time - never allowing yourself to stretch out of your comfort zone!

By tapping into that enormous reserve, you can literally do anything you really want in life!

*Get some help with being more creative if you need it and start to become the genius you really are!*

*"Avoid unhappiness – look out for triggers and steer clear".*

**…..time to reorganise your mental clutter....**
*There are many times in life when you've got too much running around in your head.*
You've got so much that needs to be done or addressed, that you get mental overload and cannot see the wood for the trees.
The trouble is, the longer it all stays there clogging up your brain, the more stressed you get about it all and in the end, you probably either procrastinate like nobody's business, or do nothing at all - because you just can't face it.
Next thing – you just can't sleep through worrying!

The only thing to be done is to reorganise those thoughts and put them in some semblance of order. Once you can see it all in a list on paper, you can then prioritise those thoughts and actions, even eliminate some, pass on some responsibility or defer things for much later.

*You can then breathe again!*

You need to make some space in your head, some room to think and get things running in a much more cohesive and manageable fashion.
Too much information does not make for a happy person!
So.... get all those jobs and issues out of your overflowing mind and onto some paper.
Everything!
Let your pen run wild. Get it out of your head once and for all. If you can't think of everything at once, then get started and add to the list as you remember things. Even add in events you know are coming up.

*It will be a blessed relief!*

Title everything into categories, such as *work, well-being, household, personal projects* – you'll know which tasks fit where. Have a page for each. This will provide importance to certain areas and also give you a sense of balance.

Once you have written everything down on each page under each heading, you can then reorganise them into order of priority.

As you do this, so you will be going through the process of clearing out all your mental clutter and also give yourself all the reminders you need for all your tasks at the same time. This will make it all the more manageable and you will be able to see exactly what needs time and attention.

You can then begin to farm out some of the tasks to others that can help, like work colleagues or family and friends. You can also start allocating the amount of time each area requires and on which date you will be able to deal with those tasks.

*Be realistic about the amount of time things take.*
Add extra time for contingency!

There will always be something that comes up that will get in the way of your plan. Don't forget to add in time for your own well-being and leisure pursuits, as well as all your personal and household activities into your schedule.
You will be able to move things around if they are less important, but make sure you get those with high priority up to the top of your list.

There is absolutely no point in not building in everything or thinking you can do things in half the time it actually takes, because if you cannot manage it, you will only defeat the object completely and end up being even more stressed than before!

Once you have got your action list sorted into *'high priority'*, *'important'*, *'needs to be done soon'*, *'pass on to someone else'*, *'general'*, etc., then you need to start getting on with it....!

Have faith in your list and when you decide to spend time on completing one of the tasks, forget about anything else on your list and focus entirely on that particular job in hand. You cannot do a job quickly and well if you only have half an eye on it because you are worrying about all the other things that still need to be done!

If you think of something else that needs to be done along the way, then write it on your list – get it out of your head-space, so you keep your mental clutter as clear as possible. Put it in order later, after you have finished what you are doing at that time.

*But, remember to be flexible – this is a moveable feast.*

It will change around naturally – but keep abreast of it all at the same time. It is a guide that can be altered.
There is no need to think that it is set in stone and everything HAS to be done according to your schedule, otherwise you will defeat the object again and only get stressed because things aren't happening exactly as laid out.
Be sensible with it.

The important thing to remember is that it's all out of your head and formed into some semblance of order. You now know what needs to be done and when – with flexibility.
As you go along – make sure you pat yourself on the back for each job well done!

*Keep yourself motivated and build up confidence in what you have done and are achieving.*

The more control you have over this, the more empowered you will feel.

*And in doing so, your overall well-being will naturally and automatically improve and your life will feel less stressed, you will sleep well, and you will really feel like you are getting somewhere again.*

Good luck!

***Read something motivating every day.
In doing this, you will constantly keep your mind at
the forefront of getting things done,
being happy, committed and determined
to achieve whatever you have in
your mind, soul and body that you need from life.***

**……stop procrastinating and start living your dreams…..**
*Procrastination is the devil of your goals.*
If you really want to get the most out of your life and actually have that wonderful feeling of achievement, one that makes you stand tall and proud and feel totally empowered, then you need to learn how to stop procrastinating and start getting on with your plans. Procrastinating can actually waste an average of 3 years of your life, or approximately 70 minutes per day!

*Imagine what you could get done in that time.*
You could write a book, make an outfit or take another step towards your dream goal.

A good percentage of people actually waste more than 2 hours putting things off and women tend to do it more than men. We procrastinate more when we're younger and this gradually lessens as we get older.
It stands to reason that when you duck out of doing things, it's highly likely to be things you don't like doing. You even avoid doing things that need an action that may lead to important results!

Making a list and ticking things off as you go is highly rewarding and is also really beneficial when it comes to focussing on your future goals more.
Try some of these tips to get your actions under-way…..

If you have something that definitely needs doing, tell someone that you are going to do it by a certain date.
By announcing that deadline, you are immediately telling both them AND yourself that you *have* to get it done – and if you don't, they will be at your back nagging you to do it!

Make a list and plan to get the most important things done <u>before</u> anything else.
You may need to prioritise your list to do this first.
Some things may *seem* urgent, but they may actually not be. Emails and phone-calls can be left to a point in the day that you choose *yourself*. Just because the phone rings, doesn't mean you have to answer it there and then. If you do, you may get distracted or side-tracked into doing something else. In which case, you are straying off your track and you won't get that *important* thing done.

*Stay focussed.*
*Getting your essential stuff done will make you feel great!*

When something needs doing, get a self-affirmation going, like "**_DO IT NOW!_**".
Saying this over and over again will really get it into your head and make you get on with it.

As you are going through your tasks, if you give yourself little rewards at certain points, it will help keep you motivated, i.e. having a coffee when you've done an hour, going for a quick walk in the fresh air when you finish 20 pages, etc.

Get your weekend planned sometime midweek. Your quality of life can improve just by you scheduling it!

*Try and stay away from those people who take up your time when you don't need it.*

Rehearse something positive to say to them if you just can't avoid them, so you don't appear rude. Think about how you work best at certain times of the day – you may be a morning, evening or night person.
Schedule all your important stuff into a time slot where you know you will accomplish it more efficiently then.
It's important learning to just get on with things, as this will obviously help you get all sorts achieved and in the long run, *make you feel on top of your life.*

People who write down their goals are a third more likely to achieve than those who just *think* about their ambitions. Putting those goals down will immediately give you a sense of the **bigger** picture. By affirming that '*this is where I want to be next month, in a year, or 5 years time*', it will focus you and give you a sense of control and motivation to get you there.

*So, if you want something – get writing!*

Break down where you want to be and how you're going to get there.

Get a sense of your skills first by homing in on what you're proud of – **all** your achievements. *Celebrate what **you** made happen* – however small!

Do some mind-mapping. Without stopping, write down fast and think **big**, all the things you want in the next 5 years.

Go wild and outrageous! No-one's judging you!

Put down all the things you'd like to change from family, career, health, social life and include everything you'd like to accomplish with them.  Rate them all in order of importance – work out your top 5 goals.

Then pick 2 you can start work on *straight away.*

Break each area down into manageable 'mini' goals, so you can see what needs to be done without it overwhelming you. Plot achievable steps into your diary and make sure you take it with you everywhere, to remind you of your action plan towards fulfilling your dreams.

Be flexible and do it your *own* way.

Don't ever think you have failed.
Just look at your list of achievements and remind yourself how great you are.

Keep your list fresh and up to date by doing more mind-mapping sessions every now and then to keep you ahead of your game, and to make you feel alive, creative and mentally alert.

*Stop procrastinating and always feel strong in the confidence that you will accomplish your goals and **whatever** you want to in life.*

**Don't get overpowered by emotions that blinker your common sense....**

**....are your habits ruining your progress....**
*Habits form when your brain is triggered, a behaviour is formed and remembered, and then it becomes routine.*
Behaviours you repeat form patterns that are carved into your brain's *neural pathways*. Once it becomes that way, your brain naturally goes into automatic and then less thinking is involved, giving it less work to do.

When your behaviour gets to this point, you have space in your brain to devote to doing something else at the same time. This lets you concentrate on that additional activity more fully, like both parking *and* listening to the car radio, for instance.
If you were to conduct a similar action whilst on holiday where you are away from the normal 'cues' for that particular habit, your behaviour is more likely to change and you would probably break certain patterns and habits in the process.

*This is why it is easier to change the way you do something and also to form new habits whilst you are on holiday and which hopefully, you would be able to carry on with when you return home.*

You can break your habits if you want to, by getting to understand them properly, with all their cues and rewards, and then changing your behaviour accordingly.
Half the time, you may not even realise what it is you are actually doing with these habits, because they have become so automatic.

*You could go on quite blindly without even thinking.*
You just need to get into a different routine and be <u>conscious</u> of it.

Because old habits are hard to break and new habits take some time to form, a lot of effort, commitment and motivation needs to take place if you *really* want to change bad habits and incorporate new, good ones.
*But, it's certainly going to be worth it in the end.*

So, through simple repetition and a little bit of self control and willpower, you *can* form new, positive behaviours.
You will need a motivator as a guide to get you there and keep you going – something that is important to you and that you are

passionate about - the achievement of a sought-after target, like a new exercise programme, for instance.

Then make your decision with a *realistic* aim for change and create an action plan that's relevant to implementing your new habit.
If your goal is too big to manage in one go, break it down into bite-sized and manageable steps to get you there.

*Don't worry if you fall off the wagon every now and then, just get straight back on it and continue on with your plan.*

If you need help from a third party, like a therapist, coach, colleague or trainer, then get it.
It's all about you succeeding in your mission.

*Imagine how empowered you will feel when you conquer all your new and positive habits you have put in place!*

Knowing that you have self-control over just one specific thing in your life will probably spur you on to changing or improving other things, because it gives you the ability to take the initiative and sustain your efforts over time.
It's good to know that if you *do* have the willpower, you can have even better relationships and will be more adept at empathising with others – which can only be good for your well-being.

*Self-esteem is a wonderful thing.*

When you've got it, you value yourself.
You respect yourself.
You have confidence in your ability.

So use your new empowered mind and strength to replace those unwanted, old, annoying and debilitating habits with some new, invigorated, inspired and motivating ones instead.
You can revamp your whole well-being in this way.

*And most importantly, be **conscious** about what you are doing!*
Be **aware** of yourself and stop if you think you are going down the wrong route again, and then re-set your new behaviours in place instead. After a few attempts your brain will recognise your better

patterns and begin doing *those* on automatic instead.
Then you can make space for more and more new and wonderful traits, until you are living your ultimate life as your ultimate self.

*How empowering is that....?!*

### ....letting go of those negative attachments...
*Having 'attachments' to wonderful things that make you happy, comfortable and loved gives you a special feeling of warmth and contentment.*
However, if you have an attachment to something negative and unhealthy that is totally holding up your life, then it is probably time to let go of it, in order to make space for you to progress forward and follow your dreams.

This negativity can get in the way of your growth and conducting your life effectively.

It could be a relationship with a certain person that's bringing you down, or a habit that you've got into a rut with but can't seem to shake off even though you know full well it's bad for you, or that awful feeling of something inside pulling you down, but you just keep allowing it to clog up your mind and get to you.....

They're all probably frustrating you and you need to be free of them once and for all.
But rest assured - it's just a *process* you need to go through in order to do that and let go.

It's a system for you to commit yourself to if you genuinely want a lot more out of your life, rather than allowing those bad attachments to rule your world, instead of it being the other way round.....!

If you are serious about doing something about it, then you need to start admitting to yourself that this attachment is *actually* a problem. No more denial or drifting along from day to day letting it get you down.

Admitting you have difficulty is the first step to moving on.
There is no need to harbour any shame or guilt about it.

Chances are that there are millions of others out there with exactly the same problem as you – but *you* are the positive one that's about to sort it out......!

Your attachment probably lives in your comfort zone, like a lovely warm blanket you've got used to. Even though you know it's bad for you, you still continue on with it thinking you *need* it in your life, telling yourself that you're better off *with* it and holding onto it for dear life, with some kind of self-satisfaction and control.

*Understand why it is there and why you haven't let go.....?*

In order for you to move past your attachment, you really need to look at how your attachment started, why you let it in, how you became attached to it and whether it is now actually doing you any good or not....?
If it's not actually working for you, it really has *no purpose in your life any more* and needs to be *eliminated*.
You need to seriously tell yourself that you don't need or want it any more.
*It has no truth for you.*

You also need to put yourself in the right mindset for letting it go completely. If you don't you will only *partially* allow yourself to let go and therefore will not be removing it at all.

Plus, you will need to tell yourself that it is getting in the way of your dreams of achieving that all important aim, and it *needs to go* – that's if you *genuinely* want to be in total control of your own life.
If those attachments are making you feel unhappy, anxious, tired, lacking in motivation and so on, then you will not be living a very fulfilling life.
Your empowerment is lost.

Be honest with yourself.
*Without honesty, nothing will change.*

What possibly started out as some kind of temporary relief has now taken over your life and become uncomfortable, causing you anxiety and affecting your happiness and ideas of fulfilling that special dream.

When you get the courage to look it in the face, it will be time to *stop rationalising why you have this attachment*. Stop trying to justify it by thinking it gives you a feeling of satisfaction and makes you feel safe.
Staying in your comfort zone, in other words.....

It's time to accept it's there and *something needs to be done about it.*

If you haven't really thought about your own well-being very much, then *now is the time to concentrate on who you are and what you want to be.*
Do you want a healthy and successful life, or do you want to be taken over by your attachments, bad habits and addictions, and consequential depression?
Start taking care and loving yourself. Shift your focus onto *you* as the priority.
If these attachments are governing you, then the chances are you've fallen out of love with yourself. They've hurt you and the reason they've become bad habits is because you no longer value yourself, and thereby do not feel you're really worth the effort.

*Well, tell yourself you are worth the investment.*
And **believe** it!

Don't think about what you are initiating as an excuse to feel like you are *losing* something. Believe that it's more for your own gain - for your health and freedom and to give yourself joy, happiness and a much better life for yourself.

*So don't see it as loss, but more as a complete benefit to you.*

Think about the control, confidence and self-esteem you will be able to take advantage of, and *not* how you are going to manage without this millstone round your neck....!
Take heart in how you will be able to breath again, live a positive life, smile and laugh at the world, have some peace and feel wonderful!
Feel how much more empowerment you will have and how that will instil so much more optimism in you!

Unchain yourself from the negative attachments and let in some light and space to enjoy your life.

*Be who you are meant to be.*

Give yourself hope.
Heal yourself.
Open up your world to new opportunities and begin doing things you've always wanted to do, but never gave yourself permission.
Believe there's a better life around the corner!
Believe that your ideas and plans *are* achievable.

Awaken all your senses and get in touch with what is on offer, what plans you can make now that you have freed yourself.
No more criticism, feeling stuck or weak, lack of motivation and constant negativity.

*Embrace your new beginnings, possibilities and your positive future!*

Write down all the wonderful things you have to be thankful for. This will help you to appreciate exactly what you *do* have and not just those negative attachments bringing you down and inducing depression.

**Feel glad for them.**

When things get a bit rough and you are finding it difficult, always distract yourself from them. Try not to allow yourself to be pulled down an ever deepening spiral that grips a hold of you.

Take heart in supportive family and friends - people who you know will cheer you up and keep your mind healthy.

If you feel yourself draining, a fabulous way of keeping yourself up is to keep yourself physically fit. It helps mentally and emotionally too and will combat negative thoughts, tiredness, stress and anxiety. You can't be lost in depression if you are bouncing around a lively fitness class!
Keep yourself clear-headed, strong and jubilant with all those happy endorphins that come along with exercise.

Always watch your diet – you are what you eat!
If you eat rubbish, you will feel rubbish.
If you eat good wholesome food, you will feel good.
**Simple**.

Calm your mind and body with deep-breathing. You'll be amazed at how this can really help you.
Yoga and meditation are also amongst the list of good, healthy things to do. A great way of releasing tension.

*Always remember that any changes you make in your life will take time.*

Particularly if it is a habit you have formed and got used to over time. But stick with it. If you fall off the wagon, just get back on it and realise it's a process that will come eventually.
Step by step, little by little.

*Every challenge in life is something new and positive and will bring wonderful opportunities and discovery.*

This is how life is meant to be, so be prepared to embrace it.
Be prepared for the transformation.
A lot of the time, attachments are just a matter of feelings. And feelings do not need to be something that you have to keep hold of forever, or allow to escalate into something that becomes out of control and affects your progress.
You do not need to allow feelings to go from zero to major anger, rage or sorrow.

You can let them go and take control of our own thoughts and reactions without taking them far too seriously.

*Because, by allowing yourself to cling to them, you end up becoming them and then they change your life – usually for the worse.*

If you are not attached to anything, then you naturally have far more freedom.
Freedom to be you.
Freedom to grow and develop.

Freedom to enjoy life and do the things you want to do.
Freedom to achieve the things you want to achieve.

*Freedom to feel like an empowered person who is proud, stands tall and looks life straight in the eye, embraces it and has fun at the same time!*


## The true definition of F.E.A.R - *False Emotions Appearing Real*


### …..step out of your fears….
*How can you be an empowered person if you are crippled by fears...?*
If you feel that your life or progress are being held up or blocked by previous failures, emotional burdens, health issues, other people's influences or any other situation that has made you fearful, then it's high time to move on from that subsequent conditioning and reprogramme your mindset.
These fears need to be eliminated.

You can stand strong and upright and be the person you know you innately should be, when you stop allowing the past to get you down and get in the way.
It probably doesn't feel like it at the time, but fear is actually just an *illusion* – it's your take on how you react to things and how you let them affect you.
They are really just stories that you have built up in your mind and that *you definitely have the power to change.*

You cannot be at peace with yourself or achieve your ultimate dreams when this burden is dogging you at every turn...

*It may take time for you to clear that clutter and reprogramme yourself, but it can be done.*

You just have to open up and allow your mindset to be freed and replace positivity where the negativity once was.

It is not an overnight task, so don't expect it to be.
It has probably taken years for your current conditioning to be firmly

instilled into your psyche and habitual ways, so you cannot expect to reprogramme all of that on a couple of nights sleep!

But, if you *want* to be a different person and achieve things in your life, then you will have to be strong, adamant, ruthless with yourself, committed and motivated.

*You need to start with this in mind and continue to have it in mind at all times.*

Being afraid is something you will obviously come across throughout life.
It would be pretty bland if you didn't get scared every now and then.

But, you don't need to have fear in your gut as part of your *everyday* life, draining your energy and taking over your thoughts, holding you back and *making you live within limitations*.
If you aren't careful, fear can grip your mind, body, soul and spirit and also inhabit your dreams.
You *can't* let it.

If your fears are controlling *you* and not you them, then you need to take a hold of them and learn to deal with them - by facing them and moving *through* them.

Most achievers in life are willing to work and move through their fears. They're dealing with their fears so that they can get where they want to be in life.

But you *can* dissipate your fears, shrink them down to nothing and remove them from being a lingering threat that's stopping you progressing.
You don't *need* to stay in that scary place any more.
There are things that you can do to help yourself, if you are willing.....
Your fears can lose their power over you if you look them in the face and write down *everything* about them. How they started, how they have held you back, what grip they have on you.

Without using any judgement at all, get it all down on paper and have a good look at what you have written.

See them for what they really are.
As you start to understand them, so they will begin to be diluted.

Begin to open up your world and start taking small steps towards facing your fears, by actively doing the things that frighten you. As you do this, bit by bit your courage with grow. Just keep telling yourself that this fear will pass.
And it will!

*You have to trust and have faith in yourself* and you will begin to expand your horizons and gain even more power over your life.
The control will be in *your* hands, **not** the fear's!

Learn to relax more by taking small breaks in your day to put your body into a more calm state, so you can start living as such.
Begin to become aware of your jaw, face, fists and heart-rate, and actively soften and slow them down.......
Become a calmer person.

How many times have you celebrated your achievements?
It's probable that you spend far more time beating yourself up when things go wrong or when you *perceive* things have failed! What message is that sending to your brain?

*Too much negativity and not enough positivity about yourself*!

It's time to strengthen your own belief in yourself by jotting down all the things you have triumphantly accomplished – no matter how small. They are all things in life that you should be celebrating and feeling proud of....even down to when you learnt to ride a bike when you were a child.

Think back and get them all out there on paper.
As you do, you will feel good about yourself and even be inspired by **_you_**!
It will make you motivated to face *any* fears you have, because you can truly see and *know* how strong a person you really are.

Amaze yourself!

If you learn to live in the *present* moment, you will not be thinking or feeling anxious about the past or worrying about what's going to happen in the future, because you will only be concentrating on what is happening **right now,** without hiding behind any negative learnt behaviour.

You can create your own brand new positive stories filled with wonderful expectations and consequences instead.
You have this option in life, because it is *yours* to control.

Instead of thinking about what you *can't* do because of this and that, think about what fantastic things you *can* do.

Life is just a series of challenges to embrace. What an adventure!

Make your fears a ridiculous joke and laugh out loud at them. Make them so silly and stupid in your mind that they are just hilarious to you. As you do this, realise that they aren't really real, just a thought process -*and then take back your power!*

Stop looking for and thinking about negative things.
Spend time away from bad news, bad people, bad situations.
Rather, think *abundantly* – you are <u>rich</u> in mind, soul and spirit.
Start to **celebrate** your life instead.

If you have the means and time, become a generous person. By sharing and giving, you will feel empowered and feel great about yourself for helping someone else and then less emphasis will be put on your fears.

Have a look at others you admire, like great achievers and follow in their path, or their bold life-style.
If they can do it from humble beginnings, why can't you....?
There is no reason why you cannot have that success, that good fortune, that joy, that fantastic lifestyle, that peace.
Focus on this and believe you can do it and be open and accepting of that fact.

Allow your fears to fade into the background as you replace that time and space in your head by learning new things, studying or developing yourself.

Then take action on these things to become truly awesome.

Give yourself a direction. Everyone needs one.
Get your ideas to fruition. Get that plan conquered.

Stand tall and proud and let go of feeling embarrassed and ignored, or constantly feeling like a failure or fearing rejection. Accept that having fears is part of life, but *get past them and move on.*

Help yourself for your own sake!
Help others.....

Passing on your knowledge, being a good leader or guiding people, will help you move on from fears and get you starting to believe more fully in yourself and what you have to offer the world.

*It feels good to help.*
You benefit yourself AND who you are helping. *Win-win!*

Visualise your goal, your destiny, your dream and you will get there. Step-by-step, day by day you will begin to see and experience your ultimate life as you see your transformation unfold before you.

*Your life is a work of art to be enjoyed with creativity and adventure.*

It's all out there to grab hold of.

There's beauty and wonder all around you - in every aspect of life. It's much better to embrace that rather than allow your fears to overwhelm you with tragedy and negativity.
Begin to get back in control of your hopes, dreams, wishes and everyday life!

*Choose to live yours fully.*
Empower yourself.

Take a deep breath and enjoy your journey! It's got to be worth a shot, don't you think?

*Because a life lived in fear, is just a life half-lived!*

**…..start planning your ambitions in your diary....**
*Take the time to plan out your chosen journey properly.*
It will be much better than it just mulling around in your head jumbling up your thoughts and never really getting very far.
By planning it out you will find that things will start moving far more efficiently and quickly than before.

Start by making a '*Mind-map*' of all the steps you need to take in order to achieve your ultimate ambition.
Go mad, that's what this exercise is all about – get it all out of your head, no matter how big or small! Take your time and think of everything...

*This will focus your mind.*

Then have a good look at what you've got down and put it into some semblance of order that makes sense to you realistically.
Then think about the time you will need to dedicate to each individual step that needs to be followed through.

Draw up an itinerary and set it into your diary.
Alternate your tasks and subjects across the weeks to make things more interesting for you to carry out, and so you don't get bored with being stuck on just one job for too long.

Set up reminders with an alarm on your mobile phone scheduler to go off at certain times so you know what's got to be done then. This will be a good prompt to keep you on top of fulfilling your tasks within your planned time-scales.

*Then get on it!*
The fulfilment of your ambition awaits!

Always remember that plans are a moveable feast. Things will happen quite naturally that may get in the way of, or alter your path either slightly or majorly.
Don't let this get you down.

*Go with the flow and get back on-board with your agenda as soon as you can.*

Don't be rigid as this will only cause stress and make you feel like you're out of control - when it's only just a blip.

If major things happen, it may make you reconsider your priorities and the plans you're working towards. This may mean refocussing or rethinking whether your ambition is *really* what you want, or can even cope with.

Maybe you should think about the following things first before you even think of embarking on anything at all....

Think *long-term* – will it work, is this really for you?
Imagine it in the future – how does it look?
How much work and cost is involved?
Is it really achievable?
Can you do it alone or do you need help?
Can you actually afford it?
Do you need to do something smaller to build up some more capital/savings first and then embark on the bigger ambition later?
Is it REALLY what you want in life?
Is this type of business or career really for you?
Are you suited to it or are you just making a rod for you own back?

Be genuinely honest and frank about things. *Don't be delusional.*

This can take a lot of courage and deep thinking.
Have a realistic look at your life, your talents, skills and your priorities.
Also, be pragmatic about not letting go of something that *IS* actually achievable with some time and effort - if that's what you really *do* want.

But, also don't just use the exercise as an excuse to cast aside something that is good and had potential just because you feel lazy, low in self-esteem or have outside forces influencing you, like doubting family and friends who just make it easier for you to think, '*forget it, I cant be bothered*"!

Because if you *do* allow that to happen, you will be losing control and allowing other distractions and influences to be the driver in your life and not your *own* needs, wants, thoughts and ambitions. You will be giving away your empowerment and ultimately your chance to fulfil your dreams and make a better life for yourself.

*And that is not what true living is all about.....*
So make your <u>own</u> ambitious plans.

### …..your horoscope inspiration…..
*Some people may think it's all mumbo-jumbo and that's fine, but there are others that find solace in horoscopes and it gives them inspiration.*
If this is you, then there are times when a horoscope can be very meaningful and have some excellent motivational intention. Some can have really powerful messages in them that really strike a cord and make you think – actually, yes, that *IS* about me and what I want out of my life!

Therefore, there is absolutely no harm in taking that message on-board and letting it help or guide you towards your dream, or even just make you feel happy for the day!

*As long as you don't live and die by it in such a manner that it affects you in a negative way, then use what it has to say to help keep you motivated and inspired.*

Keep those positive messages close by so you can refer to them when you need to, if this is something you feel will comfort you and keep you on track.

Write them down and put them somewhere where they can be seen, so they are kept at the forefront of your mind. Maybe even email the strong messages to yourself, so they can be saved as a reminder of what they mean to you.

*Use the strength of those meanings to feel empowered and uplifted as you go about your daily tasks.*

### …..don't fear the deadline……
*Just the word 'deadline' can make you want to run for the hills...!*
But some people thrive on deadlines and it's a fantastic way of actually getting things done – especially when it comes to the visions you want to fulfil.
Think about when you have something important to get to, like

going on holiday or getting ready for a special birthday party or wedding.....how fast do you move to get everything ready and organised then..?

Well you can also harness that strategy when it comes to your aspirations.

If you learn to use deadlines in a more positive way, they can be extremely powerful, because they get things done, they motivate you into action, they make you creative, they help you manage your workload and you become extremely productive.
They seriously target the goals towards building your dreams......
When used wisely, they are actually a great way to feel in control and on top of things.

Deadlines *drive* you.
They get a *performance* out of you.
They give you *energy*.
Without deadlines, you can tend to slip, slow down, be too much of a perfectionist, procrastinate and even ignore what actually needs to be done.
*Delay, delay, delay*!
Because there is no urgency, why bother now? Later will do.
Then later comes and all of a sudden it's panic and stress, there's people breathing down your neck, including your own internal nagging, you've got nothing done and you're now feeling like a failure.
But you've had all that time to get it done and now it's just wasted, gone forever!
Then other projects and requests come tumbling into the equation and before you know it, you're having to juggle several balls at once!
*Pressure*!
Down goes any feeling of being on top of things and your empowerment is subsequently compromised.

*You don't have to necessarily wait for someone else to give you a deadline, you can set it for yourself, so that you are the one in control.*

All those targets you want to achieve that you have let slip by the

wayside could well be done by putting the deadlines in yourself. That ambition you want to fulfil – start researching it and set a date for when you *definitely* want to have it accomplished by and *stick to it*.
That nagging job that has been staring you in the face every time you sit down to watch TV or play about on the internet – get planning to build it into your routine.

Get dates in your diary for exactly when you want everything done by – and *adhere to them*.

You are the only one stopping yourself!
If you want to achieve these things, then its time for action.

*Your choice...*

Having your deadline will focus and energise you into driving forward and keeping the momentum going.
You *know* you are capable of sticking to deadlines because personal scenario's like the holiday, party, wedding, etc., have already demonstrated it!
You just need to hone that and concentrate it on the tasks you want to fulfil.
Even better, actually reduce the time you need to get something done by – just like when you speed through your work on a Friday to get out of the door to the weekend!

And if you let someone know about your deadline, like a colleague or partner, then you *have* to stick to it.

You're giving yourself no option.

Publicising it in any way makes you more committed. Otherwise, if you don't do anything, you know you won't only be letting yourself down, but others too. It empowers you to get things done and forces you to focus on exactly what's required to get a successful result.

*You don't have the time to procrastinate, delay things or be a perfectionist – you just have to get the job done.*

It's a brilliant strategy.

Everyone loves a challenge and that wonderful feeling of total satisfaction when you complete it successfully.

*And the gain in your heart is worth all the deadlines in the world!*

> ***"Each day is a new journey.***
> ***Make it exciting, interesting and fulfilling".***

**…..prioritise and empower……**
*Sensibly prioritising your tasks is a powerful way to making you a more effective, efficient and smart worker.*
Doing this will inevitably give you more time to engage in all the other activities that you would dearly like to be enjoying, or putting all your aspirational ideas into fruition…..

Listing your tasks enables you to take a look at what order of priority they take and how you can spread that work to best effectiveness.

You can make a list of your duties in priority order:

1. *those that are **vitally important** and must be done otherwise there will be <u>serious</u> consequences.*
2. *those that **really** should be done otherwise there will be a <u>mild</u> consequence.*
3. *those that would be **nice** to get done but <u>nothing</u> will happen if it isn't done right now.*
4. *those that can be **delegated** to someone else thereby <u>freeing</u> you up from the responsibility.*
5. *those that you can just get **rid** of completely, because they really <u>don't matter</u> at all!*

You can head each category however it suits the tasks that need to be done.
Once you've listed all the jobs under each category, you can then prioritise those individual lists according to their level of importance. Within each task, you can break down all the actions required to complete the job.

Once you've got this done, you can begin getting the work completed.

*Discipline yourself to get started straight away and keep at it until each task is finished, ticking off each successful completion as it's achieved – even if you have delegated it out to someone else.*

Give yourself a pat on the back or a treat every time you get the result you want.
*Really feel good that you have accomplished something!*

Your lists will organically change as certain other jobs come up that become important, so you may need to revise them accordingly.

*Once you have achieved the main task of prioritising your lists, you will feel much less cluttered in your head and you will feel extremely satisfied, confident and energised to make great strides upwards to your fulfilling and successful life.*

**…...always have pride in what you do......whatever it is....**
*Whatever role you have in life, be proud of it.*
Being proud will drive you more – even if it is carrying out a menial task.
Doing it well will make you feel good about yourself and in turn the job that you do.

*Every job is useful.*

Without that specific job being performed, the likelihood is that there would be a strong impact on the rest of your organisation or environment that you work and live in.
For example, if you didn't clean the toilets, then people wouldn't be able to use them, or they'd have to suffer being in a dirty environment.
This would probably make them unhappy, causing a negative effect on their whole day and that would then, quite probably, be passed on to others around them - all because of their bad experience.
If you didn't do the filing, the whole workforce would probably be in chaos.
If you didn't pick up the rubbish on the street, the town would be in a right mess and there would probably be uproar.

If you didn't serve at that table, the restaurant wouldn't be able to run.

This doesn't just apply to lower paid jobs, even if you are high up in the corporate world, you will still have lots you need to endure throughout your day.
Perhaps you have to meet people you don't really have a lot in common with, just for the sake of increasing the company profit margin. But you still have to make sure that your role is undertaken with grace and the right mindset, otherwise the organisation would probably collapse.

No matter what your role is, it will be of service to people in some way or other, from the lowest to the highest and everything in between. It's what makes the world go round!.....

Whether it's you or someone else, these roles have their place and importance in society.

People take it for granted that these jobs will be done so they can live and work in relaxed and pleasant conditions.

*So, instead of thinking about your job as just a low rung on the ladder, or a right pain in the backside, do it well, be proud, make people appreciate you and your role and do it to the best of your ability.*

You will go home feeling satisfied having done a good days work and earned your money, feeling better for having served others in some way and that you have contributed positively to your community and the world.

*Give out and it will be given back to you – in some way or another. Be proud and feel empowered by that pride.*

**"Life will throw you curve balls.**
**They test you, but as long as you have your health and sanity, you can genuinely move on.**
**Leave the past negativity behind you and look forward to a renewed, more fulfilling and experienced life".**

### …..is trying to be perfect ruining your life….
*Trying to make everything perfect in your life can be a definite source of stress.*
If you are a perfectionist, you probably spend so much energy monitoring yourself and others so closely, that you don't give yourself any room for mistakes – it's just not part of your make-up.

Everyone slips up, but part of being a perfectionist is that you believe that, by turning your whole world perfect, you can minimise or avoid any of the pain that goes with blame, judgement and shame.

However, rather than striving to be or do your best or it being part of your normal growth, it could actually just be a shield you're putting up...

When going through life thinking you need to be this or that to be accepted, or to please others, or to be what others think you *should* be, the quest for perfectionism becomes very exhausting and unrelenting.

*You are living a very false life while you put on your mask and say "Yes" and "No" in all the wrong places.*

You go through life being something you're not, totally losing sight of who you really are and this can have a really negative impact on you.

Perfectionism has been linked to OCD, alcoholism, anorexia, chronic anxiety, social inadequacy and self destruction.
There needs to be some flexibility in your approach rather than being rigid and fixed.

*If you were to just embrace your imperfections and vulnerability, you would end up living a far healthier life mentally and emotionally.*

As such, you would be much happier, stronger and empowered.

If you are consumed by your perfectionism, instead of spending your days feeling unworthy and having that long list of prerequisites of when your life will be perfect – the 'whens and ifs' like,

*"if I get this, then"....." or*
*"when I do that, then".....etc.,*

you could instead be far more contented and satisfied with yourself by learning to take the rough with the smooth, or the blemishes with the clear days.

*You don't need to have reasons for when you will be worthy of good or happy things.*

Don't live by what other people will think, or by those unattainable expectations. Start to be more realistic and tell yourself '*I'm doing the best I can*'!

Everyone has flaws and things they don't like about themselves, but you can learn to accept those things and stop being so hard on yourself.

And, are they *really* going to change your life?

*Just be the best you can be as the person you are and you will be a lot happier and feel a lot more empowered in your own skin.*

**.....isn't it time you began to acknowledge your successes......**
*If you want to live a life feeling proud of yourself, confident, empowered, happy and fulfilled, then you need to make sure that you acknowledge everything you do well.*

That includes *all* your successes, achievements, accomplishments, everything that made you feel good and everything you were complimented for.

There's no need to boast about it and make yourself unpopular by being arrogant and over-egotistical, but, stand tall and fluff up your feathers a little bit.

*Keep telling your brain that you are good at things, that you have stuff to be proud of, that you are walking your path to your goals and destiny.*

*Why not* allow yourself to celebrate what you've done, who you are, where you're going...?

Even if you are just saying it to yourself, writing your own journal or making a list of the things you're proud of – *be thrilled, not humble.* Involve your friends and family in this exercise too – it all bounces off each other to great effect!

Are you spending too much time being self-critical, telling yourself not to get too above yourself, who do you think you are, falling off your own invisible pedestal without feeling positive about your achievements, so-much-so that you live a sad, negative life....?

*That's really not very good for your health, your state of mind , your well-being or achieving your aspirations....*

If you are on your path making the journey to realise your dreams, *any* accomplishments along the way is a sign that you are getting there, your dreams are being realised, you're on the right track to being a success and you're getting what you want out of life!

*Enjoy that wonderful feeling!*

There'll always be plenty of people around who will try to pull the rug from under you or knock your achievements through jealousy, envy or just plain negativity.
<u>But</u>, if you're feeling good and proud of yourself, you will be able to ignore this negativity and move past it in a strong bid to get on with your life with your head held high.

Unless you have a powerful support network on your side helping you to succeed, you will always have those who are willing or expecting you to fail, so you need that inner confidence telling you how well you are doing.

People will point out how things may be a bad idea, what you could be doing better, or how you are making mistakes, so, by having your list of accomplishments – whether written down or in your head, you will have the positive attitude you need to bypass this negativity.

*Your strength and empowerment will reassure you that you are doing exactly what you need to do to get where you want to be, and that you will not be brought down by those people who don't believe in you like they ought to.*

And, even if you do make mistakes or have done in the past, you will know that you can learn from them, spin them into positive lessons and use that experience to do a better job next time.
So, recognise all your positive results, all your successes, all your new skills and abilities and the power to make good decisions and perform well, *because you've earned it.*

*Along the way, it will help keep you focussed and on track to fulfilling your dreams and ambitions.*

Apart from anything else, it will seriously keep you motivated! There's nothing more motivating than knowing you are doing a really good job, ticking off all those achievements and getting closer and closer to your real life goals.

Any time you have a knock-back or someone tries to put you down, just refer to your list and it will help make you feel so much better and more confident about how well you are doing.
It will put the whole story into perspective for you and you can think -

*"Actually, I **AM** doing well, thank you very much, so you are wrong to think so negatively about me and what I am doing, because, look – I'm doing it, I'm getting there, I'm following my path and achieving my goals"*!

Don't be too shy about acknowledging even the smallest of things. It all adds up to feeling happy and successful in yourself.

Don't play down anything, just keep congratulating yourself, giving yourself a well earned pat on the back and acknowledging that you deserve this praise, because you are getting there, you are doing something with your life and *it is making you happy!*

If you have a family, think about how they will see you doing so well and how you will be passing the lesson down to your children or peers, setting an example as someone who *can*, and *is*, following their dreams or accomplishing something great in life.

*Because you are pursuing your passion and showing them that anything is possible!*

**What a fantastic inspiration!**

Start really appreciating yourself.
With each step you take and make a success of, you are moving towards higher goals.

*Be the leader of your own life.*

Don't wait for others to tell you you are good. Know that you are *yourself*.

As you tick off your successes, so you are also making your path clear to see where you are at, where you want to be and the future ahead of you.
Step away from the negativity of anything you failed at or any big mistakes you may have made, and always keep telling yourself how you haven't got where you want to be because of them.
Rid yourself of those emotions.

The brain is picking it up all the time and making you feel bad about yourself, always tapping away at you internally. It is not healthy and will not make you achieve anything at all.
This kind of internal dialogue is just counter-productive.

*Look for the more satisfying moments that affect you more deeply and sit in your psyche cheering you on.*

You can still acknowledge your mistakes and failures, it's all part of life's challenges, but view them in a healthy way.
What can you learn from them and take with you on your journey...?
How can you make better decisions next time and what would you do differently as part of your progress?
What calculated risks can you see ahead of you and work with effectively?
How can you take the more positive lead in the future?

What can you actively do with confidence that will make your achievements far more valuable?

Start creating your log of successes.

Have a special diary for them. Stick pictures and mementos inside it, giving yourself images, awards, papers or little trophies that you can refer to.
Each time you do this, each time you read them back to yourself, you are fixing them into your brain, giving yourself constant positive affirmations of how well you are doing and how far you have got.

They are constant reminders of your *personal legacy.*
Imagine what someone would think if they looked through your book or list in years to come?

They 'd say "*WOW! This person was amazing*"!

Each thing you do, each thing you acknowledge, each thing you are proud of, each thing that makes you feel happy about yourself, will collectively motivate you and increase your confidence.
*Doing so, will spill over into all the other areas of your life, like a domino effect.*

New doors will open for you as more opportunities naturally appear to you (because you will be in the right mindset to actually **see** them), your relationships will become more fulfilling, your awareness of the world and all it contains will become more heightened.
You will start to have more trust and respect for yourself and in turn, others will of you too.
You will attract more and better things into your life, your network will increase, your self-esteem and well-being will become healthier.
You will overcome self-doubt, your conviction in what you are doing and in life in general will be stronger, you will triumph where before you may have just got by.
You will acknowledge credit where it's due.
You will become less stressed and more focussed.
You will overcome barriers that seemed too high to scale before.
You will have boundless energy, as you count down to your ultimate goals.
You will feel great.

Life will feel good.
You will drive your initiatives forward.
Your aspirations will soar.

*You will feel totally empowered!*

Yippee!

**…..challenge yourself to do something new and exciting……**
*Sometimes it can be really daunting when you want or need to do something new.*
After all, you can stay within your usual comfort zone for so long, that it can require such a lot of strength to get out of it.
How are you going to live a satisfying life if you remain stagnant and disinterested….?

But, if you are *really* determined to conquer something very significant or a long-standing burning desire, then get yourself into the right mindset to do so.

Whatever that yearning is, it will be out there waiting for you – it's all about *conceiving and believing* that you *can* have that particular wish - then you are far more inclined to go for it. The more strongly desired, the more determined you will be, and the more you will overcome any challenges you may face in order to get it.
It will build character as you empower yourself to successfully achieve it.

It could be something big or something less onerous that you've always wanted to do but just never got round to doing it. It could just be a quick job or something that takes time.
You will know yourself what you want to attain. It's your choice.
Begin to build up a list of things you really want to get done or achieve in your life.
Even if you tick off just *one* of those things, *you have achieved something for yourself.*
Accomplishing that one thing you've always wanted to do, will undoubtedly make you motivated to continue on and do more things that will invigorate you or make you feel happy.

*Doing something out of your ordinary routine makes you feel alive!*

Like everyone else, you need to go through different phases in your life - whether you want to or not, it will happen.
*But you don't want to be apathetic and let life pass you by.*

So new challenges should be part of your journey and growth, with each new phase bringing you different joys and opportunities, and closer to where you are meant to be.
And each new phase will bring freshness and rejuvenation into your life and will be part of your survival. It brings out your strength and perseverance as you power towards your new goals.

*And each new goal provides you with a purpose and sense of satisfaction.*

It will bring you closer to yourself and others, helping to build better relationships – some of which will be life-long.
If you embrace change, you can develop, grow and regenerate yourself and your interests and endeavours into something wonderful.
This will give you the zest for life that you should have on a daily basis.

You will empower yourself to become responsible for your actions and your path, to overcome difficulties and face things head on, breaking out of inertia instead of just disappearing into the wallpaper.
You can then become fulfilled and happy with yourself and your life.......

*Keep challenging yourself.*
*It's revitalising!*

### "A goal without a plan is just a wish".

### …..following your dreams is the ultimate empowerment……
*What exactly are you here for?*
To help someone else follow their dream to the detriment of your own, or to make the most out of your life, doing everything that

satisfies you and allows you to walk your path to contentment and inner peace?

If you're stuck in the former dilemma, then start saying 'yes' to *yourself* for a change, ignore the demands of others and stop delaying what *you* want to do, so you don't end up regretting your life – *because how very sad would that be?*

If you are not really accomplishing anything of any importance to you, how is that making you feel? Have you stopped dreaming, lost your motivation, your reason for living, your get up and go?

Then it's time to stop listening to those naysayers, or that little voice in your head that thinks you can't do this or that, and *begin to prove them all wrong.*
It's time to be a '*doer*', become empowered, begin to create and start to change your environment and life for the better!

*Start making some real memories, make your world your own, be interesting and interested, take up challenges and start living your dream.*

Why not?

Any challenges you undertake will help you grow.
They may well be out of your comfort zone - they probably will be if you've spent all your life living in someone else's shadow, but this is good! You have to take chances in life if you want to grow and move forward.

*But remember that those chances can bring you so many wonderful opportunities.*

Of course you will be feel afraid, but this proves you are alive!
You will make mistakes along the way, but who cares? This only helps you to learn and make better choices and decisions next time.

*The greatest mistake you can make in life is to be continually fearing you will make one!*

When you think about it, it's *your* dreams and *your* actions that define you, therefore you cannot let others define you by trying to tell you what to do and not do. This will just be a lie that you are living, in someone else's name.

It's not the *true* you.

How many times do people get you wrong because you are in a totally different place to where you should be?
People will make their minds up about who you are based on what you do and the actions you take. If you want people to see the *real* you and react accordingly, then it's up to you to make sure they know the *real* you!

It's also up to you to be the real you, so you can think and feel about yourself as you want, having the confidence of knowing that you are fulfilling exactly what you should be in life.
Be true to yourself!

Additionally, and what could well be very important to you and others, is that by following your dream, making some mistakes and picking yourself up, dusting yourself off and bouncing back towards your goals, you will be inspiring to others. They will see what you are doing and achieving and will want to follow their own dreams too.

How much of a happier place would it be to live in when you see the people around you happy and fulfilled and living the life they are *supposed* to be living as well?

How much more interesting will you be as you go through your life happily living out your ambitions and feeling satisfied. Crossing bridges, making deals, making decisions, choosing, creating, meeting people, connecting, taking challenges.
All wonderful daily processes that make you feel good about yourself and your future.

Nobody said that there are really any rules in life.
*You make your own restrictions.*

Nobody is really telling you to limit yourself to the 'norm' – and even if they try, it really is up to you to stand up and be proud of your own morals and thoughts, feelings and ambitions. After all, when all is said and done, you are the ONLY one who can live your life, so it is your responsibility to make sure you do! And, not just do or live by what others are telling you to do.

It is probably only to follow their own interests anyway – if you think about that deeply enough....

What happens when you get to your dream? Is it all over?

The high possibility is that you will begin even bigger and better dreams, if not along the way, then as yours come to fruition.

*There's absolutely no harm in thinking **BIG!***

You will meet people and circumstances along the way that will undoubtedly put some fantastic opportunities your way.
And, as you are now a confident, lively, active person, you will be totally open to seeing those possibilities and making new and strong decisions about whether or not you want to follow them through.

Your mindset would have changed positively and you will feel empowered to take on new challenges in your life.

Your new-found confidence and pathway will make you feel that you, *at last,* have something to live for.
You will feel the power within you to surge ahead and make things happen for you, even if things don't turn out as they were meant to, you can still feel proud that you worked towards *something*.

And if that particular idea didn't come to fruition or become a viable option, there is a high likelihood that other things will have popped up along the way, that may even steer you in an *entirely* different direction that would suit you much better anyway!

Plus, you will have learnt so much along the way, that the skills and experience you gained will be invaluable to you in the future.

Everything happens for a reason......

Never forget that you always learn from 'failure' – if that is what you want to call it.
But, it cannot be failure if you have given it a good shot, learnt from it and you move on with pride, a new mindset, a new outlook and new skill-set.
Just see it as a good valuable lesson and experience and look forward to the next thing on your list – *always remembering that it is your life, so live it under you own terms!*

Never think that it's too late to try!

Don't sink back into your sofa in your 40's, 50's or 60's, even 70's, 80's and 90's, and think, well that's it! I've had my life!
You haven't....
If you haven't already done it, you have to create your own success in life.
Don't sit back and wait for the magic fairy to come along with her wand and do it for you. It would take all the fun out of it if that was possible anyway!
Just think – today is the perfect day to start making things happen.

*Tomorrow never comes – so don't wait till then.*

Get your action plan into action!
Following your dreams means you actually *have* them!
Okay, so you have got caught up in the '*responsibilities of life*' as an adult.
Can you remember when you were a child and you were inspired by your dreams? What actually happened? You probably started listening to others around you telling you to be happy with your lot and stop dreaming.....
How boring! How controlling! Says who?
Dream big.
Think success.
Think goal accomplishment.
Think contentment and satisfaction.
**Why not?**

Remember, at the end of the day, goals are just dreams with dates attached to them. If you believe, you can, ***do***.

If you don't believe, then it's time to change those thoughts and start rethinking how you *really* think your life should be.

*If you believe you can do anything, then you will.....*

You will, because with that belief, you will put the necessary tools and actions in place to fulfil those beliefs.
You will be motivated by your thoughts about your dreams.
Your mindset will be positive and action-led and your beliefs and thoughts will empower you to surge ahead and forward in life.

It's not just about feeling or being positive and hoping that one day '*something*' will happen or come along and change your life. It's about following through on those thoughts and putting the things in place to achieve them, using that new empowered mindset to do just that.

It may take some time. People don't just change overnight.
You will have some blips and meet some opposition along the way – from both others and yourself, because there is the possibility that you may slip back into your old ways of thinking and doing.
*It takes 40 times to make an action a habit.*

All the habits and conditioning you have learnt along the way in life, instilled by others you have been surrounded by – parents, teachers, friends, work-mates, bosses, will sit in your head and heart for a long time. But if the message you have been getting from them is negative, then it will naturally take time to rid your head of those deep and strong thoughts and emotions about your person, situation and circumstances.

*Be patient.....*

If you have a bad day, go through the motions and emotions, but don't let it rule you.
Don't let it control everything you have been working towards.
Believe that time will make things work. Get up and move forward.
Allow your mind to be controlled by your *own* thoughts, not those of others.

Remember your *goal*.

Remember your *dream* at all times.
Keep focussed and motivated by what you are trying to achieve.

A few bad days are nothing in life when it comes down to it and when you think about the successful and positive end result. Or when you think about the achievement and satisfaction you will feel, and the happiness you will give to both yourself and others around you.

If you dare to dream, if you dare to think big, if you dare to stretch yourself, things will happen quite naturally, because you will be in the right mindset and you will put yourself in the right places. You will find and make the time.
You will open the necessary doors.....

If you look at successful people, you will see that they have a natural belief in themselves. This is how you need to be if you want to get out of life, all the things you feel you deserve and believe in – whether that's a big ambition, or a small achievement, or just a wonderful sense of peace and calm.

*Visualise yourself in the position you want to be in.*

*Really* see yourself there. Hold that thought in your mind everyday. Make it something worth working towards. Make it your motivation. Make it your daily focus.
Work backwards – what do you need to get there? What tools do you need, what money do you need, what skills do you need? Make your action plan. Add some dates. Even if it's going to take several years to get there, have fun doing it!
It will be a *fantastic* journey – but it will be *yours* to savour, yours to hold onto and yours to live.
Your pathway to your own success, you own dream.

**It's all about you......**
And that's absolutely fine!

*Don't make your regrets in life that you had dreams but you just didn't try..... what a shameful waste.*

Don't be one of those people that lists all the reasons why you *can't*

fulfil their dreams, instead of listing all the reasons why you **can**!
If you need money, find it, save it! If you don't think you're talented enough – really challenge that and if you need new knowledge or skills, go out and get them – they're out there for the taking.

If you've failed in the past, don't use that as an excuse that you fall back on all the time because you can't be bothered, or you think that's just the way you are destined to be.
Learn by it and be *better* next time.
And if you haven't got enough experience, go out and get it – even part-time or for free, because if you *want it badly enough, you will do it*!

If you don't think you're lucky – then make your *own* luck – things don't happen by magic – *you* make it happen.

*Be in the right places, meet the right people, do the right things.*

If you think you are not worthy of it, think again – make yourself worthy by changing that mindset into believing you *totally* are and have the *absolute* right to be!
All such negative thoughts are defeating you before you even get started!

Think about how you will feel getting up every day and doing exactly what you **want** to be doing – how great will that feel? Doing what you love and living your life on your own terms are the best things you can do for yourself.

Your dream has been your thought – so there is a high likelihood that you will have an innate ability to achieve it. It's unlikely that you will be dreaming about doing something that is totally alien to you as a person!

The world's movers and shakers are those who believed in their dreams and persevered until they manifested what they dreamt about.

When your work is your dream you will create your best life possible.

Your hunger will be fed through the pursuit of your dreams. It will add meaning to your life and make all your efforts worthwhile.
Start to feel alive!
Don't ignore your dream to the detriment of your soul.
Don't starve yourself and your creativity.

There is a chance that your dream will be seen as crazy. It may be a unique idea that you want to follow through. So be prepared for opposition and criticism, but don't give up – *you may be the* **pioneer** *of something new and wonderful that may change the world!*
You've got to give it a try!

Don't be put off by others who are just stuck in a rut - *open your own wings and let yourself fly*!

You deserve to be remarkable. Why on earth not? People are born to be great – including you. Your dream needs to be fulfilled.
You may be someone who makes the world a better place.
How wonderful!
Don't you owe it to yourself and those who will benefit from what you have to offer?
Be courageous.
Allow yourself to grow.
Nurture that dream.
Don't limit yourself.
Unleash your passion to the world.
Leave your legacy.
Be brilliant!
Those dreamers that did take action have created everything around you. ….
Think about that!
Make some memories.
Be remembered.
Take a chance.
Take a leap of faith.
*Go get 'em!*

**Every 'No' brings you closer to that next 'Yes'!**
**If you need to speak to 10 people to get to that one 'Yes',**
**then realise that those nine people**
**are part of your path to success....!**

**…..feel empowered and get that job……**
*In this day and age of so much competition for the same job, it's essential to stand out from the crowd and get noticed - if you really want that position!*
Therefore, it's extremely important that you get yourself fully prepared and don't just fly by the seat of your pants.

Apart from anything else, knowing that you are really organised and have done your research, will enhance your feeling of confidence and empowerment when you go into the interview and present yourself to the panel in front of you.

The planning you do could be the turning point to new opportunities and life-changing outcomes, so you need to impress and show them what you have to offer.

The first thing you obviously need to do is some research about the company you are being interviewed for. They will be impressed if you know a bit about their background, details and recent activity. Apart from this, you will be able to see how you can *personally* fit within the organisation and show your prospective employers how your skills and experience will benefit them too.

During your research, you may be able to access clues via social media sites about who is interviewing you. You could discover you have something in common that you can use to your advantage. You may even find you went to the same college or worked for the same former employer as them.
Any information like this helps to break the ice!

Make sure you check through the job description to see how your abilities and experience match the role and how you can promote them when asked. This may include any responsibilities you've had or targets and results you've already accomplished using those skills.
Don't forget to prepare your own questions that you'd like to ask about the company, the role, prospects, training, etc.

Remember, it is a *two-way street* and you need to know it's the type of place and environment that *you* want to work in too.

Find out if you have to do a presentation and if so, what facilities will be available to you? Remember to take any certificates you have to show them, including ID and some spare CV's, just in case the interviewer needs a copy.

Practice makes perfect, so if it's been a while since your last interview, make sure you have a firm handshake, maintain eye-contact, don't fidget and practise your presentation or what you want to say, out loud.

First impressions make all the difference, so walk in confidently and smile.
Dress smartly and appropriately for that particular organisation, making sure you are clean, tidy and well-groomed.
Have a nice massage or new hair-do ready for the day, if it helps with your confidence and increases your feeling of empowerment.

Arrange to get there in plenty of time so you feel relaxed and not stressed from panicking. Leave some contingency time for hold-ups and delays, especially if you are travelling by public transport. Know where you're going and make sure there is parking available if you are driving there yourself.
Take the company's contact number, in case you need to get hold of someone if you cannot get there for reasons out of your control.

Do some deep-breathing before you go into the interview or meeting to help settle any nerves.

Although you may really want or need the job, if you go in with a slight feeling of it not being the be all and end all of your life and that you are just going to have a *discussion* with someone, then you may feel a lot stronger and not quite so insecure.

Obviously you want to come across as wanting the job, otherwise this will give the totally wrong impression, so be positive and professional about this and let them know that you would be a great person to have on-board and work with.

Don't act or feel desperate!

Never berate former employers or roles, as this doesn't look good and makes a negative impact.

Be ready and prepared, know the role, know the company, know your own skills, know what you have to offer, *so you feel confident and empowered and get that job* !

**Good luck!**

**....be a student for life.....**
*Stay willing and open to learning from everything and everyone around you.*
From every situation you encounter, from every problem you need to solve, and from having a healthy thirst for knowledge, you will establish room for new intelligence, new ways of thinking and your creativity will soar within every aspect of your life.

*As long as there is still something to learn, you will always grow....*

If you think you know everything already, then you will stagnate and go stale.

You can become a guru or an expert in your chosen field, or you can just be free in knowing that you are extending yourself and opening your mind to all sorts of wonderful imaginings and teachings.

*Every person you meet, every place you go to, every experience you have, will teach you something new and valuable.*

If you accept that as ***fact***, you will go into each day and each problem, knowing you will take something *special* away that you can store and use whenever you need it.

Your mind and soul are boundless and you can use each teaching to enhance and complete your life in so many profound ways – including your personal growth or the achievement of your goals and aspirations.

*Your life is your journey and you owe it to yourself to reach beyond a small, limited bubble into the real and wonderful world you are surrounded by every day.*

#### ....be a success.....get your empowering mantras going.....
*To help get you through all kinds of scenarios in your life, one of the best things you can do to keep you motivated and focussed, is to make yourself your own* **Power Mantra.**
It should contain all the things you want to be.

When you are putting your mantra, or mantras together, you *must* tell yourself that you *ARE* actually that person you desire to be - and *never* be vague about it, or the message will be too weak to instil into your brain!

*I <u>Am</u> Strong!*
*I <u>Am</u> a Successful Person!*
*I <u>Am</u> Powerful!*
*I <u>Am</u> Confident & Assertive!*
*I <u>Have</u> Excellent Skills!*
*I <u>Have</u> The Courage Of My Convictions!*
*I <u>Am</u> Empowered!*

<u>Own it!</u>

You can do this for your personal ambitions. Wherever it is you want to get with them - make yourself an appropriate power mantra. Make up a poster with your mantra on it and put it somewhere prominent where you can see and refer to it regularly.
Consult it if you feel you may be falling backwards at times.
Continually remind yourself of who you are and what you want to become.

*Stand up, take in deep breaths and really feel the words and meaning of your mantra.*

Say them out loud to yourself several times, breathing in the sentiment and making sure it goes wholeheartedly into your consciousness.
*Make your mantra <u>really</u> empower and work for you.....*

***Put motivational messages and mantras
in your phone scheduler or diary
to prompt and continuously remind you.
Make sure you look at your phone regularly,
or put alarm reminders on it,
so it pops up all the time and lodges into your mind,
keeping you continuously uplifted.***

**....master your self-esteem and get things done...**
*Having good self-esteem is one of the most important things you can have for your own personal growth, empowerment and happiness.*
If, over time, you have allowed external circumstances or other people's judgements to affect your self-confidence, then having the power to halt this self-limiting behaviour that's stopping you from progressing positively with your life, will help make you become a much more enriched person.

Having a real purpose in life will help you to build up the foundation for strong self-confidence, by giving yourself something to focus on and showing people that you have a will and desire.

By first writing down lots of ideas for your own intention, you will help give your mind a clearer picture of what exactly it is you want for yourself, including your successful outcomes.
The way you interact with yourself - your '*internal dialogue*', shows the shape of how confident you feel.

Your confidence can be shattered in an instant or boosted very easily, just by what someone can say to you – whether thoughtlessly or with conviction!

*The same is true with the way you talk to yourself – except in this case, you are stuck with it <u>all</u> day!*

The most potent way to counteract the negative internal noises is by positive affirmations – by talking to yourself in the same kind of way as you'd talk to a friend when trying to boost *their* confidence.
You need to do this on a regular basis everyday.

Write down positive phrases relevant to you and say them out loud, even look yourself in the eye in the mirror - *and really mean it* - just the same way as you do with your mantras.

This will help build up an optimistic frame of mind.

After a short time, you will begin building up your self-esteem and start to get on with using those talents and skills that you *know* you've had for years.

*How empowering is that?!*

**…..raising your confidence and self-esteem by harnessing your true potential…..**
*It stands to reason that, with improved self confidence, you will be totally able to harness your true natural potential - making life easier and enabling you to achieve your personal goals.*

By allowing your skills and talents to become more enhanced, you can begin to build up your self-esteem and start living the life you truly deserve.

You may have had your self-confidence knocked over the years, with other people's opinions and certain circumstances suppressing your self-worth. Especially if you have always had lots of fabulous ideas and no-one has had any faith in you.

But, you first need to know for yourself who you truly are and what you want out of life, if you want to get anywhere - even if it's only to be at peace in your own head.

Writing down your thoughts is important in doing this. As you open up to this, you will go on a road of discovery and begin to build a picture of exactly who you are, instead of trying to be someone else *for* someone else.

*You will begin to properly appreciate your true self and bring back a sense of the wonderful person you actually are, and as a consequence, build up your self-esteem.*

Controlling your focus and innermost thoughts is the key to understanding how to build up self-confidence.

Deliberate training in self control is the way forward.
This is not a limitation on your freedom, so there is no reason for you to fear development of it.

Far from it....

In fact, you can control your thoughts to become more free in your actions in order to really gain what you want out of life.

*This can become quite a skill, but it is worth it because ultimately, the better you become at controlling yourself, the better your life can be.*

With this ability, the development of your talents and skills will be easier and you will be far more confident about everything, instead of just randomly flailing around in the dark not really knowing any kind of direction at all.

You can go ahead with following those dreams you've had in your head, without letting low self-esteem get in the way of them. Additionally, any promises you actually make for yourself, will be fulfilled far more easily.

*Then your self-esteem will really soar.*

As you begin learning to have some control over yourself and getting to know your *real* self and individualism along the way, so you will be able to use your newly gained self-confidence to make positive moves forward in your life, and begin to have an impact on your circumstances and the people around you.

*Begin by being giving of your time and energy in such a way that it gives you a sense of purpose and self-worth.*

The more you do for others, for example, helping, empathising, being there, the more your confidence will increase, because you will allow yourself to become closer to people, instead of your insecurities keeping you at arms length all the time.

*Finding what your actual purpose is and getting nearer to others, will in turn help you to stop focusing on your own issues and negative circumstances.*

Gradually, as you practise this more and more, you will see your true-self beginning to shine through, and consequently, you could even become inspirational to others around you, as they watch your confidence grow and your transformation is realised.

*Then you can really get stuck into fulfilling your ultimate desires and ambitions.*

**Put in the work and you will get amazing results!**

**......use those positive affirmations to build up your self esteem....**
*If you want to improve your self-esteem and empower your mind into becoming a confident person and getting excellent results, then try continuously using your positive affirmations on a regular basis to train your mind into doing exactly what you require.*
You must therefore *always* visualise yourself as a successful and confident person.

If you find that you are talking negatively to yourself, you need to correct it by talking positively in an inspiring and enthusiastic way instead.

If you want your life to be a success, the most powerful way of motivating yourself is to write down your own ambitions so you can get the most out of your life.

Take responsibility for your plans by setting goals and coming up with a strategy for taking action, and be committed to it – because if *you* don't do this, no-one else will!
If needs be, find someone you can model yourself on – someone you admire with qualities you think are inspiring – then watch and learn!

*You have to totally focus on your potential **not** your limitations, build on and use your strengths, be positive and try to keep yourself optimistic.*

By concentrating on doing things you are good at, your persistence and confidence in these things will make a massive difference to how you feel about yourself.

Take stock of whether you are actually doing things for yourself or spending your life being what other people want you to be, to the detriment of your true instincts and identity. Decide exactly what it is you want to be doing and do that instead.

*You will find this to be an exhilarating sense of freedom!*

If you have had issues with your parents that have built up resentment and are, quite frankly, just getting in the way of you progress, then it's time to release that heavy burden and start living in the present!
The past is gone, but you aren't.....!
You are no longer a child, so don't let your childhood affect who you are now.

*Stand up and be proud.*

If you are surrounded by negative people who are just dragging you down, then you must start replacing them with more supportive people instead. You need friends who do not spend their time mocking and criticising you, but rather, only want the best for you.

*Remember to keep going, even when things get you down.*

You have to persist at things if you want to succeed. You are in charge of your life and your thinking, and every time you achieve something, it is a victory towards your progress.

*Life is an adventure – get out there and get excited about it, and more importantly, enjoy it – that's what it's for!*

Always remember to acknowledge your achievements – they are your accomplishments, so take credit for them, don't belittle them.

Promote your triumphs and don't let them go unnoticed or allow them, or yourself, to fade into the background.

*Because if you don't value what you do, others won't notice and they won't value you either!*

To build up your self esteem, jot down all your achievements and successes, even the small ones. Just the action of doing this will build up your confidence which will set into your mind *how perfectly able you are to accomplish things.*

Fear of rejection or having to face a confrontational situation, may bring past failures into your mind and make you think that, once again, you may not be capable of facing things. If so, then think about *all* the things you *have* done in the past that were <u>brave</u>, that were <u>courageous</u> and that you achieved *anyway.*

Think about how you got through them *regardless* and what the outcomes were.
You overcame them **before**, so you have it in you to do *exactly the same again*, if you just reframe your mindset to those previous *successes*.
If you need to rethink your strategy this time to secure a better outcome, then note how you handled it last time and how you can improve the situation should it arise again. You can make that worry a thing of the past by learning how to deal with your fears positively and optimistically instead and not think, "*Oh no, I just can't do this again....*"!

*You can* – just do it better!

You have to look at possible tricky situations as a <u>challenge</u>, rather than a problem.
Just think of them as something you *can work on and overcome*, and not something that will make you automatically sink under the strain.
Energise yourself to build up the strength to get what you want out of that challenge.

How you view a situation will have a significant impact on how you deal with it, so if you think it's going to be a problem, your mindset

will be set up for just that and you will handle it as such, possibly getting stressed and feeling helpless.
If, however, you view it as a challenge to be overcome, your mindset will be in a far more positive and optimistic place. You can then put an appropriate strategy together to reach a much more gratifying solution.

*Always make your glass half full and not half empty!*

Another valuable plan you can use if you have difficult challenges to face, is to tackle them in the morning and get them out of the way. That way you won't have them burdening your mind all day hanging over you like a dead weight. If you've got them out of the way, you will feel good for the rest of the day and this will empower you to face all your other activities far more effectively.

Is it time to forgive yourself for everything you give yourself a hard time about?
Things happen, but you have to get over them if you want to power forward.......

*Don't spend your live beating yourself up about stuff that's <u>done</u>.*

Harbouring negative feelings will hinder you and stop you achieving your aims.

*Acknowledge they happened, tell yourself you are sorry, use your positive affirmations to keep you on top and motivated..........*

*…..and then get on with your life!*

### …...how will simple self improvement tools help me achieve successful outcomes....
*If you are looking to improve yourself for personal development in order to attain higher success and fulfilment, there are approaches you can use to guarantee results.*
You may not believe it, but most successful people are just as intelligent as the average person.
The only difference is that they *expect* higher attainment, and as such, have a mindset akin to that.

Their self-belief and perseverance is all the knowledge they need to push themselves forward in life.

*They expect it to happen and it usually does because all that expectation and belief converts itself into the action required to achieve it.*

Obviously, knowing what you desire out of life and the goals you want to achieve are vital ingredients for getting to where you want to be.
So, writing down those objectives and strategies to get there is essential to that success. It will give you a clearer picture of what plans need to be put in place and how to go about building and achieving those expectations.

*With every action and individual goal achieved, you will be one step closer to achieving your happiness.*

Being balanced is essential to your growth.
Everything you do and think will have an impact on everything else in life.
So you need to be emotionally, mentally and physically 'fit' in order to drive your personal growth and thereby achieve your end game.
Being well rounded will help you feel more secure on your journey.

Writing down your thoughts and daily activities can have a hand in helping you make sense of yourself and facilitate your own enhancement and higher self-confidence.

Meditation can also help significantly, by reducing stress and any thoughts that are causing you unease. Additionally, it can bring about good physical health, encourage a lower heart rate, aide sound sleep and help speed up recovery from any illness you may have had.

*Having a balanced mind is obviously an excellent starter in self improvement and empowerment.*

Influence your subconscious mind through your positive affirmations in order to alter your personality, disposition, attributes and life as a whole, so you can accomplish the expectations you have set for

yourself. Regularly jot down and recite all the affirmations relevant to each area of your life.
The more you ingrain those positive messages into your brain, the stronger you will be in reaching your ultimate enterprise and life-style.

It doesn't matter what it is you want - wealth, success, empowerment, achievement or contentment, you can fulfil all those things and more, using these simple strategies.

**Don't forget to look up and back....
you never know what you are missing......**


**…..let positive encouragement yield results....**
*Surround yourself with positivity – of mind, people, environment and thoughts, so you can attain your highest feelings of optimism and happiness.*
Help yourself to reach this state once again, with your positive affirmations - they are like seeds planted in soil......poor soil - poor growth, rich soil - abundant growth.
The more you choose to think thoughts that make you feel good, the quicker your affirmations work.

*They truly have the force to change your subconscious.*

And there is no equipment or cost involved.
Instruct your unconscious mind for your success and confidence, because it always reacts to the instructions you give it - both negatively and positively.
Specify what you *personally* feel defines self-esteem and confidence - whether that's being able to talk to different people or having the courage to speak your mind, it's your own individual request.

Remember the simple formula - positive, no negative wording like *don't, want,* or being down on yourself. Keep them in the *present* tense, talk to yourself in the *first* person and base them on a *specific* action.

*"I AM persuasive and assertive in all my everyday interactions."*
*"I like initiating conversations and AM confident in doing so."*
*"I have a real knack for ...........(fill in what you are good at)"*
*"I AM a picture of health and fitness."*
*"Every day I AM achieving my goals towards a wonderful, fulfilling life".*

You just need to adopt this easy way of changing your mindset towards good things.
You deserve to hold your head up high, be listened to and taken seriously, be rich in abundance and have wonderful things happen to you in life......

......and why not.....?

**....the thing about confidence and money.....**
*There is no doubt that confidence can come from having money.*
It empowers you because you can get what you want when you want it, and who doesn't desire that scenario?
Money doesn't have to be the *'source of all evil'.*

Usually, it's when you don't have it that the evil comes out! When you do have it, you can live a full and happy life (as long as you have everything else in place of course – like a balanced mind and spirit), so you don't *have* to treat it as the devil incarnate.

You can use your money to fulfil some of your life's expectations, go on adventures, build businesses and be as philanthropic as you like by treating family, friends and giving to charity.

*Money is freedom and feeling free gives you confidence.*

How confident is the feeling of knowing you have the money to pay all your bills?
It feels very comfortable indeed!
Weigh that up against being in the opposite position – no money is a headache and has a terrible knock-on effect on yours and your close ones lives.

Not to mention the self-respect it gives you when you are earning money for yourself – and how confident and empowered does that make you feel?
Very good to be sure!

*Claiming control of your finances is an early step to a healthy attitude about money.*

Though many people believe confidence comes with having lots of cash, confidence accompanies a clear picture of what you have and what you need.
Earning and managing your own money gives you confidence, self-respect and that freedom and pride that someone-else's money will *never* give you.
But, be smart with your wealth.

*True wealth is experienced through a generous heart!*

It is not a sin to want money or riches, even if it's just an amount to make you feel comfortable in life.

*So continue being empowered on your path to those riches and you will undoubtedly achieve your ultimate life in time!*

### …..could self-consciousness be getting in the way of your progression....

*Being self-conscious will undoubtedly get in the way of your ambitions if you allow it to overtake you on a day to day basis.*
If there are things you want to achieve in your career or personal life, then getting over self-consciousness is something you should try to tackle.
By thinking that you are very much a *unique* person in the world – just like everyone else, and that your place here is just as valuable as anyone else's, should help you to realise that there should be no need for self-consciousness.

You will acknowledge that you have a right to express yourself and be who you are, just as much as the next person.
You should really feel proud to walk on this earth in the same strong way as anyone else.

You should be able to enjoy being *you* and others should enjoy you, enjoying being you!
If you have something of value, you should stand tall and be able to tell the world all about it, *without the fear of being judged detrimentally.*

<u>You should try and embrace all this.</u>

After all, we all breathe the same air and walk in the same light, so let this tell you that you have as much right as the next person to live on this earth in peace and harmony and at one with the sun, the moon and the universe.

Use your own precious energy to connect to others' energy to make positive sparks and allow the world to turn with enrichment and abundance, electrifying the world and making it a better place!

*Take it's astounding beauty and nurture it, so that it nourishes you.*

It gives and you receive, so you give so it can receive and this amazing cycle will truly keep us all enriched and happy and living in paradise.

Practically, getting past being self-conscious and that feeling that everyone around you is looking in your direction, may be helped by you not actually focussing on *them.*

Going about your business paying no mind to people, where you would *normally* run the 'risk' of feeling judged or criticised by them, means that you will not notice this so much.

*If you cannot 'see' them, there will be nothing to fear from them.*

You could instead be having some wonderful positive thoughts of your own. Perhaps you are concentrating on how confident you are feeling that day, or how you are creating new ideas in your mind, or thinking deeply about something fantastic you are looking forward to, or merely just walking tall and upright, playing and enjoying your favourite music on your mobile device.
You cannot see your so-called 'critics', so they cannot touch you!

*You need to conduct yourself with pride.*

Be aware of your own self in that particular moment, rather than worrying or thinking about who is looking at you or judging you in any way. Once you begin to do this and by taking small steps, you will gradually become more confident.
Then you can start making bigger strides by looking around you, taking in the scene, watching others and eventually being strong enough to look people straight in the eye, smile and really feel good about yourself and who you are.

You will be presenting yourself to others brimming with confidence and empowerment.

Little by little, by looking after yourself and your health, having pride in yourself and doing things that you love and believe in, you will be able to take on the world and move forward with the strength to achieve all the things you want in life.
Pull in your stomach, shoulders back, head up and smile both outwardly and inwardly – feel better and more confident.

*This will have a great impact on how you feel, your own empowerment and your important place in this world.*

***Take a picture of your day.***
***When you have achieved something or have something positive to celebrate, why not capture the moment in a snap?***
***Take a photo of whatever it is, so you can look back on it and smile with a wonderful sense of achievement, satisfaction and pleasure!***

**…..tricks for when you feel intimidated and unsure….**
*There are times, whether in a professional or personal situation where you may feel intimidated, unsure of your abilities, nervous, awkward or downright scared.*
You would probably love your life to flow in a more confident and

empowered way, so you can perform better at work, feel great in an interview, give a fantastic strong presentation, or look someone in the eye without feeling shy or nervous.

There are some simple ways to boost how you feel under these circumstances, that will give you the power to transform your life once and for all.

*Being prepared is an obvious one.*

Knowing what you're talking about is bound to give you an encouraging lift, so you can address people with confidence and give intelligent answers without doubt or hesitation.
So *know* your stuff.

Having confidence may mean the difference between success and failure. Feeling confident inwardly will naturally show outwardly.

*If you dream big, you need to play big and **become big**.*

Become '*big*' by moving and expanding your body, exaggerating your movements, or anything that makes you look *physically* bigger – it will help boost your confidence.

When it's time to 'perform', stand tall, keep your shoulders back and feet apart, or sit up straight in a chair with your arms loose and on the armrests.
Fill the room!
Standing upright will instinctively give people the perception that you are knowledgeable – even if you fake it!

Give a little power pose!
Just physically doing this can change your testosterone and cortisol levels, increase your appetite for risk, cause you to perform better in job interviews and generally configure your brain to cope well in stressful situations.

So, next time you feel a little intimidated or unsure of a situation, try empowering yourself with a few of these clever tactics.

*Then feel yourself grow in strength and self-assurance - enough to* take on the world!

**"Everything you want is on the <u>other</u> side of fear".**

*……tapping into your power within……*
*What do you usually think of when you hear the word '**power**'?*
It's probably something to do with control, dominance, command, *authority*, or similar.
However, this only covers *one* type of power.
Power is also the ability to face adversity, overcome fear and inhibitions, pick yourself up when times are hard. It enables you to be in touch with your inner life and have the foresight to plan ahead. It is an expression of personal will, allowing you to trust your own instincts and hunches.

*It's about directing your own life and not allowing others to control it for you.*

So then, it means you being able to walk around and feel powerful *in yourself* and not spending your life procrastinating.
Instead, you are perfectly able to apply yourself to your work, have the willpower to control your weight if needs be, not fear rejection, hold a conversation with someone new, confront people when necessary, feel motivated, and be part of the community around you.
It's an every day power, not a bullish arrogance and acting all superior over others.

It's more to do with being able to express yourself *confidently* and chart your own direction in life, by being assertive without being confrontational, and *creating a meaning to your life*.

It's an ongoing process that needs to be built up and maintained.

Apart from the obvious inner strength that generally comes with power, you need to know what your reason for living is. You need to be able to *devote* yourself to your path, commit to your activities, live in the moment and live a life without fear, anger or envy.

Also, it's to be able to love and accept love, have concern for others and try to live without too many regrets and recriminations.

When you have all this, you can feel free to pursue your own goals without fearing failure or success.

This is *genuine* power.

Those who cite dominance as power, are usually not really very high in self-esteem, and usually use this kind of power to hide some kind of underlying weakness and doubt their own popularity amongst others.

*And, vulnerability shouldn't be viewed as a weakness, but more as a strength.*

Having the ability to empathise and care for others through your own experiences of feeling frightened, overwhelmed or helpless, enables you to utilise those experiences for your own growth.
It's about gaining your own inner power through your *participation in life*, being open, having good emotions, strong ties, showing an interest in others, being able to enjoy pleasant pursuits and constructing a meaning to your life.

*Tap into your own power and start living your life to full effect.....!*

**…..using your emotional intelligence to get ahead…..**
Having good Emotional Intelligence (EI) is part of being a balanced person.
Being balanced helps in your quest for life empowerment.

Essentially, being emotionally intelligent enables you to have a much better understanding of your emotions and the ability to express them *cleverly*.
It also helps you to understand and react to others' emotions in a mature way, because you are in touch with both your own and the other person's feelings as well.

*This can certainly give you some enormous control over your life and how emotions impact you on a daily basis.*

Knowing how to deal with people's feelings is a very useful tool that you can use to help keep things balanced, without allowing emotions to go into over-drive where they can end up causing problems.

The common personality traits you would have if you are high in emotional intelligence is being more flexible and adaptable. This is because you can use your EI to adapt to new situations that come up and deal with them far more efficiently – including your own.

*Having good EI can only benefit both yourself and others.*

If you are in control of things, you will have more self-motivation, which is a good thing when it comes to battling on through tough times, as it allows you to manage your stress levels more easily. You will also have a far more cheerful disposition because of the confidence and positive outlook you generate.

Having these traits will naturally mean that you can carry yourself better in social situations, because that higher level of intelligence will mean you are far more able to communicate better.

Think seriously about how you deal with your emotional situations. If you think you need help in this area because it is just hampering your progress, then find some help from a professional, or just take a good look at how you can improve handling people and circumstances better.

Your own personal empowerment will depend on having good emotional intelligence, especially if *you want to make definite and positive moves towards goal achievement and a more fulfilling and prosperous future.*

### *"Use setbacks as challenges and lessons to learn from".*

**…..a healthy balanced life is worth more than any pot of money.....**
*Feeling empowered is totally helped by the kind of relationships you have in your life.*
In order to feel balanced and at ease, you need your relationships to

be that way too, at least *most* of the time.

Obviously there will be times when things go off kilter, but that doesn't mean it's the end of the world and it can't be fixed. And if you are in a good, balanced relationship, when things do go wrong, it will be strong enough to return to equilibrium again easily and without too much fallout.

Certainly, you don't need to spend days, weeks or months in a state of flux about difficult situations.
That's just not a healthy place to be in, for either yourself or those involved.
You really don't want issues to turn into something you dwell on *so much,* that it gets you down and puts you into depression, making you unable to get on with your life.

*You need to be in a strong enough position where it is just a normal part of life that you can work through and get over.*

You certainly don't have to stay unhappy and you don't have to think everything's falling apart and you're failing in life.
Life is a natural flow of alternating conditions, so there is no need to go into an emergency strategy and tell your brain the *negative* has arrived and will <u>never</u> go away!

When it comes to rebalancing whatever has gone wrong, you first need to see where you're at inside, and to do that, you need to *listen* to yourself, be still, focus and pay attention.
*Feel* your responses to what has happened, without reacting inappropriately and making things worse, thus giving yourself and the others involved *a chance to breathe.*

*Cultivate and learn not to respond or react immediately to negative circumstances.*

That's not easy, but in doing so, you will give yourself the space to let things become more clearer in your mind, allowing you to be more patient because when you're in this position, you are able to see the *whole* picture from a much healthier perspective.

You can then take responsibility.

When in the thick of things, you can naturally blame everyone else for what is going on. But, by not reacting *immediately*, you can give others the benefit of the doubt and find a positive and constructive way to see their side of things, as well as your own too.

*It is said that what we see in others, we bring out in them, and so it works in reverse with you too.*

You and others, can end up perceiving a situation in the wrong way. You need to see yourself and others in a positive way and not think the worst all the time.

Try not to give up on someone just because they are going through a mess and have become difficult to handle. Because if you can teach yourself to stay with them through those difficulties and hold them in your mind and heart, there's a high likelihood that they will get through those problems, come out the other side and become who they are truly meant to be.

You can be there as a solid figure in their lives, waiting for them to develop through that period, learn from it and use the experience to continue on their journey with renewed strength.

You can help build their empowerment, as well as adding to your own in the process!

However, this doesn't mean you have to automatically surround yourself with negative and pessimistic people, if they are just constantly bringing you down.
But, you can still allow them to go on their way and hope they will rise up above it and make their way in life with love and peace.

As real life has a natural way of renewing itself, it will confront you with new issues, challenges and opportunities that give you fresh insights into your relationships and how you react to people in different circumstances.

As this happens, you do need to remember to try and stay in the *present* and not harbour or bring up old wounds or feelings and connecting them to what is going on at that particular _new_ moment.

Your life cannot revolve around dwelling on the past and remembering how you were previously wronged, and then spend the rest of your time determined to make whoever you feel is responsible, pay for what they have done to you.
It's a new day with new issues that need to be dealt with accordingly.

*It's time to leave the past in the past, let go of what happened before and approach things with a new mindset.*

Remember that the other person in today's set of circumstances, has also woken up to a new day with a probable new mindset too and they should be allowed to be different from yesterday.
You need to allow both of you to grow and not be stuck in revenge mode all the time.

This is far more empowering than harbouring such negativity.
To keep your relationship alive, think about what you have given each other.
Why not do something spontaneously - just for the joy of doing it!?

Find things that have nourished your relationship, rather than everything that they have wronged you with, and in doing so, you are choosing to *feel good*, rather than focussing on the negative aspects.
You can focus on hurts and spend your time feeling sad, angry and upset of course, but isn't it *much* nicer to focus on pleasures and feel happy, joyful and contented?

*It is an open choice for you to make.*

By doing this, you take the attention off your negative inner dialogue which directly interferes with that habitual feeling of your previous suffering, and instead, it leaves you to concentrate more on what you have <u>now</u>, **right in front of you**.....

If you have a very busy lifestyle, it probably means that you don't spend as much time as you'd like with the people you love. Even when you do spend time with them, it is rushed and not enjoyed as much as it could be.

With all this in mind, always remember that no-one ever gets to their death bed and says, "*I wish I had worked harder*".
They are more likely to say, "***I wish I'd spent more time with my family and friends***".......!

So give yourself time to breath.
Step off the treadmill.
Stop chasing rainbows and pots of gold for a minute.
It's not all about the money, money, money.....

Think about how you can conduct your relationships more positively and friendly. Your brain will immediately feel freer and you will therefore enjoy your life in a far more relaxed and satisfying way.

*You will feel much more in control of your emotions and how you handle yourself and others, which has to be a very empowering feeling for sure!*

**Everybody wins!**

**…..stop and think before you act.....**
*So, how do you manage your moods when things have been perfect all day whilst you've been in you own little bubble....and then someone comes along and spoils it all?*
You've been happy, calm, motivated and feeling good and then this other person brings their negativity, bad mood, cranky temper, whinging, complaining attitude and bang!, your whole peaceful ambience, well-being and order has been shattered by those outside forces!?

Your natural response is probably to react by striking back, shouting, defending yourself, crying, stomping off, etc.... you know the thing...
But, the best thing to do in this kind of scenario, for all concerned, including yourself, is just to stop!
Before you let your emotions control your actions and mouth and you end up doing or saying something you may regret later, or cause the situation to spiral out of control and then everyone's in a bad mood....*just step off the gas.*

Rushing into an action or sarcastic comment will probably be the wrong choice, made without proper rational thought.
Because it will undoubtedly be a snap decision or judgement that may not have any reasoning behind it whatsoever!

It's a very natural response. But is it really the right one?

Can you think back to a situation where this has actually happened in your life before and it has caused more harm than good? Or perhaps you've hurt people along the way causing rifts in relationships that, if they had been handled more rationally, could easily have been avoided?

The probability is that you may not even have all the facts at hand for the reason that the other party is in a bad mood at the time, or why they're angry, upset, quick-tempered or emotional.
There could be something quite significant that has just happened to them to warrant their behaviour.

It's quite possible that if you knew the *whole* situation, you would be much more sympathetic and therefore likely to react in a more concerned or reasonable way instead.
You'd have a better understanding, make different and smarter decisions and be able to handle the situation with greater empathy.

By just stopping before you react, you can avoid blow-ups, devastation and any unnecessary heartache.

Even if the situation is an emergency, take a deep breath and think about your options.
Get some clarity to formulate a mini plan or ask for help. Give yourself the time to be able to handle the crisis rationally.

So stop, breathe, look, listen, think or get help and try to find some sound solutions and answers.

Be composed and understanding enough to consider the other side and be guided by your inner voice and calm instruction. You will save yourself and others a lot of unreasonable behaviour, thereby helping your relationships in the long run.

This is an extremely empowering and useful tactic you can perfect and that will see you through many, many real circumstances and situations that confront you in life and where you can come out the other end on the winning side!

**…....I get so angry and frustrated at times.....**
*Having pent up anger leads to frustration and bitterness.*
These types of emotions will hold you back in your pact to become happy, successful and empowered, or to achieve any kind of calm and serenity in your life.

In order to attain any or more of these positions in life, you will need to learn how to deal with negative emotions effectively, and not spend too much of your precious time on getting het up every time something goes against the grain.
Try not to get embroiled in a full scale argument with people.
*It achieves nothing and could actually end up in more hurt and upset than necessary.*

Have the strength to walk away from the situation and give it a chance to calm down.
Certainly issues will need to be addressed, but a full scale loud dispute will not get you the result you both need. So removing yourself from the situation until you are both in a rational mood to discuss things sensibly, will be the best path you can take.

You will feel more empowered to tackle the situation more reasonably and rationally when you take yourself away from the heat to collect your thoughts and give yourself some head-space. You cannot argue with yourself if you choose to move away and leave it.

In your own space, take some serious deep breaths for a while.

The upset will naturally continue to run through your mind, but try to redirect your thoughts by focussing on something else, something nice, or listening to some favourite music – whatever you think will help.
You may even want to have a little cry on your own – it will help let the emotions or frustrations out without having to share them with the opposition!

Attempting to get the matter out of your head for a while will help you to move forward with things.

In time, you will both cool down and once you are in a calmer and more reasonable mood, you will be able to deal with things much more intelligently and effectively.

*There is nothing to be gained from screaming and shouting at each other.*

It won't resolve anything and will just make things worse, even creating some horrible scars that will be even harder to heal, than the issue that caused the situation in the first place.

*The ability to deal with negative emotions should really help you come on in leaps and bounds, enabling you to really enjoy life in a much more balanced and happy way.*

**…..and you bear grudges because……**
*How much time and bitterness do you use up in your life bearing grudges towards people who may have 'wronged' you in some way?*
You've never been able to forgive them because you don't want to back down, your stubbornness won't allow you, or you have spent so long in that grudging mode that you just can't get out of it, and so you've resigned yourself to a life spent in anger and resentment?
How much energy do you think this state of flux is zapping from you?
How much happiness is it robbing you of, never allowing you to move forward from it and continually taking up too much of a place in your soul, mind and heart.

How often does it keep rearing it's ugly head every time something reminds you of that woeful situation or person, because it's eaten it's way into your psyche and changed you as a person?
You may or may not realise this, but you are actually damaging your health in the process.

How can you feel empowered in life if you allow this negativity to control you, your thoughts, your actions and your lifestyle – all to your own detriment….?

If you feel like reeking revenge on someone and even if you did manage to, how do you think you will feel once you have exacted it, after the novelty has worn off of you having '*won*'?

If you want some '*one-upmanship*' – the best way to stick it to them is for them to see you happy, having a great life, fulfilling ambitions and smiling from ear to ear as you go along your adventurous life path.

*Happiness is the best revenge!*

It's natural that you're born with an innate sense of justice.
When someone has done something wrong to you, of course you want to right it.
You could spend hours, days, weeks, months, even years hatching a plan to get back at them.

Imagine how much negative energy that it taking up, sucking the life out of you - all to the deterioration of everything else that should be going on in your life...particularly if you are the type that is very unforgiving.

But to adopt a new attitude to situations and have the ability to start using a forgiveness strategy instead of spite, hatred and revenge, *will serve you so much better.*

It's a hard thing to do and will obvious take some time and strength, but if you want a calmer and more peaceful life, then it's worth using some effort to get to that wonderful state.

'They' say that '*life isn't fair*', and we all have to get used to a balance of good and bad things that happen in life, but once you accept that and you don't live in bitterness and anxiety every time things don't necessarily work in your favour, then forgiveness can be so much easier.

*If you're spending time ranting and raving about something or someone that has wronged or stressed you, then think seriously about who it is that is **actually** suffering?*

Because those people who you think have done this to you will not be the one feeling the pain – they've probably already moved on and forgotten what they've done – that's *IF* they even realise that they have *actually* done something wrong!

So, the only person who is actually crying over the situation is you!

Errrrr.....what's wrong with this picture...?

Holding onto your pain and hurt is only heightening the damage, not to mention pushing those close to you further away, as you drag them into your emotional troubles.

For years, Buddhists have preached about the virtues of forgiveness and letting go, moving on and embracing the '**now**'.
You will suffer more anxiety, depression and negative self-esteem if you insist on holding onto bitterness, and you find it hard to forgive both yourself and others.

It therefore seems obvious that forgiveness can reduce your stress levels and promote a better mood and state of health.
A refusal to forgive just causes more stress and increases irritability.

Perhaps it is time to empower yourself, take control of your emotions and negative situations by turning them into something positive.

So, next time someone does something that you consider mean or nasty, then try to just let it go over your head, instead of building the situation into a huge mountain of frustration, bitterness and anger. You'll feel much more relaxed, healthier and happier.

*Isn't happiness the best revenge of all?*

**Who was it that said '*Life is unfair*'....?**
**You can make it as <u>FAIR</u> as you want it to be..!**

## …..I'm surrounded by selfish and self-centred people….

*Everyday you probably come across selfish and self-centred people.*

You may even be a bit selfish yourself from time to time, but hopefully, it is not a general in-built characteristic.

However, you can try to adapt the following to both your personal and work-life....

Knowing how to deal with people who think of nothing but their own needs and wants to the point where they are oblivious to the people they are affecting, or don't even care who they hurt in their quest for self-gratification, pleasure or opinion, can be a very useful skill indeed.

If you want to feel fully empowered in your day to day activities, then you really do need to have a strategy for getting past these selfish and self-centred people, whilst still keeping your patience, stress-levels and reputation in tact.

The traits of the selfish are not always easy to notice and can come in different guises.

They can even come across as lovable, nice and sweet at the beginning of your acquaintance, but they are actually very adept at covering their darker side.

And then before you realise what's happening, they can lure you under their spell, and as your relationship begins to grow, they gradually render you emotionally weak and start sucking the happiness out of you.

Once they've got you to this stage, it's very difficult to change their behaviour.

*They are only interested in their own comfort and will have no consideration for anyone else throughout the process.*

Being nice and well-mannered is okay for them, as long as they are getting something out of it. They will totally believe that they are a perfectly nice person, often completely oblivious to their own selfish character, but in the process, carelessly and intentionally trample over everyone around them.

They'll probably be fake around those they dislike – pretending to be their friend.

You'll recognise the selfish person as someone who always seems to be taking from you, without ever giving anything back themselves. Always asking for favours – whether big or small, and squirming out of helping you in any way.

They'll also probably laugh with you about others they've selfishly taken advantage of, seemingly boasting about their cleverness.

They seem to prey on the more caring and emotional people, using and abusing them until the relationship breaks down, and then they're off to find some other poor victim to damage.

However, if you yourself are intimidating or less emotional, then they would be more inclined to suck up to you and try to win your affection, instead of being selfish.

They can even appear to be needy and vulnerable to begin with, caring for you and trying to please you, only for you to drop your guard, allow them into your heart and then lovingly hand over the strings of control to them.
They will be ready to take advantage.

After they have your affections, it becomes very one-sided, their caring drops and you become miserable, unappreciated and weak. At this point, they begin to feel more important than you and become convinced that you need *them* more than they need you.

*This is the foundation of all selfishness.*

This is when they expect you to do all the giving and they, the taking.
They are skilled manipulators and liars by instinct.
They can be lazy and aloof.
Unlike a truthful person who will tell you how it is, the selfish person will probably be the one who is sucking up, complimenting, eager to please and faking their smile.
*But they will have ulterior motives.*

This type of person will never commit to doing something for you *unless there's some benefit in it for themselves.*

With you as the weaker person, your selfish 'friend' will use you, and you will then become lost and confused, wondering why you are miserable around them, yet everyone else thinks they're brilliant!

Don't expect their sympathy if they hurt you, they'll only make you feel insignificant and won't take it seriously.
You are beneath them, so they won't apologise!

You'll undoubtedly feel a lot of hurt and pain, as no matter what you do, it won't be enough. You'll be picked on, flawed and over-looked and your feelings won't be reciprocated in what has become, a *one-sided* relationship.
All your bigger gestures will just be looked upon as ordinary and unremarkable.
All their expectations will continuously increase and you will end up craving for the slightest bit of attention to get their blessing that you are doing something *right*.

If you are being manipulated or used by such a selfish person, then you need to regain your strength and stop them from hurting you.

*You need to open your eyes and realise what's happening.*
Then you need to take some action to stop it continuing!

Although it may take some time and courage, you need to gradually detach yourself from them little by little.

You will then be able to *see more clearly* just *exactly* what this person is really like, and this will give you the strength you need to remove yourself from the situation and relationship.

*You need to become empowered to be **you** again!*

During this process, try and keep hold of your personality without changing straight away, otherwise they may end up leaving before you, and in that case, you will probably end up hurting all the more.
They would have the control again!

However, <u>don't</u> allow them to manipulate you again once they see you are becoming stronger, as they begin to repeat the whole process and you become hooked in all over again!

*Don't fall for this ploy, just gradually become stronger inside, whilst pretending to be the same person.....*

Replicating their behaviour may give them a chance to see how they are behaving themselves.

Once you are strong enough and in a position to stand up for yourself, using them or acting fake like they do gives them a taste of their own medicine, helping you to get back at them and also seeing for yourself how you were manipulated by them.
This won't always feel right to you and you may find this a negative way to conduct yourself, so it's up to you if you want to test this theory or not.
It's certainly not helpful to become something you are not, and it would be much better to act in a more positive way in your bid towards removing yourself from this relationship.

*You should be able to expect some kind of appreciation for your efforts and **not** be taken for granted or made to feel worthless and low.*

No-one needs to feel distressed and shocked by someone who is arrogant, mean, egotistical, selfish, scheming and plotting, all about 'me first' and live constantly just for themselves, shunning the needs of others in their wake.

These types are fearful of losing control and so spend their time maligning other's reputation, misrepresenting situations and are unwilling to compromise in their quest to get their own way.

They also don't want to share – whether that's material things or information, even if those resources just get wasted.
They never sacrifice anything for anyone.

This is probably borne out of insecurity and the lack of knowing about the balance of 'give and take'.

Their contempt of others can also come from a lack of self-esteem inducing a negative outlook on life and as such, are not good team players.
Sometimes they have a lack of drive and motivation and therefore find it difficult to inspire others, making them unpopular in the process.

Because they are very self-centred and self-obsessed, they cannot see or hear anyone else, have no consideration or good listening skills, because they don't have compassion for anyone else, cutting people off in mid-conversation to bring the focus back to themselves.
They are not interested in anyone else's opinions, suggestions or advice and they certainly don't need your contempt.

*Don't fall into any of their traps!*

Remain unfazed by their selfish acts and damaging calculating behaviour. Although they can be very annoying to some people, the best thing to do is change the subject and move on.

If you think you've got the patience, you can always try and bring them out of their negative frame of mind by asking them why they have been rude and critical.

There may well be reasons why someone is being rude and selfish. It may be that they have some personal problems that they can't share, or they don't want to get too close to people and be hurt by them as a result.

If you are sensitive and understanding, chances are they may see their own self-interest and become less critical of others.
Keep a sense of humour around them, be kind, stay cool, but keep your interaction with them short, particularly if you find that whatever you have tried just doesn't work.

However, if the relationship is damaging you, you may have to draw a line under it and move on. See if you can do this without judging them. This will just make things worse for everyone and be less destructive in the long run.

*You can't let people mistreat you, so stop cooperating with this.*

Be wise about things.
Remember that selfish people choose to be negative and pursue behaviour that hurts others, so they can feel better about themselves – and you don't want this to influence your behaviour or be associated with it.

Never think you can change a selfish person. If they won't change themselves, then you certainly won't be able to.

*You can't really build a proper long-term relationship with someone who doesn't have the ability to love and care for you, so why bother?*
They'll just look for someone else to manipulate instead!

*When you get up the strength, remove yourself and don't look back.*
Feel empowered and positive when you do this.
Walk tall and proud.
Be brave!
Think of the end result.

**Think of life on the other side.....!**

Your life is *yours* to live and fulfil, so you deserve to get out there and be who you want to be, not be someone else's slave and dogsbody.
Make your change for the better.

*Get your empowered head on and go for it!*

**.......you don't have to put up with unreasonable people.....**
*Some people are just unreasonable.*
You probably come across them on a regular basis - but dealing with them can become quite frustrating, particularly if you really don't know how to handle them positively and effectively.
And that can seriously affect how empowered you feel....

It is important to try and stay calm when people are just being unreasonable with you, especially if you want to emerge from the situation unscathed. Under these circumstances, they will invariably be provoking a response from you and will certainly not be interested in your opinion, or what the facts are and who is actually *right*.

If you can pinpoint their argument and acknowledge their anger, you can cleverly redirect the focus back onto their behaviour, without responding in kind. Remember that unreasonable people are usually projecting their own faults and anger onto you, so are likely to hurl it your way regardless of your response.

Your first instinct will probably be on the defensive.
However, try to focus on the *real* issue, as it is crucial to maintain your *own* equilibrium whilst you try and diffuse the situation.

*Don't rise to their wrath or get into a win or lose mentality!*

You won't win with logic, personal opinions, facts or certificates, nor will treating them with the same disregard for civility and rationality that they are showing you, get you anywhere......
You need to learn to *work* with this type of person.

*Master self-control to triumph over them.*

And by showing them the level of respect that you wish to be treated with, you can move the argument back into the realm of positivity, without resorting to arguing at their volume and level - because they just see this as winning and therefore attempt to continue the conflict.

If you are having to deal with unreasonable people in authority who are giving you impossible demands that you believe cannot be realistically accomplished, then simply request all that is required to do the job, rather than just telling them how futile it is.
This way you are keeping the focus on what they want doing and giving them a stark reminder of what is actually involved to achieve this insurmountable task.

If needs be, get a mediator to take some control of the situation. Always remember when it comes to unreasonable people, that you are not the deluded person.

But you *can* emerge with your own sanity and dignity intact, if you learn how to deal with them effectively!
Don't let them walk all over you and make you feel small in any way. You have the total right to live decently with your head held high and not be made a fool of.

*Show your true worth and feel empowered – not downtrodden!*

**….oh dear....here comes the know-it-all to rain on my parade.....**
*There are times in life when you may feel intimated by someone who thinks they know everything about everything.*
It's an irritating situation that can be dealt with quite effectively without you feeling like the underdog. Good news!

The first and most obvious way of dealing with a know-it-all is just to avoid them! If you keep out of their way, they can't get at you, or irritate and intimidate you.

Keeping calm and unemotional means they will have nothing to feed off. As soon as they sense tension, you're lost. They will thrive on the 'wind-up' as well as your misery and insecurity.

Keep your pride in tact by remaining calm throughout.

If you have no choice but to interact with them for some meaningful debate or other, make sure you know what you are talking about, by getting all the facts you need in advance. Preparation will enhance your argument and enable you to put them in their place if needs be.
If they are adamant about their view, ask them to prove their source of information. If they can't, then you have won against them.

*Take the fun out of their wind-up by refusing to care.*

If they have nothing to attack due to your lack of interest, they have nothing to feed on.
If you are dismissive of them with phrases like "*whatever*" and "*if you say so*", you are not providing them with any weapons and therefore they have nothing to use as a means against you.

Have a sense of humour – they can't argue with someone who is smiling and laughing at their expense!

If you do get stuck in a conversation with a know-it-all, always remember that they will only stand to lose admiration and respect from the people they talk to, so keep that in mind.

Imagine how empowered you will feel if you can sensibly use any of these tactics and come out of the other side *winning* with such people.
Makes you smile doesn't it........

**...you don't have to be dragged down by manipulative people....**
*Winning can be the only goal for some people.*
And in their ultimate quest to get there, they can use '*covert (hidden) aggression*' to dominate and control you.
Using underhanded and deceptive behaviour, they will assert their power and hide their true intentions in their manipulation of you.

These tactics are a steady diet for this type of personality.
It's the way a manipulator prefers to deal with you to get to the things they want in life.
You need to be able to spot them and handle them effectively, so that you can carry on building your dreams and following your aspirations.

The following are their tactics that you need to look out for.....
In their process of victimization, your manipulator is not necessarily obvious in the way they behave and as such, you as the 'victim', can *feel* something going on, but can't pin-point the evidence of aggression, and, unable to validate your feelings, you can become quite defensive.

*If you are under the spell of the manipulator, their clever ploy is that they don't appear to be fighting in any way, so their tactics are hard to recognise.*

Because of this, they seem to make just enough sense to put you in doubt and question your gut feeling, and in the process, you are taken advantage of.

Because these features make them highly effective psychologically, anyone can become vulnerable and emotional and therefore unable to think clearly.

A manipulator can easily home in on and exploit your weakness or insecurity – whether you are aware of it or not. They can recognise them and know all the right buttons to push.

Your gut feeling may be quite sensitive and as such, you will probably be in the habit of giving people the benefit of the doubt, thinking that there must be something softer and more vulnerable 'underneath'.
All whilst trying not to admit to the real conniving and ruthless character of the manipulator and their underhand agenda.
You won't want to appear to them or others as harsh, judgemental or negative and you may tend to doubt *yourself more,* than you believe the true nature of their intentions.

If you want to feel more empowered around these types of people, it is fundamental that you are able to recognize their agenda and learn how to handle yourself more confidently.
So you can free yourself from their control and dominance for good. In the process of doing this, your self-esteem will be given the boost it needs.

When you try to protect and defend yourself, you naturally and quite unconsciously go into your own *automatic defence mechanisms*.

Your manipulator will use a variety of mental behaviours and manoeuvres to help ensure they get what they want.
Rather than defending their ego from a sense of guilt or shame, the manipulator will usually be fighting for their position, gaining power and removing any obstacles that get in their way.

*You need to spot the tactics they are using to maintain their power over you – one of which is denial.*

They will refuse to admit that they have hurt you or done anything wrong, denying any kind of insensitivity or ruthlessness - even though they clearly have!
They can convince you that to their merit, that they are only acting

on loyalty, concern, passion and conscientiousness.
Then you end up looking like the fool because *your* behaviour and *insinuation* 'seems' inappropriate and unjustified! And when you confront them, they play innocent and you end up retreating with feelings of guilt.

This just leads to them carrying on as though they now have permission to do so, aggressively pursuing their personal agenda! They can go about their business thinking they are acting in honour, nobility, purity and honesty. They will always have a high awareness of what might hinder or advance their cause – even sometimes changing tack completely in it's successful pursuit.

*Playing dumb is another clever tactic.*
Being oblivious to any kind of warning, plea or wish by anyone else, they refuse to pay any attention to anything that will distract them from their goal – resisting and refraining from changing in your favour. Even though they will know full well what you may be after, it's futile because actively listening to and heeding your suggestions is an act of submission to them.

From their point of view, they don't need to listen, submit to, be guided or directed by anyone else, because they would be losing their power and control over the situation, because they will usually view you as <u>less</u> clever, powerful or capable than them!

*Another effective tactic of theirs is rationalisation.*
Your manipulator makes sense of their behaviour, persuading you by rationalising in such a way as to convincingly justify and explain their actions enough, so you fall for it!
In doing so, they manage to keep you off their back.

They also send out subtle messages that makes you feel ashamed that you are not operating in their 'honourable' way. This intention makes you feel guilty for not being as conscientious as they are '*pretending*' to be.

Your manipulator is then free to pursue their own goals without interference and quashing any qualms of conscience – that's if they actually *have* any!

*Changing the subject to cause a diversion is another notorious move your manipulator will use - particularly if you try and pin them down to a single issue or behaviour you don't like.*

They will change the subject, dodge the issue, throw a curve ball, just be evasive - anything to distract from focussing on their behaviour or question, or to receive any kind of consequence. This then just keeps them free for self-promotion.

They can cleverly side-track you down a road where they can shift the focus onto *your* 'negative' behaviours instead, and in doing so, completely divert the attention away from them and give you the run-around, so that a straight answer from them is never actually achieved.

If you're not being given a <u>direct</u> answer, it's highly likely that you are being given the slip!

*Your manipulator will be prone to lying and cheating in their quest for getting what they want.*

They have very subtle ways to go about it so you don't find out until later that you have been duped! Look out for them distorting or withholding the truth from you and being vague to direct questions.

If you need to obtain specific information – ask for them to confirm it.
*Frequent intimidation with subtle, indirect or implied threats, or guilt-tripping and shaming to keep you anxious, apprehensive and in the 'under-dog' position, is another manipulative behaviour to keep you self-doubting and in a state of anxiety and submissiveness.*

To them they are illustrating a comparison between their and your characters.

And, because you may have more of a *conscience*, your manipulator will use this trait to make you feel bad by suggesting you don't care enough, or that *you* are selfish.

In fact, the total opposite is true and applies to *them* more - however they would <u>never</u> admit to any wrongdoing whatsoever.

*Making you feel inadequate, ashamed and unworthy is another technique, using subtle sarcasm and put-downs to increase fear and self-doubt.*

In doing so, they foster a continued sense of personal inadequacy in you, as the weaker party, thereby allowing them to maintain a position of dominance. It can be done just by tone of voice or glances, questioning your credentials, position, authority or certainty about a particular issue.

*Also, gaining sympathy and compassion by playing the innocent victim of unfair treatment and unwarranted hostility, is another crafty behaviour used to get something out of you.*
By relying on your less callous and hostile personality, they can convince you that they are truly suffering and that they wouldn't want to see anyone in distress, and in doing so, it puts you on the defensive.

*Yet another tactic used, is to make out that they are only being aggressive to defend themselves, and as a consequence, putting you, the victim, unconsciously on the defensive.*
This masks your manipulator's intent and bullish behaviour and in the process, gets you to back off.

*Claiming to be of devoted service and obedience is also a very cunning ploy.*
They will maintain they are working hard and tirelessly towards a more noble cause. But all the while they are just working towards their own self-serving agendas and ambitions, in their desire for power and the dominant position. Far from being the humble and submissive servant, the only master they serve will be their own desire, loudly professing subservience in their fight for dominance.

*The art of seduction is another surreptitious characteristic used to get you to lower your defences to gain trust and loyalty.*
Knowing that people want approval, reassurance and to feel valued and important, they will tell you that you are of worth, knowing full well that you can also be emotionally needy and dependent.
On their mission, they are very adept at being attentive, charming, praising, flattering or overtly supportive of you. In doing so, you end up giving them your loyalty and confidence, all whilst behind the scenes things will always turn out *their* way.

*Finding a scapegoat to get them off the hook by projecting the blame onto you is yet another crafty manoeuvre used expertly and subtly, but is quite hard to detect.*
Some people are capable of being totally kind from the outside, but

beware - they can be vicious on the inside! Or they may seem sincere, but are really quite evasive. Others seem very hard-working, yet are totally untrustworthy.

<u>*Look out for these traits and be very wary of them*</u>.

Use your intelligence and own clever manoeuvres to dodge these situations. Don't be drawn into their web or sucked into their wily ways!
They are only after satisfying their own agenda.....and you need to satisfy your *own*, not get blocked or shut down by these people!

As well as knowing how to handle a manipulator, you may find yourself in a scenario where you have to ascertain what someone's *true* character is, so that you can make the right decisions and gain some kind of empowerment for yourself.

There are some helpful tricks you can use to try and establish their *real* traits.....

1. If you want to know what their *real views are* on life, strike up a debate about something.
   *They'll soon show their true colours.*
2. See how they *change their inner state* if you verbally challenge them.
   *Things will come out.*
3. See how wise they are by discussing certain strategies with them.
   *Watch exactly how clever they are.*
4. Find out *how courageous they are* when you tell them about dangers and difficulties ahead.
   *How do they stand up?*
5. Watch their *true nature come out* after they've had a few drinks!
   *Alcohol makes you talk!*
6. Give them a chance to show *how virtuous they are* by getting them to handle money.
   *Always a temptation!*
7. Check their *competence* by giving them a job to do.
   *This will show their true skills.*

8. Watch *who they make friends with* during a time when their fortunes are low.
   *Their position will tell a lot of home truths.*
9. See *who gets their charity* when they have plenty of money in the bank.
   *If anyone does at all......*
10. See the *types of people they employ* when they get to a high enough position.
    *Who will they help out?*
11. Observe *their ethics* during times of difficulty.
    *A sure fire time to show true characteristics!*
12. See if they would *take up a bribe* during times when they are down on their uppers.
    *Another way to open up the truth flood-gates.*
13. Check *how steadfast they would be* if they were tempted by seduction.
    *Some people can easily be pulled down in certain circumstances....*

If you recognise that you may be dealing with a manipulative person, albeit slick, subtle and adept, *listen to your gut and true sense of empowerment and make sure you are not taken in by them*!

Employing some of these tactics will help your life run more smoothly and with strength and clarity.

Or do you recognise these characteristics in yourself?
How does this picture make you feel as a person?
If you find there's more negative traits in there than you like, then perhaps it's time to start being a little nicer in life.....

*If you change your thinking to a more positive perspective, things will naturally come to you without employing these under-hand tactics – so maybe it's worth taking that journey instead.*

It'll also make you a lot more friends along the way too......!

**Life is meant to be lived,
so no matter what is thrown at you,
move through it with grace and dignity.**
*Never, ever let anyone take away your mojo –
it's yours to be proud of.*

**….don't be too timid to ask for that money or favour you're owed or need....**
*There will probably be a time in your life when you need to ask someone for money.*
This could be quite an embarrassing prospect for you because it can be such a sensitive issue.
In these circumstances, you will need to take a deep breath, dust off your '*killer instinct*' and become strong and empowered in order to achieve a positive outcome!

Similarly, there will be other times when you may need to develop and use this approach to help you get over some of life's obstacles – not just for money.

However, there really is no actual *mystery* to how to get money or favours from people - other than merely <u>*asking*</u>!

The **big secret** is to *ignore* whatever emotions you have going on at the time, put them aside and just focus on the task of getting that money or outcome.
So don't think about embarrassment, guilt, nervousness, fear, intimidation, or any other feelings that may come along with such a task.....

*Your goal is to get that money or favour fulfilled, so you need to <u>whole-heartedly</u> go after it!*

You must totally ignore any other state of mind you happen to be in, detach yourself from anything else going on in your life and concentrate solely on your objective.

*Just take a deep breath and do it!*

With this kind of totally focussed mind, you can actually develop that perfect killer instinct and use it to make all sorts of other important advances in your life.

Make your actions and words *totally effective and powerful* for you. *Be strong and give it a try – you've got nothing to lose and* **everything** *to gain!*

> *"Each day is a new journey.*
> *Make it exciting, interesting and fulfilling".*

**…..my finances are all over the place.....and it's getting in the way of my progress.....**
*There is nothing less empowering than being pulled right down by problems with your finances.* Finding yourself in this situation could be due to having so many debts that you just can't handle, or burying your head in the sand and ignoring certain financial circumstances, or perhaps you just don't focus realistically on what's what with your money!

Just think about how much *better* you would feel if you didn't have this depressing millstone hanging round your neck, dominating your head-space and nerves every minute of the day and night!

*You would be able to breathe again, feel calmer and more at ease with yourself and the world.*

How empowering!

If you are someone in this unfortunate financial dilemma, you probably secretly already know that things need to be put in order - especially if you want to walk around with your head held high.
*That said, there's no time like the present to get around to sorting it all out.*
Your first step towards doing this is to establish how much you're spending each month - *particularly if you're <u>overspending</u>!*
If you feel out of your depth, get some expert help in to sort things out for you – it will probably be money well spent and may even be a saving in the long run!

Look at it as a sound investment, rather than an unnecessary or unaffordable cost.

Try the following strategy:

Make a list of all your monthly outgoings – mortgage or rent, household bills, travel costs, food, entertainment costs, etc., plus any money going into a savings accounts or towards credit cards and loan repayments.
Remember to factor in your one-off yearly costs, like car insurance, MOT and holidays – dividing by twelve to give you an approximate monthly amount.

Then separate the costs into *essential* and *non-essential*.

To do that, ask yourself what would happen if you *couldn't pay* for something, i.e. clearing a credit card debt versus missing a payment on your mortgage - which is far more serious, as you could lose your home!

Once you've completed this exercise, you will have a much clearer picture of your finances and you can begin to write up a realistic budget.

Whilst going through this process, see if you can cut back in certain areas to *free up money* that can be used to address any outstanding debts.
There are probably many ways you can cut waste if you look at things properly....
*Really consider deeply* where these areas are – it could be the difference between you being in the black or the red - so it's really worth the effort!

If you find that you don't have enough money to stretch to addressing your debts, you *must* contact your lenders to see if you can rearrange some monthly payments.
If you <u>talk to them</u>, you will get much more of a chance to work something out, rather than if you just ignore the situation and allow things to build up into an *unnecessary negative headache*.

Debtors *can* be approached if you are <u>honest</u> with them, because they would rather receive *something* every month than have to keep chasing you for payments you just cannot afford.

*Plus*, if you just *leave things without dealing with them sensibly*, you will end up in much more hot water and owing far more, because they will increase what you owe by adding on *extra* costs for administration, debt collecting agency fees or even court costs! You will then end up having to pay off your debts for **so many more** months, or even years, rather than if you had just acknowledged, confronted and sorted the whole situation out up front instead.

*It's all just wasted money! You might as well just make a pile and set fire to it!*

Throughout your budgeting process, any costs you can actually *eliminate completely* should be highlighted, like the gym membership you never use, or seemingly small things like takeaways and cabs - things that build up quite substantially without you even realising it!

Take the time to assess your bank and credit card arrangements.
Is it possible to extend your overdraft limit with your existing bank or think about moving accounts to a more competitive bank?
What about the interest on your credit cards - are you paying more than you need to?

If you've got a large amount of debt, try switching to a 0% balance transfer card or a lower rate card – saving you on interest every month, thereby giving you less time to pay it off.
Once your debt is eventually paid up, you can start thinking about what to do with your money.

If it allows, it may be time to start putting your dream into action with any surplus cash you can squirrel away towards your ultimate goals and ambitions. Or if you are already in business, how you can expand or develop your enterprise in some lucrative way.

It is a very liberating feeling to have some savings building up in a specific savings account, because you *know* you have a backup to use when you need it.

But can you improve on or create a new saving habit? Even if it's only £25 a month at first, it will soon build up..... It will take some discipline, but saving or investing your money is the best way of ensuring you're financially prepared for the future.

It's your safeguard that you are moving towards what you should really be doing with your life – whether that's setting up in business if you aren't already, learning a new skill to get your dream off the ground, or just settling down somewhere in peace and quiet and eliminating the stresses out of your life – something you may have been yearning to do for so long.....

The best thing to do with your savings initially is to build up an emergency pot of 3-6 month's salary in an account that you have easy access to, particularly if your financial priorities are looking after your family or clearing a very large mortgage.
Knowing you have this pot behind you will make you feel a whole lot more secure should you be in a situation where you lose your job or income, or perhaps decide to go it alone.
At least you know you will have this period covered.

Once you have your security savings for emergencies sorted out, it's best to put any more savings aside in an ISA, as it is a tax-efficient account and you will earn all the interest on it. Standard savings accounts are taxed on any interest you get.
Set up a direct debit each month, so you know it's going out of your account and you can't squander it away on unnecessary frivolities.

You could go for stocks and shares if you have more time, but this is risky, and if you want to keep your nest-egg for certain activities, like setting up your business or changing your lifestyle, then this is something you will need to think about very carefully. You can reduce the risk if you choose collective investments which give you exposure to a selection of companies, instead of individual ones. *Get some expert advice on this.*

If you want to go down the conventional pension route to secure yourself at retirement, as opposed to other ways of making money for this period, such as investing in property or making good business choices that reap rewards that you can rely on for your future instead, then start saving for it as soon as you can.

Some employers promise to match or exceed your contributions. You can also benefit from tax relief on your contributions into your pension. If you are already on top of your pension, make sure you check it annually to ensure you are not investing in any flops!

*Every saving you make on your food, bills, utilities and holidays, or business accounts, can be helping you save for your long-term future and accomplishing your goals and dreams.*

Be disciplined and focussed about it.
Make it your mission to get past any financial headaches and to secure some backup funds, so you feel empowered to proceed in a much more positive way and *really* get what you want out of your life!
It's in your hands.....

### ....a few tips for your finances....
*Here are some things to consider when it comes to looking after your money.*
Ensure you don't land on your uppers if you were to lose your job, by never depending on that one single income.
Make an investment or find a simple way to create a *second* source from somewhere.
You will be glad you did if something was to go wrong.

*If you are a spendthrift, you should know that if you continually buy things you don't actually need, chances are that you will end up having to sell things you **do** need.*
Rein in the spending.

*When that rainy day does actually come, will you have anything to fall back on?*
Some financial experts believe that the priority shouldn't be to save what is left after <u>spending</u>, but to spend what is left after <u>saving</u>.

*Are you a risk taker?*
Well, if you are, remember - never test the depth of the water with both feet!
Some investments will sound wonderful, but always think first – should you put all your eggs in one basket....?
If the investment fails, what are you left with?

*Everyone has certain expectations of each other, but think about this – honesty is a very expensive gift, so don't expect it from cheap people.....*
You will reap benefits if you bear these few golden nuggets in mind the next time you are feeling frivolous about your financial decisions.

*Being on top of your personal money situation is a wonderfully empowering feeling.*

Enjoy it!

**…..money gives you freedom as well as riches....**
*When it comes to money, it shouldn't purely be what is driving you in life.*
It is your *goals*, your *adventures*, your *inspirations*, your *peace* and *contentment* that should be the *real* motivation behind valuing the cash....
The proper reason why you require money is actually to fulfil these desires.
Money gives you freedom because it provides you with the means to do what you want, when you want.

*It gives you peace of mind.*

Peace of mind in the knowledge that you can pay those nagging bills that stress you, that you can have that holiday you *so* need to give you time to relax, you can get that beautiful home in your chosen location that allows you to live in calm and relaxation, or you can have the cash for adventures to explore this wonderful world and funds that can thrust your entrepreneurial spirit towards a thriving business.

And if you have a humanitarian or philanthropic nature, cash to be able to dedicate a portion of to help your favourite charity or a community project that's close to your heart.
Or perhaps just to be able to give your family and friends when they need help.
You may even just want a *little* money to give you the freedom to live in peace and comfort and just 'be'.....
*It doesn't have to be millions to be satisfying.*

Indeed, some people do not want or need to be striving to get to the millions.

*Rich can mean different things to different people.*

It doesn't *have* to be 'Trump-style' to give you what you want in life. Although it *could* be!
Rich to you could mean rich inside, rich in relationships, rich in satisfaction, rich in peace and harmony. Whatever it is to you, this is your own individual goal.
And a little money can give you that bit of comfort and happiness.

*Money can mean empowerment in the way you personally believe it can.*
So don't look at money as the 'root of all evil', or for driving yourself to the bitter edge in it's pursuit, just for it all to pile up for the sake of it, or merely for pure arrogance and self-importance.

*It can be the gateway to all good!*

Use money *effectively* to achieve those important dreams you have in life.
Strive to do and be who you genuinely *should* be, by making enough funds to fulfil your own state of inner excellence and to feel free, calm and totally true to yourself......

*Money is a just the medium towards achieving the lifestyle you so desire.....*

**....attracting money and abundance....**
*Money is abundance, but that's not all abundance is.*
It can be wealth in the form of knowledge, health, creativity, confidence, love, peace, happiness, family and anything else you care to mention that you want or need in your life, every day.
Abundance is also relative.

*If you have never had anything, then any more than a little can actually feel like huge abundance.*

If a homeless person has never had shelter, then a home, no matter how ramshackle, can feel like total enrichment.

A hungry person who is given a regular meal, feels abundance in that nourishment.
A couple desperate for a family being given a child will feel they have been blessed and filled with abundance.
And still, a person striving to climb a career ladder to the top, or an entrepreneur endeavouring to make their business thrive and make a good life for themselves, will feel like wealth and success is their abundance.

It depends on your individual circumstances....

If you want to improve your own situation, then you will need to put yourself in a place where you can enable those riches and abundance to come your way.
No-one has a magic wand to wave over you, so to make it all happen, you will need to have some kind of dedication or commitment.
Unless, of course, you are relying on pure luck.....

So to get started, you need to establish, within reason, what it is you want, or how much you need to earn to achieve your desire and then put a deadline on it.
This doesn't mean you should be ridiculously unrealistic about it though!

For instance, if you've never earned a million pounds in your life, then the chances are, under *normal* circumstances, you're not remotely likely to earn that much within the month!

*Having your goal in mind makes it easier to acquire money or even manifest prosperity once you've made up your mind that you're going to do it.*
So then – make up your mind!

Maybe you've already had a set of important circumstances in your life, but perhaps on a different level, that you can refer to as an example?

For instance, have you been in a situation where you've absolutely *had* to raise some cash come hell or high water *as a matter of*

*urgency,* and it was essential to find some doable way of achieving it?
Perhaps you needed to find a small car for a brand new job, without which you wouldn't have a chance of fulfilling the role.....

*Therefore, you expected to find it somehow, and you did.*

When you have a goal such as this in mind, you will know that the *specific goal itself* is what you focus on, rather than the money. You had an 'obsession' or necessity that needed to be realised. Concentrating *directly* on a specific goal focusses your mind on what it is you want and then you build up an intense desire to manifest it.

The money itself is a means to that end and is not the main obsession.

Obviously money isn't going to come out of thin air without some sheer hard work. But in order to attain your goal, you need to keep concentrating your energies on how to attract money to accomplish it.
Even if your current earnings might not be enough, your subconscious mind will eventually start coming up with ideas and you will begin to gain momentum, thus encouraging you to work even harder with what you have.
As you open your mind, far more opportunities will present themselves and you will be in a much better position to follow them through.

*Your expectations and obsessions will lead you along the pathway of attracting money to achieve your aim.*

Once you get into this *mental mode*, you will gain empowerment over your life and goals.
Your financial status should feel much better and the knock-on effect of that will give you a real sense of satisfaction and peace inside.
You will be much better able to cope and happiness should ensue as you take control of your situation.
Life will feel more enhanced and the follow-on consequence within your circle will be immense.

Everyone will gain from your new way of thinking and experience a real sense of this *new* you.

Pass on your wisdom so that others can benefit from your knowledge and overall enjoyment of life alongside you......

Abundance will come as a part of the *law of attraction* as you open up your natural *flow*.
You will enrich your life both from a monetary aspect and of fulfilment in so many other ways – ways that you choose to follow.

*Your path awaits, so go and grab it with both hands.*

**…..so see money for what it really is.** ….
*Enjoy it, make it work for you, allow it to contribute to your life, but don't let it take over your whole life - as it can be fickle.*
It is not really part of who you are - you didn't bring it with you at birth and you won't take it with you at death.
So, keep an indifferent attitude toward it.

*Your whole life is not always about financial reward.*

Some rewards like joy, happiness, fun and love, can be far more gratifying than any abundance of cash.

So it's not *all* about money or worldly success, but rather it's about a fulfilling life and your own *personal* success.
Obtaining prosperity is not about what you are willing to do to gain it, more importantly, it is about what you are willing to *give up* in exchange for it.

*If you are so focussed on making a living – you don't see anything else.*

So focus on your goals and happiness instead.

Use money as a means to an end – so you get what you truly want out of life and don't see it just as the sole purpose for living....

*You will definitely feel the total empowerment in this....*

**…..do you want to be rich…….or are you just where you're meant to be….**

*Most people think they want to be rich, but in reality, they are just where they are intended to be financially.*
That may be hard to swallow, but realistically, if you weren't, you'd be doing something to make it different…..

Money has a definite way of making life more convenient for you. It may not buy you happiness, but it can buy you a certain *lifestyle*.

But in order to gain prosperity, you will most likely need to give something up in exchange for having that wealth in your hand…..

If you're not there yet, then there's a strong possibility that it's because you don't want to give up certain '*stuff*' in order to get to your prosperous future, like the time, effort, partying, friends, particular creature comforts and pass-times, etc.
Quite probably because you can't be bothered.

*And, that's why people are mostly, where they 'should be' financially.*

Even when you do have money, it's a bet you complain it's still not enough….
The more you have, the more you want.
And, if you lose it, you wish you'd appreciated it more when you had it!
So, if you *do* want it, you have to establish in your mind exactly <u>whether or not</u> you are *willing* to go that extra mile, out into the big wide world and actually *fight for it*….?

If you want to be something successful, then you have to make the effort.

*And that's all about having the right mindset to go forward and make your fortune.*

Once you establish that specific mindset, when you do make money and are unfortunate enough to lose it, you will *know* that you have the capacity to make it again, because you will have the confidence, ability and **will**.

Fortunes are made and lost every day.....

If you find a role in life that you enjoy, you *should* be able to make a good livelihood out of it.

*Most successful people will be following this strategy.*

The money will take care of itself because you are using your innate given talents and expertise to *earn your path to wealth*.

Any job just taken for security alone or that initially pays well, will likely not fulfil you and therefore your enthusiasm and creativity will begin to wane, consequently making you mediocre and with little reward to show for it.

*You need to use and nurture your unique spark of brilliance –* something that is in everyone - in order to establish and accomplish something that cannot be done by someone else.
Find your *USP*....

*Striving to discover exactly what* **that** *is should be part of your vital drive and desire in life.*

And, whether you realise it or not, whatever that is, may constantly be trying to *reveal* itself to you, but you could be missing it all the time, because you are *so* focused on making a living that you just don't notice!
However, if you've become stagnated and you *really* want to make some kind of wealth, you need to set your sights much higher than you already probably do, because you will never make any money or success from having mediocre ambitions.

*Weak dreams inspire weak efforts.*

Here's a point to think about in this situation - don't fight your battle at the *bottom* of the pyramid – because that's where most other people are and it's already much too crowded!
*It's much easier nearer the top.....*

Also, it's usually much harder to scrape a few pounds together, than it is to acquire an abundance of money – in much the same was as it's easier to sell an expensive luxury car to someone with money, than it is to sell a beaten-up wreck to someone who just can't afford it!

*Apply this sentiment to life in general and begin to value yourself and what you have to offer.*

Be unique in your abilities and think big in your ambitions.
There is always someone out there looking for your talents.

*Remember - the world is full of many varying statuses and levels of wealth.*

If you have a real valuable offer, someone will be able to pay for it if they really want it, *so don't sell yourself short*.
Feel proud of your efforts.
Believe in yourself.
Don't be bottom of the pile.
Push yourself and make your fortune – whether that's monetary or satisfaction and fulfilment.

*The world is a big place, so why not be a big player in it......?*

>  **"Accelerate your growth, evolve with abandon,
> be inspired and allow, live and love your purpose".**

**….using meditation and visualisation to achieve abundance…..**
*Participating in meditation and visualisations will undoubtedly make you feel a lot more spiritual and 'connected' to the world and all it's beauty.*
The more you dedicate yourself, the more you can allow the essence of these practises to flow freely through your conscious mind.
Then gradually, from this *connected* position, you can feel more secure in the knowledge that life is really working in your favour. You will be able to *feel* the energy radiating through you and channelling your *higher* spiritual self.

Be genuinely open to this flow and with little effort your goals will be

realised, as things _naturally_ twist and turn to your benefit, removing the stress of struggling.
Things will feel far more harmonious and at ease, because you will stop 'blocking' the process.

If that sounds a bit far fetched to you because you haven't ever really indulged in this kind of thinking before, then at least give it a try and see how it works out for you.

Take it earnestly and you will be amazed by the results......

Life is a journey and your destination will clearly be in sight as you relax with this flow, so make sure you enjoy it and are willing to change yourself where appropriate along the way.
As part of this process, you should not allow any strong emotions to get in the way of attaining your goal, otherwise you will be working _against_ yourself and this flow.
You will just be energizing the _negative thought_ of <u>not</u> achieving anything, rather than energizing the _actual goal_ itself.

If you are very emotionally attached to your goal - enough for your fears and feelings to negatively overtake your actual progress, then you may need some help figuring out why you are allowing them to get in the way of achieving your ambition.
Seek assistance with this if needs be.

Also, help this situation by continuously practising your positive affirmations to help build up your confidence and make you feel more secure. Tell yourself that the universe is looking after you, that it will always provide for you and you have everything you need.....

_Love yourself._

Tell yourself to relax, let go and allow things to flow towards you.
If you find yourself continuously 'butting up' against your desires, then know that there are forces telling you that actually _this may not be the right way to go_. The universe could be showing you that there may be _something better and more suited to you out there instead_ - something that you may not have even thought of yet....

Remember – everything happens for a reason.......

Never forget that everything is out there for the taking, including all your own true desires - you just have to prepare yourself emotionally, spiritually, mentally, intellectually and physically to *believe and accept it.*
Using your visualisations and power mantras, you can bring forth a sense of prosperity and abundance into your life.
You need that *strong belief* that there is enough for everyone out there - *and you are no exception!*

*The universe is filled with absolute abundance.*

You don't need to be spiritual to realise this.
You have to stop thinking that life is hard, that you are thinking in a selfish way, or that you have to sacrifice to gain anything. If you do, you are concentrating on *lack* and not *abundance.* These are very limiting thoughts and totally against how the universe naturally works, and this flow....

Everyone is meant to be prosperous, you just need to understand and learn how material and spiritual wealth is harmoniously balanced and how the earth nourishes you.

*You should also learn to enjoy the simple things in life.*

Once you have everything you basically need, you can spend time expressing yourself creatively, enjoying the experience of abundance in a balanced way, without constantly thinking about material wealth as a means to happiness.

You need to appreciate what the earth has to offer in it's beauty, nourishment and infinite good, so that you can believe in all great possibilities and flourish accordingly.

*Begin to imagine yourself as a whole and successful, fulfilled person, satisfied with your life.*

You have to believe that the world is a good place in which you, and everyone else in it, can create the life you want individually, so that you can find true happiness.

Visualise yourself doing exactly what you want, living the way you want, loving your life in absolute fulfilment and satisfaction.

**Just try it.**
*See what happens......*

However you look at this, even if you think it is a bit far-fetched, just by the action of being relaxed, positive, confident, optimistic, balanced and open to what the world has to offer and being accepting and grateful, it stands to reason that more is going to come your way.
This is because you will be in a more open and accepting position to welcome all of those things and put greater effort into achieving what you want in life....
It doesn't necessarily *have* to come from any spiritual state – it's just a matter of common sense really.

*Once you sign up to this way of thinking, true empowerment will ensue and you cannot fail to live in true happiness and abundance.*

**…...so then, you should not continue to look at wealth as elusive....**
*If you adopt the belief that abundance is just never going to come your way, then it will become harder and harder to find the riches you desire.*
On the other hand, if you look at the Universe as the rich source of unlimited bounty that it is, you can open the flood-gates to all the resources you need.

*Embracing this belief puts you in a position to be receptive and welcoming to it....*

To fulfil your chosen purpose and gain the tools and funds to achieve it, make an important pact with yourself at the beginning of each year, or when you personally think your new year should begin – perhaps that's *NOW*!

Think about what it is that you would like to achieve in *this* new year and what *this* year is going to mean to you....
Have a little mind-mapping session with yourself, thinking hard and deeply, get it all out and then whittle everything down to a serious

ultimate aim that has a deep-seated passion and yearning for you.

*It has to be realistic to you and your inner desires.*

Commit it to some paper or electronically, so it's available for you to focus on regularly and it keeps your goal continuously in the front of your mind. Look at it religiously, reflecting and updating it every month, so it instils fresh motivation and keeps the momentum and excitement going all the time.

*Make sure you write it down in a* **positive** *way and mean what you say!*
Upbeat, positive affirmations are the way to do this – no '*ifs*', '*ands*' or '*buts*' used in any way. This is your *own* selfish goal or ambition for *you* to achieve, so make your <u>own</u> mind up.
Perhaps you desire a year of working towards your wealth and freedom.

Maybe you want to achieve something specific in this particular year that you have been meaning to do for a long time, but keep putting it off.

Remember, the more you achieve for yourself, the happier you will be, and in turn the happier you will be around your colleagues, friends and family, which can only benefit all of you.

If there are some sacrifices you need to make in order to get these things done, then think carefully about what they may be and how you can make them without upsetting too many people around you – bearing in mind that these sacrifices will be made in order to improve the lives of those around you too.

*These ambitions and achievements – your 'inner wealth', don't necessarily need to be about work.*

They could just as easily be about adventure, fun stuff, family or health and fitness.
It's up to you – *your life, your choice.*

To help you focus and concentrate, you can always meditate to enhance your state of positivity concerning having abundance and prosperity – on any level. You can then relax whilst visualising yourself in your ultimate existence, being in a wonderful environment that fits you personally, with all the family and friends you need, doing the work you love, being outwardly expressive and creative and being rewarded for your efforts, having a deep satisfaction of life and feeling peace and harmony.

Whatever your chosen desire is. Whatever your chosen state of wealth is.....

To move away from that built-in notion of prosperity being elusive, your positive affirmations should be to continually tell yourself that the universe is rich in abundance with plenty for everyone, that you deserve to live in a prosperous and happy way and that you will easily be rich, wealthy and successful (*in all things*).

Adamantly state that you are absolutely enjoying the fruits of it! Refrain from thinking that you are unworthy and cannot have what you want and instead move *into* accepting and believing fully, that you are *totally* able to have the best in life.

Accept you are a deserving person, no matter what life has thrown at you previously (*ignore that – it's past, gone. This is your* **new** *life!*).

Begin to love yourself and try to stop those negative feelings about yourself rearing their ugly head at any given moment. What purpose does that serve towards going the right way up to attainment? Start appreciating yourself more.

Once you love yourself, you will have the strength necessary for believing that you really do *deserve* to have a wonderful life.
You can appreciate who you are and love who you are, whilst at the same time, realise that you will always have room to develop and grow.

Even if you feel you are lacking in skills or ambition, or any other problem or issue you may have about yourself, through using your positive affirmations, you can imagine yourself as being adept, capable, victorious, thriving and happy.
The more you imagine yourself as such, the more your brain will

listen and react by helping you make any changes you may need, or just allowing you to feel happier in your own skin - exactly as you are.

*Continuously keep that positive energy flowing around you.*

Remove any unnecessary troubling feeling of being hard-done-by and put upon. This just causes you to reverse or block up the *good* energy that allows wonderful things to flow to you quite naturally.

*It's a wonderful mindset with wonderfully beneficial outcomes!*

As you begin to accept and allow favourable things to happen to you, so you will start to feel in a more generous and benevolent position that inspires you to want to give good things out too.

Therefore spreading the positive energy flow around you and others, and as a consequence, keeping more people happy and peaceful.

*The more you share, the more you will benefit from the world and the giving becomes it's own reward!*

Be open to both receiving and giving – not only to and from others, but to and from yourself too. Give in any way you feel fit, however small, and demonstrate you have faith in an abundant world.
The more you give and receive, the more empowered and connected you will feel.

*This is the ultimate way to live in total inner wealth and prosperity.*

Why not experiment with this philosophy and see how it can benefit everything you are involved with!

**Make yourself valuable.**
**Everyone wants to feel and be valued.**
**By making yourself have a worth, no matter how small,**
**you will have a value that people will want**
**and that will make you feel really good about yourself.**

## ....look after yourself, for your own sake......

### .....take control of your health to keep on top of your game.....
*Anyone who wants to actually feel in control of their life and empowered to get on with things and make some proper progress, should seriously consider that being fit and healthy is an absolutely vital component.*

If you don't do anything about your health and are just disregarding the effects of an unhealthy lifestyle with bad food and no exercise, then you will not be at the *optimum condition* necessary to really live life to the full, or to be alert and fit enough to take advantage of all the opportunities that come your way.

*You need to take care of your body, after all, it's the only place you have to live in.....*

And when you put it like that, it sounds serious enough to make sure you do something about it, doesn't it?

*Why abuse or neglect the very thing that keeps you alive?*

Looking after it does not have to be a big chore. In fact, once you get going, it becomes fun and a *natural part of your life!*
Feeling wonderful by putting good energy into your body with nutritious food and vibrant exercise, is not a luxury for the few, it's available to *everyone, everyday.*

If you are living in a competitive world, then keeping yourself fit and healthy will help you in your quest for having a sharp mental state and give you the ability to flourish on your own, as well as amongst others.
People naturally thrive on competition and so you need to stand up to any intimidation or confrontation you may be subjected to.

As they say, in that kind of environment, only the strong survive, so never lose sight of your objectives, and look after yourself so you can keep at the top of your game...

No-one should really be scared of going that extra mile in order to get there. Not if you have the right mindset – which includes having a fit and healthy body – both inside and out.

If you are feeling lethargic, uncomfortable, depressed and fatigued as a result of a poor lifestyle, how are you realistically going to be able to take the bull by the horns and really make the most of those opportunities that come your way, as well as sustain what is required to follow them through and maintain the momentum...?

Looking after your health doesn't have to be complicated, difficult or scary, you just need to tailor a few basic principles to fit in with your own life.

Get yourself into that right frame of mind by telling yourself that this is seriously what you want in life and then *be prepared to embrace it.*
If you go into it with your mind closed and are critical of living a 'healthy and fit' life, then you will be lost from the start.
You will be allowing something else, like poor eating and laziness to control *you* and in turn, your attitude to your life.
It will be taking a hold of *you*, not *you* it!

The tough part will always be getting started......
There may well be a few false starts – but expect it and don't give up just because of 1 or 2 blips.
*Get back on the horse and ride it out.*

No-one will expect you to get it right first time, but every little helps and bit by bit, you will gradually get there and be on the right track to good health and the ultimate lifestyle for you.

*Maximising your well-being is what life is all about and getting the most out of it is your responsibility, so you can make sure you actually **live** it.*

You are here to enjoy your life after all – and that doesn't mean eating as many pies and cakes that you can cram into your mouth and just spending your days loafing about on the sofa. Nothing is stopping you doing that on *occasion* – you're human after all and you don't want to take all the fun out of life!

However, you can guarantee that eventually, once you get started on properly looking after yourself, you won't want to live like that forever-more anyway. This is because you will feel yourself healing from the inside out and every day you will become stronger, more vibrant and alive and ready to take on the world!

When you start to appreciate the impact that fantastic feeling of heightened alertness, awareness and wakefulness gives you, you won't want all those rewarding benefits to stop, nor will you want to go back to your old lazy way of life again!

*And why would you......?*

Additionally, exercise releases *feel good* endorphins and once you get those hormones rushing around you regularly, you will want that fabulous natural 'high' sensation to continue on forever!

Ideally you should be doing around 30 minutes of moderate exercise, 5 days a week – enough to increase your heart rate and leave you panting, but still able to talk.
Exercise at a time that suits you and make sure you do something you *enjoy and know you will stick at!*
Exercise should be **_fun_** and with so many activities around to tempt you, mix and match until you come up with your own perfect fitness set.
Remember, it isn't all about knocking yourself out in the gym!
Even housework is a form of exercise! But to make it interesting, you could try dancing, zumba, water sports, cycling in the countryside, playing with the children – anything where movement is involved.

*It all adds up to keeping fit and your ultimate road to total health and fitness!*

If you're starting from scratch, change your diet *gradually* to incorporate some good nutritious food and give yourself some stress-free space, freedom and peace for yourself, as this all contributes to a better, more wholesome and satisfying way of living. Plus, the more relaxed and balanced you are feeling, the more likely your head is going to be in the right place to embrace and be more accepting of this new life-style and mindset.....

It may all take some trial and effort, but it will be worth it in the end. If you build it up little and often and it leaves a smile on your face, then you're on the road to making the most out of life and enjoying it more!

All you have to do to have a fulfilling, great life and enjoy a feeling of total wellness, confidence and happiness, is <u>join in</u>.

And that's the ultimate empowerment......

*So go on, be good to yourself and you can live so much more energetically and vibrantly.*

This will have a wonderful knock-on effect with all the rest of your day to day activities. In the long-run, you will feel the total benefit within your output and performance in all aspects of your work and personal life.

*You can then begin to follow a wonderful life-style and reap the rewards you so deserve for putting in all that hard effort.*

**....*If you are not enjoying wonderful health,* then it's time to consider if any conditions you have are actually getting in the way of your progress....**

**....start by addressing your ailments.....**

If you have any ailments that need addressing, then it may be time for a visit to your doctor.

If you think that your ills are seriously getting in the way of doing your job or fully progressing with your life, then don't suffer in silence - get help if you need it!

There's no need to be shy about it – your doctor sees all sorts of scenarios every day. They're there to help you.

Don't be a martyr to your aches, pains and illnesses, because by dealing with your health problems, you can be free of them blocking your path and stopping you doing things.

You will ultimately feel better and be in a much healthier position to tackle everyday tasks and forge ahead with your ambitions and achievements.

Your head space will be freer to think about other things, like how you can improve your life in so many ways. Then you can live far more happily and get on with developing your ultimate life-style. So take the plunge, make that appointment and sort it out today. Your well-being is important!

*You cannot be totally empowered if you are constantly worrying about your health!*

### ....then consider your medication....
*Have a serious look at the potential impact any medication you are taking is having on you.*
It's quite possible that the side effects could cause any number of symptoms, including mood swings, depression or feeling flat and these could well hinder your progress and thought patterns.
If you suspect this may be so, then check with your doctor to see if there is an alternative medication you can take that will not have a negative affect on how you successfully get through the day.

Being brought down by these adverse conditions is not in the least bit empowering.

*If you can remove those ill feelings, you will feel so much more alert and able to really get on with advancing your life towards where you ultimately want it to be.*

### .....could a food intolerance be hindering your progress......
*Don't underestimate the impact that food intolerances can have on your progress and general well-being in everyday life.*
In the same way that you may be effected by certain medicines that could be stopping you getting through the day in a focussed or motivated way, so food intolerances can easily play a large part in hindering your thinking and ability to move forward.
If you are serious about fulfilling your ambitions and desires and you think you may be suffering from any kind of intolerance, whether from a food or otherwise, such as chemicals, etc., it is certainly worth a trip to the doctor to get it evaluated.

*You may not even realise you have an intolerance until you pay particular attention to it. It may actually be the very thing you love and crave the most!*

Certainly, an intolerance to dairy and/or egg can have a lot to do with feeling low, depressed, anxious, 'fuzziness', poor concentration, lethargy, tiredness and lack of motivation and focus.
It can also result in irritability and mood swings – quite severe in some cases.
The pain that comes with wheat and gluten intolerance caused by bloating and IBS symptoms, can also interfere quite seriously with your schedules.

*These things and more, can definitely cause a huge hindrance in your working and personal life.*

Trying to act professionally when you have a terrible bout of IBS, or putting up with an intolerance that causes you to feel thick-headed, nauseas, moody or low, when you're in the middle of an important meeting, or whilst trying to reach a deadline, can really impede trying to achieve your ambitions within the time-frame you have set for yourself.

If you think that you are being bothered by any negative reactions to a food and the symptoms that come with it, then you could rectify it by an 'Elimination Diet'.
This is not necessarily the easiest of things to embark on, as it may take a bit of time and a lot of commitment to truly establish what particular foods you are intolerant or allergic to. It's also quite possible that it may not be just one single substance that you are affected by.

An elimination or allergy diet can isolate food allergies and food sensitivities (intolerances).
These are quite different to each other.

A food ALLERGY describes an immune system response and can be very serious, like having anaphylactic shock or severe swelling that can cause real problems.
Whilst a food INTOLERANCE is an adverse reaction to a food and, although debilitating and upsetting, will not really harm you, but will still be irritating and mood-affecting.

There are a number of medical symptoms that may be related to

foods, such as candida, irritable bowel syndrome, diverticulitis, asthma, eczema, migraines, unexplained rashes and lactose intolerance.
These can also be accompanied by other symptoms, such as 'puffing up', itching, catarrh, fatigue, aching joints, brain fog, sleepiness, dry skin, altered mood and much more.

*All debilitating things that will obviously affect your day to day living, work and progress.*

Eliminating foods from your diet to establish the correct intolerance/s can be quite tricky.
If you have an intolerance to a particular food, the chances are that it may actually be one of your *favourite* things you like to eat that is causing the problems, so it will be very hard to give it up for a while.
Not only that, but there is also a high possibility that you will get withdrawal symptoms from removing those foods from your daily diet.
Some of these may be quite nasty, like severe headaches, shaking, low blood sugar, lack of concentration, fatigue, lethargy and irritability.

But they will only last a couple of days, so if you *expect* this to happen you can be prepared for it.

However, it will be worth it in the end, because when you find the offender and remove it from your diet, you will be absolutely **_amazed_** at how much better you feel!

You will hugely benefit from eliminating all the unpleasant side effects from your body.
Your life will open up and you will feel much more able to get on with the things you want out of living.

Of course any elimination diet should be done under strict control and with advice from a health professional.

Failing all of this, there are some clinics and services that can do a blood test for you to establish what you are allergic or intolerant to, but do some good research on this, as some of them aren't really that helpful and they cost money.

But, however you look at it, if you think it may be a problem, for the sake of your own progress and sanity, get down to a doctor or nutritionist for some advice. The symptoms could be zapped within days if it is easily diagnosed and merely a question of removing the offending item from your diet.

*You will be astounded at the transformation that just eliminating the culprit will make and you will have a much bigger spring in your step and zest for life!*

You will wonder how on earth you had survived all those years tolerating it!

*Empowerment will be much easier to achieve and you will be able to race ahead with your goals with so much more vigour and enthusiasm.*

Or you can merely go about your day feeling so much happier and healthier in yourself!

**...one thing that you may want to eliminate is caffeine....**
*Like everything health-related, the thinking on what the effects of caffeine have on your well-being changes all the time.*
Therefore, keep up-to-date with the latest theories and try to come to some sensible conclusion for yourself as to how, or if, it may actually be affecting you personally.

In the meantime, some of the evidence currently shows that there are a range of health conditions that *could* be aggravated by consuming food and drink containing caffeine and with advice from your doctor, you could find it better to eliminate them from your diet If you are suffering from any of the following, you may want to consider if caffeine is making it worse:-

*Acid indigestion, anxiety, stress, irritability and nervousness, candida or yeast problems, colitis, diverticulitis, diarrhoea and other irritable bowel symptoms, chronic fatigue syndrome and other auto-immune disorders, diabetes or hypoglycaemia (low blood sugar), dizziness, meniere's syndrome or tinnitus, gout, heart disease or heart palpitations, high blood pressure, high cholesterol, insomnia and interrupted or poor quality sleep, liver disease and gallbladder problems such as gallstones, kidney or bladder problems including kidney stones, nutritional deficiencies, including essential mineral depletion, migraines or other vascular headaches, osteoporosis, skin irritations, rashes and dryness, ulcers, heartburn, stomach problems such as hiatus hernias, urinary tract irritation and exhausted adrenal glands.*

If you are one of those people who thinks they can have several shots of espresso before bedtime and are still able to sleep, then the chances are that your sensitivity to caffeine has diminished and are probably at risk of your adrenals giving up responding!

That being so, you may have *less resistance to stress and it can leave you vulnerable to health hazards*, such as environmental pollutants, some inflammation, fatigue and autoimmunity related health disorders.

Don't be fooled into thinking that 'decaf' doesn't contain caffeine, as most still contain some trace amounts up to around 10%.

It may be that if you are in your 40's, you can no longer tolerate the same level of caffeine as you could when you were younger. The production of DHEA, melatonin and other vital hormones will start to decline and caffeine speeds up that downhill drop.

Caffeine also dehydrates the body and contributes to the ageing of the skin and kidneys.

If you *are* currently a caffeine freak, it should be time to cut right back, particularly if you can identify with some of these health problems.

*The effect of the caffeine 'hit' will not really be working at it's best if you are a serious drinker.*

Cut back by gradually replacing your cup with half caffeinated/half decaffeinated coffee, decreasing the caffeinated amount bit by bit, until you are only drinking decaffeinated.
Then see if you can get off it altogether..... Try an alternative beverage instead.

Be prepared to have some withdrawal symptoms for a while, however, they aren't as bad if you do it gradually as mentioned.

*Then you can use the 'benefits' of a cup of fully caffeinated coffee to sharpen your mind and lift your mood when you need it.*
**Good luck!**

**...stub it out......**
*Everyone knows that smoking has a detrimental effect on their health and will therefore have an impact on their day to day well-being.*
Every day, more and more evidence is being revealed concerning the effects of smoking, and to be up to date on these matters, you should keep up with current thinking.

But as it stands, all the debilitating factors that come along with smoking are known to interfere with you conducting a full and happy standard of living, health-wise.

So, it makes good sense then, that giving up tobacco in any form, should be a priority - *if you are serious about living a fulfilling, healthy and empowered life.*

And the same premise goes for other drugs and alcohol too....
Contrary to the popular belief that smoking *relaxes*, regular smokers are actually more likely to develop mood and anxiety disorders.

*Cutting out cigarettes is harder if you are a smoker under a lot of stress.*

It's an easy crutch to fall back on when life's getting you down or you're feeling sad, tense, angry or even just bored. Smoking becomes a 'learnt' behaviour when something triggers one of these emotions in you. And even if you're depressed, you are far more likely to take up the habit, than those who don't suffer with this problem.

You probably believe that the act of smoking actually calms you. However, if you are one of these people, you should be aware that smoking helps to transform saliva into a deadly cocktail that damages cells in the mouth and can turn them cancerous, not to

mention all the other hazards that the toxins in cigarettes cause....
there's lung cancer, wheezing and puffing, lack of energy, the smell, etc....you know the thing......

*These are all good reasons for you to give up the weed and not allow it to control you or take your power away in doing so.*

As long as you are damaging your insides like this, you will never be in a wonderfully fit and healthy state of well-being – which in turn, will naturally affect your life and how you live it.

*Be empowered and talk yourself out of that habit!*

Get some professional help if you need it.

Take the plunge **now** and see how your life unfolds in a much more fulfilling, miraculous, positive and vibrant way.....
Plus, think about how much money you will be saving that you can put towards living out your dreams.....!

**Can you see yourself on the other side.....?**

**.....kick that stress out of the water.....**
*There is nothing less empowering than suffering with constant stress.*
It's different to pressure.
Pressure can be motivating, but stress is when the pressure exceeds your ability to cope.
You may suffer from *work-related* stress, but when you add on home and social life obligations and commitments, it's not surprising that you can be pushed to the limit.

Developed in order to help you to deal with danger, when you get stressed, your body releases *adrenaline*, which in turn, creates *noradrenaline* and *cortisol*. These three hormones together divert resources to the places where they are needed the most.

Typical signs of stress include a change in behaviour, getting ill all the time, over and under-eating and lacking in concentration.
Chronic stress could eventually lead to gastrointestinal problems such as IBS, ulcers, colds and flu, heart disease and even cancer.

It is best to identify what and why something is stressing you, what your options are for dealing with it, and then find a suitable solution. Sometimes the easiest way to identify the cause is to relax yourself, as that will enable you to really look objectively at your problems.

Therapies, meditation or yoga can help, as well as exercise, which is the single best thing you can do to reduce your stress levels and the best thing you can do for your health *full-stop*, plus it will put you in the *right frame of mind to deal with your worries*.
Managing stress is simply a matter of managing your body's chemistry.

There is a whole range of supplements that can help you do this, so get help from a health professional regarding these.

Under stress you may overeat, which causes weight gain and can lower your self-esteem, which just adds insult to injury.

Alcohol also depresses your mood and immune system and long-term use of stimulants such as coffee, tea and caffeinated drinks will keep you awake and disrupt sleep patterns.

Listening to music can also help change your mood and encourages more positive thoughts and has a beneficial effect on mental health. And if you dance and sing along with it, you're adding more of those happy endorphins to uplift you even more!

Reduce some of the stress you give yourself through having <u>unrealistic</u> expectations.
Time and again promises get broken, such as losing weight or agreeing to do something for someone that you know you wont be able to fulfil....
Then you just end up feeling inadequate when you cannot stick to the agreement, because you make your own laws only to break them, then you judge and punish yourself and feel miserable!

*But you create your own life, so you can make or break your own rules any time you want!*

However, if you just accept that *everyone has inadequacies*, then you can give yourself a little lenience when you 'fail' at things, without spending time beating yourself up about it and then feeling ashamed and consequently stressed about it all. (Not that *failing* means that at all – everyone takes at least *something* out of every experience to use for the next one!)......

This also goes for those deadlines or duties you may have given yourself that turn out to be unrealistic. Like giving yourself so many tasks or goals to achieve, that in the end you can't do any of them because they're all so '*pie in the sky*' or just unrealistic to accomplish.

You can also have blocks in your life, or times when you just feel sluggish and need to down tools, because you're just not being very productive.

*Just embrace this time.*

Instead, use it to re-energise, have some 'down-time' and recoup. It's probably a sign you need a break anyway.....
Sometimes you get less done when you are over-tired and over-stressed, so use the time off to reflect, relax and get yourself ready for the next phase.
Then you become totally motivated and inspired and really feel yourself *buzzing and in full production mode*!

Anyway, as a self-esteem booster for you, you should know that a lot of people only fake it when they aren't necessarily feeling that confident, inspired or even secure in what they are doing.

It's a clever tip – fake it until you are feeling stronger – you'd be amazed by the amount of people in the world doing this!

*You can even fake feeling empowered – until you literally really do....!*

## …..getting past depression and health worries so you can conquer your dreams...
*Do you find some mornings you leap out of bed, whilst other days you just want to hide under the duvet?*
It may be depression - a debilitating condition that increases

irritability, restlessness, sadness, loss of interest, fatigue and feelings of worthlessness.
It can also decrease sex drive, energy levels and sleep.
It can hurt physically by contributing to headaches, back pain, digestive problems, bodily aches and joint pain.

Depression and other health concerns are all culprits that can hinder your progress.
To feel more empowered, you need help to get past these anxieties and awaken from a life of merely *going through the motions* – whether that's through self-help or from a professional.

Take the time to re-kindle the *belief in yourself* and remove the constraints and negative influences derived from certain life circumstances, such as, how you were brought up and educated, and other people's expectations of you.
With some simple strategies using diet, exercise and emotional support, every day can be a bit happier.

Work out where the '*gaps*' are in your life, like what needs enhancing and filling with more joyful and satisfying things.
Bring back your natural 'innocent' happiness.
Remember when you were a child, before you had any of the worries you find yourself with now. And never forget that *you* are in control of how you feel.....

Don't spend too much time judging what you *don't* have, but rather what you *do* have. This in itself will help remove some of the stress or pressure that you may be feeling – things that may be assisting in a downward spiral of depression and lack of sleep.

*If everything was taken from you right now, you would be so grateful for what you actually did have.*

So, why not be contented with what you have then, particularly if all your high expectations are causing you far too much stress and pressure anyway?
Doesn't that make sense to you.....?

If you feel that you may have any underlying health problems that could be getting in the way of your ambitions, motivation, focus or

coping strategies, then maybe a trip to the doctor would be advisable.
Doing this will help to eliminate any of the those negative factors from your life, which in turn, will help you to move forward in a much more productive and positive way.

Take the time to address those nagging issues that have been persisting for years. Those where you have just not stopped and given yourself the time to sort out due to one thing or another getting in the way.
Get any medical help you need before you take these problems into old age when they get progressively worse, or you even end up with them for life.
This will certainly help your well-being and enable you to live a much more active and enjoyable life well into retirement.

*Additionally, it will give you the physical tools to progress forward in a much stronger, more optimistic and fulfilling way, both personally and on your ambition pathway.*

Even if you discover you have a problem like depression, if it is *clinically proven*, a small 'crutch' for a short period to mend the problem, could be just what you need to nudge you forward and on your way.

If it is determined that you are not clinically depressed, then motivational options like visualisation and meditation, etc., should be really helpful in assisting you to eliminate negative thoughts and replace them with more positive thoughts and actions.

These are some options to help you on your path to success with a more healthy, stress-free and happy frame of mind.

You may eventually find that you aren't able to achieve your *real potential* because of a constantly busy life, stress, toxins or even just by going on 'automatic', where you're not really thinking about how your body is reacting and functioning on a day-to-day basis.

*Also, a large part of your life quality depends on the correct balance between the right diet and exercise.*

And that's not just about cleansing and balancing for general health and medical reasons, it's more about considering how *beneficial* it is to your *overall well-being and ability to take on life at your* **fullest capacity**.

Cleansing your mind, as well as your body is necessary for reducing unhappiness and stress.

Learning to programme this healthy way of living into your mindset, will become the tools for habits that will stay with you forever.

Because exercise helps to create new neurons in the brain and also boost blood flow to it, it increases the levels of the key mood-regulating chemicals, dopamine and serotonin.

So, get some *enjoyable* exercise into your daily schedule.

Also, make sure you eat from the 4 main groups everyday.
Food gives you the energy required to keep your body working **efficiently** – it's not just for making your belly feel full!

And energy creates energy when you exercise!

The most harmful foods to a *good functioning body and mind*, are sugar and saturated fats.

Because the state of your mood is a combination of how much energy you have and how positive you feel, it reflects your physical and mental well-being and how much you can do.

If your mood is low or you're feeling depressed, your physical health will also be affected – mainly because you may lack motivation to take any exercise or eat well.
This becomes a vicious circle - if you don't eat well you have less energy and your mood dips further, making it harder to motivate yourself to take the steps you need to look after your health.

To help your body stay on top, use water to rehydrate, cleanse and flush out toxins, as well as dilute the effects of too much caffeine, which reeks havoc with your moods and concentration.

There is always a reason for your mood, so if you're feeling low, it's important to try to look at why you feel the way you do, rather than just accepting it.

A *comprehensive* whole lifestyle approach will obviously have many other health and 'feel good' benefits too, which will obviously make mood swings far more manageable.

*Once you know why you're feeling depressed, by targeting the cause and using the help of some of these clever tactics, you can get your life back on track and on the road to much greater achievement.*

### …..depression medications – can they work for you…..
*You may need to go down the route of taking medication as a short-term measure to help with depression, so you can see some light at the end of the tunnel.*

However, you should bear in mind that any tablets you are prescribed may take several weeks to achieve their full effect. You may also need to try a few different types before you find the right one for you.

But, once they do begin to work, you will find enormous relief - so it's worth the wait.

You will need to see your doctor to wean yourself off them gradually once you start to feel better, rather than just coming off them abruptly, because you may get some unpleasant withdrawal symptoms otherwise.

If you think you are suffering from depression, don't just ignore it! You don't *have* to live with it and can be helped.
Nobody needs to live with the debilitating symptoms it presents and allow it to control you, rather than you conducting your life in a normal and positive way........

### ….use mood management to change your mindset....
*If you're not feeling well, the success of getting anything accomplished could be detrimentally affected.*
But there are ways to manipulate your mood and help you feel more uplifted.

One tactical way you may wish to try to improve it, is through music. It does depend on what you listen to, because different types of music will have a distinct impact on your feelings and well-being.

For instance, you can use loud fast music to exercise to as it will stimulate and motivate you, or you could listen to Mozart to uplift you and relaxation music to calm you.

Food can also have a major affect on your mood, some with depressing outcomes and others proactively enhancing how you feel. Look up which foods can do this.

Food intolerances can be a real problem. You'll probably know if you have any and how they affect you...

You might find that trying to impress people makes you act more cheerfully around them.
You're also probably happier around other happy people, however similarly, you can be depressed by other depressed people, as you tend to be influenced by other's moods.

*So if you want to be a happy person, then steer clear of negative depressed people that make you feel down.*

Additionally, you are more likely to feel upbeat if you have successfully accomplished something good, as opposed to feeling more moody if you haven't been able to achieve anything.

As sadness can be a state of mood that can be *normal* to some, but abnormal to others, if you do start feeling sad for no good reason and it is affecting your day-to-day activities, it could well be a symptom of depression or a related illness.

If you suffer from SAD (Seasonal Affective Disorder), it can be treated. Your doctor may recommend therapies that teach you how to refocus your behaviours or emotions.

Also, stress reduction through meditation, exercise or mindful behavioural methods can help keep symptoms at bay and lift you up.

*All of these types of mood enhancements will obviously have a positive impact on how empowered you feel and in turn, how you conduct your life far more successfully.*

#### ….help yourself with food for happiness
*Comfort foods – they're there to comfort – right.....?*
Well, they can certainly help you increase your weight, if that's comforting enough?
However, there are some foods that can actually *help* specific areas of your health.

If you're into your comfort foods, particularly the fatty and sugary types, you probably use them to help manage your moods. This is because sugary foods give you an instant high-energy lift.
But this is closely followed by a crash in your blood-sugar and mood.

*Therefore, keeping your blood sugar on an even keel is very important.*

To do this and help moderate your mood and cravings, eat frequent small meals.
Include in them, more complex carbohydrates, like whole-grains, brown bread, rice, crisp breads and oat-cakes, because these foods take much longer to be absorbed by your body and will provide a steady stream of energy throughout the day.

Some mood stabilising nutrient-rich foods include oily fish, nuts, seeds and green leafy vegetables that contain Omega-3 fatty acids. Decreased levels are linked with depression and other mental health conditions.

B vitamins, particularly B6, can be found in whole grains, pulses, orange juice and lean meat, and together with Zinc, which is in beef, chicken, pork, chickpeas and Brazil nuts, make *serotonin* - one of the brain's natural 'feel good' substances.
Citrus Fruits containing Vitamin C, also helps turn *tryptophan,* an essential amino acid, into serotonin.
Greens, nuts, pulses, seeds, fish, dried fruit and bananas, sardines, pulses, nuts, bread and soya milk also contain Magnesium and

Calcium, which work together for healthy nerve function and to reduce anxiety.
Always check the latest thinking on this information.

These are all far better ways of helping to maintain your mood and lift any signs of depression, rather than feeding yourself with junk and so-called *comfort* food.
Not least to mention that eating wonderfully nutritious food feeds your brain and body and gives you that fantastically invigorating feeling of health and vitality!

*Now isn't that more empowering than feeling all sluggish, down and out of control.....?*

**…..getting active to produce those 'feel-good' chemicals....**
*Never underestimate the power of activity and exercise to boost your mood!*
Just getting outdoors and walking in a green environment can start you on your way.
You will feel less blue after a simple 'green' walk. The change of scene, fresh air and beauty of the surrounding area all give you a different perspective on life and will help to re-energise your state of well-being.
Exercising at least 3 times a week for 45 minutes to 1 hour, is the optimum way to induce your feel-good *'endorphins'*.

*Make sure you do something you really like and enjoy so it keeps you motivated – that's if you want to stick at it and keep the favourable results and benefits continuous.*

The positive effects on your mood will begin as early as the very first session, because physical activity promotes the production of those natural *happy* chemicals - usually within 20 minutes.

*Don't look at activities and exercise as a chore.*

Rather think of it as being fun with lots of advantages and promoting happiness and strong well-being.

Look forward to it!

Once you get into the swing of things, you will miss it when you don't do it!

*What a wonderfully natural way towards building your ultimate empowerment!*

### ...what about the help of any emotional aids.....
*Everybody needs the chance to talk about their feelings and engage with other people.*
When you're feeling depressed, sometimes this is the last thing you feel like doing. However, it's probably one of the best things you *can* do....
So, ask your doctor if they can give you a referral to a psychotherapist for some 'talking therapy', such as *cognitive behavioural therapy* (CBT).
There are also some *self-help* groups that could also be extremely supportive, so check what's available and most appropriate to you.

Activities like yoga or dance that engage the body and mind can work wonders, especially alongside the social interaction that comes with joining a group, or even with friends, family and children.
Find things that really suit you.
There may be lots out there you don't know about until you ask, so don't suffer in vain.

*The sooner you get yourself sorted, the sooner your road to empowerment begins to steer towards the light......*

### ......are your negative beliefs and ideas about yourself really worth the creedence....
*If you have constant negative thoughts and beliefs about yourself, you need to learn to challenge them to see if they are actually true and if they really merit the emotional bashing you give them.*

When your inner voice is being critical of you, stop and ask yourself *exactly what evidence* you have to support those thoughts....?
Where have they come from, are they actually *real*, have you carried them around since something happened years ago that is now not really at all relevant?

If you actually *challenge* the beliefs you hold about yourself that perhaps you are useless or incompetent or unattractive, or any of the other negative thoughts you have when you are feeling low, you can then begin to *change* those beliefs and ultimately build your self-esteem back up. Because you can do something positive about the reason why you feel them.

*You can fight back.*

If you need professional help to change your negative thoughts and any other unhelpful behaviour that's affecting your life, then talk to your doctor or health consultant.
Using these steps will help you feel calmer and more positive. Over time you will find you can set yourself proper goals for the future and actually begin to achieve them.

**Empowerment!**

**…..using energy to deal with emotional stress....**
*Keep a close eye on how emotional stress can affect your general health.*
Manage it by '*cleaning up*' any strong, negative emotions and judgements as they arise.
As soon as you start to feel your energy going sideways, you should try to get yourself back to '*neutral*' and **refocus**.
Doing so can empower you away from those bad emotions and judgements that you automatically make, because of built up memories and conditioning of past experiences.

Learning to do this can quite literally transform the way you conduct your life.
Having the power to go *back to neutral* will put your mind and thoughts on hold, so that you can dissipate your feelings, put a pause on your reactions and thoughts and bring in your '*heart intelligence*' to stop draining your energy.

This is so beneficial for your wellness……

When you spend too much time on *judging*, your system feels *bad* as the negative energy backs up inside it – which won't help in certain situations when you need to have a clear head.
By bringing your mind and heart back to neutral, it alters your

emotions and physiology into a calmer state, thus enabling you to see more options available to you with better clarity.

To do this, you need to **_stop_** and start a slow, deep breathing pattern - this helps to disengage you from your stressful thoughts and feelings.
Continue this until you have completely relaxed and neutralized your emotional state.
Flipping out just adds to any negative situation, which in turn causes you to contribute to a badly affected inner state of well-being.

*You need to choose to step back from your emotions when you start to feel them heating up.*

This type of breathing will help you draw the energy out of your head where negative thoughts and feelings get amplified.
Just having the *intent to disengage* can help you release a lot of your emotional energy.
Although it doesn't mean irritability, anxiety, or other stressful feelings will have totally evaporated. It merely means the charged energy has been taken out and you have stopped accumulating stress.

*It will give you a chance to regroup your energies and refocus.*

Basically, you've taken the heat out of the situation!
At the end of the day, if you want to become a more relaxed person who is not governed by stress, judgement, anxiety and heartache, you need to ask yourself if you *really* want to keep draining your energy by getting so het up and projecting negativity during certain situations all the time?

As you build your ability to realign your emotions you will have much more energy and empowerment to do the things you *really* want to do and not be governed by continuously holding onto upsetting situations that just bring you down and zap your spirit and motivation.

*That is just wasted energy and there's nothing at all empowering about that.....*

## Pass on a Smile –
### you will set off a chain of events and positive energy!

**...this anxiety is controlling my life.....**
*There will be days when you just cannot get on with your life or follow your goals, because you seem to be consumed with anxiety and depression for no apparent reason, and you cannot understand why.....*

It might seem like the last thing on your mind, but it could just be the food that you ate recently giving you a bad reaction. Then again, if could be that you are letting silly things get to you, like simple administration tasks.

Or it may be that age-old scenario of 'robbing Peter to pay Paul' in an attempt to resolve your finances......

However, an imbalance in your brain chemistry could also be the reason why you are more prone to chronic anxiety – and this may be genetic. The root of your anxiety may come from any number of conditions that have affected you throughout your life so far.

Today's stress can come from workloads and deadlines, road-rage, potential redundancy, paying bills, etc., and when your body is under this kind of constant low-level stress, it can eventually lead to a state of anxiety.

*But, a stress response can be necessary during certain times, like giving a presentation for instance, because it keeps your brain alert and gives you the motivation you need to get through it.*

Symptoms of stress and anxiety can include a sense of panic, palpitations, tremors and sweating.

If you can't fall asleep at night because you're worrying, or you regularly have nervousness causing a pounding heart, sweating palms or butterflies in your stomach, you're probably experiencing anxiety.

*It can be very disruptive, but you can control it.*

If you _are_ suffering from anxiety, think about how you got to this point?

Also, think back to times when you've had similar incidences to deal with in the past. Can you remember how you managed to sort everything out in good time and then wondered what all the stress and fuss was about?

*Did you come out the other side relatively unscathed having survived what you thought at the time, was a monumental problem?*

Consider how you managed to overcome those hurdles – maybe by yourself or with a little help from friends and/or family. It could just have been that you were able to sort things out in your head merely by taking a nice walk, or distracting yourself in some way by doing something you love, or even just relaxing for a bit, while you take stock?

*If any of these schemes worked for you back then, they can work for you again....just have faith in those previous courses of action.*

If you are now in an anxious dilemma or could be in the future, then think about applying any of those proven strategies, so you are ready to cope with your fretful situations when they arise.
Whatever you do, don't sit on your problems for long, otherwise you run the risk of them magnifying in your head and driving you mad!

*Just by removing yourself from a difficult situation for a while will do you a power of good.*

A simple coffee can actually lift your depression temporarily and make you feel more positive, giving you the pep and momentum you need to sort things out, and give you the confidence to look your mood or problem in the face and confront things once and for all.

Talking things through with a neutral friend can also remove some of the burden from your shoulders. They may also help you to see a way through, even coming up with a solution that you may not have thought of yourself.
Make sure you use someone who has a rational and calming presence so they put you at ease and do not judge you in any way.

If you really feel that you need professional help for your anxiety, then Cognitive Behavioural Therapy may work for you as it gets you to talk through your anxieties and trains you to challenge and look at your thoughts more rationally.

*It examines the real evidence for your concerns and helps you to look at them more realistically.*

If you really do need it, medication can at least help ease your feelings of anxiety and get you over the worst, so you can function more normally and conduct your life more successfully.

Remember to exercise, including relaxation activities like meditation and tai chi, and also eat a healthy, balanced diet.

It's very important to keep your blood sugar from getting too low and worsening the symptoms of anxiety, like making you feel shaky and jittery.

Remain as sociable as possible and get a good sleep pattern, as this can make the world of difference in helping to keep you calm.

Alcohol is certainly *not* the best way to deal with anxiety – even if you think you can bury your problems with it.

*It actually works in the opposite way by* becoming addictive and acting as a depressant.
Remedies may help so go to a professional who can give you proper advice relevant to your own personal situation.

The sooner you <u>stop</u> and deal with your anxiety problems, the sooner you will be in a wonderfully strong position to think about following those dreams you have been harbouring and wishing you could get on with once and for all......!

*Your empowerment depends on it.*

**…..my sleep pattern is affecting my day to day functionality...**
*Sleep is vital for your health and is as important as your five-a-day.*
Not getting enough sleep can seriously affect your ability to function and cope.
Your physical and mental well-being hinge on the amount and quality of sleep you get each night.

Your personal and work life will obviously be affected if your sleep patterns are having a detrimental impact on it.

*Your ability to reach your goals, whatever they may be, will be hindered by the seriousness of this problem.*

How empowering you feel will definitely be lacking if you are not feeling awake and alert.
So it is very prudent that you make the effort to address it – that's if you *really* want to live the life you long for.

If you suffer from insomnia you will obviously have difficulty falling asleep, waking up during the night, trouble getting back to sleep, waking up too early or still feeling tired when you rise.

'*Primary*' insomnia is not directly associated with any other health condition and can be more serious and more difficult to treat.
'*Secondary*' insomnia is caused more by lifestyle or health problems, such as back pain, depression, arthritis, cancer, heartburn, pain and taking medication or other substances, and usually passes once the stress or health issue has resolved itself – if it can be.

It's important to sort out your sleep problems quickly, because lack of it increases the risk of obesity, diabetes, cardiovascular disease, anxiety and it can also affect your relationships.
During sleep, your body performs several functions such as recuperating and renewing.

*Don't let insomnia rob you of a healthy well-being and state of mind.*

If you want to have a normal, successful and satisfying life, you need to have some strategies to help you balance being mindfully awake and having restful sleep.
Whatever you do, get some assistance - it can only help - especially if you are stuck in a rut and it's actually blocking your progress.

There are many tips out there for helping you get a restful night, so do check them out.
How can you expect to get your life in order if you are crippled with stress and anxiety or sleep deprivation?

Make sure your empowerment in tip-top shape by getting the assistance you need.

Your future only relies on _you_.....

**You can only feel _one_ emotion at a time....
So therefore, if you are falling into anxiety, fear and seeing 'lack' instead of 'plenty' –
recall something that made you feel
deeply grateful and pleasant
and spend time with those feelings instead.
Practise doing this often and whenever you need to.
You will reap the benefits of a much more
positive mood and thankfulness.**

**….memory getting in the way of your progress......it's not just your age.....**
If you are getting on in years, you may be susceptible to some memory lapses, such as struggling to remember names and numbers, but it may not necessarily just be down to your brain slowing down with age.
It's more likely to do with _information overload._
Holding too much in your brain gathered over many years, may not be allowing you to decipher problems as easily as when you were young, when you had less stored away in there.

Your mind is too _cluttered up_ and you probably find it difficult to rid yourself of _irrelevant_ information, so that it enables you to just process what needs to be done _there and then,_ more simply instead.

When you were young, you could probably hold lots of information in your mind at the same time as you could mentally manipulate it, but now it may not be as easy.
Therefore, you need to stop filling up your mind, so that it doesn't interfere with any task in hand.
So if this is a problem for you, then you need to '_de-clutter_' your mind - just like you do your cupboards!

Get rid of any previous information you've got stuck in your head, so you can get things done more efficiently.

When it comes to any tasks that need lots of thought, try *not* to think about anything else at the time, other than *exactly* what needs to be done *then*, and using *only* the information you need to tackle it with. Stop wasting your precious head-space on other things that aren't relevant to what you are trying to achieve at that particular moment.

So, on a positive note, it may well be that your memory problems may not simply be just your mind slowing down.
Additionally, to help ensure your memory is kept in tip-top condition, get lots of sleep, drink plenty of water and take up yoga and meditation, including deep breathing.

*This will help keep your mind calm and clear and give you the skills to keep 'unclouded' mentally.*

Learn a language or an instrument and solve puzzles like crosswords, as this can help keep your mind young and active. Socialising can also aid your mental sharpness.

If you want to keep your empowerment strong well into your old age, keep that brain decluttered of old information.
Use only the details you need to get you by and save some mind space to tackle life with more verve, energy and confidence.

*Imagine how much freer you will feel in yourself....!*

> **"Teach yourself how looking within, clearing the clutter
> and learning a brand new approach
> can change your life forever.
> Make it one that works and transforms the way
> you think and feel and lets you
> take on life with passion and vitality.
> Venture into bliss, venture into
> serene happiness and abundance.
> Life and this world are for living.
> Take the step, take the leap of faith".**

**....using holistic therapies to relax, de-stress, balance and empower you....**

*It's such a toxic and stressful environment you live in nowadays.*
All sorts is thrown at you, like pollution, chemicals, pressure of work and commitments, etc., and you can suffer a whole range of health symptoms because of it all.
Then they are probably only treated by your general doctor to *mask* the problems, rather than actually getting to the *crux* of what is really going on inside your body, making it difficult to know how to manage your own health properly.

*Holistic therapies can help to detect the root cause of disorders which can then be treated, instead of purely dealing with the 'symptoms'.*

If you are suffering from stress, tiredness, fatigue, medical ailments, or just feel that you need to recuperate, relax or feel invigorated, then you may find the holistic way of great advantage.

Certain therapies are aimed at examining your behavioural patterns and eliminating any false beliefs you may hold, enabling you able to move forward and become free from anxiety, stress or limiting negative thoughts.

By using a holistic method, you can get relief from a wide range of conditions, such as IBS, depression, anxiety, headaches, insomnia, hayfever, candida, eczema, asthma, joint and muscle pain, PMS/menopausal complaints, fatigue and many more conditions.

Part of your own life empowerment is obviously to feel your best.
In order to perform at your optimum level and achieve that enriched lifestyle, you will want to do all you can to feel totally balanced and at one with yourself and your surroundings.

You will want to feel vibrant, invigorated, prepared and ready to take on anything that is thrown your way, and be totally alert to all opportunities that present themselves to you.

*This is the only way to move forward and upward with your life.*

If you don't know enough about these types of therapies to

encourage you to participate in any of them, then perhaps the following information will at least give you some insight into how they can be beneficial to you.

These treatments can encourage self-healing, enabling you to gain a sense of well-being and taking care of your body, mind, spirit and soul.

You can explore or indulge in any of the following holistic therapies if you want to gear yourself up to feeling fantastic.
*It's entirely up to you.*

### ....using spa's to enhance your sense of well-being.....
*Are you exhausting yourself continuously, day in, day out?*
You probably already realise that if you constantly run at 100mph without a rest, then your body is either going to shut down or burn out.
It's time to get back to *you*, unclog your brain, rejuvenate your system and remove the physical, mental and emotional pain that goes along with it.

One of the best ways to put your system back in order is through 'Spa Therapy' which includes massage, steam rooms, sauna's and jacuzzi's.

As stress is a large factor in many illnesses, it's not surprising that relief is the main priority of most people who use a spa, because it de-stresses your mind, body and spirit.

So, if it's just a quick stroll down the road to your local spa, or off to the other side of the world to relax for a week or more in wonderfully peaceful surroundings, take full advantage!

Consider the following benefits that a proper spa treatment can give you:-

A spa increases the body's energy flow, improves flexibility, reduces high blood pressure and hypertension, heals emotional distress, reduces the effects of ageing, soothes tired muscles, tones and nourishes your skin, detoxifies your body, stimulates circulation, reduces weight-related problems, reduces insomnia, stress and fatigue, enhances spiritual awareness and simply helps you feel better about yourself.

Try out your local facility to see what it's all about to see if it suits you as a significant part of your empowerment schedule.

*Your mental and physical health should be important to you if you want a clear head and strong mindset that enhances your life and contributes to successful outcomes.*

**…..massaging your way to good health and empowerment....**
*One powerful way to help you de-stress and feel good as part of your empowerment and healthcare programme, is through massage.*
It can play an important part in keeping you healthy and youthful throughout your life and into old age, keeping you well in mind, body and soul – all of which have a huge impact on how you carry out your daily life as successfully as you possibly.

Massage helps to eliminate anxiety and pressure and undoubtedly will help you to manage physical and emotional stress, as well as relieving and reducing many other conditions, such as pain and degenerative diseases.

It can also enhance your sleep quality and reduce fatigue as well as give you greater energy, improve your concentration, increase circulation and detoxification, and even give you a sense of perspective and clarity.

There are many types of massage, such as, Swedish, Shiatsu, Trigger Point, Neuromuscular, Cranio-Sacral, Deep Tissue, Myofascial Release, On-site (chair or corporate massage), Sports, Acupressure, Reflexology, Rosen Method, Tapotement, Aromatherapy, Indian and Tibetan Acupressure Head Massage and many more.

If you haven't already, perhaps it's time to start exploring this obviously beneficial method of de-stressing and relaxing, as part of your regular empowerment programme.

## ....using Reiki energy to heal you.....

*Reiki is a natural healing energy that not only works on the physical, but on every level of your body.*

It is the combination of 2 Japanese words - Rei meaning *"universal"* and kei meaning *"life force energy"*.

Reiki treats your body, mind and spirit, bringing harmony and balance and encourages your body to heal itself.

There are many benefits, including stress, tension, anxiety and pain relief, balancing emotions, inducing relaxation, balancing your body's chakras, providing a closer connection with inner wisdom and helping to ward off illness and fatigue.

All of these elements will allow you to respond more calmly to all the events you are faced with in your life.

*Perhaps this kind of therapy could help you get on the right track to feeling fully empowered again..?*

## ....using Kinesiology to rebalance and get you back to normal....

*Kinesiology is a way of communicating directly with your body to find out what you need for optimum health.*

Kinesiology uses simple, safe and precise muscle testing procedures to find your problem areas, getting to the cause or root of your problem and not just the symptoms.

It uses specific massage points, nutrition, energy reflexes and emotional techniques to balance you holistically.
It looks at one organ of your body or aspect of your health.

If you have any minor imbalances and they're not corrected, they accumulate and cause other areas to compensate, which then compound each other and this leads to functional changes, giving rise to discomfort, pain and even allergic reactions.

*If these warnings are ignored, disease can follow.*

Kinesiology looks at your emotions and anxieties, specific personal dietary intake, supplements for any nutritional deficiencies you may have, structural imbalances and energy blocks, thereby balancing you as a *whole* person and enhancing excellent health and well-being.

*You may find that this kind of rebalancing is just what you need to build up your empowerment.*

**...a little hypnosis could help you on your way to success.....**
*Hypnosis is a technique that can be used for many undesired ailments and behaviours.*
It can assist in manifesting any new aims and desires you may have, such as motivation, empowerment, weight loss, quitting smoking, healing, relaxation and stress relief.

Through hypnosis, your subconscious mind can be influenced into accepting new *positive programming* in order to effect change in you.
When you are in a hypnotic state, you are also more susceptible to suggestion and can then be reprogrammed to change old beliefs, patterns and feelings, replacing them with far more optimistic affirmations instead.

If you feel any of your ailments can be treated in this way so you can get your *mojo* back, perhaps it's worth a consultation with a qualified hypnotherapist.

Anything that helps you become you again and gives you the power to enjoy your life fully, will help you on your path to ultimate fulfilment.

**....Acupuncture – get the needle to stop your needling.....**
*Acupuncture is based on your balanced flow of energy in order to determine good health.*
Over 1000 acupoints just under your skin can be stimulated through the insertion of needles to enhance this flow, correcting and restoring the balance of your health.
You can benefit from improved well-being and the quality of your life that may have been affected by your life-style, diet and thought patterns.

All kinds of ailments and imbalances can be improved through the power of acupuncture. Your weakened immune system caused by stress, illness, allergies, toxins, etc., can be strengthened, as well as the added side effect of achieving emotional balance and relief from depression, anxiety, frustration and worry.

*Don't live in misery by letting your symptoms get the better of you and in the way of your dreams, especially when there is plenty of help out there just waiting to give you a supporting hand.....*

**…..Emotional Freedom Technique could be what you need to boost you…..**
*Based on the same electromagnetic energy that flows through your body and the 'meridians' used in traditional acupuncture, 'Emotional Freedom Technique' is also used to treat physical and emotional ailments.*
Simple fingertip tapping rather than needles, is used to regulate your health.
This helps to heal and bring about optimal health, by restoring the balance of your mind and body, through 'clearing' the short-circuit emotional blocks from the body's '*bioenergy*' system.

No matter how good your diet and life-style is, if you don't have good emotional health, you will not achieve ideal healing, because of the barriers causing emotional 'dis-ease'.
EFT helps to remove any negative emotions you may have, reduce pain and food cravings and implement positive goals.

Perhaps EFT is a way forward for you....?

Why not at least give it a try and see if it helps lift you into a more positive state and mindset that allows you to achieve your goals.....?

**…..the importance of good breathing to help you through your day….**
*There are so many benefits to accurate and deep breathing - from living longer to balancing moods and performing at your best.*
Through proper abdominal breathing techniques, your nervous system is soothed and blood pressure reduced, thereby allowing you to manage any stress and anxiety effectively.

When you are stressed, tense, angry or scared, it is quite typical to

breathe in a shallow way and hyperventilate, which can just prolong anxiety.
During this state, your body constricts, your muscles get tight and as your breathing becomes shallower, you will not be getting the right amount of oxygen that your body needs.

Slow, deep breathing into tight areas can actually release that tension, relax your mind and body, bring about more clarity, relieve emotional problems and clear uneasy feelings.
As well as this, it can ease your pain, improve circulation and massage vital internal organs, including strengthening and toning your abdominal muscles.

A lot of your body's toxins are released through breathing.
Good breathing can increase oxygenation to your brain and all of the cells in your body, as well as strengthen your immune system and metabolise vital nutrients and vitamins.
It also boosts energy levels, improves stamina, cellular regeneration and elevates your mood by inducing neurochemicals in your brain.

There are many ways to do your breathing exercises, so find some that really suit you.

Give yourself the time to regularly schedule it into your day, *as part of your programme to mastering your stress and empowerment, improving your relationships and feeling much stronger.*
You will then develop a feeling of true relaxation.

*This will cross over into your day-to-day functioning, bringing about more peace and a renewed ability to carry out everyday activities and interactions with people, enabling a more balanced outlook and view on your situations, challenges and life as a whole.*

### ...can zero balancing bring about a better look on life......
*Zero Balancing uses a hands-on system as an innovative 'body-mind' therapy.*
With comfortable finger pressure and gentle traction, it focuses on key joints of your skeleton that conduct and balance forces of gravity, posture and movement.
It also concentrates on areas of tension in your soft tissue to create points of balance around which your body can relax and reorganise,

allowing you to experience deep relaxation, 'internal organisation' and improved function.

In doing so, Zero Balancing helps *unblock* your body's energy flow and increases vitality, thus contributing to better alignment and posture and allowing for more freedom of movement.
It opens up 'stuck' areas in your body's 'shock absorbers' so that aches and pains can be relieved and the quality of your life is generally improved.

*A session will leave you with a feeling of wonderful inner harmony and organisation.*

If you want to induce a deep state of relaxation, renewal and all over feeling of wellness, then Zero Balancing will help you feel far more vital and alive.
It will support positive changes in your behaviour or attitude whilst focusing on your personal goals, by realigning your energy to remove old patterns so any resistance to change can subside.
With the help of this system, you could truly add to that sense of empowerment.

So, to benefit from a bit of Zero Balancing strength that enables you to progress forward with your life more successfully, why not give it a try and see if it gives you that extra boost you are looking for.......

**......get relief with body stress release....**
*Every day you are being exposed to different types of stress through physical injuries, strains, bad posture, chemical pollutants in the air, additives, colourants in food, harmful chemicals in everyday products and mental and emotional stress.*
Your body is designed to adapt to these stresses in a positive way, but sometimes you can just find yourself totally *overloaded* and in an effort to cope with this, your body will tend to store the stress in your muscles.

This is called *body stress*.

It can cause pain, stiffness, postural distortion, numbness and cramp.
Tension in your muscles can put pressure on your nerves which

disturbs your body's communication system and reduces the efficiency of your body's natural self-healing ability.

Body Stress Release (BSR) is a complementary health technique that can help anyone, including pregnant women to infants and the elderly.
BSR helps locate stored tension and by working with your body's natural desire to be stress-free, it uses a gentle and effective technique to help release the tension from your muscles and relieve your aches and pains.

Freedom from body stress promotes a better quality of life physically, mentally and emotionally.

Once your stress is reduced and your body is back to normal, you will benefit so much from the freedom this will give you.

*You will be able to get your work done far more efficiently and arrive at a much more empowered feeling over your life.*

### ….get a better sense of mental clarity from craniosacral therapy….

*Are you spending your life feeling tense, so-much-so that it's affecting your overall well-being and sense of confidence?*
Then perhaps you could get some help with *Craniosacral Therapy* (CST).
It not only works with your head, but you as a *whole* person, inducing positive changes in your body, mind and spirit.

During and after sessions you may find a comforting inner peace, sense of relief, deep stillness and relaxation, 'connection', a feeling of acceptance and being more fully 'alive', and as though you have been put back in one piece and are 'whole' again.

You can have CST for long-standing physical and emotional problems or ongoing support in your busy life to help meet your daily challenges.
It is non-invasive, gentle and suitable for letting go of any tension and fear held in your body, so it induces calmness.
It supports your body's innate ability to balance, restore and heal

itself, and also helps to reduce stress and builds your 'underlying' energy.
As well as noticing physical and emotional improvements, you may also find that you have more awareness of your own needs, strengths and quality of life.

*This will obviously carry over into a feeling of more empowerment in your life, as this clarity stimulates a stronger mental and emotional awareness.*

### ....can homoeopathy help you move on with your life.....
*Homoeopathy has been around for as long as conventional medicine, but with the added benefit that it is non-toxic and does not cause any side-effects.*
It is suitable for all ages and is successful in helping a wide range of ailments by using a gentle, individual and respectful approach.

The selection of remedies used is based on the principle that '*like treats like*' – that is, a substance that causes symptoms when taken in large doses, can be used in small amounts to treat those same symptoms.

If you have any ailments that are seriously getting in the way of your goal-setting, then perhaps a consultation with a Homoeopath could be beneficial in getting you motivated again...

### .....a Chinese medical diagnosis could be just the help you need to get on with your life...
*Traditional Chinese medicine is a well respected and sophisticated 'diagnostic' procedure that is based on the signs and symptoms of the 'bigger' picture of your health.*
Looking at any 'patterns' of disease you may have allows for a very personalised treatment to be formulated.

The diagnosis is collected by a series of *looking, listening, smelling, palpation* and *questioning*.

Your eyes, hair, complexion, facial expression, postural tendencies and general deportment are examined.
Rashes and lesions are checked, as well as any pain and swelling in your tissues.

Your tongue is assessed for vitality and the state of your fluids, hormones and stomach 'qi' is also observed.

The unique sound and clarity of your voice and breathing are also evaluated.

Body odour, breath and faecal, urine and vaginal discharges are looked into for underlying disease, and hands and abdomen are palpitated for tissue tone.

Your pulse is taken to determine the state of your vitality and balance in your body as a whole, along with your blood tested for overall constitution.

Your practitioner takes clinical data about you to achieve a successful personalised treatment, including asking about perspiration, energy, libido, appetite, digestion, elimination, body temperature, menstrual patterns, reproductive history and family medical history.

*So you are very much treated as a whole person mentally, emotionally, physically and spiritually.*

With such a comprehensive overall look at every aspect of *you*, the many benefits of a diagnosis could help you get past so many issues that may be hindering your health and stopping you from getting ahead.

So a trip to your local Chinese Medical Centre could give you the boost you need to power on and get ahead with your plans.

**It's quality, not quantity that will do most to improve your life.**

***Be calm.***
***Slow down.***
***Breathe....***

*There are so many different therapies out there that could help eliminate symptoms that are hindering your steps towards a happy and fulfilling life.*

Some, you may find quite surprising.....

So, to help increase your sense of empowerment, see if any of the following therapies can help you on your path to peace and contentment, which in turn becomes an important aid towards achieving a successful and enriching life.

### .....can flowers benefit your mood and well-being.....
*Flowers can play a positive role as part of the natural therapies - from their visual beauty to their scent and colours.*
The essential oils used in aromatherapy are extracted from flowers.

Through the neurochemicals released in the brain from their smells and colours, flowers may help treat and remedy depression, fatigue, tension and cramps.
Negative emotions, fear and anxiety are also reduced and immune systems strengthened, lessening the incidence of falling ill.
Flowers can induce calm and happiness and help to clarify moods, as well as activating your imagination and attention.

The colour of flowers have stimulating effects, for instance, the red rose (of passion) is said to increase adrenaline and raises energy levels, yellow (sun) helps you feel optimistic, blue induces calm, relaxation and good sleep through the production of melatonin, and violet decreases tension and nerves through the stimulation of the pituitary gland.

As flowers have such a therapeutic and positive effect, they make you feel better and as such, your confidence will increase too.

*Every little favourable and pleasing thing you surround yourself with, or beneficial experience you add into your life, will contribute to an overall feeling of positivity and wellness – and that in itself, will add empowerment to how you conduct yourself in the long-term.*

### ....build your own energy and confidence through colour therapy.....
*Do you go about your life not even thinking, noticing or appreciating colour– even though it is there in front of you every minute of every day?*

Colour is an important aspect of everyone's surroundings.
The *energy* of colour is something that can affect both your feelings and physical responses and because of this, you can use it for many benefits.

Colour Therapy has been used as a powerful and non-invasive holistic form of therapy for years, using the energy that comes from the varying wavelengths of light from which colour is made up.

With every colour having it's own individual significance, it can be interpreted in a variety of ways from person to person, taking into consideration their uniqueness, situation, culture, history and geography.

When employed correctly, those different frequencies of light that affect all living cells, can have a profound healing effect on you and everything around you, because you, and everyone else, have their *own* vibration & frequency.

Used as part of everyday life, your problems can be treated with this kind of therapy - even for general relaxation and healing, or to positively stimulate your health and well-being.

Working with the appropriate colours can help to dispel your negative feelings, free any blockages and re-balance your body mentally, emotionally, spiritually and, in turn, physically.

There are many different ways of giving and using colour, including; Solarized Water, Light boxes/lamps with colour filters, colour silks and hands-on healing.

*Heighten your awareness of the energy of colour and see how it can transform your life.*

The wonderful colours of this earth and nature are here for a reason and purpose, not just by chance and you should make colour a part of your everyday life, not just a short experience with a therapist.

Colour, therefore, is an important aspect of daily life.
It can bring about good mood, confidence and self-expression.

*Being empowered is all about this and therefore it should be given serious consideration as an everyday enhancement used to your advantage.*

### ….laughter – it's free, it's a natural high and good for boosting your mood…..

*Think about how great you feel when you have a real good laugh about something……*
It's like a natural high – medicine for the soul!
And, it's a *great* way for you to feel less depressed and lonely.
People will far rather have a laugh with someone than sit down and cry or moan about things.

*The chemical reaction that goes on inside your brain when you laugh is powerful.*

Electrical impulses are triggered in the brain to release a natural form of tranquillizer and pain relief, as well as those feel-good *endorphins*, and it also eases tension.
Physically, laughing can be a really good full body workout.

*Be happy AND work out!* **Bonus**!

It probably improves coordination of your brain functions, which increases alertness and memory and helps clear your respiratory tract from coughing.
Laughter also increases your blood oxygen and strengthens internal muscles by tightening and releasing them.
Laughter is healthy for you in a variety of ways, such as boosting your immune system and reducing stress.

If nothing else, it is fairly obvious to most people that laughing is a really good thing that can lead to more confidence and social interaction – which is excellent for your path to empowerment.

*Think about all the other positive benefits this can then lead on to….*

### …..creative therapies…..not just an exclusive club….

*As a natural part of your natural birthright, creativity should not be viewed merely for the elite to enjoy or classed as some distant, out of reach prospect.*

It should be seen as an *essential* element of life that can enhance productivity, increase happiness and benefit many health matters.

*Use creativity as part of building up your state of empowerment and confidence.*

**…..get creative – it can keep you healthy.....**
*Being creative is really good for your health - emotionally, mentally and spiritually.*
It's an excellent way of reducing stress, plus it's really important to have some fun in life.

**Why not?**

If you want to sing, dance, knit, learn a new language, garden, do crosswords, art, yoga, cookery, play an instrument, go on a course, whatever it is that you're interested in, *go for it!*

Creativity is brilliant for improving overall well-being, as it boosts self-confidence and also makes you a more interesting person.

Keep happily balanced and challenged by being productive alongside being creative and indulging in leisure activities.

Take time to rest and rejuvenate, as well as setting time aside to do something stimulating and fun.

*And in any case, all work and no play makes for a very dull and unbalanced life.*

Mix it up by doing something that you feel comfortable with, so you can relax into it, but that also keeps you sharp, stimulated, motivated and gets your creative juices flowing.
Use your brain more, gain new skills, enjoy and make it pleasurable.

*It's one of the best investments for both your mind and spirit that you can make in your life.*

**Have fun!**

## ....art ....it's therapeutic and confidence building....
*Empower yourself to be the person you really want to be through the therapeutic art of art!*
Do not underestimate the special value and benefits there are in indulging in a bit of artistry to free your mind and spirit..
It can relieve stress, relax you, take your mind off problems and allow yourself to get lost in the moment, while you express yourself through the creation of something wonderful.

Painful emotions can be helped through the expression of art, and in doing so, take them out of your internal mind and into your work . Your self esteem and self awareness can be increased and even self-control can be encouraged through working with art materials.

Through artistic creation tapping into your unconscious, you can rediscover yourself and your strength, increase your skills and get your brain and senses working more fully.
It can instil a positive mood and lift suppressed thoughts and memories.

Even your energy and vitality can be increased through art and it can provide relaxation, reduce anxiety, worry and tension.

*What a wonderfully fun, hands-on, active and productive way to empower yourself all through the expression of art!*

## .....sing yourself into a more positive state of mind.....
*Singing is an excellent way of lifting your mood.*
Even if you're not good at it, it sends positive chemicals racing round your body, is a great mood enhancer and an excellent way of building self-esteem.
Not only is it good for you, but it's also great for your well-being and a surprising way of increasing your sense of empowerment.

Singing has the same kind of positive and enriching effect on your health and happiness as laughter, exercise, play and being outdoors, providing you with physical, emotional, mental and spiritual benefits.

The physicality of deep breathing during singing will help to increase the amount of oxygen delivered to your brain, causing a sense of alertness.

The stress and pressures of life are left behind as you become absorbed in the activity of singing, because you get distracted whilst you are focussing on something different from your normal daily routine instead.

Emotional blockages and repressed feelings can be unlocked and it has the ability to make you cry, laugh, feel free and ignite your passions.

Just like in exercise, those feel-good endorphins are released. They are also a natural pain-killer as well as an aid to help grieving and loss.

Singing can act as a form of meditation, as you allow yourself to feel spiritual, take your mind away from issues and problems in your life, move you beyond self-importance, allowing you to let go and feed your inner soul.

*So singing is very empowering, creating a mass of positive energy alongside a healthy mood enhancing state that you can really enjoy and gain immense benefit from.*

**…..seeing the world through a lens….**
*Do you spend far too much time walking around missing all the beauty around you, or if you do spot something you admire, you lose it in that moment…..?*

Well, why not make a memory of it, so you can keep that special association forever?

As you are moving around during your day, capture things that intrigue and interest you by taking photos of the world you are connected with – even if it's just on your mobile device.

*It will make you more aware of your surroundings, structures, art, environment and nature, bringing you closer and more in touch with **your** world.*

Feeling *connected* is an important part of your empowerment……
And every way that you add to that feeling of strength and positivity within you, will ultimately prove to be a additional bonus to your life as a whole.

Once those chosen moments have been lovingly captured, you

could even use the pictures to create a beautiful personal art project, or maybe just reflect on them and remember those unique experiences that made you feel so in awe just at those particular times......

*Whatever you do, you just don't know what wonderful things those special captured moments might then lead on to...*
*They could be part of your next big inspiration....*

**…..the personal advantages of owning a pet.....**
Pet owners will know that there is no denying the therapeutic benefits that their beloved animals give them.
This is partly because being affectionate sooths....both you and your pet.
Interacting, playing and walking your pet gives you the stimulus and fantastic access to physical exercise, unconditional love and social interaction.

Additionally, the companionship, the fun you have with your pets and also having something to look after, can ease your loneliness and depression, reduce stress and anxiety, build confidence and self-esteem and instil a positive mood.

Looking after your little best friend can give you a sense of self-worth, boost your morale and optimism and can also help your immune system and increase energy.

*The health benefits speak for themselves.*

A pet can help lower blood pressure, elevate serotonin and dopamine levels, which help you to relax and keep calm, and lower your triglyceride and cholesterol levels – the indicators of heart disease.
Pets can reduce the feeling of isolation and help you to stop focussing on issues and problems, at least for a while, because you have something else to care about, something that *needs* you, and in turn makes *you* feel needed and wanted.

*So, therefore, perhaps having a beloved pet by your side would be a perfect way to help your health, vitality and confidence, which in turn can go a long way to building your empowerment.*

**…..get out in your garden and on your way to fulfilment....**
*In your bid for optimum health, you have to seriously consider connecting to nature.*
Getting access to the great outdoor environment is a wonderful way to lower your blood pressure and reduce stress levels.
Being outside has such a positive effect on your emotions and is essential to your overall health and well-being, not to mention a crucial way to get your vitamin D allowance.

Like everyone, you are connected to nature, so even spending time in your garden is an important way to maintain this vital connection. Not only that, but gardening can help combat anxiety and moderate depression, so-much-so that outdoor activities are now labelled as *eco-therapy,* because of their positive health benefits and ways to lift your spirits.

Gardening is a powerful tool to improve the quality of your life and can increase confidence and self-esteem.

This could be one of the activities that helps you overcome certain issues that may be hindering your progress.

*So perhaps it may be the type of thing that suits you and gets you back on your route to empowering happiness and ultimate fulfilment.*

**…..eco-therapy – it's about all of us....naturally.....**
*You are part of the 'web of life' and as such, are not isolated or separate from the whole environment all around you.*
Therefore, you should adopt a healthy relationship of *mutual harmony* with nature and the earth and as you connect with it, so you can subsequently experience better mental and spiritual health.....
Because everyone is *personally connected* with the whole of this planet, in order to keep nature beautiful and fruitful, including maintaining it's welfare and prosperity, you have to consider the needs of both it and all others in the world.

*It seems obvious to say, but as we take care of the earth, so we care for ourselves.*

Many mental health professionals are now incorporating aspects of *ecotherapy* into their existing practices and private 'eco-therapists' are helping to empower people, based on the theory that nature *heals*.

A dose of nature can have the power to reinvigorate you, improve your mood, ease anxiety, tension, stress and depression, helping your self-esteem.

Find a nice location where you walk and commune with nature, quietly observing the beauty of the world around you, as you slow down and realise your deep connection with it.

*Whatever fits your goals and lifestyle, can be found in ecotherapy.*

**"Increase the pleasure of living and lessen the pain of life!
Doing pleasant things helps to buffer stress
and will keep you in a better frame of mind".**

**….make play part of your day....**
*You may not think that play has any part in empowerment, but the benefits over-ride that thought.* Play is vital and important in your life.
It makes you smarter, more productive and improves relationships. If you don't already, you need to start playing, as obviously, it's fun and makes you feel good.
The simple act of doing something you enjoy is pleasurable, that stands to reason, but playing has a profound biological process that makes you more switched on and innovative and it increases creativity.

*Therefore, you really shouldn't leave it as the last thing you do – which most people are guilty of....*

You don't *have* to make it about being competitive, productive or as some kind of lesson.
After all, life is so much more than a mechanical existence, or just a dutiful responsibility that is formally organised and rigid.

*You should make play a part of your daily life towards being a fulfilled human being.*

Take time to rediscover joy and really feel *free* to do and be what you choose.
Nothing lights up your brain like play does and you will be surprised to find that, with enough play, the brain actually works better.

*Play should be a state of mind, rather than just an activity to mindlessly go through.*

Never feel stressed about playing, or think it's hard work or a competition. That just takes the fun out of it and all the fantastic benefits that you should be gleaning from it.
It isn't something that you should feel *bad* about – that wouldn't be play and fun then, would it?

At the end of the day, if you go without play for too long, and you just work, work, work, you will end up saying, '*is this all there is*'? And that really is sad.....

*Play = empowerment.....!*

**…..tapping into the power of your senses…..**
*Slowing down and actually getting in touch with your senses has powerful benefits.*
Sound, touch, sight, taste and smell make up the five senses and they are obviously all significant and share important features.

**Smell** *consists not only of the sensation of the odours, but that of the experiences and emotions associated with the smell itself, that can evoke strong emotional reactions.*
The smells you like and dislike are based purely on emotional associations and the effects of a scent are similar to the effects of music on your mind and body.
The smell cells in your nose are linked to your 'limbic system' – one of the oldest parts of your brain that governs emotions, behaviour and long-term memory.

Aromas can impact on almost everything from your dreams,

emotions, driving, stress, gambling, pain, concentration, memory and romance.

Exposure to certain fragrances may sometimes be responsible for altering your mood and they can also benefit health and well-being, thus improving the way you feel.

The positive emotional effects of smells and fragrances also affect your perceptions and evaluations of people and environments.

Marketing machines use different smells to affect how and what you buy and how much you spend or risk.

There are a whole range of scents that have positive benefits from chamomile, coffee, eucalyptus, lavender, peppermint and many more.

Check them out and see how they may help you feel calmer, more refreshed and energised, or make you sleep better.

The more help that scents can provide you, so the more you will be able to function better and as such, feel far more empowered in your day to day dealings.

**Sound** *and healing have a long association and like light, sound is composed of frequencies and is a form of energy.*

Tibetan religious rituals use bells specifically for healing as their resonance has the power to affect the body's energy and heal it.

Sound therapists can help you benefit from it's healing remedies – should you wish to explore this form.

Laughter, music, loving words, the beauty of your natural surroundings are all joys you can appreciate as part of the gift of sound and taking advantage of all these can only add to the wonderful feeling of happiness and strength.

**Taste** - *what you put into your body via your mouth is just as significant as what you experience or consume through your eyes, ears and nose.*

Food and drink are not simply calories. They are matter – condensed energy that burns in your body to provide fuel.

It keeps you alive!

The sensations of taste respond to that sour, bitter, salt and sweet found in food and drink and which you can use as a way of creating great pleasure – to be enjoyed and savoured.

It is a way of making you feel good, whether eating alone, as a couple or in groups. You can use the occasion to uplift you and really instate a wonderful feeling of goodness and happiness.
This kind of experience can only add to that feeling of feeling alive and grateful.

Throughout the ages, food has also been used across the world as medicine to help and heal.
So therefore, appreciate your food as you savour each mouthful and adopt a sense of gratitude for what you have been provided by the earth.
Feel connected to it as you acknowledge and value it's advantageous offering to you.
This has an empowering effect on your emotions and relationships, so you might as well make the most of it and allow yourself to totally submerge yourself in it's fantastic benefits.

**Touching and seeing** follow the same appreciation as all the other senses.
To be able to see the world around you, to engage in it's colours and textures, light and form and everything else around you is a positively natural joy.
To be able to touch and feel and allow yourself to be submerged in warmth, textures, soft and hard, cold, dense and light are all part of this world's present to you as a human being.

You can benefit greatly from being shown how to fully appreciate these wonders you have been given. In doing so, all of the senses can be fully tapped into and you can feel at one with who you are and your place on this earth.

Learning to appreciate all of this can lift your spirits greatly, making you feel worthy and valued and thus, add to your own sense of empowerment.

*Look, smell, touch, listen and taste the world – it's all out there for you to take full advantage of......!*

## ...energy is in and around us all.....
*Energy is present in the wind blowing through the trees and in falling snow.*
It's in laughter and tears and the sun shining down on the ocean.
It's in our emotions and in our feet as they carry us across the grass.
It's there as the waves crash against the rocks and as you hold someone's hand.
It's in the gaze into someone's eyes and the connection between us all.
And just as your favourite place lifts your spirits and creates positivity, so a room where there's bad feeling has an atmosphere of negativity.

Energy is in everything.

*Choose yours to be positive.....*

## ....knowing your body energy......
*The energy of your body is complex and has two main aspects - energy within your body and energy emanating around your body.*
The quality of each layer of your energy is different and acts uniquely - moving from the outside in towards your body.

The spiritual body, which is the furthest away from your physical core, is your realm of spirit and intuition and is faster than the speed of light.
This energy expresses itself as your flash of inspiration, your instinctive intuition or immediately recognising trust in something.

Your 'mental' energy is the action of thought and is not as fine or quick as your spiritual energy.

In energetic terms, you require sustained mental and emotional development to open the pathways to spiritual understanding.

Immediately surrounding your physical body is the energy band known as your *emotional* body, where emotions and their impact are held, felt and exert their influence. Your emotional body holds both your emotional history and capacity.

Maintaining clear energy in your emotional body contributes to a caring behaviour, which is essential to the world's survival. Balancing the energy of your emotional body helps you find productive ways to deal with your feelings and desires.

*Learning to feel your own energy within you and around you will give you a full sense of connection and as such, give you the empowerment you need to feel strong and is something that you can use to your benefit at all times.*

### ....using the power of energy in prayer....
*A prayer is like a special energetic message.*
If you pray regularly, you will know it's power and know that it works. This isn't merely *wish* fulfilment - it's a way of you connecting with a much *deeper* layer of meaning and '*causality*' in your universe – one that recognises the existence of a greater *whole* that you are surrounded by and that influences you.

*And everyone is part of this.*

Prayer doesn't have to be religious.
The most effective prayer you can make is the prayer that comes from your heart.
There are no special formulations to remember or books to research.
It is just an expression of your heart.

'God' can be a shorthand to this. It doesn't have to indicate a deity in the sky or some overwhelming authority figure. Nor is it preferable to any of the several other expressions used, such as 'The Light', 'The Creative', 'The Source', or the many more given names that are equally as relevant.

Radiate your positive energy out across the universe with your message using love, feeling and sincerity and you will find a *true* connection that lives within you, bringing you a real sense of peace and belonging.

*You can physically feel this if you give it wholehearted depth of sincerity and belief.*

Use this energy to power you on through all aspects of your life and also to show gratitude, thanks and love for what you have in your life, as well as all your influences and relationships that support and guide you.

*Boost your empowerment through your own prayer that you can make up specifically relevant to you personally.*

Or perhaps you would like to use some of the following prayers to help inspire and connect you:

*"Show me the stars in the sky and the sun in the mist and the world beyond the world of the everyday.
Teach me tolerance, wisdom and always love.*
***Thank you".***
(Universal Prayer).

*"Teach us the wisdom of the seasons and the secret of night and day.
Teach us the meaning of the clouds and the feelings of the waves.
Teach us the power of the wind and the silence of the mountains.
Teach us the stillness and action, love, laughter, pain and despair.
Then teach us stillness again.
Teach us to find you and ourselves.*
***Thank you".***
(Secret Wisdom).

*"Lead me from death to life, from falsehood to truth.
Lead me from despair to hope, from fear to trust.
Lead me from hate to love, from war to peace.
Let peace fill our hearts, our world, our universe peace, peace, peace".*
(old Hindu Prayer).

**…..cleanse and clear your energy to restore balance and empowerment in your life…..**
*Everything is energy!*
Nature has it's own vibrations, as do people, places and buildings. Buildings and people are the same with regard to energy in the sense of both experiencing positive and negative energy.

*As you go through your day, you spend it picking up other people's energy.*

Some people can drain your energy, making you feel not yourself. Events in your life all shape your vibration, whether good or bad.

*You need to have positive energy to feel empowerment.*

Too much negative energy in and around your own energy field can bring you down and will stop it flowing properly, becoming blocked and constricted and holding back any proper progress in your life.

*This is why you may need to have this energy cleared.*

The blocks can be caused by emotions like fear, guilt, self-criticism, sadness, anger and resentment, all of which will cause you to close down spiritually, emotionally, mentally and even physically.

When you feel ill, you seek healing through a doctor or therapist. Therefore, you can just as equally clear out these blockages and get your energy moving again and well-being restored.

*Cleansing your energy improves your health, speeds recovery and protects and supplies you with much stronger energy.*

It makes you feel more relaxed, more vitalised and more refreshed. In order to do this, you first need to *accept* how you are feeling, and once you have done this, you will feel a release of tension.

You need to look at the root of your problem and begin to understand it – this could even be from a long-term limiting belief or attitude to something. By unlocking that emotion, you accept the issue and in doing so, you can get the energy moving positively again.

This then gives you the chance to look clearly at what it was that caused the problem in the first place and what gave you the negative attitude and emotion that goes along with it.

Once done, you can begin to dissolve it and move on.

If you are spending your life thinking that you will never amount to anything because you are not worthy, or life and people are cruel, or you believe you've done things that make you think you don't deserve good things, or you're worrying that you might get hurt or fail if you try, or you just aren't in control of yourself so you'd be powerless to do anything with your life anyway, then you are *putting limiting pressure on anything positive ever coming your way.*

But even if you *do* have all those feelings, by acknowledging them and coming to terms with them, you can at least begin to take on some coping strategies and do something about them.
This includes giving yourself the chance to *let go* and realise that these feelings or beliefs are destructive and self-defeating. Because then you can work with that acceptance, instead of allowing those beliefs to control you.

It is important to understand that they are *just beliefs* and are not necessarily the truth, and therefore can be worked on and changed, so they no longer stand in the way of your progress, or any kind of empowerment that you need to get on with your life.

If you know these feelings are overriding your development and causing resistance to achieving what you want in life, then it may be helpful to write down all of the reasons why you think you can't have what you want.
This may be laziness, lack of money, believing it won't work, or that you're scared, for instance. Then look carefully at those reasons you've given and ask yourself if you genuinely *do* believe them as the truth.

*Come to realise that because of all these beliefs, you are putting unnecessary limitations on yourself and they may be stopping you fulfilling your dreams!*

From this, make a list of those negative attitudes about yourself, your relationships, the world, other people and your life and look at what emotional power they have over you.
Allow it all to flow out of you, accepting any emotions that come with the process and understanding any *programming* that is controlling you.

Spend time doing this, then symbolically destroy the paper that you've written on to acknowledge that they do *not* have to have any power over you at all.
Once done, you can then replace those negative, restricting thoughts with good positive affirmations that are *far more* constructive.

If you feel that you have been harmed or angered by particular relationships through their mistreatment of you, or you are filled with resentment from certain injustices, then it's time you put this to bed too and release yourself from this hurt.

*No good can come of it, but you can clear out those feelings.*

List all the people that have caused you this pain, including what it was that they did to you. Closing your eyes and visualising each person, one by one, have a conversation with them, explaining why and how they have hurt or angered you, forgive them and release all the negative energy that has existed between you.

*Ask them to be happy and then move on.*

Destroy your list meaningfully, telling these people that you forgive and release them, throwing the paper away, showing that you are letting go of those past experiences, resentment and hostility.
You may need to do this several times before the feelings and negativity go completely, or if some of your emotions are very strong.
You may even need help from a third party to get you through this.

There are other exercises that you can do to cleanse yourself from the bad energy that causes you problems and re-place it with new pure, clean and good energy.

*One way to do this is to visualise the bad energy leaving your body and going down into the earth.*
Give it a colour that you feel resembles it.
Then breathe deeply and visualise new energy from the fresh air moving into your body or going through the top of your head. Give the new energy a wonderful new colour.

*Another way to cleanse energy is to picture yourself standing in a waterfall.*

Visualise you are sweating bad energy off your body and it is flowing away in the stream below. Now see your body absorbing clean pure water from the waterfall, or that you are drinking it – replacing the water you lost through sweating.

*A third way of cleansing is to get any kind of salt.*

Put some in your cupped hands and rock them side to side 6 times. Then say out loud *"all that is within that did not come from me, I command that you go back from whence you came. All of which is not of God, leave me"* (whatever 'God' means to you).
Then open up your hands leaving some salt in each.
Close your hands then wave them up, across, in front of your body and to the back of your head, down the front of your body to your toes, up the back to your waist and back, in front of you, cross your arms and then discard the salt.

If you are experiencing too many negatives in your environment, including any buildings you frequent or live in, it is advisable for you to have them cleared too.

You may want to clear out the vibrations from previous occupants and personalise it with your own. Make sure your living and working environment is clear of surplus 'stuff' that is no longer needed, so the energy flows freely through and around, and you feel like order has been restored.

*This can be extremely therapeutic.*

Usually, various techniques can be used with clearing a building, including a blessing of the space which recharges and renews the energies, thereby attracting a more positive and lighter flow of energy.

*This can create a more loving and harmonious environment, energising it and bringing in more productivity, creativity and balance.*

Whatever it is that you feel needs to be cleansed or cleared, the sooner you deal with it, the quicker all negative energy around you can be *replaced by positive good energy and you can once again live life to your fullest potential with a feeling of true empowerment.*

Get help if you need it!

**....learning how meditation and your chakras help your balance.....**
*Practising meditation is not about seeking exotic experiences, but rather, it's about finding balance, harmony and true joy in life.*
It can be more restorative than sleep.

The Chinese and Indians believe that your energy moves like a life force through your body along invisible lines known as '*meridians*', and certain places in your body function like energetic fuse boxes, i.e. your '*chakras*'.

*Their smooth function is regarded as crucial to well-being.*

The purpose of meditation is to access your chakras and your body's energy.
This helps release the elements of your personal history that have settled in the form of obstacles, marks or blockages in your energy. Once released, your health and well-being will become significantly changed for the better.
Having energy is related to some of your mechanical processes, like eating and digesting, consuming and burning fuel. But the energy within your body is also affected by other energy bodies and by your chakras.

Your body has 7 key chakras and many smaller ones - each of which relate to a particular area of your body and affect it's overall functioning.
Chakras interact with the emotional, mental and spiritual energy bodies.

Here is a description of your chakra's and their individual components, including what functions they are related to:-

The **base** or **root** chakra, '*I AM*' – seen as the colour red and sounds '*OO*', is found in the coccyx/perineum and is the root of the body associated with the immediate family.
It has strong connections with the feet, legs, buttocks and hips.
It is related to the quality of being grounded, having a strong presence – both physical and psychological.
It's mantra is '*I am here now*'.

The **second** or **sacral** chakra, '*I FEEL*' – is orange and sounds '*OH*', is found in the sacrum/pelvis, and is associated with a larger social unit.
It affects an individual's views and reactions towards physical relationships with others, influencing issues relating to sexuality, reproduction, self-esteem and earning a living.
It also concerns artistry, creativity and the power of imagination and is related to lunar energy and water.
It's mantra is '*I am a force of attraction*'.

The **third** or **solar plexus** chakra, '*I DO*' – is yellow and sounds '*AW,*' is found in the solar plexus/upper abdomen and is involved with 'gut knowledge' – which represents power and authority and affects the stomach, internal organs – pancreas, spleen, liver, kidneys, gallbladder and intestines.
It is linked to your responses to adult situations, such as meetings or office politics.
This is the seat of willpower and personal identity with strong ties to the ego and pride and to fully awakening oneself as an individual, aggressive mental energy and fire.
It's mantra is '*I know who I am*' and '*I am power*'.

The **fourth** or **heart** chakra, '*I LOVE*' – is green and sounds '*AH*', is found in the chest and symbolizes maturity and involves one's relationship to the larger world, as well as to individual loved ones.
Physical problems are associated with the heart or breasts.
This is the centre of love, affection, caring and connectedness with all life.
It channels healing energy from the heart, as well as instilling a deep sense of calm, peace and oneness.
It is considered to be the vital link between human and higher spiritual chakras.
It's mantra is '*I am love*'.

The **fifth** or **throat** chakra, *'I SPEAK'* – is blue and sounds *'EH'*, is found in the throat/Adams apple and is linked to eating and self expression and relates to the mouth and throat.
It involves communication and truth, creativity and taking responsibility for oneself and one's development.
It's mantra is *'I am knowledge'*.

The **sixth** or **brow** chakra, *'I SEE'* – is indigo and sounds *'IH'*, is found in the forehead and includes the nose, eyes, ears and brain – all the organs of perception and of the ancient eastern concept of the 'third' eye, often regarded as a 'magic' eye with the special ability of second sight.
It's mantra is *'I am wise'*.

The **seventh** or **crown** chakra, *'I UNDERSTAND'* – is white or violet and sounds *'EE'*, and is found in the crown/slightly above the head and is closely associated with the finest energy, allowing only the purest, most spiritual input into the body.
It is influenced by the dominant chakras below and affects the quality and amount of energy absorbed through the crown chakra and how it is used.
It is the centre for transcendental insight, spiritual revelation, divine communion and cosmic consciousness.
It is commonly understood as the chakra of enlightenment.
It's mantra is *'I am divine'*.

To start a simple form of meditation, use a quiet room with soft, ambient lighting.

Sit in a firm but comfortable chair, with your posture upright and symmetrical.
Gently tense and relax your muscles in your feet and slowly work your way up to the top of your head.
Next, find a spot on the wall in front of you and focus on it. Begin to turn down your *internal dialogue.*
Take six deep, slow breaths and gradually soften your focus, slowly closing your eyes.
Focus on the sounds outside the room and then within the room.
Listen to the sounds within your own body – your breath, your heartbeat and the faint ringing in your ears.

*This is where you want your attention to be.*
Slowly breathe in and out.
You can use a word or mantra to focus on your breath.
Continue for as long as you feel is comfortable for you, gradually building up your time until you feel totally relaxed and connected.

There are many forms of meditation, but you can use this method whenever you want. You can even practise it whilst waiting for something important like an interview or test, when you are feeling stressed, or just when you want to have some inner peace.

*The more you practise it, the more you will glide through your days appreciating everything around you, building up your confidence and generating a wonderful feeling of real empowerment.*

**…get yourself grounded and look forward to more inner peace..**
*Being grounded is all about feeling balanced and at one with the earth and your existence in it.*
If you are unbalanced, your energy field will be affected, out of alignment and you will feel ill at ease.
One way to become balanced is by opening up your *chakras* from root to crown and reconnecting your body with the earth energy, allowing universal energy to flow in efficiently.

You can do this either through meditation or a simple, quicker exercise.
A very *simple* grounding exercise involves the visualisation of yourself as a tree:-

Close your eyes and visualise roots growing out of your feet and extending them into the ground, into the earth's crust, down into the centre of the earth and anchoring them there.
Using the meditation method, you need to make sure that your feet are planted on the ground through standing or sitting, whichever is your preference and what is most comfortable for you.
It is important that your feet are on the ground, so it can connect to the earth effectively.
Closing your eyes, take 2-3 cleansing breaths, then continue to breath deeply.
As you do so, imagine your legs are the trunk of a tree with its' roots extending into the ground. Through your roots, draw up nurturing

minerals back up to your feet and through your entire body. If you have fears and anxieties, rid them out of your body through your leaves like a tree expels its' carbon dioxide. As they move out of the leaves and into the air, imagine them condensing as water and falling to the ground to be absorbed.
Continue repeating this until you feel yourself rid of your toxins and you feel calm and grounded.
As you finish off and come back to reality, tell yourself that you are coming back into yourself, l, 2, 3 and open your eyes.

If you are new to this, expect it to take some time to perfect....
It may even be a few years before you can truly be free of whatever negative thing you have to get out of your system. You may even be revisited by it.
However, by using these practised strategies, you will be in a much stronger place and position to be able to face them head-on and move forward.
You do need to deal with any negativities you may harbour if you sincerely want to get past them and surge ahead with your life's goals.

*You will then have a new, more powerful mindset that will set you up for life and personal achievement, as well as possessing a lot more serenity and inner peace.....*

**…..try quantum cleansing to detox your mind…..**
*Quantum cleansing is a type of meditation that can 'detox your mind', easing depression, improving mental functioning and reducing stress and anxiety.*
It can reduce *'Quantum Toxins'* - the thought patterns or attachments to negative feelings that can actually influence your physical chemistry.

Taking the time to do just five minutes of meditation every day is thought to enable you to come back into the *present moment* and in doing so, encourage you to make better decisions and give yourself the chance to truly experience your life to the fullest.
*Total empowerment.*

Here is one of those meditations that you can practise as a special treatment for your mind…..

Sit comfortably and upright in a chair, feet flat on the floor under your knees, hands on your thighs, arms relaxed.
Look straight ahead and take a deep breath.
Sense your feet on the floor. Then move your attention to your calves, still breathing.
Repeat this for each area of your body, letting your awareness sense each part intensely.
The more you practise, the more you will strengthen your ability to direct and hold your attention.
If your mind starts to think about other things, steer the attention back to your body, say thanks for sharing and move on with the meditation.
This is normal.

Becoming aware is all part of bringing back your energy to yourself, rather than your state of mind robbing you of it.
Teach yourself to move away from distracted and habitual thought patterns and into the present moment instead.

Use this method anywhere, especially when stressed or nervous, like at a job interview, when your thoughts unconsciously spend way too much time and crucial energy having expectations, judgements, measurements and negativities.
Just redirect your attention and breathe....

As you get better at it, you will gradually clear out quantum toxins, cleansing your mind and using your energy far more efficiently and effectively, so you can become more productive, make better decisions and become anxiety-free.

A 'crowded' mind can zap your energy, release ageing free radicals in your body and cause mental stress and pressure, because of all it's 'over-thinking'. Only invite in those thoughts that you *want* to take up your energy.

Removing unwanted things from your personal space will help you to claim back some of your energy – so get rid of what you don't need, is broken, you don't use or wear - give them to charity.
To remove repetitive unwanted, annoying thoughts, repeat them slowly over and over again until they just lose their appeal.

*You will then realise that they are really unproductive and will eventually fade away.*

Keep a notepad by your bed for when you have a head full of stuff that needs to done. Write them down, get them out of your mind and save them till the morning - then get a good nights sleep instead!
Use things to calm you like essence oils, massage, taste and sound and redirect energy away from your mind by activating your senses instead, helping you to dissolve those annoying thoughts.

Also, meditation, yoga, music, dance, walking and reading will get your creative juices flowing and take your mind away from your aggravations for a while – a perfect distraction.

Take time to actually *listen* to your body's needs and wants – you may not even realise that you are burnt-out, stressed, rushing about, hungry or thirsty, or just in need of a good, healthy stretch!

*Stop, listen, feel and act!*

Just take some big, long, deep breaths.....*and relax.....*

*Taking the time just to listen to yourself, be calm, rest, look after yourself and your body and mind, is all part of your total life empowerment helping you to be you, and nobody else except you.*

**....love is healing....healing is love.....**
*Healing is about becoming whole.*
It's about allowing love into your life and coming to know exactly what that means.
When you think about it, love transforms everything in life, including your reactions to events and people.

When you know *real* love, you will understand it is impossible to actively want to hurt others or to turn pain against yourself.
Living in a world of love will give you so much peace and tranquillity, by knowing you are able to give *and* receive it.
Allow yourself the time and space to love and be loved.

*Put yourself into a position to accept it into your life.*

Feel it and let it feel you.
Be calm and gentle.
Withdraw from selfishness and greed and open up your heart to others and yourself.

*When you are at this state of 'whole', this is when you are truly empowered.*

### ....crystals may help you to heal and transcend....
*Within alternative medicine, crystals are prized for their healing properties because they essentially emit energy and can be programmed and empowered to help you.*
Crystals and minerals are associated with their healing colours, each pertaining to your various chakras - or energy centres of your body.

Using their own distinct vibrational frequencies, 'Gemstone Therapy' works to strengthen your body. When placed next to you, the vibrations within the aura of the crystal causes your own aura's vibrational rate to change.

If you are going to use your own crystals, once you have chosen the right ones for you, they should be 'cleared' of any leftover negative energies by being cleaned.
You then need to direct positive energies toward your crystals through chanting or affirmations.
You can promote healing in a specific area of your body, or form a vision in your mind of what you would like to happen.

*Any kind of healing you get from crystals will ultimately help you become more balanced in the long run, and as such, help you on your route to total happiness and fulfilment.*

Which adds to part of your overall empowerment programme.

### ....give yourself a real sense of tranquillity......
*Spiritual healing has the ability to change you physically, mentally, emotionally and spiritually.*
This is because a healer helps you to see things from a new and

more positive perspective.
Sometimes the changes can be quite subtle, but they can also be quite noticeable and profound.

Your healer can guide you from sickness to recovery through *spiritual 'awakening'* and the benefits can leave you with a feeling of peace and calm.
They can help to remove any blockages causing problems in your growth and life, by using a combination of talking and energy healing to bring about restored balance.

*This kind of healing may be advantageous to you on your pathway to contentment and may be just the tonic you need to help you feel more empowered.....*

**...recharge your batteries....renew yourself.....**
*Of course you'd love to live with inner peace and tranquillity, enjoying each moment of your life, relishing every challenge thrown at you.*
*That is the ultimate aim....*
But you probably have a busy and hard-working life to lead and as such, there are times when you feel stressed, angry or ill at ease.
It's at these times when you need to calm down, take stock and recharge your batteries - that's if you want to enjoy a more balanced life, with good health and strong relationships that aren't negatively affected by your grumpy, tired moods.

When was the last time you stopped to look at or smell the beauty of a flower or looked at the trees?
Are you so busy running around like a mad thing, that you hardly give yourself time to breathe?

Then how about you take some time out just for *you?*

However you like to relax, allow yourself this time to re-energise, so you are fighting fit and raring to go at the next challenge that faces your day.

*Not only will you feel good, but everyone around you will feel the knock-on effect of your revitalised state and mood as well.*

Try listening to some of your favourite music, or take a wonderful walk along the beach, collect shells and breathe in those sea ions, just stand and watch the water ebb and flow over the pebbles, or even play with your pet or give your baby a cuddle.

Why not smile at people and children as you pass them, get out into the great outdoors and see nature at it's best, or have dinner with some really close friends, plays games or your favourite sport, do some yoga, meditation, sleep or pray, pick up that book you've been meaning to read for ages, laugh yourself silly at a funny film or go to a show?

Or how about something creative like a bit of artwork, or dancing and singing, have a relaxing bath with scented candles, maybe book a holiday, getaway or a spa?

*All these things will give you a wonderful feeling of vibrancy and serenity.*

Whatever it is that you know will make you recharge your batteries and you can enjoy in peace without any stress, is obviously going to help and uplift you.

*And don't make it just a 'one-off' - make it a regular thing!*
Build it into your week or even day. ….

Use some of these tactics if you feel stressed at any time and unable to cope, or you feel your heckles are beginning to rise. Just remove yourself from the situation and get some fresh air, deep breathe, look at nature, the sky, the trees, walk and daydream, or even simply make a cup of tea!
Put things into perspective.

*Give yourself time to calm down and reflect.*

You may even get the answer or solution to the problem or situation you are removing yourself from when you will have a clear head and can see things much more rationally.

Remember, what doesn't kill you makes you stronger and if you feel strong, you will be able to handle situations far better.

With a much more relaxed mind, you will have the right head on you to approach situations with ease and confidence.

*A calm mindset.*

Even the strongest of people can have their moments!
You have to give yourself a break and time to refocus, recharge and move forward.
Removing yourself from problematic situations works.
Get out, go for a drive, crank up the music, have a break without your phone or laptop so you can get a *fresh* perspective. Go on holiday if it's doable – if not, make it so!

Rustle up some endorphins with a gym session, exercise class, swim or brisk walk. Allow your brain to drift off for a while and clear the cobwebs. You'll feel much more confident afterwards or you may even find answers while you in the middle of it!

Get yourself a motivational book that you can dip into whenever you need a confidence boost and reminder about why you are doing things, how brilliant and brave you are, how to trust your own instincts and that you are on your way to bigger and better things.

*A problem shared is a problem halved, so find someone you can talk things through with.*

Start giving yourself permission to escape.
*Go out and play!*

Whatever you choose to do and is far removed from your daily grind - do it and reconnect your soul with your happy self.

**Feel like *YOU* again!**

*Get your empowerment back to where it's meant to be!*

**…..remove, remind, unwind….**
It's only when you remove yourself from the hustle and bustle and the stress and strain of everyday life to a place of peace, calm and beauty, that you realise there's more to life than endless striving, arguing, bitterness and tension.

You get a chance to breathe, stop, sit, look, listen, watch and relax.
You can then *really* see the wood for the trees.
Put things into perspective.
Truly smile for a change.
Take in the air, the ambience, the freedom and the positive vibrations in the atmosphere.
Draw in the energy.

*Realise why you're here.*

Think, contemplate, extend your mind.
Allow the peace in.
Watch things growing, nurtured by nature.
Understand the situation you are in.

Think about how to make changes, be creative, look for solutions.
Bring your life into focus......*real focus*.
Understand the need to shake those shackles and <u>be real</u>.
Be true to yourself.
Come to terms with your inner self.
Your reason for being.

Is it really necessary to live in conflict and stress?
Are you going against the grain of your true meaning and soul?
Can you make your life better?

No more rose-tinted glasses, driving hard towards alien goals that are meaningless to you at the cost of your health and sanity.
Start living in a place of quiet contentment, your own mood – made through genuine self-satisfaction and enrichment.

Make a space for yourself in life and in this world – one with true meaning and value.
One worthy of your innate skills and talents.
One where your energies are balanced harmoniously.

*One where you truly live as you.*

> **Insanity = doing the same thing over and over again
> and expecting different results.**
> *Albert Einstein*

### ....step out of the gloom and into the room....

*Do you spend far to much time obsessing about food, fat, your weight, attaining success or your multiple failures, instead of imagining what your life could be as joy, energy and happiness?*
*Then it may be time to shift your focus to a fresher look.*
*It's time to connect your mind, body and spirit.*
*Time to feed your soul.*

### Every day...

It's time to dance, to listen to music, to dissolve all your inhibitions in a hot bubble bath, to laugh at a comedy, light a candle, smile at people, pass on the gladness, breathe in the moment - it's yours to keep.
Time to meditate with the silence of the rocks and sand, to read and be inspired, to explore, discover and have fun.

*The universe is your playground.*

Open your eyes to the beautiful day, remove your own restrictions and those being put on you, pass on some love, start things anew with a deep sigh.
Look at the flowers – take in their beauty, sing with the birds, begin your day with fresh eyes and end it with knowledge and wisdom.....

*Just have fun – don't think about it.*

Stop worrying – it doesn't help anything.
Laugh at mess and then reorganise yourself!

*Feed your soul....it's important.....*

### ....find your unique blessed place....

*Do you have a special place that's just yours?*
Somewhere you can be at peace and have time in relative quiet to just *be*, think, reflect, contemplate, clear your mind and just relax.....?
If you don't have one, then find one that *fits* and is especially for you.

*This is your **'unique blesséd place'**.*

Use it to look at your life, put things into perspective and come up with ideas, or just to feel free. Free of everyday 'noises', stresses, people and the day-to-day grind.

Use it to get away from having to achieve, manage, decide, lead, direct, operate, implement.

This is *your* place that no-one can take away from you.
It's yours to keep and yours to just be *you*.

Look *outwards* and be at one with nature.

If you practice meditation, you may want your unique blesséd place to be your personal '*expression of intention*', where you use chosen objects to create a space that allows you to increase your awareness of your spiritually and connect to what is sacred to you.

These items could be anything that resonates with you, like crystals, pieces of nature - like stones, sticks, beach items, or treasured possessions and photographs – anything that holds a deeply felt meaning to you upon which you can stop and reflect.

You can either arrange them somewhere indoors like an altar, or take them outside to your special place with you, wherever you feel calm and safe.
This 'sets an intention' for space and silence within yourself so that you can awaken, expand and feel connected.

Use your unique blesséd place to become at one with yourself and the universe.

*Come away feeling renewed and calm, with a stronger sense of inner empowerment.*

**…..your prayer to the universe….**
*To help you on your road to empowerment and positivity, you can make up a prayer to the universe asking for what you want in life – a bit like a mantra.*

Examples of these could be:

"*I ask the world to bring me peace and harmony. I am at peace with myself*", or

"*I ask the world to bring me confidence and success. I have the confidence to push myself forward in life and be a success*", or

"*I ask the world to make my body fit and free from pain. I am rich in fitness and pain free*".

After you have decided what your prayer is, you follow it by giving thanks, for instance:

"*Thank you for giving me all these wonders and riches*".

You can make it up as a poster and put it in a prominent place where you can see and reflect on it regularly.

Make it into your mantra, breathing in the words so they penetrate deeply into your mind and body.

*Each time you say and look at it, it will help you to connect, feel inspired and more empowered to better your world.*

**….why not begin your day more happily…..**
*Start your day on a positive note, by setting up a good mood as soon as you open your eyes...*
Upon wakening and whilst still in bed, put yourself in excellent spirits ready for the day, by announcing to yourself and the universe what you want for that day – whether that's how to feel or any actions you desire.

For example, you could start with:

"*I am happy, happy, happy!*", or
"*This is going to be a great day full of achievements and happiness*", or
"*I am calm, confident and relaxed*".

Whatever your choice for the day is.

You can keep repeating any of these to yourself throughout your day whenever you need to.

Then whilst you are still in bed, give yourself a full stretch from top to toe, stretching your legs individually from the hip to the point of your toe, then pulling your toes back, circling your toes and hands, stretching your lower back, curling your hips up and back, stretching out your arms, your shoulders and neck, until you're *fully* stretched. Then take in three full, deep breaths.

Whilst you're still lying in bed or when you get out, do some limbering arm circles, tall stretches, side and shoulder stretches, or vitalizing yoga moves, so you're ready to get up and take on the day!
You will feel much more invigorated and ready for any challenge, rather than just grumpily dragging yourself out of bed stiff and full of aches, and huffing and puffing your way through breakfast!
*Give it a try and see for yourself how much better you feel...*

### ....start your day feeling more alive....
*To continue generating your good mood, free up 10 minutes of the morning after you wake up to do something that's motivating and invigorating, so you start your day off full of positivity.*
This could be anything from doing a balanced series of exercises like sit-ups, stretches, isometrics, pilates, yoga, meditation, cycling, or a short run.
Or perhaps taking a walk somewhere nice, maybe with your dog, or putting on some favourite music, turning it up loud and singing or dancing to it!

*Anything that you love and lifts your mood and that will start your day bright, happy and motivated and will keep that feeling going for the rest of the day.*

And while you're at it, how about changing your morning alarm to something that's soothing, if it isn't already....?
When your alarm goes off in the morning, it is the start of your day and if it's annoying, loud, aggravating or depressing – that's how you begin! Boo!
So, change it to something that makes you feel good instead,

makes you smile or laugh, or just feels pleasant about waking up and embracing the day!
Use your mobile device if needs be – it usually has a good range of sounds you can choose from.

*Feed your soul on a regular basis.*

Be thankful and appreciate what you have got and not what you don't have.
Make space for yourself - everyone needs it to keep their life balanced.
And you owe it to yourself.
Be selfish sometimes!

*Boost up your empowerment!*

**….doing something charitable makes you feel good.....**
*Giving back and being of service to others can be a wonderfully rewarding experience.*
Doing something for someone else or for your community, really does make you feel good. Knowing that you have made someone else happy or done something that makes your environment better, not just for yourself but for others around you, will give you a huge sense of satisfaction and achievement.

Helping in any small way, or just smiling at someone as you walk past them, or maybe giving directions to someone who is lost, for instance, gives you enormous contentment knowing you have helped them with their day.

*You will feel good and so will they, and as a result, you will both probably have a much better day.*

Making unselfish gestures for others, no matter how small or insignificant generates fabulous positive energy that lives inside you and them for hours, and this great spirit will probably continue to be passed onto many others as well throughout the day.

So think about how this 2-way process impacts your soul and that of others.
Make it a way of life – to be unselfish and considerate at times.

*And then keep 'passing it forward' to help create a more wonderful world.....*

**…..leisure time....measure time.....**
*No-one can continually rush around at a hundred miles per hour and get away with it for long, without it having an damaging impact on their health.*
If this is you, you need to learn to take five minutes of every working hour to relax and unwind. Stop what you are doing and make a hot drink, do some relaxing deep breathing exercises, stretch your muscles, or do some yoga, for instance.
These short breaks actually enable you to have better concentration and will improve your general productivity.

Also, spend 30 minutes each day doing something *enjoyable* that's not on your 'to do' list or related to work.
Soak in a bath with some lavender essential oils, have a massage, or just sit drinking a cup of chamomile tea.

*Basically, just do whatever it is you enjoy and makes you relax.*

If you can't, don't or won't do this, then it would explain why you may be feeling tired, stressed, down and unfulfilled.

Don't think of it as only '*allowing*' yourself to do something you enjoy, or want to do once all the '*have to do*' stuff is completed, as you may find it all overtaking your life.
If you do this, it will never be the 'right' time, as the list of things *to do* will always be long and active!

Don't feel guilty if you have a good time, it is *your* life to live at the end of the day.

*Life isn't all about work, work, work!*

Reward yourself for things you achieve - you deserve it.

And if you feel good about who you are, you're more likely to take care of your health and well-being and also have better control over your life.

*Every little addition to looking after your general demeanour is a step up on your empowerment ladder – so be good to yourself.....*

**…...be calm enough to actually enjoy your life….**
*What does worrying and stress actually get you in the end?*
Running around frantically, getting embroiled in problems – perhaps some that don't even concern you or that you have no control over anyway, is a fruitless task and will drain you of all your energy.

Slow down and actively *be calm*.

You will be in a much better place to take on challenges, deal with issues and also enjoy your life, if you can approach things with a *lighter* attitude.

*So learn to take deep breaths and go with the flow, stop giving yourself a hard time and racing against yourself.*

Calm down your 'inner noise' and you will begin to accept yourself as who you are much better. You will be surprised at how easy life feels and things start to come to you, you start making the right choices and feeling happier in your own skin.

Remember, you can do *anything* you want to - if you make the right choices for *YOU*.

Remaining calm is a strength.

*Don't feed negativity with more negativity – what's the point?*

**….flowing good energy into your environment with feng shui...**
Bringing complete balance into your life is all about enabling total life empowerment, so you can live in ultimate fulfilment and satisfaction.
This means getting your environment in good order too.

Feng Shui has long been known as the '*art of placement*' and it's purpose is to bring balance, harmony and beneficial energy to the environment where you live and work. It can have a tremendous impact on the quality of your life.

The Feng Shui basic principle is that the energy of all things in the physical world, including cars, computers, rocks, houses, people, land and furniture, connects and moves everything through the 'cycles of life'.
You can have a personal response to them, just as those things that give you comfort and well-being lift your energy levels, whilst other unhappy associations will draw your energy down.

*Everything is related to everything else, making all things in your life important.*

When you change one thing, a series of events changes everything else – like ripples in a pool, they spread out and affect everything in it's contact (*cause and effect*).

The *Chi* (energy) in everything is constantly changing - your mood, the seasons, your body, your community, nurturing and supporting your growth.

The objective of Feng Shui is to create living environments that are comfortable, organised and in harmony with your inner being, using the principles of this Chi energy.

You are able to enhance your life with living spaces that nourish and empower you, by surrounding yourself with the things that you love and using your environment to enable you to be a creative, healthy and happy individual. Just like when you surround yourself with chaos, unwanted clutter and disorganisation, you are easily overwhelmed, frustrated and stressed.

As you become more positive and clear, you attract good relationships and prosperity into your life, as well as increased energy, good health, awareness of synchronicity and most of all, a feeling of empowerment and increased self-esteem.
*Thus improving all aspects of your life.*

At the simplest level of good feng shui principles - '*everything is alive*' and you can start by arranging your furniture to let the energy flow better round your house and work space.
By letting go of things that no longer enhance your life, you are

putting '*conscious intention*' into your environment and opening your space to tremendous amounts of energy to flow through your physical surroundings and into your life.

*There are many things you can do with Feng Shui that could make a difference to your life, and anything that helps the energy flow more positively in your life, will help your overall balance and sense of empowerment.*

There are plenty of books on the market that will give you a lot more information about Feng Shui and all the benefits it can give you, so if this interests you, then check them out!

**…..your road to taking care of yourself.....**
*Part of feeling empowered is to make sure you are at peak health and fitness, so you can carry out your life in ultimate confidence and substance.*
If you *really* want to optimise your physical and emotional health, it stands to reason that you need to adopt a healthy lifestyle, by putting your well-being at the top of your list of priorities.

In other words, *you need to take care of yourself.*

Put yourself first and in doing so, you make yourself available to others from a much better place.

Stress reduction is foremost, because alongside it comes addressing anxiety, panic attacks, sleep problems, headaches, stomach upsets and sexual problems.

Apart from removing all negative aspects from everyday living, stress can be helped through exercise, meditation and yoga. These activities all have a hand in helping to relieve tension and enhance your mood, making you feel much calmer and enabling you to confront any issues you encounter.

Successful continuous motivation comes from getting yourself motivated in the first place!

*Energy creates energy, and the sooner you get started on moving yourself, the sooner you will understand what this means....*

A great way of producing endorphins, which are your *natural high*, is getting involved in activities and exercise that will automatically make you feel better and stronger.
This will also induce a much better mood and make you feel more confident, awake and alert.

As you become stronger with exercise, so your heart and muscles get a good work out and they become stronger too, increasing your metabolism. This makes you continue to burn more calories even after exertion, thereby keeping your weight maintained, as well as helping you to feel fitter and more confident in yourself.
Exercise may well help you to reduce pain, stress and anxiety and will certainly help you get a better nights sleep.

*So, it's definitely a win-win situation.*

Any type of activity will work, even gardening, walking and playing helps.

*Also, food can have a surprising affect on your mood and health – both positively and negatively.*

As already discussed, limiting sugar, alcohol and caffeine is definitely a good strategy, as they obviously aren't good for you.

Alcohol depresses the nervous system and affects the chemicals in your brain, so this needs to be reduced or even eliminated, if you want to know which way is up!

Maintaining a healthy diet is a sound path to take if you want to live well.
Limiting processed foods, red meats, high *bad* fats and puddings and replacing them with fruit and vegetables, whole-grains, low fat dairy and lean poultry and fish in the right amounts, is a much better way forward to glowing health and vitality.

Ensure you spend time with positive friends and family who can build your self-esteem and make you feel good.

Having a good listener can help relieve pressure and negativity. Or work with a therapist if you need someone to give a sympathetic ear to your problems – someone who can help you see a more optimistic way ahead.

*In other words, look after yourself and your body will look after you – both inside and out!*

Every step of keeping your health, fitness and well-being in optimum condition will help you on your path to ultimate empowerment.

*A healthy body, mind and spirit is definitely the way to move you through life to the very best of your ability, allowing you to grow and develop towards your dream aspirations.*

**....know your body....heal yourself....**
*Knowing how your body works is the best way to approach. succeeding in your health, fitness and empowerment programme.*

If you have the knowledge to gain a *good* understanding of what happens to your body when you do certain things to it, such as eat and drink particular foods or do various exercises, or what you put into yourself, such as drugs, nicotine and alcohol, etc., then you will be in a *far* more *intelligent* position to manage your well-being **overall**.

This knowledge and understanding will help you develop the right kind of mindset to enable you to programme into your brain, the best strategy for your health.
This will then mean that you can make *much better choices* about your wellness and lifestyle, so you can *really* start living the happy and contented life that you want.
There are many theories and ways to help you maintain good health, and whatever you choose to try, do give it a <u>decent</u> amount of time to see the results materialise, before you decide whether it's actually working for you or not.

*Whatever positive steps you decide to take will only be of definite advantage to you in the long run and will have an enormously beneficial knock-on effect, leading to increased levels of empowerment to drive you onwards and upwards in the direction of your life's ultimate plan.*

**…..the importance of human growth hormone on your health and fitness….**
*Human growth hormone (HGH) that is manufactured in your pituitary gland, is a vital part of the endocrine system and controls a range of your bodily functions.*
It is said to be the *master* hormone and may even have a hand in controlling several of your other hormones.

The stimulation of your HGH contributes to many benefits including, reduced body fat, increased muscle mass, higher energy, rejuvenation of vital organs, restoration of youthful immune function, stronger bones, lower cholesterol, lower blood pressure, smoother, firmer skin, sharper vision, elevated moods, promoting rapid hair and nail growth, improving circulation and protection from the consequences of ageing.

*As you age, so the production of your HGH declines and your levels of HGH will be negatively affected by stress, emotions, diet and lack of exercise.*

A deficiency can be addressed naturally with a change in lifestyle, including stress management, decent sleep and a good nutrition and exercise plan, to help cause the pituitary gland to secrete more of the hormone.

If you feel you may have a deficiency and it is interfering with your health and progress, then please visit a health professional or look into more information on Human Growth Hormone.

*Anything that is slowing down your route to a successful and fulfilling life, will have an impact on your empowerment, so seek help if you need it.*

**….break hard habits and take back your life….**
*Habits come in all shapes and sizes and can obviously be good or bad.*
It's the bad ones that will be having a negative effect on your day to day living and as such, probably impacting on how successfully you conduct your life.

Your road to empowerment means that you need to rid yourself of habits that are getting you down and blocking your way to happiness and fulfilment.

It is estimated that, to form a habit, you halve to perform something 40 times and then it becomes one, so actually breaking that habit will obviously take time.

Eating habits are usually performed out of comfort, probably due to stress and anxiety-related issues, or to induce a feeling of warmth and pleasurable feelings.

Getting that '*hit*' is something that makes you feel better and any thought of breaking it could fill you with discontent and make you feel very uneasy. After all, you're giving up what you have really loved for many years and in doing so, it's taking away your 'comfort blanket'.
So, you cannot expect removing that comfort blanket to be easy and an overnight success.

*That would be delusional and optimistic and down-right near impossible anyway.*

So don't expect it!

On your journey to feel wonderful and vibrant on a day to day basis, you need to embrace the fact that it will be a slow and gradual step by step process.

*Expect fails and days when it all goes pear-shaped.*
That's fine.
Everyone has days when they feel down, disillusioned and apathetic.
But don't give up the ghost and let that control you. It's just a small relapse, that's all.
*Get straight back on the wagon and start peddling again!*
Don't use it as an excuse to slip back into your old ways. That will only make you feel worse and you will kick yourself for it later!

*As soon as you notice it coming, re-frame your mind and get back to your strategy.*

Don't just say you'll just start again tomorrow, because tomorrow never comes and you will just give into the temptation more.

**Start again _NOW_ - it's the best place to start!**

Don't make yourself have to rev up the momentum again or begin making excuses. You *really* don't want to undo all that good work you have already done towards your *wonderful journey to ultimate well-being*.

Remember, these things have built up in your internal system and brain over years, so your body won't be able to cope with a sudden elimination.....
You'll get withdrawal symptoms, cravings, headaches and emotional traumas.
You're essentially taking away a crutch that you have lived with for years, bound together physically and emotionally, and even mentally.
You've got used to that crutch at certain times of the day, like that coffee in the morning, or that puff of nicotine at various 'important' times of the day.

*You've become used to these things as a natural part of your daily life!*

Whilst you adapt to living without these things, expect to feel terrible, emotional, irritable or angry.

*If you **accept** it, then you can **cope** with it so much better.....*

Cut back *gradually* – where YOU are the one in control of IT, not *IT* in control of YOU!
Feel empowered as you, bit by bit, beat this thing that's had a hold on you for so many years – that's lived in your brain and gradually damaged you in so many ways.

Eventually, you will be rid of this monster you've allowed to live within you and you can feel fabulous about how you've taken back your mood, your emotions, your weight, your lungs, your health, your well-being and your pocket (these habits usually come with a hefty price-tag!).

*Get yourself into the right mindset.*

Tell yourself that you are a *healthy* person and you're living your life *exactly* how <u>you</u> want it!
You are full of vitality, energy and vibrancy.
This is YOUR life and you are taking it over!
**Bye bye negative habits**!

Here's some help on how you can eliminate some of those bothersome habits:

**Caffeine** – gradually reduce your caffeine intake by going *half & half* – that is, half caffeinated and half decaffeinated when making each cup of coffee.
After a week or so, gradually reduce the caffeinated and increase the decaffeinated coffee so that you are eventually only making decaffeinated cups.
Then start making the cups smaller, followed by reducing the amount of cups you drink per day (as even decaf contains about 10% caffeine).
This method will reduce any negative withdrawal symptoms you may get from removing the caffeine completely from your system in one go – like nasty headaches.
After a short time you will begin to feel so much better, less edgy and nervy, less moody, less tired and have a much lesser feeling of dependency on it.

*You will feel in control instead of it controlling you.*

Start to lessen the association with that cup of coffee as well, such as,
"*I can't do anything until I've had my coffee*", or
"*I hope there will be coffee at this meeting*", etc.

Try to disassociate it by distracting yourself from that dependency and replacing it with something else that's good instead.
Try another drink like herbal tea, water, juice, etc. Not cola's though, as they contain lots of caffeine too!
So, you can also use this strategy to get off that fizz too!
Then, once you get to this new point, you will be able to enjoy the

*occasional* cup of coffee when you fancy it, without it taking a hold of you and being an addiction!

After you've eliminated the caffeine, you will be amazed how that 1 cup makes you feel – spaced out, 'zooming', wide-awake followed by a slump, hyper followed by depression, shaky, confused, not being able to concentrate!

*And you will wonder how you managed for so many years to pump that dreaded stuff into your system continuously!*

Learn to use it to your advantage, not your downfall.!
One cup can be great if you need to have a sharp mind in a meeting, because it can give you that uplift when you need it, and can also lift a mood when you feel depressed.
**But!**
*Don't fall back and start using it more and more to get those effects, because it will just be totally counterproductive!*

**Good luck**!

**….and what about foods you are sensitive to…..**
*How can you live your life effectively if you are feeling sluggish, out of sorts, low in mood or angry, etc….?*
Being addicted to certain foods can be the very thing that you may well be intolerant or sensitive to! Sometimes, the more you want something, the more it is affecting you – your mood, your energy, and your ability to think and act.

*You can simply overload your system with the same things and your body can begin to rebel.*

If you love eating cheese, eggs or wheat products like bread and cakes, and you find you get depressed a lot, irritable, apathetic, tearful, headachey, sluggish, aching joints, lacking in concentration, catarrh, itching skin and a host of other 'ailments', then check that you don't have an intolerance to these, or other addictive foods or drinks.
It's not the same a having an allergy, which can cause far more severe reactions, but all the same, the symptoms could be affecting your whole life and well-being <u>without you even realising it</u>.

*But, you can have a similar reducing strategy as you did with caffeine, but with those sugary, fatty and salty foods too, or foods you may be intolerant to.....*

If the main reason for your habit breaking is to remove those addictive foods from your life so you can gain the upper-hand once and for all, you can also go on an '*elimination*' regime.
This is where you remove certain possible 'offenders' from your diet, so it allows you to pin-point which are the culprits and which aren't, and then you can stop eating or drinking them.

*You will be absolutely amazed how differently you feel when you do!*

There may be more than one thing that affects you, so it is a fine balance in getting it right, but with a little patience and steadfastness, you will get there.

If you are in any doubt and need help, then see your GP or nutritionist.

Once you find and eliminate the culprit/s, you will begin to notice the difference in how strong you feel, inwardly healthier, outwardly shining, fitter, livelier, more vibrant, back in control and ready to take on the world!

Additionally, once you get away from the junk food and replace it with delicious nutritious food instead, you will feel the difference it makes to your health and general well-being.

*Either way, when you're there, you will be in a fantastic position and ready to take on the world!*

**Go!**

**….kick out those drugs, smoking, alcohol and other habit-forming vices forever......**
You can also use the same kind of thinking and reduction strategy as applied to both caffeine, food and drink, if you want to permanently remove any other vices from your life too.
If you cannot do it on your own, then get some professional help.

If you are really serious about gaining control back and having renewed vigour, vibrancy and vitality in your life, then look on this as a '**challenge**' to a _better_ way, rather than something you are just going to hate doing and will probably fail at.

## Get your head into the right mindset!

_Tell yourself that you <u>want</u> to be healthy and feel alive again and_ **look towards the end result** _– a new, happier, livelier you who is living your life as you truly want!_

Picture how your new life will be.
Picture yourself doing it, being it.....

You can then get on with the things you _really should_ be doing, without being taken over by the negative feelings and the head-lock that those vices have had you in all these years!

_Take back your life_ – **start now**_!_

### …..do you need an energy boost.....
_If you feel low in energy and it's zapping your productivity and creativity, you need to pinpoint and understand where and how this is happening, and then begin to make inroads into recharging your batteries._

Take a look at the most common culprits within your diet and lifestyle and see if any of these things are actually affecting your energy stores.

Anxiety, stress and worry are seriously draining, as well as dehydration, too much alcohol and caffeine, strict diets, blood-sugar swings from eating sugary foods, lack of sleep and even boredom.

Keeping a diary showing your moods and bouts of fatigue can help identify any patterns happening.

To get a good understanding of how and what is affecting you, you will probably have to do this for about a month and then once you get help to correct it, you can once again get back on track with your life.

*There are ways out there to help you deal with the problems that are zapping your energy, so get some!*

It may even be as simple as taking a supplement, getting out in the fresh air more, drinking more water, changing your routine or eating a better diet that includes a sustained supply of good energy throughout the day!

**Remember - energy creates energy!**
Get exercising and your body will get the wake-up call it needs.

*All of these things will improve your energy stores and thereby give you the boost you need to empower yourself forward and truly live life as you should be doing!*

**…..feed your body well and it will look after you...**
*Believe that whatever you do to your body and whatever you put into it, you **become** it.*
If you feel bad, likelihood is, you are treating your body badly.
But you *can* change this, if you really want to......

Your skin replaces itself every 35 days and your liver about every month.
Your body regenerates new cells from the food you eat, so what you consume literally becomes you!
You have choices in what you are made of, so make them good ones, if you want to get the best out of your body.
You are what you eat.

*Empower yourself with good food!*

**….antioxidants – they are important for keeping you young....**
*If part of your empowerment is to feel as young as possible for as long as possible, then you need to know about antioxidants.*
When your body cells use oxygen, they naturally produce 'by-products', some of which are '*free radicals*'.
Antioxidants found in food, act as scavengers to prevent, slow down or repair the oxidative damage caused by those free radicals.

Heart disease, diabetes, cancer and macular degeneration are contributed to by this damage, so it's important to try and avoid or

repair this as much as possible. Antioxidants may also help your immune defence system and as such, help to lower the risk of infection and cancer.
Antioxidants also minimize the exposure of oxidative stress caused by things like smoking and sunburn and can help boost your skin from within.

*Get your antioxidants from good nutritious and fresh foods instead of supplements.*

The top antioxidants are vitamins A,C,E and Selenium found in a variety of foods, such as some fruit and vegetables, nuts, seeds and oils.
Check out what foods you really like that contain these wonder nutrients and get eating!
*You can keep yourself young and healthy by looking after your antioxidant supply!*
And that means adding to your overall feeling of empowerment.

*You owe it to yourself.*

### ....restock your stores to re-energise your life......
*Are you a bit complacent about the importance of vitamins and minerals in your diet?*
Maybe it's because you don't fully understand their function in your body, or realise how **crucial** they are to your actual well-being?
Or maybe you don't realise they are **essential** *for achieving your optimum state of health*, so you can make the most out of your life.....?

*Making the most out of your life is a major part of empowerment.*

Vitamins contain substances that are **required** just for normal everyday growth and the maintenance of your health.

### Without them you would become seriously ill.

They are a *vital* part of what your body is made up of and they help to protect you from diseases like cancer and heart disease.
If you think you may be deficient in any way, then see a health professional.

This is also particularly pertinent if you rely mainly on processed or fast foods, regularly skip meals, have a food intolerance or allergy, are vegan, or if you have been ill.

Begin to retrain your eating habits and follow a more wholesome diet that will replenish your stock of vitamins and minerals on a constant basis.

*Once you start to replete your stores, you will definitely feel the difference in yourself, which will obviously have a positive knock-on effect to your day-to-day living and overall progression.*

**....knowing the efficiency of your vitamin & mineral stock.....**
*If you are lacking in a bit of knowledge about the importance of specific vitamins and minerals and how they help your body maintain full health and vitality, then here are a few basic but useful details and some examples of their job and purpose, that you may find informative.*

Vitamins are defined as 'water-soluble' and 'fat-soluble'.
Water-soluble vitamins are the B & C group and fat-soluble are A, D, E, F and K.
The fat-soluble vitamins require some fatty foods to be eaten to ensure they are assimilated properly into your system, so they can do their job properly.

Water-soluble vitamins are not stored in the body, so must be replaced daily because you extract what you don't use in urine and perspiration, etc.
Some vitamins are destroyed by absorbing oxygen from the air, some from heat and water in cooking and preparation and some by light.

There are many books and information about vitamins and minerals which tell you exactly what they are good for and what foods you can find them in.

As with any kind of medication or supplement, if you have any doubts or questions about your intake or deficiency, please consult a professional for proper advice.

*Make sure you have your recommended intake of vital nutrients, so you get the most out of your body and can therefore maintain a good healthy life-style that will help you conduct your affairs with strength and vigour.*

### ....a healthy gut means a healthy outlook....
*If you want to help ward off a host of ailments, including memory loss and frailty as you get older, then you need to get some 'friendly' bacteria into your gut.*
Those good bugs in your intestines help you keep fit through the release of energy from your food. This keeps your bowels very healthy, your brain working well and even possibly strengthen your muscles.

You can make that good bacteria thrive through eating a variety of fresh foods.

There are also several friendly bacteria supplements available on the market you can try, like 'pro and pre-biotics', if you feel that your diet is lacking in any way.
As with most things, the thinking on how and if these things work changes all the time, so do get the latest up-to-date information before making any hasty decisions.

*Anything you can do to make your feel strong and in control of your life, will help you on your path to a successful, empowered and positive outlook.*

### ....get your daily dose of youth....
*No doubt you want to live long and healthy so you can fulfil as much as you can, be as active as possible and really enjoy yourself?*
Diet can help enormously in fighting ageing on both your appearance and the actual effects time has upon your bones, muscles, skin and brain.

It's so easy to make *wise* adjustments to your diet by including some of nature's 'wonder' foods.
In order to help you age with strength, grace and a feeling of empowerment, here are just a few good suggestions about what you can eat every day to achieve youthfulness.

Red watermelon can provide protection against sunburn - a chief cause of skin ageing and also helps to repair skin cells.
Pro and pre-biotic yoghurt strengthens your body's immunity against illness and is great for healthy digestion and when eaten regularly, has good anti-ageing properties.
Omega-3 fatty acids found in oily fish can aid some of the symptoms of rheumatoid arthritis, helps preserve eye health and maintains levels of good fat within your skin.
Vitamins C and E together possess anti-ageing qualities, including helping wrinkles.
Beta-carotene, folic acid, zinc, potassium all boost your body's natural defences against the elements and infection.
Avocado provides potassium, which reduces the risk of blood pressure and fluid retention, vitamin E, which helps maintain skin health and oleic acid - a healthy fat that boosts your body's good cholesterol levels.
The high levels of vitamin E in seeds provides protection for your cells, as it helps to neutralise free radical toxins which cause damage to your skin.
Garlic, with it's strong anti-oxidants has fantastic and varied rejuvenating health properties and can combat the effects of ageing, rejuvenate your skin, increase energy levels and also counter the formation of cataracts. It also fends off chronic illnesses related to age, such as heart disease.
Cruciferous vegetables like broccoli, can ward off the effects of time on your body and can stimulate a wide range of antioxidant defence pathways, maybe even interfering with the age-related decline in immune function.
High in vitamin A & C, Barbados Cherry or 'Acerola' juice, will keep you looking young because of it's many skin boosting nutrients, as well as helping you to sleep more soundly.

*Obviously keeping yourself youthful will have an impact on how you feel about yourself, giving you confidence to push yourself forward and stand up and be counted.*

Why not give it a try and see if it adds to your sense of empowerment.....?

### …..you are what you eat – and it comes out in your skin…

*Feeling good, as well as looking good, is all part of being self-confident and assured, and that has an important impact on your overall empowerment.*

You must have realised by now that when the food you eat is bad, you feel bad.

But, you can also *look* bad because what you put inside your body has a huge effect on the look and feel of your skin.

It's true when they say '*you are what you eat*', because food can really help to make you look and feel beautiful both inside and out. If you really do want that additional positive element to feeling empowered, then this means watching what your put into your body.

So, as well as spending so much time and money on lotions and potions, think about the importance of choosing the *right types* of food that nourishes you from *within*.

It can be far more effective in keeping you looking youthful and lovely than any facial.

You can get lots of further information, but just as an example, to have or maintain a good skin, choose foods rich in antioxidants like vitamins A, C & E, essential fatty acids, selenium, omega-3 fats, DMAE (2 dimethylaminoethanol) and lutein, as well as barley grass and blackcurrants.

Reduce high GI carbs and increase low GI carbs.

A balanced diet packed with vitamin-rich fruit and vegetables will help keep you looking fit, healthy and gorgeous.

Your skin, hair, nails and eyes, not to mention your weight, can all positively benefit from optimum nutrition.

*And looking and feeling your best will naturally enhance your feeling of empowerment.*

### …..and there are foods that really don't help your health or your look….

*There are many things that can stop you from feeling good about yourself and as such, block how empowered you feel about your life.*

Some of those things could be the food you eat.

If you want to feel and look good, there are foods that you should think about avoiding, because in doing so, you could feel more in control of your moods, actions and weight, as well as your skin, hair, nails and eyes, etc.

The biggest culprits are excess salt, alcohol, trans-fats and other offending ingredients – because they are just an enemy of your overall look.
Alcohol is toxic and terrible for your skin, as well as being full of empty calories that just lead to certain weight gain.
Too much sugar will also make you gain weight, but it can cause wrinkles too, because it alters your collagen and elastin.
Snacks like crisps, chips, biscuits, etc., are all high in *'trans fats'*, an extremely bad type of fat that will not only make you gain weight, but is also known as a leading cause of heart disease and has been linked to other life-threatening conditions.
Too much salt is obviously a big *no-no* and avoid nasty additives, such as tartrazine and carmoisine.
Abstain from processed carbohydrates that contain sugar and stick to *complex* carbohydrates instead, such as wholegrains and wheats, fresh fruit and vegetables.

These should be an essential part of your everyday diet anyway.

Look into the effects of soya, as it may now be in question - it can be found in a lot of processed foods.
Beware of soft and fizzy drinks - the acidity gets to your teeth and soft drinks can cause serious cell damage.
Stay away from foods and drink containing Sodium Benzoate, as it can switch off vital parts of your DNA which can lead to accelerated ageing.

*If you want to have optimal health and that wonderful feeling of looking good, walking tall and strong and being able to feel the power in that strength, then thinking seriously about what you are putting into your body just makes good common sense......*

**…..stop, think….trans fat…I don't need you in my arteries….**
*You may not already know about 'trans fats' – but if you are concerned about looking after your health, then you really should find out more.*

There are a lot of warnings about eating *saturated fats*, but trans fats come with an even *bigger* health risk.
Like saturated fats, trans fats **raise** *bad* cholesterol (LDL) and increase the risk of heart disease. But *unlike* saturated fats, trans fats actually **lower** *good* cholesterol (HDL) too and do even more damage.

*So it is the worst kind of fat you can eat!*

Small amounts of trans fats occur naturally in beef, lamb and full-fat dairy products, but most of it comes from processing liquid vegetable oil by adding hydrogen, so it becomes a solid fat called '*hydrogenated*' oil or fat.
Meant to enhance a lot of processed foods, they actually travel through your digestive system into your arteries and turn into *sludge*.
*You should therefore severely limit your consumption.*
Even if the food label states that it's *partially* hydrogenated, it will *still* be a trans fat.

<u>So take care!</u>

Those tempting foods are not all about the high amount of calories they contain, they could be detrimental to your heart and overall health too.

*And without your good health, you have no true empowerment......!*

**…..how superfoods can turn you into a super-person....**
*Generally, the better your health, the more able you are to thrive in a competitive environment and be a success in yourself.*
That's because you will be more alert and capable of carrying out daily challenges and go after what you want in life.

*So, the better your nutrition, the better your life!*

Superfoods are full of health promoting nutrients packed with lots of vitamins and minerals and including them in your diet can help in your mission to achieve your *ideal* state.

They help to boost your health and vitality, promote healing and protect you from illnesses like heart disease and cancer. They can nourish the nervous system and your brain and enhance your skin, bones, muscles, veins and arteries.

In your quest to gain optimum health, you need to consume a vast range of nutrients and the best way to cover this is to eat foods of varying colours.
In doing so, you will ensure the efficient working of your *appestat* and therefore maintain a good weight and stay in good shape.

Here are some of the more common super-foods that you have easy access to every day and should be enjoying for their fantastic health-giving qualities.
They encourage ultimate health and well-being, so make sure you get a good range in your diet.

*Almonds, apples, apricots, artichoke globes and Jerusalem artichokes, asparagus, avocados, bananas, barley, baked beans, broad and green beans, bee pollen, beef and lamb, beetroot, blackberries, blackcurrants, blueberries, broccoli, brown rice, cabbage, carrots, celery, free-range chicken, chicory, chlorella and spirulina, dandelion, dates, free-range eggs, game, garlic, grapefruit, grapes, kiwifruit, leeks, lemons, lentils, melon, millet, oats, oily fish, olive oil, onions, oranges, peas, sweet peppers, potatoes, pumpkin seeds, rabbit, radishes, raspberries, spinach, sprouted seeds, strawberries, sweet potatoes, tomatoes, turkey, turnips, walnuts, watercress, whole-wheat, wheatgerm and yoghurt.*

Imagine how wonderful you would feel every day if you were to pack your body full of all these fabulous nourishing and wholesome nutrients!

As well as superfoods being rich in health-giving properties, herbs and spices can also have a beneficial effect on your digestion, alongside having many other excellent uses.

You can find out more about all the wonderful benefits of each individual food and how to prepare them, in the many other books available on the market.

*Whatever you eat, savour and enjoy your food – it makes you who you are and gives you the best possible strength for your road to an excellent empowering life-style.*

## ….water....the elixir of life....your friend and saviour.....

*If you want to be fit and healthy.....then seriously consider your water intake.*

Your body is made up mostly of water and is therefore in need of constant replenishment in order to remain hydrated.

*Of all the nutrients there are, water is the most important.*

It helps to produce energy, aids your nervous system, is an effective shock absorber, as well as acting as a lubricant for your joints and eyes, prevents constipation, as well as the severity of colds and flu. Every system in your body depends on water to carry out it's normal daily functions.

It can even help your concentration, overall daily performance and keeps you alert, vibrant and healthy.

Every day you lose water through sweating, exhaling, exercising, urinating and bowel movements, so you need to replace this in order for your body to operate properly and efficiently.

Dehydration can affect your athletic performance, cause tiredness and dull thinking and even affect your chance of kidneys stones. Signs of dehydration include excessive thirst, fatigue, headache, dry mouth, little or no urination, muscle weakness, dizziness and light-headedness.

*Water is therefore absolutely **crucial** to good health.*

As well as liquid drink, food also contains up to1 pint of water and usually accounts for 20% of your daily fluid intake.

There is no need to do any *extra detoxing* by drinking lots of water, because as long as they are functioning normally, both the kidneys and liver do a *fantastic* job of doing that naturally – *it's their job!*

If your urine is colourless or slightly yellow and you feel well, you are probably consuming the correct amount of water for your needs. If your urine is dark and smells strong, you probably need to drink a bit more.

So, use water in order to function efficiently, enhance your brain power and overall health and physicality, if you really want to add to that feeling of total empowerment.

*It is the **elixir of life**, it's costs you nothing and is available on tap, so take advantage of all it's <u>free</u> benefits!*

### ….your weight versus your life….
*Part of your path to feeling totally empowered may be to enhance how you feel about your body image.*
And that could be having a new perspective on *who* you are, or losing or gaining weight to make you feel better about yourself *personally.*

Additionally, being the correct weight for your size and life-style is an important aspect of carrying out a healthy lifestyle and being in control of what you want to achieve.
This could be events such as going on adventures that require a good level of fitness, or perhaps having an active job that requires you to be flexible and in top form, or even just being healthy enough to enable you to reach all your aspirations with relative ease.

Knowing and understanding how your body works so you can get the most out of it, is a very good starting place.
Additionally, having a healthy view on yourself without feeling any pressure from anyone, including you, is also much better for you, both emotionally and mentally.

*If you know that you are where and what you want to be, then that can only be an entirely positive component to your feeling of overall empowerment.*

### …..having a healthy body image….you are you….
*With the pressures of the media splashing beautiful images of celebrities across the world, it's hard to believe in yourself if you are consumed by hang-ups.*
But it *is* possible to develop more of a good image of yourself, *if you*

*are prepared to try.*

If you want to feel strong and empowered, then you can tune into the more positive aspects of yourself and move away from the more unrealistic negative thoughts and feelings you have.

You don't have to constantly bring yourself down by believing that you have to be perfect, just because you've just seen, what looks like, a wonderfully sculpted body on the front of a magazine.

But you *can* make the effort to be the best you can be – for **you**, so you *feel* better and more confident about actually being *who you are*.

You *can* break out of that internal dialogue that makes you think there is some kind of expectation required from you to be the '*ideal*' person.
This kind of expectation will only affect your self esteem and body confidence.

*But, you can reverse this and develop a far more positive way of thinking.*

One exercise you can try that may help you, is to get a group of friends together in a relaxed environment with some nice refreshments, and have an open discussion about what everyone's individual views are on body image.
This has to be carried out in a trusting, respectful and helpful way.

You will probably be amazed at how different everyone's perception is!

This method can build strong and healthy representations that will make you feel much better about yourselves, and also make you realise just how unique and individual you *all* really are.

Write down who you think represents what you class as a 'good' body image and what this means to you and why.....?
Are you all constantly worrying about your body, continuously dieting and always comparing yourselves to others?
Or do you all have a good balance of exercise and nutrition?

Rate yourselves out of 10 for a good body image and discuss how you feel about that.
Swap tips and skills on how to look after body and health, and what strategies you use to help you feel good.

*Everyone has things about themselves that they are proud of, so write down 10 qualities that you love about yourself.*

This could be anything from being kind, calm, witty, happy, your eyes, your sense of style, etc. Anything you possess will be essential to understanding who you are and building your self-esteem, as well as helping to increase your body confidence.
Once you have done this, you can list the top *3 things* you could realistically do something about, and then **stick** to it.
Have a clear idea and identify how you will do those things and by when.
Let people know that you are going to *do* them so you are totally committed – then **go for it**!

*Focus your mind on this and what you want in life.*
Doing so will give you more courage to make things happen, which in turn will make you feel totally empowered and in control of yourself.

*Then your image of yourself will be a positive one that you can build on and become that whole, unique individual you deserve to be!*

### ....weight control – it's all about understanding how the 'appestat' works...
*Knowing how your appetite operates, is an intelligent way of understanding what you are actively doing with your body, particularly when it comes to you weight and health.*
If you want to successfully lose or maintain your weight, this is the *clever* way of 'dieting' – if you want to call it that.

Eating is controlled by your brain and the '*hypothalamus*' has an important function relating to your weight, regimenting your appetite and adjusting the metabolic rate at which you burn calories and produce energy.

Your **'appestat'** regulates cells with the aim of ensuring you eat and nourish your body **only** when you need to and makes you **stop** when this job is complete.

But when you go on a crash diet with very little calories, your appestat will start running and because of the drop in food intake, your metabolism will automatically begin to slow down, because you need to *conserve* energy.
Fatigue will usually follow - something you will feel when you haven't had enough food to sustain you.

### *Your energy levels drop.*

In effect, the less food you eat, the less weight you lose, because your metabolism will slow down if you drop your intake too dramatically.
What happens then, is when you start eating normally again, your metabolism is still running at the low and slow emergency rate and as a result, you will put more weight on than before! Oops!

Basically, any diet that is working **against** the natural function of your appestat, will just not work.

If the mechanism of your appestat isn't working correctly because of a malfunction, your weight can seriously fluctuate.

Trying to avoid becoming overweight or obese is not about removing total fat or carbs from your diet.

*The secret (which isn't really a secret at all....) is to give yourself all the proper nutrition so that your body can function at it's **utmost**.*

Without that and a proper functioning appestat, trying to fight obesity is like wading through treacle.
If you listen to nature, i.e. your health feed yourself properly and nutritiously, you can ultimately prevent obesity happening to you.

*It's just a matter of understanding what's going on inside your body......then you can live a wonderfully healthy life.*

**....and how does serotonin help.....**
*Serotonin is a 'neurotransmitter' - a chemical that communicates information throughout your brain and body.*
It is one of your body's natural mood-enhancing compounds and when stimulated, creates an extraordinary sense of well-being. It is responsible for making you feel content and satisfied after you've eaten.

A lack of serotonin can often be accountable for food cravings and can also be the cause of you feeling down and having mood swings and depression.

*The most natural and powerful way of stimulating the production of serotonin can be through food and exercise.*

To keep your immune system healthy and operating at full capacity, you need a healthy gastrointestinal tract, as a lot of your serotonin lies in the gut.
Blood sugar fluctuations cause insulin releases, and these spikes can lead to a surge of adrenaline, which then interferes with your serotonin production.

The best way to avoid this and still get your 'hit' and boost serotonin, is to choose carbs that are *slow-burning,* such as wholegrains and oatmeal. They also contain '*tryptophan*' that converts to serotonin.

Reduce stress, sleep well, get some sunlight and fresh air, laugh and have some fun, enjoy your relationships, love a lot, drink only very moderate amounts of caffeine and alcohol, and exercise to elevate serotonin, endorphins and dopamine – all good mood-enhancing chemicals.

*Get that serotonin flowing around your body – the better you feel, the more empowered your life will be!*

**....getting your healthy dose of energy keeps you on your mettle....**
*If you want to keep your energy at optimum levels so you can conduct your life from a much more lively position, and in turn, get things achieved, then knowing what can give you that vitality is extremely helpful.*

It will also give you more of an understanding about what is zapping your energy as well.

How are you supposed to be enthusiastic about anything, if you are constantly feeling tired and listless?

Because serotonin increases when you eat carbohydrates, very high levels can leave you feeling tired. Cancel this out by adding a small amount of protein, like eggs, cheese or fish to your starchy meal.
It's typical to crave sugary snacks when you're tired, because it gives you that quick energy boost, but then your insulin goes into overdrive and you feel even more lethargic and hungry.

*Stop this by eating fruit instead, because it releases energy slowly.*

Caffeine drinks that give you an instant high can be addictive because you become dependent on that energy kick. However, it *is* a toxin to the body, causing it to use it's own energy to eliminate it, thus completely defeating the object.

*So, only use it in moderation as a pick-me-up.*

To avoid being sluggish and tired, keep hydrated with plenty of water.
Being lethargic could mean you have a vitamin deficiency, so eat lots of fruit, vegetables, nuts and wholegrains or take a *good* supplement - with advice. Vitamins B & C and Co-enzyme Q10 claim to combat fatigue.

*Deep breathing will help you wake up your lethargic body and sharpen your mind, as it is great for getting the vital oxygen into your body that you need for good energy.*

So there are definitely plenty of healthy ways of giving you a boost of energy.

*If you are serious about increasing your empowerment, so you can get on more effectively and bring your plans to life, then following some of this energy advice may be a way forward you need.*

**....one potato, two potato, three potato, four....whoops..carb overload....**

*So, what happens to your body when you eat too many carbs?* Well, it can only store a limited amount of carbohydrates before "carb saturation" causes an imbalance.

Unfortunately, if you love a dinner of rice, pasta, bread, and other carbs, once the *glycogen* levels are at capacity in both your liver and muscles, whatever you don't 'use' gets stored and converted into fat.

*So, although carbs are fat free, don't think that any excess will not make you fat.*

All your efforts to eat low-fat or fat-free products to lose weight will be completely sabotaged!

Add to this dilemma, any food that is high in carbohydrates will generate a rapid rise in blood glucose, which causes the pancreas to secrete insulin into the bloodstream, that then lowers the levels of blood glucose.

Insulin is essentially a storage hormone and one of it's functions is to use the excess carbohydrates and save them as fat in case of future famine.
So the insulin that's stimulated by excess carbohydrates aggressively promotes the accumulation of body fat.

*Therefore, the message your body gets when you eat excess carbohydrates is to store fat!*

Additionally, the increased insulin levels tell the body not to release any stored fat, making it impossible for you to use your own stored body fat for energy.
So, all the excess carbohydrates you eat will not only make you fat, but will also make sure you stay that way!

Take care with your 'carb-loading' if you want to maintain a good level of health and vitality.

*Every little action you take towards it will positively benefit you on your path to feeling terrific and totally empowered.*

### ....use your sugar intake wisely....
It's the fats, proteins and carbohydrates that you eat that creates sugar in your body.
Any natural or refined sugar you add to food will get into your bloodstream first, followed by the sugar in complex carbs such as wholegrains and vegetables, then by the sugars created from fats, and finally the proteins.

An instant surge of sugar will circulate in your bloodstream from large amounts of refined carbohydrates, like sweets, cakes and biscuits. When this happens, insulin is pumped out via your pancreas to destroy it, causing your sugar levels to drop dramatically.
Because this happens so quickly, a message is sent to your brain to demand more sugar to lift your levels back up, and hence you reach for your next sweet treat.

*This, in effect, causes you to be trapped in a vicious cycle of nutritional imbalance and as a consequence, you pile on* the pounds!

So, enjoy a sweet treat every now and then ***but*** don't let it become a staple part of your diet!
Take control and don't allow that sweet craving to take over your entire body and govern you.

Be empowered over your appetite!
*Be empowered over your life!*

### .....get balanced.....get on it.....
*If those slumps in the day are getting in the way of achieving your goals, then there are ways to keep this in check.*
Eating a good breakfast can keep your sugar levels balanced and stop the sweet cravings and those unpleasant sugar highs and lows.
Make sure your concentration and performance are at their optimum by keeping your energy levels up, through eating regular nutritious meals throughout the day.

*Avoid junk – all kinds!*

A varied, well-balanced diet will ensure there are no vitamin and mineral deficiencies leading to potential health problems.
Eat at least five portions of fruit and vegetables a day, have plenty of fibre, keep salt, saturated and trans-fats to an absolute minimum, add one or two portions of oily fish each week and some good quality lean protein, with complex carbohydrates and a daily probiotic.
Keep your fluids up, especially your water intake.

Stick to these principles and you won't go far wrong.

*If you do this, you should be nicely balanced and ready to take on the world!.*

### …..**protein....built to last**.....
*Your body is made up of proteins which are crucial to your daily functioning.*
They help create chains of enzymes and antibodies that fight illness.

Good protein intake benefits you by giving you lean muscle mass, improving your strength and balance, helping against fluid retention, assisting in healing injuries and also adding to your zest for life!

You need around 0.8grammes for every kilogramme that you weigh, so therefore, if you weigh 70kg, you will need around 56g per day.
If you do regular intense exercise you need more, to compensate for the increased muscle breakdown that incurs during and after the activity.

As you can't store protein in your body, if you have more than you need in one day, it doesn't roll over to the next.
Also, as you age, your muscle mass starts to decline and the lower your levels of lean muscle, the less your body's ability to burn calories, which can lead to higher fat levels.

*So, make sure you don't leave this very important element out of your diet if you want to feel fit, healthy and able to function at optimum levels.*

## …..the news about your weight issues….

*Having confidence in how you look and feel is all part of that great sense of empowerment.*

So, if you have any issues with your size that are bothering you, then knowing what may be causing that extra weight, could be extremely helpful in your quest for achieving your ideal figure and long-term goals.

*It may be because your hormones are playing havoc.*

The hormonal chemical changes that happen in your body can knock you out of balance and make it harder for you to lose weight. High stress levels cause your body to release *cortisol*, which helps sugar to be released into the bloodstream and this puts you on edge, which makes you reach for food.
Also, the fatty, sugary comfort eating you do when you are stressed will produce excess insulin and as a result, your body becomes resistant to losing weight.

To try and reverse this, you need to reduce your stress levels, sleep well, eat healthy nutritious food and get a good amount of exercise. This will put you on the road to getting yourself back on track and feeling in control once again.

Additionally, if you always remember the saying '*you are what you eat*' and get into your mindset that if you eat bad, you feel bad (even if it's not right at that particular time you are eating), you would then be constantly alert to what you are putting into your body.

A lot of body fat comes from sugar, or glucose - and all starch is simply glucose molecules. It's rare that you will increase your weight through disorders, it's more likely to be through the imbalance of calorie intake versus energy output.

*If you eat just one extra biscuit a day than you need for energy, you can gain up to a stone in just 6 months!*

If snacking is a problem, then make sure they are nutritious ones. Don't allow yourself to get so *ravenously* hungry that you end up reaching for *bad* foods.

## This is a killer!

Use snacks to your advantage, as they may actually help you to *lose* weight, rather than gain it! This is because snacking helps you stop binging and craving those bad foods and keeps your sugar levels balanced and your energy up.

Become active to burn more calories and speed up your metabolism.
*Don't eat mindlessly – that is - without thinking about what you are doing, otherwise you won't realise when you are full.*
And eat *slowly* and really *enjoy* your food.

Keep the tit-bits at bay – you could be eating *several hundred calories* and *adding a pound or two a week* if you're not careful!

High calorie coffees (the milky types) and alcohol will also add insult to injury with your weight, so avoid them wherever possible.

Get your quota of sleep too, as losing those valuable zeds can change your ability to produce those hormones that regulate appetite.
*Leptin* tells your brain when you are full, and *ghrelin* makes you feel hungry.
More ghrelin plus less leptin = weight gain.

*Keep hydrated, as thirst can often be confused with hunger.*

Water is an excellent appetite suppressant, as well as helping to speed up your metabolism and boost energy levels – especially ice-cold.

Artificial sweeteners found in diet fizzy drinks can encourage sugar cravings and increase appetite – *actually having the opposite effect of being '**diet**'!*

Your weight may be a medical problem, as some conditions like thyroid problems, polycystic ovary syndrome and insulin resistance can all cause weight gain.

Plus certain medications such as some drugs used for high blood

pressure, steroids for inflammatory conditions and antidepressants can all affect your weight too.
So talk to your doctor about it.

*Keep a log of your food and drink intake.*

You may be very surprised how much you consume, especially when you add in all the little nibbles you have throughout the day! Write down on paper exactly what you are eating so you can *realistically* see what's actually going into your mouth.

This will highlight whether there's too much junk and not enough good nutrition in your diet – the type of *essential* food that keeps your body working *efficiently*.

Don't lie to yourself – remember to include <u>*everything*</u> – even the little mouthfuls here and there.....

*You're only fooling <u>yourself</u>, nobody else!*

Also, check the amount of calories in the food and drink that you are consuming, as you may be deluding yourself about the *actuality* of the number they *really* contain.
Once you get the whole picture down on paper and you are no longer deceiving yourself, make all the fundamental changes necessary to put you on a healthy track.

*Start saying 'I **don't**' and not, 'I **can't**'!*

In doing this, you are not acting as though you are depriving yourself, but rather you are more in *control* of your options, which in turn gives you a sense of empowerment and determination. Saying, *'I can't'* just signals **loss** or **lack**.
For instance, "*I can't have that....*", replace with "*I don't have that.....*"!

See the difference?

If you are a 'yo-yo' dieter, when you lose weight your metabolism slows down and you will experience hormonal changes that will increase your appetite again once you've lost the weight.

It will help your self control *and* waistline if you seriously consider how you are going to feel *after* that high-calorific snack **before** you actually eat it, rather than just what it will taste like at that particular moment.....!
Once the 5 minutes of savouring that chocolate bar has passed, the time spent afterwards when those debilitating feelings of the highs and lows, guilt, disappointment and any negative symptoms you might get from that food kicks in, *will certainly not outweigh that quick fix!*

A good tip is to eat your protein first, as this speeds up the signal to your brain that you are full, which will stop you over-eating.
*Wait for* **15 minutes** *before you go for a 2$^{nd}$ helping or pudding after you meal.*
The likelihood is that once your food has had a chance to be digested and go down, you won't *actually* feel hungry any more.
Repeat to yourself - "**Let it go down, let it go down**", like a little mantra!"
It *really* works!

Gradually reduce the time you finish eating at night until you stop eating anything after 8pm.

Before long, this strategy will just come naturally and you will no longer yearn or crave for food any more, because you can convert that thought into *logical and sensible thinking* instead.

Remember – ***Eat until you're satisfied, not until you're full***!

Get exercising!
Do something you really enjoy and can stick to.
Mix it up with different types of workouts to make it more interesting for you, so you make keeping fit a stimulating part of your life.

As you grow older, from your 30's, you begin to lose muscle mass, so you will need to do some 'resistance' training, such as weights to keep your muscles toned and strong.

*You need good muscle tone to help you burn fat!*

Whilst you are doing this, you will begin to see all the wonderful effects it will have on your health, weight and how you are feeling. Sluggishness will be eliminated and replaced by more enthusiasm for vibrant exercise and total well-being and vitality.
You will also get a lot more energy and start to flourish into who you *really* want to be – just by looking after yourself!

*And that is a brilliant feeling of total empowerment!*

**….keep telling yourself you can and you will.....**
*If weight-loss or fitness is one of your empowerment goals, then affirmations are known as being a fundamental tool in accomplishing great lasting results and achieving far more dramatic success rates.*
When you devise your affirmations, don't make the mistake of telling yourself that you want to '*lose* weight', as this trains your mind and subconscious into thinking that you are 'losing' something.
Tell your mind that you want to be an ideal or healthy weight, or fit and healthy.
You can see the difference......

What you need to ingrain into your mindset is that what are doing is making a '*programme of positive lifestyle changes'*.

You need to accept and understand that you will need to adapt and alter your routines to incorporate a more healthy attitude about your diet and exercise.

**So you need to get into the *right positive mindset* for health and fitness.**

If you have the right head-space for it, then it will work far better for you than just blindly going on some random fad diet that may or may not work.
This is because you haven't trained your brain to accept that you are now a *healthy living individual* and not just an overweight person that is constantly on a diet depriving yourself all the time.

*You need to set your mind to you being an <u>achiever</u> and someone that embraces a healthy lifestyle, who enjoys exercise and that wants to live life to the **full**.*

So, decide on the changes you need to make and begin to *tell your subconscious* **exactly** what actions you need to take to achieve them, and then put some positive affirmations into place. Remember, you are talking to *yourself*, so make sure your affirmations are in the *present* tense, that is, what you are right **NOW**.
*So* make them *affirmative* without using any negative wording like, 'stop', 'won't', 'quit', 'lose', 'no', 'not', etc.

So, some examples could be:

*"I AM a healthy person because I eat good wholesome food and AM achieving my target".*

*"Through the zumba classes I AM attending, I AM speeding up my metabolism and achieving my ideal weight".*
*"I AM totally energised and full of confidence because I AM fully committed to my active life-style".*

In doing this, you are reconditioning your subconscious mind with *positive statements*.

But in order to get to your goal, you must make the conscious commitment to making your healthy eating and exercise a *normal* part of your routine.

*Do everything you can in your day-to-day life to make living this new life just part of who you are and not something that makes you constantly complain, as this will only cause you to fail.*

Say your affirmations as many times as you need to every day. During classes and at the gym or however you exercise, you can push yourself using your positive affirmations to keep you motivated to achieving your fitness goals.

Follow this *properly* and with **commitment** you will get there, step by step, day by day.

*Don't rush it – have faith that it will come.*

If you fall off the wagon, don't despair, just get back on it and carry on.
Everyone's done it.....
Don't keep saying "I'll do it on Monday or tomorrow", because tomorrow never comes....!
**You can do it !**
Have faith in yourself!
It's all about the right mindset...

*Feel empowered to get that goal!*

**.....so, which type of exercise is best for me.....**
*You can exercise for all sorts of different reasons.*
It could be to increase aerobic fitness, to increase strength and muscle tone, to increase flexibility and mobility, to lose weight, to help relaxation, to maintain good health and to stay fit and young for as long as possible.

*And also to make you feel happy and empowered!*
Those endorphins do a brilliant job of that when they're released through physical activity.

Each type of exercise benefits your health in different ways and the best way to ensure all-round fitness and health is to do a mixture of each type.

**Isotonic or aerobic** exercise moves your joints and muscles in your arms or legs.
*This type of exercise requires energy.*
For improved fitness levels and overall health you need to do regular aerobic exercise that raises your heart rate and makes you slightly breathless.
When you exercise aerobically your body uses 'glycogen' and fat as fuel.
As you breathe more heavily with exertion, carbon dioxide is expelled from your body.
Aerobic exercise burns fat, improves mood, strengthens your heart and lungs, reduces the risk of diabetes and gives you a better quality of life.
Probably even extending it!

Examples of aerobic activities include running, walking, swimming, cycling, dancing, skipping, aerobic classes and team sports, such as football, hockey, etc.

**Isometric** exercise is also called *strength* or *resistance* exercise and involves mostly muscle work to build up strength, helping to improve your posture and balance and giving your body a more toned look.
Additionally, muscle burns more calories than inactive tissue, even when you're resting, thereby helping you to stay at a healthy weight.

This kind of exercise includes weight-lifting, athletic throwing events, some gym equipment, including free-weights and weight machines, rock-climbing, boxing, wrestling, martial arts and exercise using your own body-weight, including using rubber fitness bands

**Flexibility** exercises include stretching to maintain flexibility and suppleness, without which your muscles would be at risk of becoming shorter and less elastic.
You should aim to do some flexibility exercises daily.

Yoga, Pilates and Tai Chi gently ease, stretch and also concentrates on your breathing.
These types of activities are great for increasing flexibility and strength, relaxing you and improving your circulation as well as giving you good balance and posture.

Try mixing up all of these types of exercise to feel wonderful overall and to stretch that feeling into your general well-being and continuing sense of confidence and empowerment.

*Be fit for your personal achievements and overall success......*


**....yoga helps you relax and improves your life.....**
*You are probably aware that when you have a more relaxed disposition, you can make far better decisions.....*
*Plus, you are able to cope much more easily when your head is in the right place!*

In this physical state, you are in an enhanced position for having total empowerment over your life and therefore, your dreams and goals.

*Relaxation is the key to finding a sense of calm and peace in everyday life.*

It can help improve your relationships, increase your work output, enhance your physical health and nourish your soul.

Yoga can help you do that, but you need to get the right kind of yoga that suits you and your own purpose.
There are many different types to choose from, some of which are very energetic and physical, whilst others are a lot more gentle and relaxing.

*Whichever you decide on, it won't take you much time at all before you begin to see the astounding advantages it will bring into your life.*

Very quickly you will find the strength physically, emotionally and spiritually to lift you up, fill you with the confidence you need to surge ahead with all your wonderful plans for utmost fulfilment, satisfaction and happiness.

**And there's nothing more empowering than that.....**

**....the last word......**
*You are here to fulfil YOUR own life!*

It's your responsibility to get the most out of yourself and your innate talent, by making it as good as it can be for the time you are given on this beautiful planet.

This may mean you being selfish, but it's really just you looking after yourself, which in turn will benefit those around you in so many ways too. All the relationships around you and all the connections to you, will feed through via your positive energy just by looking after yourself first.

*It has a knock-on effect.*

When you are happy, well and relaxed, so you pass that influential positivity onto those you come into contact with.
If we all looked after ourselves by feeding our soul, creating positive vibes and making the right choices, then the energy flow between us all will always be positive and when energy is positive, happiness can be spread.

**Think about it.....**

If you are around happy, energetic people who smile and laugh their way through life, who conduct themselves well because they have made all the right choices in life for *them* as an *individual*, then you will naturally feel their high, their good energy flow, their internal peace and their calm.

*It passes on naturally.....*

Even if you only smiled at someone as you walk along, they will usually smile back.
This puts you in good spirits and makes you feel nice, and so will they. Then you're all set up for the day and will continue to smile at others who smile at others, who smile at others, and so on...

*The positive energy is passed on and on and on.*

When anyone feels good and calm inside, it projects outwardly too. You will skip through the day doing tasks in a relaxed manner, feel confident and get jobs done more efficiently. Therefore passing on good work, which in turn also has good energy.
Your boss, partner or whoever is close will be happy with you, and so the vibe has been passed on through so many other varying ways.

So, as each day passes, make the right choices for *you*, so you become happier, things work out better for you, ambitions are fulfilled and success is imminent - whether that success is in business, personal achievement or just your own inner peace and contentment.

Then everyday you can wake up feeling good, fresh and motivated from all the achievements you have made and the happy energy you've passed on to others.

They in turn will pass their positive energy onto others in their own surroundings and so the world will turn in a much better way. Thoughtfulness, charity and consideration will be amplified as patience and goodness radiate out from your inner happiness and positivity.
All this is passed on and more and more circles of optimism are rotated round and round.

*All because of the good choices you made!*

When you feel happier and lighter and your positive energy is flowing so freely, you will open up to how your heart is feeling, how love flows through it and you will build better friendships and relationships.
Bringing you back to the very basics.
By sharing what you have, you'll become more receptive to the Universe's bounty.

Allowing you to clear the clutter of past negative relationships, events and experiences from your head and heart and making way for renewed thoughts and opening up to a realm of possibilities and opportunities.

*Your world will begin to see wonderful prospects.*

These opportunities will open out into more choices.

Choices you will be willing to consider and take on in order to be more successful in your life.

*Unblocking your mind will allow you to think more clearly, see more clearly and decide more clearly.*

Why use up your energy in a bad way?

Negative thoughts, bad feelings or nastiness all zap you from within. Quickly replace that bad energy with good thoughts to stop the rot setting in and spiralling out of control.

Think of something wonderful, whether it is something you have personally experienced or something you wish to experience, or be near, such as a beautiful waterfall or landscape, a wonderful time with your partner or an invigorating activity like skydiving.

You choose.....

*Anchor this thought and feeling in your mind and use it every time you sense you are falling back.*

Be prepared to make some initial sacrifices as you go on your path to fulfilling your ultimate life.
This will be inevitable.

It may be in terms of time, effort, finance, relationships, changes to your life, including relocating.

But come to terms with the fact that if you want to get somewhere in your life that is ultimately '*you*' and where you want to be, changes *have* to happen and sometimes that means making certain choices that may not be popular, but in the long-term will reap rewards.

*Be really honest and frank with yourself.*

Whatever is negative and stopping you going along your path and reaching your ultimate self will be hampering your progress and you need to make the right choice about whether or not it really has a place in your life?

**Remember, your choice, your life......**

**Live it!**

**<u>LIVE EMPOWERED</u>!**

*...and Grow Your Wings....!*


**....did it do anything for you.....**
*I hope you have found something useful in this book that helps you on your road to true empowerment.*

*Do check out more information on any of the subjects discussed, especially if you feel you need that extra helping hand to move you forwards and upwards.*

*The most important thing is that you are your real self, true to who you are and fulfilling your life in the most spectacular way possible.*

*Always remember that it is your life to live and in looking after yourself and your interests you will always feel in control and as such, empowered by what you are working towards.*

*Your body is the only one you live in, so look after it and it will look after you for many, many healthful years......*

*Never let anyone steal your mojo or make you feel wrong or worthless. Let those people get on with their own life and you move happily through your own.*

*Always remember you are a valuable and unique individual and you have every right to be so.*

*Be open to the fantastic opportunities that present themselves to you.*

*Using your new intelligent mindset, feel positive in your decisions to follow them through.*
*Use your intuition and allow the universe to guide you on your way.*

*Take the bull by the horns and allow yourself to be free in your own mind, body and spirit and take that leap of faith in yourself.*

*You deserve it.*

*Good luck with your life.*

*I hope it is strong, content, peaceful, invigorating, satisfying, full of fun with wonderful relationships – but make sure you concentrate on yourself first.*

*Follow your dreams and be lucky, be happy, be thankful, be healthy and most of all.......*

*be **empowered**.....*

## A Power Mantra

(insert your own words....)

*I am strong!*
*I am powerful!*
*I am confident and assertive!*
*I have excellent skills and talents!*
*I deserve to be taken seriously and respected!*
*I have the courage of my convictions!*
*I deserve rewards for my contributions!*
*I am forward thinking and innovative!*
*I am rich, wealthy and successful!*
*I am me and that's the best I can be!*

***I am empowered!***

## A Prayer to the World

(insert your own words....)

*I ask the world to bring me peace and harmony,*
*I am at peace with myself.*
*I ask the world to bring me confidence and success,*
*I have confidence to push myself forward in life and be a success.*
*I ask the world to bring me happiness,*
*I am happy in my skin and I bring happiness to others.*
*I ask the world to make me healthy,*
*I am rich in health, I am rich in vitality.*
*I eat to live, therefore I only eat what I need to live.*
*I ask the world to make my body fit and free from pain,*
*I am rich in fitness and am pain free.*
*I ask the world to bring me energy and strength,*
*I am rich in energy and strength to carry me through life.*
*I thank you for giving me these wonders and riches, which I take and appreciate.*

**<u>Thank you</u>.**

Printed in Great Britain
by Amazon.co.uk, Ltd.,
Marston Gate.